THE MEASURE OF AMERICAN ELECTIONS

Policy making in the realm of elections is too often grounded in anecdotes and opinions rather than in good data and scientific research. To remedy this, *The Measure of American Elections* brings together a dozen leading scholars to examine the performance of elections across the United States, using a data-driven perspective. This book represents a transformation in debates about election reform, away from partisan and ideological posturing and toward using scientific analysis to evaluate the conduct of contemporary elections. The authors harness the power of newly available data to document all aspects of election administration, ranging from the registration of voters to the counting of ballots. They demonstrate what can be learned from giving serious attention to data, measurement, and objective analysis of American elections.

Barry C. Burden is a professor of political science at the University of Wisconsin–Madison. He is the author of *Personal Roots of Representation* (2007) and coauthor of *Why Americans Split Their Tickets* (2002, with David C. Kimball). Burden has written or cowritten more than thirty-five articles in peer-reviewed journals, including the *American Political Science Review*, the *American Journal of Political Science*, *Legislative Studies Quarterly*, *Public Opinion Quarterly*, and *Electoral Studies*.

Charles Stewart III is the Kenan Sahin Distinguished Professor of Political Science and the former head of the political science department at the Massachusetts Institute of Technology. He is the author of *Budget Reform Politics* (1989) and *Analyzing Congress* (2nd ed., 2011) and the coauthor of *Fighting for the Speakership* (2013, with Jeffrey Jenkins). Stewart's writing has appeared in the *American Journal of Political Science*, the *Journal of Politics*, *Political Research Quarterly*, *Legislative Studies Quarterly*, the *Election Law Journal*, and *Harvard Law Review*.

CAMBRIDGE STUDIES IN ELECTION
LAW AND DEMOCRACY

Recent developments have pushed elections scholarship in new directions. As a result, interdisciplinary work has flourished and political scientists and law professors have developed a more sophisticated sense of the relationship between law and politics. This series seeks to create an intellectual road map for the field, one that systematically examines the issues confronting both mature and emerging democracies. It will chart those new intellectual paths to spur interdisciplinary work, to identify productive ways in which scholars' research agendas connect to policy makers' reform agendas, and to disseminate this body of work to the growing audience interested in the intersection of law, politics, and democracy.

The Measure of American Elections

Edited by

BARRY C. BURDEN

University of Wisconsin

CHARLES STEWART III

The Massachusetts Institute of Technology

CAMBRIDGE
UNIVERSITY PRESS

CAMBRIDGE
UNIVERSITY PRESS

University Printing House, Cambridge CB2 8BS, United Kingdom

One Liberty Plaza, 20th Floor, New York, NY 10006, USA

477 Williamstown Road, Port Melbourne, VIC 3207, Australia

314-321, 3rd Floor, Plot 3, Splendor Forum, Jasola District Centre, New Delhi - 110025, India

79 Anson Road, #06-04/06, Singapore 079906

Cambridge University Press is part of the University of Cambridge.

It furthers the University's mission by disseminating knowledge in the pursuit of education, learning and research at the highest international levels of excellence.

www.cambridge.org
Information on this title: www.cambridge.org/9781107699915

© Cambridge University Press 2014

First published 2014

A catalogue record for this publication is available from the British Library

Library of Congress Cataloging in Publication data
The measure of American elections / edited by Barry C. Burden and Charles Stewart III.
    pages   cm. – (Cambridge studies in election law and democracy)
Includes bibliographical references and index.
ISBN 978-1-107-06667-0 (hardback) – ISBN 978-1-107-69991-5 (paperback)
1. Elections – United States.   2. Elections – United States – Management.   3. Voting –
United States.   I. Burden, Barry C., 1971–, author, editor of compilation.   II. Stewart,
Charles Haines, author, editor of compilation.
JK1967.M43   2014
320.60973–dc23   2014002757

ISBN 978-1-107-06667-0 Hardback
ISBN 978-1-107-69991-5 Paperback

Contents

Figures

Tables

Contributors

Stephen Ansolabehere, *Harvard University*

Lonna Rae Atkeson, *University of New Mexico*

Barry C. Burden, *University of Wisconsin–Madison*

Paul Gronke, *Reed College*

Thad E. Hall, *University of Utah*

Michael J. Hanmer, *University of Maryland at College Park*

Paul S. Herrnson, *University of Connecticut*

Eitan Hersh, *Yale University*

Douglas Kruse, *Rutgers University*

Christopher B. Mann, *Louisiana State University*

Lisa Schur, *Rutgers University*

Robert M. Stein, *Rice University*

Charles Stewart III, *Massachusetts Institute of Technology*

Gregg Vonnahme, *University of Missouri–Kansas City*

Acknowledgments

Although our names are listed on the cover of the book, *The Measure of American Elections* is the product of many people and institutions. This book would have been impossible to produce just a few years ago because of a lack of data and intellectual community. Things have changed in dramatic fashion over the past decade.

The contemporary study of U.S. election administration can trace its origins to the meltdown in Florida following the 2000 presidential election. The recounts and legal disputes that took place over the thirty-five days between Election Day and the Supreme Court's resolution in *Bush v. Gore* illuminated just how little systematic knowledge existed about how states and localities manage elections.

The academic community responded in part through the creation of the CalTech-MIT Voting Technology Project (VTP) in 2001 and launch of the *Election Law Journal* in 2002. These new initiatives helped bring together scholars from multiple fields and established connections among scholars and election officials, the legal community, and advocates. The CalTech-MIT collaboration also led to the creation of a new metric, the "residual vote," to evaluate how successfully ballots were being counted.

The Help America Vote Act (HAVA) of 2002, passed into law as a direct response to the 2000 election, created the Election Assistance Commission and an invaluable source of data: the Election Administration and Voting Survey (EAVS). The EAVS has improved significantly since its first administration in 2004. It has become an indispensable source of data on election administration, covering everything from voter registration to provisional ballots and voting technology.

With growing availability of data came further initiatives to use those data to evaluate election administration. An opening salvo was the publication of Heather Gerken's *The Democracy Index* in 2009. The book proposed an index that would rank states based on how well they conducted elections. Among others, the book inspired the Election Initiatives team at the Pew Charitable Trusts to assemble an advisory group of scholars, election officials, and other experts to consider development of a similar index. (Charles Stewart III was heavily involved in that effort.) After two years of study and development, the group issued the first ever Election Performance Index (EPI). An elaboration of Gerken's initial proposal, the EPI produced performance scores for the states in the 2010 and 2012 elections. The scores drew on indicators from the EAVS, the Census Bureau, existing Pew reports, and the Survey of the Performance of American Elections (SPAE), funded by Pew and developed by the VTP research team. Release of the EPI was testament to the power of data to reveal truths about election performance and serve as a value diagnostic for improving elections.

As the EPI was coming to fruition, we convened a conference at MIT in the summer of 2012 that brought together the expert scholars who appear as contributors in this volume. They were asked to produce "white papers" on specific measures that had been considered for inclusion in the EPI. The careful scrutiny applied to those measures helped inform which elements appeared in the EPI and led to this edited volume. It is testimony to the integrity of the authors of the chapters that follow that all approached their intellectual task impartially and without anticipating what the Pew EPI development team wanted to hear. It is testimony to the rigor and thoughtfulness of the Pew Election Initiative team that they supported this project without hesitation from start to finish.

The burgeoning science of election administration continues to develop. The EAVS provides more complete and higher-quality data with each election cycle. The SPAE has now gathered survey-based measures for multiple elections. These two sources, along with the Current Population Survey, permit tracking of indicators over time in a way that was never before possible. States and localities are improving the transparency, reliability, and validity of the data they collect. A second edition of the EPI will be released in close chronological proximity to the publication of this volume, updating the analysis to include the 2012 presidential election. President Obama's bipartisan Commission on Election Administration's report, issued in December

2013, further highlighted the power of scientific analysis of election data to identify concerns and best practices for improving elections. Indeed, the Commission was given advance access to this book manuscript and heard testimony from many of its contributors.

There are many people to thank for their involvement in the project. The twelve experts who contributed to the volume represent the best in scholarship on election administration. We are grateful for their contributions. David Kimball, Martha Kropf, Michael McDonald, and Quin Monson provided excellent oral and written feedback as discussants at the MIT conference where the chapters were first presented. Stephen Pettigrew, a PhD student at Harvard, provided superb research assistance in support of the entire project. Justin de Benedictis-Kessner and James Dunham, PhD students at MIT, pitched in to provide invaluable assistance during the summer of 2012. Data-hungry researchers at Pew were especially helpful in providing an interface between the data sources and state election officials. Aleena Oberthur and Andreas Westgaard deserve a special note of commendation. Daniel Guenther of MIT helped to facilitate the production process.

The Election Initiatives team at the Pew Charitable Trusts has been pivotal in advancing the study of election administration. Their financial support made the EPI possible, facilitated the MIT conference, and has underwritten other valuable data-driven projects, including dissemination of election information to voters and modernization of voter registration. In particular, we single out David Becker, Sean Greene, and Zachary Markovits for their efforts to bring together scholars, practitioners, and advocates as part of a continual effort to improve elections.

This book is published as part of the Cambridge Studies in Election Law and Democracy series. We appreciate the endorsement of the series' editors, Guy-Uriel Charles, Heather Gerken, and Michael Kang. Finally, we thank the Press's law editor, John Berger, for his support and assistance with the project.

Introduction to the Measure of American Elections

Barry C. Burden and Charles Stewart III

How good are American elections?

Where would one start in answering this question?

Whenever this question is posed, it is common to answer it from the position of deeply held beliefs, but rarely from the position of a systematic analysis of facts. These beliefs might arise from partisanship: a good election is one that my favored candidate wins. These beliefs might be chauvinistic: a good election is one run according to the rules of my community.

Rarely are these beliefs rooted in hard facts.

When facts intervene, they rarely are presented in a systematic fashion. Opinions about levels of voter fraud might be attributable to a viral YouTube video. Concerns about the effects of a new voter identification law might be informed by a reporter's interview with an activist who is eager to share stories about how voters she has talked with will be disenfranchised on Election Day. Satisfaction with a new electronic voting machine may be illustrated by a picture of a smiling citizen coming out of the precinct with an "I Voted" sticker stuck to her lapel. Disdain about the ability of local governments to run elections might follow from a newspaper article detailing yet another season of long lines when waiting to vote in Florida (or South Carolina or Maryland or …). At its worst, this approach is evaluation by anecdote.

Consider instead how the question about the quality of American elections would be framed if first we asked about other policy domains: "How good are America's prisons?" or "How good are America's schools?" or "How good is America's health care system?" Some people surely would respond based on fact-free beliefs; others would respond with a random story about the experience that one's cousin had with one of these institutions. However, it would not be difficult to discover that in

2007 (the most recent year for which data are available), 15.5 percent of all parolees were reincarcerated, that Connecticut had the highest reincarceration rate (29.9 percent), and that Maine had the lowest (o percent).[1] Nor would it be difficult to find out that Alaska's fourth graders ranked last among the fifty states in the reading portion of the 2011 National Assessment of Educational Progress and that Massachusetts ranked first; that the gap between girls and boys was greatest in Hawaii and smallest in Texas; and that the gap between whites and blacks was greatest in Connecticut and smallest in North Dakota.[2] A brief Internet search would reveal that in 2008, the infant mortality rate among the fifty states ranged from 3.87 per 100,000 live births in New Hampshire to 9.95 per 100,000 in Mississippi (Mathews and MacDorman 2012, 6).

In other words, an obvious way to begin addressing questions about the state of public policy in these other important areas would be to draw on a large body of data about the performance of these institutions and policy systems.

None of the statistics just referenced is the be-all and end-all of the question about how well the prison systems, schools, and health care systems work in the states. The point is that in each of these policy domains, significant effort is poured into defining measures of policy input and output consistently across states, multiple measures of system performance are regularly reported through a federal agency, and entire professions have grown up to analyze these data. Despite the fact that answers to policy questions about criminal justice, education, and health care are legitimately informed by ideology and deeply held beliefs, even committed ideologues typically ground their appeals in statistics when they argue about policy; some will even be convinced they are wrong if the facts are against them. The data provide a common starting point.

This returns us to the original question: How good are American elections? If an American wanted to argue this question based on facts, he would most likely go to the turnout statistics and discover that in 2012, 58.2 percent of eligible Americans voted, ranging from 44.2 percent in Hawaii to 75.7 percent in Minnesota.[3] Compared with other nations, U.S. turnout was in the lower half of 112 countries

---

[1]   Probation and Parole in the United States, 2007 – Statistical Tables, http://bjs.ojp.usdoj.gov/index.cfm?ty=pbdetail&iid=1099.

[2]   The Nation's Report Card – National Assessment of Educational Progress, http://nces.ed.gov/nationsreportcard/naepdata/.

[3]   United States Election Project, http://elections.gmu.edu/voter_turnout.htm.

with presidential elections in recent years – ranked seventy-fourth (right between the Democratic Republic of Congo and Romania), above the European nations of Poland, Serbia, Portugal, Slovakia, Ireland, Austria, Macedonia, and Lithuania, but below the nations of Moldova, the Russian Federation, Montenegro, Finland, Ukraine, Iceland, France, Kazakhstan, Armenia, Cyprus, Tajikistan, Belarus, Turkmenistan, and Uzbekistan.[4] An American with a bit more perseverance might also discover that when asked in a national survey in 2012 whether they were confident that their votes were counted as cast, 63 percent stated they were "very confident," ranging from 80 percent in Vermont to 54 percent in Washington.[5]

An American who was interested in understanding in a more nuanced sense how well elections are run in this country would *not* find much in the way of defining consistent measures of election administration input and output across states. Nor would he or she find much effort at reporting such statistics even *within* states, much less a profession devoted to the proposition that elections would function better if we understood systematically the facts associated with election administration. Indeed, this American would find that states differ in how they even define critical aspects of election administration, including such fundamental measures as turnout. Sometimes even a state's chief election officer lacks the authority to require local election boards to report to him or her basic statistics about election administration beyond the bare facts of the election returns themselves. This American would also discover that the National Association of Secretaries of State (NASS), which is the organization of top state constitutional officers who most often are ultimately responsible for the conduct of elections, has led a campaign to abolish the U.S. Election Assistance Commission (EAC), the only federal agency that gathers statistics about election administration nationwide.

In other words, while there are scientific professions devoted to the study of corrections, education, public health, transportation, and many other critical functions of state and local government, there is no scientific profession devoted to the study of election administration.

This book is part of an effort to change that.

---

4 International Institute for Democracy and Electoral Assistance, Voter Turnout Database, http://www.idea.int/vt/viewdata.cfm.
5 See "2012 Survey of the Performance of American Elections" (Stewart 2013).

In particular, the chapters in this volume are devoted to the study of ten areas of election administration through the lens of hard data and social science. The topics cover the waterfront in the field of election administration and policy, ranging from the registration of voters to the counting of votes. None of these chapters is the final word in any of these areas. They are something more important: in many cases, they are the *first word* in starting a conversation about the systematic analysis of election administration and policy in America.

FIRST THINGS FIRST:

ESTABLISHING THE VALIDITY AND RELIABILITY OF AMERICAN
ELECTION ADMINISTRATION

In the areas of public policy that aspire to be data driven, great attention is paid to the validity and reliability of the key measures employed in the field.

Validity may be defined as the degree to which a measure actually describes the underlying concept it claims to measure, rather than something else. In other words, it refers to how well an observable quantity describes an unobservable theoretical construct. For instance, we cannot observe someone's intelligence directly, but we can observe how well she or he performs on an IQ test. A robust literature and scholarly debate has grown up around the question of how valid IQ tests are as an indicator of (unobservable) intelligence.[6]

An example of the application of the concept of validity to elections is in the area of absentee ballots. For example, a valid measure of absentee ballot usage should track actual usage, even if it sometimes misses the mark somewhat. Similarly, the measure of line lengths is highly valid if it approximates the actual waiting times, rather than being consistently too high or too low.

There are many methods used to establish validity, including such things as relating a measure to other variables known to affect or be affected by it. This is often an interactive process of moving back and forth between measures and their actual scores (Adcock and Collier 2001).[7]

---

[6] Within political science, the classic statement on validity and reliability is Carmines and Zeller (1979).

[7] This sort of refinement is discussed in some of the chapters that follow. Here we mention two examples. The absentee ballot rejection rate is an important measure that could be computed

In contrast, *reliability* refers to the degree to which a measuring procedure yields the same results when the procedure is repeated. A highly reliable measure produces similar results when applied multiple times in the same setting. For example, a reliable measure of a state's absentee ballot usage will yield a similar conclusion even if different staff members provide the data. Likewise, a reliable measure of polling place lines based on surveys of voters will show consistent times if the survey is repeated. Although low reliability does not affect accuracy of a measure, it does affect its precision. That is, while the answer might be right on average, the high degree of variability makes it difficult to discern the signal amid the noise. One way to increase reliability is to bring more data to the table by adding observations or combining measures into a summary index.

In psychometrics a great deal of attention is paid to whether respondents give the same answers when given the exact same battery of questions on different days. Similarly, a diagnostic medical test that gives the same results when repeated on the same individual in rapid succession is said to be reliable.

Measures of validity and reliability are generally measures of *degree* and not absolutes. It is well understood that reliable measures may fluctuate from one moment to the next, as when the results of an aptitude test vary depending on whether a student is well rested, under stress, or hungry. Thus, the standard is rarely perfection when it comes to assessing validity and reliability, but the closer we can come to perfection, the better.

On a scale where 1.0 indicates perfect reliability, most of the state measures used in the chapters that follow correlate between the 2008 and 2010 elections at levels between .7 and .9. Where the correlations are lower, it is sometimes a sign of poor reliability stemming from a small sample size. Aggregating over multiple elections will remedy this problem. In other cases, it is a sign that what the measure is capturing has changed between the presidential election and the midterm election. Several of the Uniformed and Overseas Citizens Absentee Voting Act (UOCAVA) and absentee ballot measures are of this variety.

---

as a share of absentee ballots cast or of all ballots cast. Which is used depends on both theory about the denominator of interest and also empirical information about which offers greater discrimination across states. Voter confidence is also of keen interest. Survey questions often ask whether the respondent is "very confident," "somewhat confident," "not too confident," or "not at all confident." Where to "cut" these four categories to create state-by-state percentages is partially a result of trial and error to find the most meaningful division.

In some fields, the reliability and validity of performance measures are based on a deep body of scientific research, stretching across
decades and thousands of researchers, supported by billions of dollars
of basic research. Consider, for instance, a study to assess the quality of
medical care received by Medicare recipients in each of the fifty states,
which was published in the *Journal of the American Medical Association*
(*JAMA*) in 2000 (Jencks et al. 2000). To assess the quality of medical
care received by Medicare patients, this study examined thousands of
randomly chosen patient records, drawn from patients in every state in
the nation. The basic question asked of these records was whether the
patient in question was treated for his or her conditions in a way that
reflected the consensus of appropriate care in a particular field. The
overall index of patient care was based on rating twenty-four indicators
of patient care such as these; the conditions covered by these indicators
affected 85 percent of Medicare beneficiaries.

The validity of the measures chosen by the researchers in the *JAMA*
study had already been established in the medical community, based
on hundreds of studies of the relationship between the care patients
received and how well they fared after their treatments. For instance,
these previous studies had established that one valid measure of the
quality of care of Medicare recipients was what percentage of those
admitted to hospitals because of acute myocardial infarction (better
known as a heart attack) later received prescriptions for aspirin upon
discharge.

The reliability of such an indicator would be more difficult to measure, because it is based on the assessment of patient records. Although
there may be *general* guidelines for care of patients, there also may be
well-established contraindications for applying that regimen to a *particular* patient – such as if the patient is known to be violently allergic
to the drug of choice. Here, judgment must be applied to the coding
of patient records in the making of the index. This is where reliability
comes in.

Two physicians, and certainly two research assistants, reading the
same patient medical records might come to different conclusions
about whether a particular patient is a candidate to receive treatment
consistent with the conventional standards of care. If they each read
the same record and come to different conclusions, we would infer that
this method of coding whether patients received good hospital care
based on their records is unreliable. Conversely, if the coders frequently
agreed, we would regard this measure as more reliable.

The reliabilities of the measures used in the *JAMA* study were assessed precisely according to this logic. Reliability was established by testing to see whether two independent coders came to the same conclusions about whether to include or exclude a particular patient record from the study. Part of the study's report included measures of inter-rater reliability for each of the indicators.

The effort just described to compare the quality of hospital care received by participants in the Medicare program across the fifty states rested on decades of medical research that consumes billions of dollars in taxes and private foundation support each year. The study of election administration barely has thousands of dollars devoted to it each year, so the reliability and validity of any measures of election administration quality that we consider must be viewed as provisional.

To continue with the medical analogy, election administration is similar to the earliest days of public health studies, when the only measure of health care quality was the mortality rate – the number of deaths divided by the number of people. This was a crude measure, but it was powerful. It could establish, for instance, that modern sewer systems improved the health of city dwellers, leading to greater attention on public works projects aimed at improving the quality of life of everyone and, ultimately, promoting economic growth.

As the raw mortality rate was used increasingly to compare health care outcomes across geographical units, hospitals, and demographic populations, it became clear that the validity of the crude mortality rate could be improved by adjusting based on the risk of dying, which might be quite independent of the quality of health care (or other public health factors). For instance, the mortality rate of a city with a high fraction of elderly residents would be higher than that of a city with few elderly residents, even if the sanitation facilities were equivalent in the two places. Thus, as the field of public health has advanced, the mortality measure has been improved by adjusting for risk factors such as age. In doing so, the new risk-adjusted mortality statistics have become even more valid measures of the underlying health of a given population.

Election administration is still in the "raw mortality rate" phase of measuring outcomes in its policy domain. Few measures of performance within election administration are widely understood and accepted.

Indeed, it could be argued that there is only one widely known measure of performance in this area: the turnout rate, which shares many of the advantages and disadvantages of the raw mortality rate. On the plus side, the turnout rate is intuitively understood and easily calculated.

Most of the country understood, for instance, that it was bad when only 25 percent of Mississippi's voting-age population (VAP) turned out to vote in the 1960 presidential election. The country also understood that when the turnout rate in Mississippi rose to the 60 percent level in 2012, this was a valid indication that the state's electoral system had improved over the intervening half-century.

On the negative side, the raw turnout rate does not take into account the "luck" or "skill" that might be involved. For instance, what do we make of the fact that the turnout rates of Hawaii and Texas in the 2008 presidential election were 44 percent and 50 percent, respectively, despite levels of educational attainment – a factor that strongly predicts whether an individual will vote – being much higher in Hawaii (90 percent high school graduates) than in Texas (81 percent high school graduates)?[8] Would we consider, on a risk-adjusted basis, that turnout in Texas was actually *much* higher than in Hawaii, because efforts to get voters to the polls in the Lone Star State must battle against lower educational levels than those in Hawaii? Or what about the comparison of Minnesota and Mississippi? In raw turnout terms, it is no contest. The Minnesota turnout rate was 75 percent in 2008, whereas Mississippi's was 61 percent – a fourteen-point deficit for Mississippi. But if we account for different levels of educational attainment using a simple technique that relies on linear regression, the tables are turned, with Minnesota suffering a five-point turnout deficit in "risk-adjusted turnout" in comparison with Mississippi.[9]

As far as we are aware, no report of turnout rates that compares the states has ever reported turnout rates adjusted for "risk factors" such as education so that the effects of policy or other systemic factors on turnout can be better understood. The best studies to this point are multivariate analyses that attempt to control for "luck" factors, such as the demographics of the state's electorate or efforts by campaigns to turn out voters. At least turnout levels of the states are periodically reported to the public and discussed. The same cannot be said of a

---

[8]   Educational attainment levels are taken from the 2011 American Community Survey (three-year series).

[9]   The method of risk adjusting here is based on a simple regression method, in which we regress the turnout rate of each state on the percentage of residents twenty-five years of age and up with a high school diploma and then generate the residuals of the regression. In this case, the Minnesota residual is +5.8 percentage points, and the Mississippi residual is +10.4 percentage points. The regression equation in this case was Turnout Rate = −84.8 + 1.68 H.S. Graduate Rate, with standard errors of 15.9 and 0.18, respectively. The R-squared statistic was .63, with 51 observations. The regression was weighted by turnout in each state.

long list of other measures of election administration that could easily be constructed from official sources, such as the rejection rate of provisional ballots or the nonreturn rates of absentee ballots.

The ideal measure is one that is both reliable and valid. That is, it has a high level of precision and a high level of accuracy. It is possible for a measure to do well on one dimension but poorly on the other, or poorly on both. A digital watch is highly precise, but it can be inaccurate if set to the wrong time; likewise, a mechanical watch without a second hand might be highly accurate while being far from precise. A key purpose of this volume is to evaluate a variety of election-related measures on these two dimensions. It is important to note that for the purposes of evaluating election performance, an invalid measure is not necessarily useless. If a measure of provisional ballot usage, for example, systematically underestimated the actual use across the states, it would be less valid but could still be used effectively to rank order states. In contrast, a valid measure with low reliability would produce problematic rankings because of the excessive noise in the indicator, but it could still be used to describe how states perform on average.

WHERE ARE THE DATA?

SOURCES OF DATA FOR THE ASSESSMENT OF
AMERICAN ELECTIONS

This volume begins the process of assessing how elections are conducted in America by identifying a manageable set of candidate indicators, subjecting them to scrutiny, and examining them for what they tell us about elections in America. If we agree that data-driven scrutiny of American elections is to be commended, we need data. Luckily there are plenty of data out there, oftentimes hiding in plain view. The remaining chapters of this book rely on these data sources to quite a detailed level. Here we introduce the reader to the most important.[10]

There are four major sources of data available for the assessment of American elections:

1. The Voting and Registration Supplement of the Current Population Survey (CPS), conducted by the U.S. Census Bureau.

---

[10] A more detailed examination of many of these data sources may be found in Pew Center on the States (2012).

2. The Election Administration and Voting Survey (EAVS), conducted by the U.S. EAC.
3. State and local election board records.
4. Academic and commercial survey research.

The Voting and Registration Supplement

Ever since the 1960s, the U.S. Census Bureau has conducted a survey every other November about voting in the most recent federal general election, as a supplement to the Census Bureau's monthly CPS. The primary purpose of the CPS is to help determine the unemployment rate and other economic statistics at the state level. The biennial survey that studies voting is called the Voting and Registration Supplement (VRS). The main CPS contains a treasure trove of information about the participants in the survey, including information about their ethnicity, education, housing, income, and (since 2010) disability status. Thus, it is possible to study the relationship between important demographic characteristics of American adults and the likelihood they will be registered and vote, and even the means used to register and to vote. The overall survey sample is quite large. In 2010, for instance, nearly 80,000 respondents were asked whether they voted in the most recent federal election, ranging from 578 in New Mexico to 5,862 in California.

Compared with other survey research that focuses on election behavior, the VRS is actually quite limited in what it asks about voting – some would say "focused." It does not ask respondents whom they voted for. (This being a survey conducted by the federal government, it is easy to understand why.) Nor does it ask other questions that political scientists studying participation might want to consider, such as interest in politics, knowledge of politics, or stances on important issues. It essentially only asks respondents whether they voted and if they are registered; if they report they did not vote or were not registered, they are asked why not. Those who say they voted are asked what mode they used to vote (in person on Election Day, in person before Election Day, or via the mail). Finally, they are asked how long they have lived at their current address and how they registered to vote.[11]

[11] This description of items is based on the 2010 VRS. While the items change infrequently, there is some fluctuation in questions from time to time. For instance, after the controversy that arose in 1980 over Jimmy Carter conceding defeat in the 1980 presidential election before the polls had closed on the West Coast, the VRS asked respondents that year what time of day they voted.

Despite the relatively limited range of questions about political participation asked in the VRS, it is the most important data set available for the study of who votes and who is registered. Some of the most authoritative studies of voting turnout have relied heavily on the VRS, beginning with the classic book *Who Votes?*, by Raymond Wolfinger and Steven Rosenstone (1980).

Because the VRS has such an enormous sample size and is paired with a larger survey that asks a number of sociodemographic questions, it is a good tool for helping us understand individual demographic circumstances that might get in the way of citizens participating in elections. As an example, consider the question of voting by the disabled, a topic covered by Lisa Schur and Douglas Kruse in Chapter 8. When a respondent to the VRS states that she or he did not vote in the most recent election, a follow-up question asks why. One of the response categories is "permanent illness or disability." Because the CPS also asks respondents if they have one of six different disabilities, it is possible to gauge the number of eligible voters who fail to vote because of illness and disability.[12] In 2012, this amounted to 43 percent of all disabled non-voters, or a total of over 1.4 million people. Furthermore, we also learn that among the disabled respondents reporting that they *did* vote, 28 percent said they voted by mail, compared with 17 percent of those who did not report a disability.

The VRS has shortcomings. It relies on respondents to recall their past behavior, and we know that recall about voting can be imprecise and inaccurate. Indeed, we know that people tend to overreport whether they voted because of a social desirability bias. Unfortunately, the VRS has never undertaken a "voter validation" study, in which researchers verify the vote history of respondents, so the precise nature of the overreporting bias is unknown in this study. The VRS does significantly overreport voting rates, although less than in other surveys. For instance, in 2012, 62 percent of VRS respondents said they had voted in the most recent election, when in fact only 58 percent of the voting eligible population had voted in that year; the corresponding rates were 54 percent and 41 percent in 2010.[13] Thus, overall participation rates

---

[12] The disabilities that are asked about are difficulty dressing or bathing, deafness or serious hearing problems, blindness, difficulty doing errands, difficulty walking, and difficulty remembering or making decisions.

[13] Unless otherwise noted, the turnout rates used in this book are taken from the United States Election Project Web site (http://elections.gmu.edu/index.html), maintained at George Mason University by Michael McDonald.

will be elevated when we use the VRS. Still, the VRS is an invaluable resource for the *comparison* of demographic groups or geographic areas, where the overreporting problems presumably wash out.

The Election Administration and Voting Survey

The EAVS was begun by the EAC in 2004 as the only national census of information related to election administration in the United States. A biennial project, the EAVS collects information from approximately 4,600 local jurisdictions that conduct elections in the United States – mostly counties but also municipalities in New England and the upper Midwest, where counties play a secondary (or no) role in conducting elections.[14]

The EAVS arises out of the EAC's mandate to produce periodic studies of election administration issues. The EAVS is actually an amalgam of three surveys. One section deals with voter registration statistics and is used to produce the EAC's biennial report to Congress under the National Voter Registration Act (NVRA) of 1993. Another section focuses on ballots sent out and returned from overseas and military voters, for the production of the biennial report mandated under the UOCAVA. Finally, sections on domestic civilian absentee ballots, election administration, provisional ballots, and Election Day activities fill out the rest of the survey. The complete survey contains more than 400 separate items, though most items only pertain to a subset of local jurisdictions.

Without the EAVS, we would not know how many voters are registered nationwide; how many registration forms were processed (or rejected) in a two-year period; how many absentee ballots were sent to voters, returned, and accepted for counting (or rejected); how many polling places there were on Election Day and how many people staffed them; how many provisional ballots were handed out and processed (including how many rejected); and which types of voting technologies were being used by local governments.

Indeed, the volume of information in the EAVS has overwhelmed the election administration community, which has not leaped to the task of using the data contained in it. The surprising lack of eagerness among

---

[14] By focusing on counties as the jurisdictions of interest, the EAVS collects data from approximately 4,600 administrative units. If one instead focuses on municipalities rather than counties in states such as Michigan and Wisconsin, where election administration is often in the hands of city, village, or town officials, the number of jurisdictions is closer to 10,000.

the election policy community to use EAVS data in their research is no doubt attributable to the survey's rocky start in 2004 and continued struggles with data gathering in the election administration domain, some of which are discussed in the following. Still, as many of the chapters in this volume demonstrate, the EAVS often is the only source of data we have to study important questions of election policy.

Consider, for instance, the simple controversy that arose in the 2012 general election in Fulton County (Atlanta), Georgia, when 11,000 provisional ballots – 2.8 percent of all ballots cast – remained on the table at the end of Election Day.[15] Was this unusual or not? Without comparative information about the usage rates of provisional ballots in other counties throughout Georgia or throughout the country, it was impossible to know. With data from other counties, it *was* possible to put Fulton County's experience in some perspective.

At the time the Fulton County controversy arose, it was too early in the vote-counting process to make good comparisons using 2012 election data, so the best one could do was compare Fulton County with other counties of similar size in the previous presidential election in 2008. Using the EAVS, we see that among the twenty-three counties with between 400,000 and 600,000 voters in 2008, only four had provisional ballot usage rates above 2.8 percent. Two of these counties were in Ohio (Franklin and Hamilton) and two were in California (Contra Costa and Sacramento), both states with very high provisional ballot usage rates overall. In 2008, California's provisional ballot usage rate was 5.8 percent, while Ohio's was 3.6 percent. In contrast, Georgia's usage rate was 0.4 percent.

Only by reference to the EVAS was it possible to see that the number of provisional ballots issued in Fulton County in 2012 was unusually high, both in comparison to counties nationwide of a similar size and in comparison to the number of provisional ballots one could expect in Georgia as a whole.

If the EAVS is the only national census of election-administration-related statistics, what accounts for its underutilization in policy discussions, aside from the fact that it is not well known? Three things undermine the quality of the EAVS as a data source – or at least introduce challenges that must be kept in mind when using it to draw general

---

[15] Ray Henry, "Fulton County Sorts through Provisional Ballots, Certifies Election Results," *Augusta Chronicle*, November 10, 2012, http://chronicle.augusta.com/news/metro/2012–11–10/ fulton-county-sorts-through-provisional-ballots-certifies-election-results.

conclusions about elections in the United States. The first challenge is the high rate of missing data, especially from the earliest years of its administration. The missing value rates from 2004 are so high that the data from the first year of the EAVS are almost impossible to use for most applications. Things got much better in 2006 and 2008. According to Pew's *Election Administration by the Numbers* report, among the most important data contained in the EAVS, 28 percent was missing in 2006, dropping to 15 percent in 2008. Conducting a similar calculation for 2010 and 2012 lowers the missing data rate further to 6 percent.

The presence of missing data from the EAVS also raises a shortcoming in the reports issued by the EAC using the EAVS data – the EAC makes no effort to impute missing data in those cases where a jurisdiction has not reported the required information. Furthermore, in calculating *rates*, the EAC sometimes uses a numerator that is based on data from one set of jurisdictions and a denominator that is based on data from another set. As a result, there is a significant absence of basic quantities reported by the EAVS and a significant number of rates that are inaccurately calculated.

Consider, for instance, the important question of how many absentee ballots are rejected because they are received after the deadline for counting. In 2008, the EAC reported that almost 75,000 absentee ballots were rejected for this reason, amounting to 18.4 percent of all rejected absentee ballots.[16] However, eight states either did not report the number of late-returned absentee ballots at all or reported a value of precisely zero. Of the forty-three states and the District of Columbia that reported some count of the number of late-returned absentee, in fifteen states fewer counties reported the number of late-returned absentee ballots than reported the total number of absentee ballots returned; in two states, more counties reported the number of late-returned absentee ballots than reported how many absentee ballots were returned overall.

In all, only twenty-three states were able to get every county to report *both* the number of absentee ballots rejected *and* the number rejected for missing the deadline. Among the states in which *all* jurisdictions reported both the number of rejected absentee ballots and the number rejected because they were late, the rejection rate for being late was an aggregate 36.3 percent – twice the rate reported by the EAC.[17]

---

[16] U.S. EAC, 2008 *Election Administration and Voting Survey: Survey of Key Findings*, p. 41.

[17] As further demonstration of the improving nature of the EAVS data, the EAC's report on the 2012 election estimated that 32.1 percent of absentee ballots were rejected for being late, a figure much closer the aggregate number from 2008.

A second challenge facing the use of the EAVS is the lack of a common vocabulary across states when they refer to basic features of voting. A good example is the term *early voting*, which was used in some form by twenty-three states in the 2012 EAVS.[18] At the same time, Kansas calls it "in-person advanced voting," Ohio calls it "absentee-in person," and North Carolina calls it "one-stop absentee voting."

The EAC's 2012 summary of what states mean when they label someone an "active voter" yields a dizzying array of definitions, which range from "a voter who is not inactive" (Alabama and Florida) to "registered to vote" (most states) to "legal resident of the state" (West Virginia) to simply "not defined by statute" (six states).[19]

A final challenge in using the EAVS to assess the quality of elections in America pertains to the fact that in many states, the chief election officer does not have the authority to mandate that local officials report to them the data necessary to fill out the EAVS survey instrument, or even to comply with national election laws, such as the NVRA. The uneasy tug-of-war that exists between state and local election officials (LEOs) is one of the little-known dramas in the management of elections across the United States. Most state election officials would probably like to receive better information from their local units about how they are performing. However, lacking the ability to sanction local units for not reporting information to the state, there is often little a secretary of state can do if a local election board simply refuses to report information beyond what is required to certify elections.

Despite these challenges, the EAVS remains the most important national data set documenting the activities of local election units in federal elections. States are slowly but surely adapting to the survey instrument. The data are more complete with each passing election. The mean state completion rate rose from 86.1 percent in 2008 to 94.2 percent in 2012. As long as the dislike among the secretaries of state for the EAC does not spill over into the demise of the EAVS, it will only improve its usefulness as time moves forward.

State and Local Election Boards

If there is one thing that citizens know about elections, it is that they are used to choose political leaders. Political scientists know elections for

---

[18] U.S. EAC, 2012 *Statutory Overview Report*, pp. 10–11.
[19] Nine other states report that the term is "not defined by statute – understood to mean registered to vote."

another reason: they are the source of a lot of data. Data are a natural by-product of elections, of course, because elections involve counting up the number of marks made on paper (literally or metaphorically) and then figuring out which candidate or ballot proposition received the most marks for a given contest.

Before the 1890s, little election data was shared widely with the public. Newspapers were the primary vehicles for communicating election returns; state governments rarely disseminated accounts of election returns for even statewide office, broken down by town or county. This all changed in the 1880s and 1890s, as a series of reforms, most notably the Australian ballot, swept the American states. The key feature of the Australian, or secret, ballot is that the ballot papers are printed by the government, not by the political parties. So the government would know which candidates to put on the ballot, it was necessary that access to the ballot be regulated and, in turn, for the activity of political parties to be regulated. As a result of the interest in regulating elections more directly, a related reform in most states was the requirement that the state also begin publishing election returns and related election statistics – such as the number of eligible voters or poll taxpayers – broken down at a finer level of disaggregation. States also needed to determine who was eligible to vote. Around this time official voter registration standards became more widely established.

With such statistics regularly reported, it became possible for average citizens to monitor the conduct of elections in their states and across states. To this day, many state libraries stockpile detailed election reports from other states. Stuffing ballot boxes became more obvious, as it was now easy to compare the total ballots cast for an office and the number of eligible voters in a precinct. Falsifying returns became harder, as it became easier to compare election returns in a precinct across time.

Fast-forwarding to the present, state and local election departments continue to spew forth incredibly detailed election reports after each election. With the spread of recordkeeping technologies such as desktop computers and spreadsheet programs, it has become easy to not only gather election reports quickly, but also to disseminate reports worldwide. States such as Idaho – small in population and far from the nation's industrial centers – post spreadsheets online that provide detailed election returns and turnout statistics for each of their precincts. Many large states with greater capacity, such as North Carolina, provide public sites for the download of similar data for anyone around the world who would use it.

The explosion of the public reporting of election-related statistics by states and localities was begun over a century ago for the purpose of allowing the public to monitor the conduct of elections and to deter fraud in election administration, under the premise that many eyes make for cleaner elections. Nowadays, much of these data remain unused, except by political parties, candidates, and consultants who are looking to find pockets of potential voters to exploit. Yet the older performance-related use of these data is still very much a possibility.

One notable way that data generated by states and localities during elections can be used to assess how well elections are conducted is through the calculation of the "residual vote rate." The residual vote rate is the centerpiece of Chapter 9, by Charles Stewart, which examines the performance of election machines.

One way to define the residual vote rate for a particular contest is the following:

$$Residual\ vote\ rate = \frac{Overvotes + Undervotes}{Turnout},$$

where the denominator is based on total turnout in the jurisdiction. An over-vote occurs when a person casts too many votes for an office; an under-vote occurs when a person does not cast the number of votes allowed for an office. Most often, the residual vote rate is calculated for the presidency, at the state level, but in principle it could be calculated for any electoral contest at any unit of aggregation.

As discussed in Chapter 9, the residual vote rate was pioneered following the 2000 presidential election as a way of identifying places where problems with voting machines might lead to confusion or outright malfunctioning. Through the use of the residual vote rate, it was possible to document the degree of improvement brought about by retiring old voting machines and replacing them with new ones in recent years.

The residual vote rate is currently the most frequently used measure that comes from official election sources, but one could imagine other uses as well. For instance, it is possible to use significant discontinuities in the support for political parties from one election to the next to spot places where there may be partisan tampering with election returns or voting machines (Myagkov, Ordeshook, and Shakin 2009).

Election returns are useful for studying the quality of election administration only if the data are reliable and reported. The residual vote rate, for instance, cannot be calculated if an electoral unit does not report how many people turn out to vote, which remains the case in three states. Nor is the residual vote rate helpful if an electoral unit counts write-in votes but does not publish them. More broadly, electoral data are the most useful if they are reported at fine levels of disaggregation – hopefully at the precinct level – and if they are reported for all modes of voting (Election Day, absentee, or early voting). The state that is the model of electoral data availability is North Carolina, which provides highly disaggregated election returns for all state elections on a relatively easy-to-use Web site.

Academic and Commercial Survey Research

Finally, academic and commercial public opinion surveys occasionally contain questions that gauge directly the experience of voters with the apparatus of elections. Election administration per se has rarely been the subject of public opinion surveys, although there has been greater interest in the topic since the 2000 presidential election. Since that election, for instance, public opinion surveys have begun asking respondents whether they are confident their votes will be counted (or were counted) fairly in the election. Analysis of such questions is the focus of Paul Gronke's analysis in Chapter 10 about whether Americans regard elections as being run fairly.

The most extensive public opinion project focusing on election administration is the Survey of the Performance of American Elections (SPAE), which was conducted on a nationwide basis in 2008 and again in 2012, but was also conducted in two odd-year gubernatorial elections and in the 2008 "Super Tuesday" presidential primary. Using the SPAE, it is possible to get a more representative view of how Americans view their own elections experiences than press accounts of the experience provide. The overall survey results are often quite at odds with the view of Election Day often conveyed by the press, where disorder and chaos are rampant. In 2012, for instance, despite the fact that there were reports of long lines at many polling places and continued distrust about the performance of electronic voting machines, 78 percent of respondents said their polling place was run "very well" (the top response category) and did not see any problems when they went to vote. Less than 2 percent of respondents stated they saw either minor or major problems that interfered with the ability of people to vote.

The SPAE is nonetheless a useful tool for identifying some problems that arise when people vote, such as the presence of long lines. This provides answers that are not as uniformly positive as the verdict on how well polling places are run. In 2012, 13 percent of American waited in line for more than half an hour to vote, for instance. This metric about long lines is revisited in the chapters that follow, both in Chapter 7, by Robert Stein and Greg Vonnahme, and in Chapter 9, by Stewart.

Summary: Data Used in Measuring American Elections

As this overview of data sources indicates, if we want to provide a portrait of election administration issues in the United States, we have a lot to work with. Because we strove in this volume to make the analysis from chapter to chapter as comparable as possible, we focus on data measured at the state level, although we could push the analysis down a further level and examine counties or even precincts.

HOW TO EVALUATE STATES

Although the science of assessing election performance is new, we are able to draw on massive literatures on measurement theory to evaluate the data considered in this book. Scholarship on measurement provides valuable guidance on how to judge the quality of individual metrics and how best to pool those items into scales and indexes to determine how well they tap into underlying dimensions. We will not devote space in this chapter to reviewing decades of research on measurement, but it serves as an informative backdrop for what follows.[20] More recent work in the social sciences provides a specific framework for how to aggregate disparate measures into a common dimension of evaluation, a central issue for those trying to measure election performance.

Most of the chapters in this book analyze data on the states. This focus is in line with Gerken's vision of a "democracy index," but it also recognizes the fundamental autonomy that the U.S. Constitution bestows on state election practices and reflects where the most abundant data are being collected. It also provides a common denominator for connecting measures across chapters. State data are also more

---

[20] For example, see Gerring (2012), King, Keohane, and Verba (1994), and Zeller and Carmines (1980).

likely to be collected over multiple years and generally have higher levels of reliability. Yet our state focus should not preclude collection of measures at a lower level of analysis. Many states exhibit tremendous variation across counties and municipalities within their jurisdictions. The stark differences between large urban centers and less populated rural areas within a state are often dramatic. Indeed, several chapters make brief excursions to examine data at a lower level of analysis before returning to the states.

We should note that it is generally preferable to draw data from disparate places rather than a single source. Any one source of information may have idiosyncrasies owing to its methods or purposes. Multiple measures drawn from the same source will often appear to go together because of common error variance rather than true connections among variables. Creating a portfolio of indicators with differing origins helps balance against the possibility of a systematic bias tainting the collective assessment.

Leaves on a Tree

In providing a data-driven assessment of election administration and policy in the United States, we can choose to set our sights broadly or narrowly. We can assess the current state of American elections as a whole, such as when a college calculates the cumulative grade point average for a graduating senior, or we can assess individual aspects of elections at a fine level, such as when a college professor assigns a grade to a student's paper. The chapters that follow take a middle ground, by analyzing a limited set of measures associated with particular aspects of American elections, such as absentee voting and provisional ballots. Here we offer some thoughts about assessing elections at a more general level.

Given the fledging nature of election performance data, it might be tempting to gather all the measures one can find and then add them up to produce an overall assessment of the states. This has been done in some other policy areas by a variety of advocacy groups. But this approach violates best practices in the social sciences. Rather than falling prone to a haphazard search for measures, we follow scholarly practice to determine whether a global evaluation is even possible. We begin with the idea of election performance, then distill this notion into four concepts, and finally collect and evaluate a series of measures thought to tap these concepts. Only then do we consider the possibility of combining the measures into an aggregate metric using various methodological techniques. This approach avoids the concerns raised by Alvarez, Atkeson, and Hall (2012) about jumping immediately to an overall index that fails to provide useful diagnostic information to election administrators seeking improvements in performance. Regardless of how much aggregation occurs in the production of a broad index, we continue to emphasize the value of individual measures.

We adopt Munck and Verkuilen's (2002) analogy of measurement as parts of a tree. They describe the broad idea as the "trunk" of the tree and its major conceptual parts as "branches." The specific measures of these concepts are "leaves." Compared with branches, leaves are more numerous and more tangible. That is, as one shifts from the trunk to branches to leaves, the level of abstraction decreases and the number of components increases, just as a tree becomes more differentiated as one moves from the ground upward to the tips of its branches. Once the leaves are selected and scored, they can be reaggregated, or "rolled up," to generate higher-level metrics.

Munck and Verkuilen apply this approach to the operationalization of "democracy" at the national level. This is the tree trunk. They then apply Dahl's (1971) distinction between "contestation" and "participation" as the two major concept branches. Each concept then implies several measures, or leaves. For example, the level of "contestation" is evaluated with measures of freedom of the press and the right to form political parties.

We decompose the broad idea of election administration performance into four concepts. These are Gerken's (2009a) three dimensions of registering, voting, and counting, as well as a fourth dimension, data transparency. This framework implies that a state's election performance is exemplary if it scores well in registering those who want and are eligible to vote, facilitating voting by those who are eligible and wish to do so, tabulating ballots accurately, and providing thorough public access to data and other election information. A poorly performing state would fare badly in each domain. The more difficult cases occur when one wishes to assign an evaluation to a state that does well in some domains but less well in others. In some settings we go further and divide each of these concepts according to whether they emphasize voter access or ballot security, the two concerns most commonly highlighted in policy discussions about election reform.

After gathering measures for each of these concepts, it is crucial to assess their reliability and validity. This is the task of the chapters that follow. What they do not attempt is a complete aggregation of measures (although the authors do investigate connections among measures within a topic area). Aggregation is a more difficult process than is commonly assumed. As we have noted, simply adding up the measures to create a single index can be problematic. It does not reflect the distinctions between categories, it overlooks the relationships among measures, and it forces all the measures to be equally important. Working downward to the leaves and then back up to the idea permits the researcher to test whether an undimensional factor underlies the measures, rather than beginning with the assumption that a single "democracy index" metric would adequately reflect the full range of election-related things that states do.

A Look at Two States

To illustrate how the approach works in practice, we compare two Midwestern states, Indiana and Minnesota. Leaving aside questions of reliability and validity for individual chapters, what do measures say about how these states perform in terms of registering, voting, counting, and data access? Can these leaves be reaggregated into a reasonable summary indicator for each state?

Before examining the data, we need to highlight the issue of missing data. If one wishes to examine the raw values of the measures, the data largely speak for themselves. In contrast, if one wishes to rank or score states, missing data create a methodological fork in the road. We could assume that the data are missing completely at random, in which case the states with data could be ranked or assigned to percentiles. The percentile approach is common in other domains, such as educational testing. A downside of having at most fifty-one units (fifty states plus the District of Columbia) is that it is impossible for a state to be in the first percentile no matter how well it performs. If the analyst wants to penalize states for missing data, they could be ranked below all those with data. But in addition to artificially compressing the range of scores, the problem of ranking all states with missing data on a particular indicator below all states without missing data is that this strategy imports the data transparency concept into every substantive measure of election performance. This muddies the interpretation of an analysis of states that seeks to understand how well they perform particular election-related tasks. To avoid imposing any assumptions about missing data now, we simply present the raw values for each measure and the state's rank among those states reporting data.

Table 1.1 reports nineteen measures of election performance, divided into the four categories. Before discussing how Indiana and Minnesota stack up on all nineteen of these measures, we should say a word about what they are and how they were constructed.

Between 2010 and 2012, the Election Initiatives project of the Pew Center on the States conducted a series of meetings with an advisory group, composed of two dozen election officials and academics from across the country, to explore the possibility of releasing an Elections Performance Index (EPI) building off the ideas first articulated by Gerken (2009a). To make these deliberations tangible, the advisory group discussed a long list of measures – nearly fifty in all – that could potentially be included in such a performance index. The nineteen measures reported in Table 1.1 were discussed at an intermediate stage of the advisory group's deliberations. They are greater in number than the indicators that eventually were reflected in Pew's initial EPI, which was released in early 2013.[21] However, the measures in Table 1.1 all provide interesting insights into election administration and policy at the state level, even in cases where they were not included in Pew's EPI.[22]

What do the data say about Indiana and Minnesota? Starting with registration, it appears that Minnesota is performing better than Indiana. It ranks first out of all states in terms of the registration rate. Indiana's registration rate, which is almost nine points lower, puts it forty-second among the states. The gap is somewhat narrower when it comes to the rejection rate for absentee ballots, although Minnesota's tiny value of 0.3 percent puts it ahead again. Here is where data completeness affects a substantive measure; only forty-four states provided this information to the EAC. Lastly, Minnesota also comes out ahead when looking at the percentage of people who report being deterred from voting because of registration problems. Minnesota is well above the median state on this measure, while Indiana is just below it.

---

[21] See http://www.pewstates.org/research/data-visualizations/measuring-state-elections-perfor mance-85899446194.

[22] The measures are calculated as in the 2012 EPI. For EAVS-based data, a state is only considered to have an entry on a particular measure if it is reported by at least 85 percent of its local jurisdictions (weighted by voter registration). Contributors to this volume frequently use a different standard for what is considered "complete" and may compute rates such as absentee ballot rejections based on different denominators. A more detailed discussion of the measures is included in the Appendix to the book.

TABLE 1.1. *Comparing two states in 2012*

	Indiana		Minnesota	
	Rank	Value	Rank	Value
Registering				
Registration	42/50	78.4%	8/50	87.7%
New registrations rejected	28/28	71.7%	2/51	.01%
Provisional ballots cast	15/48	.2%	1/45[a]	0.0%
Provisional ballots rejected	14/40	.2%		–
Registration a reason for not voting	28/51	6.5%	2/51	1.2%
Online registration available		1		0
Voting				
Turnout	42/51	55.1%	1/51	75.7%
Absentee ballot rejections	39/44	.5%	35/44	.3%
Absentee ballot nonreturns	2/45	.7%	11/45	4.3%
UOCAVA rejections	46/46	20.6%	34/46	7.6%
UOCAVA nonreturns	3/47	13.5%	15/47	21.1%
Disability a reason for not voting	10/51	17.9%	24/51	14.7%
Polling place a reason for not voting	35/49	3.4%	3/49	.7%
Time waiting to vote	41/51	15 min.	14/51	6 min.
Counting				
Postelection audits		0		1
Residual vote rate	39/48	1.5%	6/48	0.5%
Confident vote was counted	19/51	91.9%	29/51	90.5%
Data access				
EAVS completeness	23/51	99.3%	1/51[b]	100%
Five online lookup tools	1/51[c]	5	1/51[d]	4[e]

Notes:
- Data are not available for that measure.
[a] Four states are tied at this value.
[b] Fourteen states tied at this value.
[c] Eight states tied at this value.
[d] Seventeen states tied at this value.
[e] Minnesota does not have provisional ballots. Therefore, whether the state has a feature on its Web site allowing a voter to check on the status of his or her provisional ballot is irrelevant. Minnesota is ranked at the top of this measure because it has 100 percent of the lookup tools relevant to it.

States are not ranked on the dichotomous postelection audits and online registration measures.

The denominator of each ranking fraction is the number of states for which data are available.

"Registration Rate" is based on citizens in the CPS.

"Registration a Reason for Not Voting" is the average over the 2004, 2008, and 2012 elections.

In terms of voting, Minnesota also beats Indiana on most measures. Most obviously, the 2012 turnout rate was almost twenty-one points higher in the Gopher State, ranking it first in the country. Yet this higher turnout rate did not result in longer lines, which averaged a third of the time it took to vote in the Hoosier State. Smaller percentages of people in Minnesota reported that they failed to vote because of a disability or something problematic about the polling place. Although Indiana reports a lower nonreturn rate among absentee and UOCAVA ballots, Minnesota rejected smaller shares of those ballots that were returned.

For the counting category, Minnesota performs better on all three measures. The state conducts postelection audits, whereas Indiana does not. In terms of outcomes, Minnesota's residual vote rate is one of the best in the country at 0.5 percent. Indiana's is one of the worst at 1.5 percent. Voters in both states are quite confident that their ballots were counted as they intended, although Indiana ranks slightly higher.

Finally, the states are similar in terms of data completeness in the EAVS, with Indiana falling just short of 100 percent completion. Both states provide all the online lookup tools that are assessed and relevant to the state.[23]

The impression that any reasonable observer would take from these indicators is that Minnesota is performing better than Indiana, and in some cases by a substantial margin. It is true that Indiana is ahead in a few categories, so the measures are not unanimous in their verdict. But the collective judgment of the metrics strongly suggests that Minnesota is in a better position. If the "leaves" in the table were aggregated up to the four larger categories of registering, voting, counting, and data transparency, Minnesota should be ranked more highly in each. If the states were students in a class, it would be natural to assign Minnesota a better letter grade.

How to Aggregate

Not all state comparisons will be as clear-cut as the difference between Indiana and Minnesota. There are likely to be states that perform much better in one category than another. This makes the task of aggregating more difficult and the decisions made along the way more consequen-

---

[23] Minnesota does not have a provisional ballot lookup tool on its state Web site. However, Minnesota is exempt from provisional ballot requirements of HAVA because it has Election Day registration (EDR).

tial. Smart analysts will disagree about the placement of some states in any global evaluation. So how does one proceed?

The most agnostic approach is to report the raw, disaggregated measures as they are. Every state's score on every indicator is listed. This approach is most transparent and imposes the fewest assumptions. It allows each state to have a unique "profile" just as each sound has a unique wavelength and amplitude, or an image has a fingerprint in the form of a color profile. By faithfully reflecting each of the various performance metrics, this approach also provides election administrators with task-specific feedback that will help them make surgical improvements to the most problematic aspects in their state. Officials in Indiana, for example, will learn that waiting times and registration problems deserve real attention, whereas absentee rejection rates are lesser concerns.

At the same time, this wide-open approach comes with liabilities. It does not apply any judgment about the quality of performance. Thinking of this task like evaluating a student, this approach reports the grade on each assignment without trying to render a final grade that summarizes the student's overall performance throughout the course. Because it throws a bundle of scores at the states, it might be unwieldy. By not providing a more global assessment for each state or ranking them in any way, it fails to encourage accountability and competition as Gerken's democracy index proposes to do. State officials might be able to avoid culpability for poor performance by directing attention toward a small number of measures on which they fare well. Reporting all the data also implicitly suggests that each measure is equally important. Ironically, this is one of the complaints about a summary index.

The solution to this messiness is to impose an aggregation rule, that is, to roll up the many leaves into a smaller set of concept branches. This necessarily involves the trade-off of adding assumptions about how measures should flock together and the relative weight that each should get. We believe that any aggregation exercise should also be accompanied by the raw data so that scholars and policy makers may benefit from learning about performance in specific domains and evaluate how the states would rank if a different aggregation rule were used.

The simplest way to combine individual measures of election performance into a small number of aggregated measures is simply to calculate the average value of each individual measure for each state. Although highly intuitive, this approach immediately comes up against the problem that the individual indicators are measured using different scales. Consider, for instance, the registration-related measures in Table 1.1. Five of the six measures are percentages, while the sixth, whether a state allows online voter registration, is a dichotomous variable equal to 1 if the state allows this, 0 otherwise. Also note that each of the five percentage measures vary across different ranges. The registration rate, for instance, varies from a low of 70.9 percent (Hawaii) to a high of 92.4 percent (Minnesota). On the other hand, the percentage of new registrations rejected ranges from 0 percent (New Hampshire) to 71.7 percent (Indiana). The average of these two percentages produces nonsense; even more nonsensical would be taking an average of all six measures grouped together under "registering" in Table 1.1.

Faced with the prospect of combining disparate measures into a single index, scholars generally "normalize" the measures in an attempt to get them all on the same scale. Without relying on higher statistical techniques, such as the one discussed later in the book, three normalization methods are typically used in situations like this. First, one can simply do the aggregation based on the rank ordering, rather than on the raw values. The best-performing state on a particular measure is assigned a value of 1, the second-best-performing state assigned a value of 2, and so on, until the last state is assigned a value of 51 (counting the District of Columbia as a state). The intermediate scale is then an average of all these rankings.

Second, one can transform the raw measures into the *percentage of the range*, so that the lowest-ranking observation is set to 0, the highest-ranking observation is set to 1, and every other observation is assigned a value between 0 and 1, depending on where in the interval that observation lands.[24] Third, one can transform the raw measures by first converting them to *z-scores* and then taking the average. A *z-score* first subtracts the raw score for a state from the average of all states, then divides this by the standard deviation across all states. This provides a handy normalization for comparing across measures.

A more sophisticated form of aggregation is to apply a data reduction technique in which the measures "speak" about how they go together. Exploratory factor analysis is a prime example of this. The exploratory version of factor analysis does not impose any constraints or other theoretical knowledge, instead asking the data to reveal what latent structure

---

[24] More formally, if x is the raw score for a state, x_{low} is the minimum value among all states, x_{high} is the maximum value among all states, the transformed value is defined as $(x - x_{low})/(x_{high} - x_{low})$.

exists. The method uses correlations among variables to identify dimensions underlying the observed data. This has the benefit of generating empirical weights or "loadings" that indicate how important each variable is to a factor. It also provides direct evidence on the dimensionality of the latent data structure, as indicated by the eigenvalues, which indicate how much variance each factor explains.

In contrast, confirmatory factor analysis uses the researcher's theoretical knowledge to guide the analysis. The researcher posits which factors organize the data and then estimates them in a more structured fashion. As in the exploratory version, the analysis itself provides evidence for how well items in a factor cohere and what weight or loading each should get. Ansolabehere, Rodden, and Snyder (2006) apply confirmatory factor analysis in their study of political polarization in the electorate. They use several surveys, such as the American National Election Study (ANES), to find questions about issues and then code them as either "economic" or "moral." Returning to our tree analogy, one might say that ideology is the "trunk," economic and moral issues are the "branches," and the individual survey questions are the "leaves." For example, the economic issues scale from the ANES includes items asking about spending on various programs, trade-offs between the environment and jobs, and feelings toward unions. Factor analysis of these items produces only one major factor (eigenvalue). The items all have similar weights, with loadings ranging from a low of .35 to a high of .67. More heterogeneous loadings or a greater number of factors would have produced a more complex interpretation of the data.

Collapsing leaves in this way is theoretically satisfying but does require making assertions about the importance of measures and how they should cohere. This is easier to justify the better developed the theory. In election administration, the state of theory is rapidly improving, although it remains uneven. Indeed, the purpose of this volume is to advance the science of measuring election performance. This exercise necessarily involves the interplay of evidence, experience, knowledge, and theory.

Applying a scaling approach to our 2012 data reveals that scale reliability is intermediate for the registering branch ($\alpha = .62$) and the voting branch ($\alpha = .54$) and much lower for the counting and data transparency branches ($\alpha = .36$ and $.35$, respectively).[25] The overall scale built

[25] The measure of scale reliability we use here is Cronbach's alpha. In performing this scaling exercise, we have to deal with two practical issues. The first is the fact that many of the EAVS-produced scales are highly skewed. To account for the skew, we perform the scaling

from the aggregation of these four branches has an overall reliability coefficient (Cronbach's α) of .40. The overall scale reliability is actually greater (α = .68) if we skip the intermediate "branch" step and instead aggregate all the leaves in one step into an overall score. Over-time reliability among 2008, 2010, and 2012 is quite high within each of the four concepts and for the overall scale, regardless of whether it is computed in one step or two.

Based on this initial examination of data from 2008, 2010, and 2012, the measures work together to render a fairly consistent verdict about state election performance. However, the measures of reliability cited earlier are, at best, weaker than one expects in highly developed areas of the social sciences, such as psychometrics. There are good reasons to believe that the coherence among measures will increase as data quality improves and data access and transparency practices in the states catch up to recent expectations about data availability. Still, there will be cases where states' rankings do not tell a unified story. A state might fare quite well in terms of registration but poorly in terms of counting. If these cases are common, one might refrain from emphasizing overall scores and instead focus on the four branches. An even less aggressive approach would rely only on leaves, which we believe should always be available regardless of the amount of data reduction taking place.

Nonetheless, there are good reasons to generate global evaluations, if we are cautious in interpreting them. Even the student whose scores on individual assignments and exams are uneven will still receive a final grade. That grade will be the instructor's best summary of the performance over the year, including assumptions about how much each score should contribute to the final judgment. The student will learn from the many marks through the year where he or she excels and where improvements are necessary. By receiving a final grade, it is possible to compare across students, for students to compare their performance across subjects, and to track performance as students move from one grade level to the next. The grade point average, which may be considered a sort of "meta" evaluation, goes a step further.

In the end, this book emphasizes the leaves over the branches, or even the trunk. The main reason is that each of the chapters focuses on an aspect of election administration and policy that can be thought of as a self-contained whole. If a state wishes to improve its standing

by first converting the raw scores to ranks. The second issue is missing data. To address this issue, we impute the average rank on a measure to replace missing values.

in how its election administration is regarded, the most likely successful strategy will be one that is focused on particular areas that need
improvement, rather than scattershot across all areas. In this early phase
of building a data-driven science of election administration, a lot is to
be gained by shining a spotlight on different aspects of election administration, one at a time.

OVERVIEW OF THE BOOK'S CHAPTERS

Each of the chapters in this volume evaluates measures of an aspect
of contemporary election administration. Chapters largely fall within
one of the four broad categories of registering, voting, counting, and
data transparency. These categories make intuitive sense and Gerken
has provided a sound rationale for the first three being distinct. They
also capture the essential steps in the workflow of election administration. There are sure to be cases where indicators cross these bound-
aries, reflecting the fact that performance in one domain often has
consequences for another domain. For example, more generous use
of absentee and UOCAVA ballots (voting) tends to result in higher
rejection rates for those ballots (counting). In addition to assessing the
reliability and validity of specific measures, the authors get to the meaning of those measures. They reveal the ways in which measures result
from such things as a state's demographic profile or election laws. The
authors show how multiple measures may be used in tandem to tell a
coherent story about the electoral ecosystem in a state or locality. Here
we review them according to whether they focus on registering, voting,
counting, or data transparency.

Chapter 2 ("Registration and Voting: A View from the Top"), by Barry
C. Burden, launches the empirical portion of this book by examining
the most fundamental statistics in the study of election administration
and policy making: registration and turnout rates. This is an appropriate starting point, not only because registration is a precondition to
voting (except in North Dakota) and the turnout rate is such an easily
grasped measure of the health of a democracy, but also because there is
so much more to these measures than first appears.

To study registration and turnout rates, we first need to agree to how
to measure these quantities. Without digging deeply into the manner
in which states report registration and turnout data, academics, policy makers, and courts have too easily taken at face value the official
reports issued by state and local election departments. This is especially

problematic in studying registration. In the management of the states' voter registration rolls, America's dynamic population encounters a combination of bureaucratic inertia, antiquated administrative procedures, and provisions of the NVRA that conspires to produce registration lists that are bloated by the presence of deadwood. On top of this, states define voter registration in different ways, and the science of estimating the number of eligible voters – which forms the denominator when we calculate the registration rate – is still evolving. Thus, comparing a 75 percent registration rate in one state with an 80 percent rate in another can be an exercise of comparing apples to turkey basters.

Burden's analysis alerts the reader to nettlesome measurement issues attendant even in the most basic indicator of electoral performance. He makes a strong counterintuitive argument that the most valid and reliable measure of the registration rate in the United States is based on survey research, not on official registration records. Having settled on a firm strategy for estimating how many eligible Americans are actually registered to vote, and how many vote, Burden provides insightful analysis into the possibilities and limitations for using policy choice to increase turnout and registration. In particular, demographic characteristics of a state and its policy choices have little effect on registration rates but considerable effect on turnout.

In Chapter 3 ("Voter Registration: The Process and Quality of Lists"), Stephen Ansolabehere and Eitan Hersh pick up on the registration list themes initiated by Burden and engage in a thorough exploration of state voter registration lists with the assistance of a unique resource – an aggregated nationwide list of voting-age Americans constructed by the political consulting firm Catalist. Their chapter provides a nationwide view of the accuracy of information contained in voter lists. It is a novel approach to the study of voter registration lists and is one of the first academic studies of voter registration that takes advantage of the "big data" revolution in American campaigns (Issenberg 2012). Beyond taking advantage of a remarkable data set, Ansolabehere and Hersh provide a useful taxonomy of registration lists based on their functions (to map voters onto precincts, authenticate voters at the polls, audit election results, and prevent in-person voter fraud) and a series of measures that help to illustrate how well the states' lists may be suited to these tasks. Finally, they make a strong case for paying attention to the complexities that attend the management of registration rolls and caution against generalizing across functions in assessing how well a particular state's voter registration list is suited to the tasks at hand.

In Chapter 4 ("Provisional Ballots"), Michael J. Hanmer and Paul S. Herrnson address an issue that has vaulted to prominence since the 2000 election: provisional ballots. A provisional ballot is issued to a person who tries to vote but is not listed on registration lists or whose eligibility is otherwise questioned by poll workers. The provisional ballots must be then verified after the election when a voter returns to show identification. Although mandated at the federal level by the Help America Vote Act (HAVA), implementation has varied significantly across the states. A high usage rate, for example, has the benefit of providing a fail-safe option for would-be voters and preventing fraud, yet it also indicates problems with the registration files provided to poll workers. They argue that the usage and acceptance rates be considered jointly; a rise in use generally translates to less frequent acceptance. They also recommend that data be collected on the reasons why provisional ballots were issued and why some were not counted.

Despite the nuances of provisional ballot activities, state-by-state data from the EAVS show that a few states are out of line with national norms. Whereas most states have usage rates below 1 percent, a handful of states give provisional ballots to between 4 percent and 6 percent of voters, and a few go even higher. Perhaps most concerning are states that do not conform to the general positive relationship between usage and acceptance. Both usage and acceptance rates are quite reliable over time, suggesting that state-specific factors are behind them.

Hanmer and Herrnson conclude by showing that key factors driving these patterns are whether states allow a provisional ballot to be counted if cast in the wrong precinct and whether those who request but do not cast absentee ballots must vote provisionally. These two provisions account for more than a percentage point difference in usage rates and twenty- to thirty-point differences in acceptance rates. In addition, states that used provisional ballots before HAVA mandated that all states use them issued more and accepted more for counting. This suggests that election officials in states that adopted the provisional ballot mechanisms because of the HAVA mandate are responding somewhat haltingly to this policy change.

We learn from Christopher B. Mann's Chapter 5 ("Mail Ballots in the United States: Policy and Administrative Challenges") that all absentee voting is not created equal. He argues that measures of absentee ballot usage are highly reliable and valid, but that rejection rates and the reasons for these rejections show surprisingly high volatility across the 2008, 2010, and 2012 elections. These fluctuations can only be understood in the context of which policy "regime" produces them. The four regimes Mann identifies are (1) absentee voting by excuse, (2) voting by mail without excuse, (3) permanent voting by mail, and (4) postal voting. These policy differences allow us to understand state differences: Wisconsin had twice the percentage of mail ballots as in Minnesota because Wisconsin belongs to the second regime and Minnesota belongs to the first. Useful comparisons for election administrators are thus among states within the same regime. One would not expect the universal use of mail voting in Oregon to hold in Pennsylvania, where voting is largely constrained to take place at traditional polling places. Acknowledging the regimes also helps make sense of disparate statistics. For example, the nonreturn rate for absentee ballots in 2010 was a mere 0.5 percent in Idaho but 30.8 percent in Utah. Once we know that Utah allows voters to put themselves on a permanent absentee ballot list, but Idaho does not, it is easy to see how this difference has come about: many people who register to vote in presidential elections continue to receive ballots in midterm elections in Utah without returning them.

While they also vote using absentee ballots, overseas voters who are covered by the UOCAVA present a distinct set of challenges to election administration and policy, which are explored in Thad Hall's Chapter 6 ("Voting from Abroad: Evaluating UOCAVA Voting"). Overseas military voters played a bit part in the 2000 election drama in Florida, but they have taken on a bigger role in national policy making since then. Indeed, aside from HAVA, the most important election reform at the national level since the 2000 election was the Military and Overseas Voting Enfranchisement (MOVE) Act of 2009, which was aimed at streamlining the process of getting ballots delivered to overseas voters in time for them to be returned and counted. Hall assesses the degree to which states and localities vary in how they handle requests for UOCAVA ballots and in how successful they are in getting those ballots counted. He documents the continuing difficulties that overseas voters have in returning their ballots, even in the wake of the MOVE Act. He also demonstrates that states can take steps to increase the successful participation of overseas voters even further, by liberalizing their ballot transit rules and (perhaps) liberalizing their registration facility rules.

In Chapter 7 ("Polling Place Practices and the Voting Experience"), Robert M. Stein and Greg Vonnahme report on research that establishes the relationship between where and when voters cast their ballots, on the one hand, and how satisfied they are with the experience, on the other hand. The past decade and a half has witnessed a revolution in the modalities of American voting. Rather than an election *day* we have an election *period*. This development has not gone completely unnoticed – witness the attention to early voting in the 2008 and 2012 elections as auguries for who would win the election – but the subject of whether early voting and easier access to absentee ballots leads the electorate to be more confident in the outcome has been largely overlooked in the rush to make voting more convenient. Furthermore, as Stein and Vonnahme make clear, once a state has decided to go all in with early voting, there are better and worse ways to do it, if the goals are to improve the voter experience and voter confidence.

In expanding their prior research, which had been focused on just two states, Stein and Vonnahme show that voter experiences are more positive in states in which voters have greater opportunities to vote before Election Day and when they have opportunities to vote in places they might frequent in their everyday lives, such as shopping centers. Voters who avail themselves of voting early do report a better experience than those who show up on Election Day, and they are willing to trade off waiting longer to do so in return for the greater flexibility in choosing the most convenient day on which to vote.

Lisa Schur and Douglas Kruse provide an insightful look into the experiences of disabled voters in Chapter 8 ("Disability and Election Policies and Practices"). Frequently overlooked in standard histories of the HAVA is the priority placed on increasing access to the ballot among disabled voters, particularly through HAVA's requirement that all precincts have voting systems that are "accessible for individuals with disabilities, including nonvisual accessibility for the blind and visually impaired, in a manner that provides the same opportunity for access and participation (including privacy and independence) as for other voters" (HAVA Sec. 301(a)(1)(3)(A)). Despite mandates for accessibility, Schur and Kruse demonstrate that turnout rates for disabled voters continue to be below those for nondisabled voters, especially among those with cognitive impairments and difficulty going outside alone. They provide compelling evidence that turnout among the disabled is increased when absentee balloting is more readily available to all voters, indicating that vote-by-mail systems can help reduce the turnout gap between people with and without disabilities.

A key measure of vote tabulation is the residual vote rate, examined in Stewart's Chapter 9 ("The Performance of Election Machines and the Decline of Residual Votes in the United States"). Developed by researchers after the 2000 election, the residual vote rate is the percentage of ballots cast that are not counted. In 2012, the nationwide residual vote rate was about 1 percent, suggesting that 1 out of every 100 votes was lost. Stewart shows that the residual vote rate is a valid measure of technological problems, such as poor ballot design and flawed counting procedures. This is clear from analyses showing higher rates for punch card machines and absentee ballots compared with lower rates for optical scan machines, where voters are often given the opportunity to correct over-votes and under-votes. The shift of states away from punch cards and lever machines toward optical scan and direct recording electronic (DRE) voting machines has contributed to a declining residual vote rate over time. Yet in the 2012 election, the rate varied significantly across states, from trivial levels in DC, Nevada, and Wisconsin to rates above 2 percent in states including Kansas and Missouri, all the way up to 3.5 percent in Nebraska.

Voting technology is behind much of this variation. Voting times also correlate with technologies, as the residual vote rate might suggest, with paper ballots being faster and touch screens taking longer. Shifts from one technology to another create more problems as election staff and voters adapt to them. By drawing on more granular data from Florida and Massachusetts, Stewart demonstrates that even within a state, the types of equipment and preparation in setting them up affect the residual vote rate. Stewart concludes by pointing to what appears to be a practical lower bound on the residual vote rate of about 0.5 percent, thus providing a reasonable standard for judging residual vote rates generally.

In his analysis in Chapter 10 ("Voter Confidence as a Metric of Election Performance"), Paul Gronke takes on an important metric that has emerged to assess elections across the country – answers to the survey question asking whether people are confident their votes were counted as they intended. A survey question such as this could serve as a convenient summary statistic of the electoral process, much like the "presidential approval" question helps summarize citizens' assessments of the president, but only if it can be deemed reliable and valid as discussed in this chapter. Gronke casts a skeptical eye on this question, but he ends up acknowledging its usefulness for guiding policy makers toward improving elections in the eyes of voters.

The usefulness of the idea of voter confidence is undermined somewhat by the tendency of voters to approach the question through the lens of loser's remorse or winner's triumph. Voters for winning candidates are more confident their vote was counted as cast than voters for losing candidates. At the same time, Gronke demonstrates that there are lessons for the LEO who wishes to improve the confidence of voters in the administration of elections. For instance, voters who encounter competent poll workers and machines that work, and who wait in short lines, have a better feeling about their vote being counted than voters who face surly poll workers, broken machines, and long lines. Election officials cannot (and should not) be in the business of ensuring that every voter votes for a winner; however, they can be in the business of improving election administration, which has demonstrable effects on boosting confidence among the electorate in the legitimacy of the outcome.

In Chapter 11 ("Election Data Transparency"), Lonna Rae Atkeson examines the rapidly changing environments of accessibility and transparency. She contends that an open election system boosts public confidence and provides valuable information for a range of stakeholders. Unlike other domains of election administration, where policies are a matter of debate, there is little disagreement that more information is a good thing. Indeed, one goal behind the creation of the EAC was to promote sharing of data. States have improved their reporting to the point where more than 90 percent of the most important items in the EAVS was complete in the 2012 survey. Yet the validity of these data is open to question; it is often ambiguous whether a missing entry means that a state did not collect it or could not calculate it, or if the item is not applicable. And when the full EAVS is evaluated, completion rates drop to between 70 percent and 86 percent, depending on the section. Overall completeness in 2012 ranged from the District of Columbia's nearly perfect record to New York, which provided only a bit above 40 percent of the data requested in the EAVS.

The other component of Atkeson's analysis is the availability of online information for the public. Drawing on the Pew study of state election Web sites and an original study of Internet searches, she finds that states with higher levels of EAVS data completeness also made it easier to find voter information using Google searches. Importantly, she discovers that neither completeness nor online information is a product of state characteristics or demographics. Rather, both appear to be the result of "time and resources" that state officials devote to their online presences. Yet she finds modest correlations among her usability and search measures, the availability of online tools, and data completeness. These are areas where improvements are happening most quickly and dramatically.

CONCLUSION: COMMON THEMES

Each chapter in this volume offers a unique portrayal of a different aspect of election performance, yet when looking across the chapters this volume, several common themes emerge.

First, and most positively, the quality of election data has now developed to a point where it is possible to conduct systematic evaluation of election performance. While the research and policy communities should continue to press for more and better data, recent advances allow us to understand what is happening – and why – in a way that was unimaginable just a decade ago. Having more complete data on a wider range of measures makes evident how much the states vary and why. As noted at the outset of this chapter, this permits valuable insights into which state and local innovations are successful at improving elections. Although a state will often perform relatively better on some measures than others, it is safe to conclude generally that some states are doing better than others across a range of measures. States that succeed in one area tend to thrive in others areas.

Second, the measures often confirm folk wisdom about particular election and states, but the data also turn up some surprises. The regularities are reassuring. For example, changes in several indicators between the 2008 presidential election and the 2010 midterm elections could have been predicted in advance. In the more intense presidential campaign environment, absentee ballots are more likely to be returned and turnout increased. Simultaneously, more voters have trouble finding their polling places and a large share of absentee ballots are rejected. These swings reflect well-known cycles in these two rather different electoral environments.

But the data also reveal the unexpected. Common sense would expect more people to say their voting was hindered by disability or illness in states where heath outcomes are poorer. Indeed, Alabama, Kentucky, and West Virginia rank near the bottom in terms of state health outcomes and display some of the highest disability and illness problems in voting.[26] What is surprising is that Connecticut and Massachusetts have similarly large percentages of voters citing disability and illness problems, yet these states have two of the best health outcomes in the country. Clearly more is at work than simple demographics, such as the accessibility of older public buildings in the Northeast. Likewise, it is

---

[26] See www.americashealthrankings.org.

not surprising that "battleground" states, such as Florida and Virginia, saw longer lines at the polls in 2012. But the intensity of the campaign is not the full story. The swing states of Iowa and Wisconsin both had average line lengths of less than ten minutes even though uncompetitive states such as Maryland, the District of Columbia, and South Carolina averaged more than twenty minutes.

Third, a state's data do not necessarily tell a single story about election performance. An individual state will sometimes vary in how it does at the four broad categories of analysis: registering, voting, counting, and data transparency. The same appears to be true when it comes to other dimension of our analysis: security versus access. This book project has made clear that there are more and better measures of voter access than of ballot security. Although indicators of provisional ballot usage might be considered on both sides of the ledger, in general there is better data on how voters interact with the system than on how the system protects its integrity. We hope that this book will help spur more effort on filling out the needs for security measures as it pushes for more comprehensive election performance data generally. The substantial variation in outcomes the authors observe across the states demonstrates that no state need be locked into subpar performance. The fact that other states – even those in similar circumstances – are able to produce higher registration rates, fewer rejected ballots, shorter lines, fewer people deterred by disabilities, and lower residual vote rates should encourage state and local officials to continue pursuing improvements.

Fourth, election performance is often, but not always, resistant to change. State indicators are rather sluggish; they display a great deal of inertia in terms of evolution over time. For example, state voter turnout in 1980 is correlated with turnout in 2008 at .56.[27] States that used provisional voting before HAVA required all states to use them have the highest usage levels of all the states. This suggests that ingrained political cultures, demographics, and folkways have a constraining effect on election performance. However, the slow pace of change also makes it easier to spot more abrupt turning points in election performance. As long as the campaign environment does not vary significantly between two elections, when an indicator shifts in a state from one election to the next, it may often be attributed quite clearly to changes in election administration because other background factors were roughly held

[27] This implies that knowing turnout in 1980 only explains 31 percent of the variance in 2008 turnout (.56 × .56), leaving the remaining 69 percent to demographic changes, electoral politics, election administration, and unexplained factors.

constant. Thus, when a state experiences longer lines or higher absentee rejection rates, it is not hard to detect and diagnose.

Thus, taken together, the chapters in this volume demonstrate that it is possible to conduct a thorough, detailed analysis of the administration of elections in the United States using a varied collection of data and techniques that is not difficult to assemble. It is our hope that the works in this volume will seed an enhanced interest in improving elections in the United States in a way that arises out of a common understanding of what needs our immediate attention as a nation.

2

Registration and Voting: A View from the Top

Barry C. Burden

Voter turnout may be the most widely hailed indicator of the robustness of a democracy. While it is true that lack of participation in a democratic system might sometimes indicate contentment, democratic reformers generally believe that more voter involvement is a good thing. Federal and state reforms have sought explicitly to increase registration and turnout rates. Initiatives such as the Voting Rights Act and provisions for overseas voters have been targeted at specific groups in society, while others, such as "motor voter" legislation and Election Day registration (EDR), have been aimed at the electorate as a whole. This chapter assesses levels of voter registration and turnout across the states, with a focus on the 2008 and 2010 elections, and how those rates are shaped by demographic, political, and policy factors at the state level.

This "view from the top" produces several conclusions. First, and perhaps surprisingly, a measure of registration based on the Current Population Survey (CPS) is often superior to one based on official state reports. Second, there is a great deal of inertia in turnout rates and especially registration rates, suggesting that state efforts to influence these rates have only limited effect in the short run. Third, there is substantial variation across states, more so than over time, indicating that state factors are quite important. Fourth, although registration and turnout rates are correlated, states vary significantly in the degree to which registrants actually vote. Fifth, turnout rates, and to a much lesser degree registration rates, are influenced by state election laws, suggesting they are appropriate indicators of election performance that can be influenced by state policy makers. Finally, there has been a convergence of

I thank Michael McDonald and Charles Stewart III for helpful feedback on an earlier draft of this chapter.

states over time in terms of turnout that is likely the result of changes in demographics, campaigns, and election practices.

WHY FOCUS ON REGISTRATION AND TURNOUT RATES

The narrative of electoral democracy in the United States documents the long-term increase in voter turnout, largely made possible by the extension of the franchise to more groups (Keyssar 2001). Over the broad sweep of history, it is clear by this standard that the American system has become more democratic. Turnout is thus considered a key barometer of the health of a democratic system. Simply put, people are more likely to participate if they are confident in the system and find it relatively easy to take part. Although turnout is affected by many things outside the control of the election administrator, high turnout is frequently regarded as a sign that the democracy is functioning well.[1] One might even view turnout as a sort of "grand indicator" that encompasses all others, coming as it does at the end of the electoral cycle, which includes many registration and balloting activities. Turnout is the product of many intervening indicators, such as how absentee ballots are handled, the conditions under which provisional ballots are counted, early voting options, disabled access to the polls, and other polling place practices.

Close behind turnout as a broad indicator is voter registration. In most jurisdictions in the United States, people must register with the government before they are permitted to vote.[2] As with turnout, high levels of registration indicate a more successful election system. Widespread registration signals that citizens who wish to vote have at least met the prerequisite of being registered and thus have the opportunity to cast ballots. These are the fundamental standards outlined in Gerken's (2009a) proposal for a "democracy index" of election performance.

Recent years have seen important developments in the administration of both registration and turnout. In terms of registration, the 2002 Help America Vote Act (HAVA) mandated that each state create a computerized, interactive, and centralized registration database. This was a substantial undertaking for some states. The databases now in place are a mix of "bottom-up" systems controlled primarily by local

---

[1] Indeed, some scholars have argued for compulsory turnout as a way to improve citizenship (Lijphart 1997). For a contrary view arguing against full participation, see Brennan (2011).

[2] North Dakota is the key exception.

election officials (LEOs) and "top-down" structures maintained by a central state authority. These databases still vary in terms of their quality, as Ansolabehere and Hersh document in Chapter 3, but they are surely improving.

Before HAVA, the last major federal effort was the 1993 National Voter Registration Act (NVRA). The law was intended to increase registration rates by offering registration opportunities as part of other government interactions, such as getting or renewing a driver's license, hence the name "motor voter." The law also limited how often states could "purge" voters from registration lists (normally after they fail to vote in two federal elections). Research on the effects of NVRA has generally found positive effects on registration but mixed results when it comes to turnout (Franklin and Grier 1997; Highton and Wolfinger 1998; Rhine 1995). In retrospect, lackluster findings appear to have been a result of incomplete implementation whereby some states were not in full compliance with NVRA. This suggests that measuring state performance is better done with outcomes such as registration and turnout rates rather than laws.

States have also been seriously experimenting with the voting process since the 2000 election. The movement toward "early voting" has increased substantially, with roughly one-third of voters casting ballots before the traditional Election Day in 2008. Some of this is facilitated by such things as early voting centers, but in other states voters may vote by no-excuse or even permanent absentee and never have to visit a polling place. More recently, a number of states have tightened voter identification laws. The states remain a patchwork of different registration and voting practices.

Technological developments have also spurred change. A small group of states – twelve as of the 2012 election – has adopted online voter registration. Automated, paperless registration systems and portable voter registration have also been offered as ways to increase registration rates (Ponoroff 2010). As of 2008, about half of the state Web sites permitted voters to check their registration status online and two-thirds allowed voters to find their polling places (Pew Center on the States 2008). A mere two years later, only nine states did not permit online registration checks and just two lacked a way for voters to look up polling places (Pew Center on the States 2011).

Registration and turnout are likely to reflect all of these developments at the federal and state levels, as well as factors beyond policy makers' immediate control, such as demographics of the electorate and the activities of candidates and other groups. Before considering the impacts of these variables, the measurement of registration and turnout must take center stage. This basic science of measurement establishes performance levels that may then be connected to state practices and resources.

MEASUREMENT CONCERNS

In an ideal world, registration and turnout rates could be computed in a straightforward fashion. The analyst would divide the number of registrants or the number of voters by the total eligible to do so. These intuitive definitions are complicated by five factors.

First, registration is dynamic. Unlike turnout, which is tied to a discrete event and thus contained to the voting period, registration may be done at any time of the year. Although surges in registration occur in the days leading up to an election (Gimpel, Dyck, and Shaw 2007), potential voters are in fact registering continuously throughout the year. People become newly eligible when they reach the voting age, meet residency requirements, or have post-felon voting rights restored. In addition, about one in five states has some form of EDR that gets processed after the election is over. Further, states operate on different schedules for purging the voting rolls of people thought to be deceased, ineligible, or recently moved. As a result, there is no ideal time for taking a "snapshot" of registration rates across the states. The data are out of date as soon as they are collected.

Second, states define "registration" in different ways. Like other elements of election administration, the creation of registration standards developed idiosyncratically with little coordination among states. Some states have partisan registration; others do not. Some distinguish between "active" registrants who have recently voted and "inactive" registrants who have not, while other states ignore this distinction. Among those that do distinguish, states are inconsistent in whether their official registration numbers combine both types or only include the active registrants.[3] North Dakota has no formal registration process but does

---

[3] Consider a recent summary of the situation provided by the U.S. EAC (2011a, 6): "States report their registration numbers for different purposes and in different ways. According to EAC's 2004 survey, while 26 States used only active voters in their total number of registrations, another 20 States included both active and inactive voters, and four States left the decision to the discretion of local officials. EAC asked each State to report its number of 'registered and eligible' voters and then asked for separate totals of active and inactive voters. In

maintain a voter list that gets updated after the election. In short, even what it means to be registered is not the same across states.

Third, turnout may be defined in terms of the total number of ballots cast or the total number of ballots counted.[4] The former is the most inclusive definition because it counts all the people who participate in any fashion, even if their votes are not ultimately tallied. The latter is narrower because it focuses only on valid votes cast and counted. The distinction might seem trivial, but the difference can be quite meaningful. The number of counted votes is almost always lower than the total number cast because of under-votes, over-votes, or problems that prevent ballots from being counted. Indeed, the difference between ballots counted and valid votes is the basis of the "residual vote rate," the percentage of ballots that are not counted (e.g., Stewart 2006). As Stewart's chapter in this volume explains, residual votes are caused by a combination of factors that are either under the voter's control (e.g., intentional under-voting) or beyond their control (e.g., machine errors). It is thus difficult to say with certainty whether total participants, total ballots, or only counted votes should be the measure. This point is heightened in midterm elections, when each state has a different array of races on the ballot that are more likely to be skipped than would a presidential contest.

The fourth question is which denominator to use to measure registration and turnout rates. Neither the states nor the federal government reports the number of people eligible to vote in a given election. For many years the standard definition used the Census Bureau's estimate of the voting-age population (VAP). That practice became increasingly problematic as the number of ineligible felons and noncitizens increased, thereby understanding the turnout rate. Michael McDonald now routinely provides a better estimate that he calls the voting-eligible population (VEP). The VEP makes reasonable adjustments to the VAP to account for felons, overseas citizens, and, most importantly,

---

addition, the survey asked States how they reported the number of registered voters for 'other official purposes.' A total of 16 States responded that they only use active registered voters. Thirty States reported using both active and inactive registered voters, and four States had some jurisdictions report using only active voters while other jurisdictions reported using both active and inactive voters. North Dakota does not have a voter registration requirement and therefore does not make a distinction between active and inactive voters. The remaining two States did not respond to this question. Furthermore, in 39 States, the number of 'registered and eligible' voters for the November 2010 election equals precisely the number of inactive plus active voters."

4   In addition, votes counted may be based on the "highest office" on the ballot or valid votes on any portion of the ballot.

noncitizens (McDonald 2002; McDonald and Popkin 2001). The VEP measures show turnout in recent elections to be several points higher than previously thought.[5] McDonald's VEP has become the standard denominator for analyses of voter turnout and may be used for computing voter registration rates, as well.

A fifth and final concern is about the quality of state voter files. Although most states have highly accurate records on who is registered and who has voted, I will demonstrate that a handful of states are reporting numbers that are clearly in error. This in turn motivates a search for unofficial sources that might be more accurate.

THE MEASURES

To compute registration rates, two data sources are used: (1) an "official" measure based on the number of active registrants reported by states to the Election Assistance Commission (EAC) and (2) a "survey" measure based on the number of self-reported registrants in Census surveys. Although both are federal government sources, there are important differences between them that warrant extended discussion.

The "official" measure comes from the EAC's reports on the impact of the NVRA and is based on data reported by chief election officials in the states. These reports are generally provided in the months following the general election. The total number of active registrants is divided by McDonald's VEP. The "survey" measure is based on surveys conducted by the Census Bureau as part of the CPS. The CPS includes a Voting and Registration Supplement (VRS) in November of even-numbered years. This supplement's sample is the "civilian noninstitutionalized population living in the United States." It is based on extremely large samples – more than 100,000 people – to produce reliable state-level estimates.[6] Respondents are asked whether they were registered and voted in the most recent election.[7]

---

[5] The McDonald data may be downloaded at elections.gmu.edu. One limitation of the VEP measure is that it is not available below the state level before the implementation of the American Community Survey in the mid-2000s or below the national level before 1980. The Census Bureau is now reporting the citizen voting-age population (CVAP), which is a significant improvement over the VAP.

[6] Within most states the margin of error is between 1.5 and 3 points.

[7] Those who report voting in variable PES1 are assumed to be registered. Respondents who are coded "no answer," "refusal," "don't know," or "out of universe" in PES2 are omitted from the calculations, as are "ineligible" respondents in PES3.

Both registration measures have advantages and limitations. The "official" measure represents the best estimates from the states, based on their voter registration lists. These lists have been improved tremendously over the past several years, but they still suffer from a number of problems. In addition to the dynamic nature of the data, the lists show evidence of having duplicate records and deceased voters, as documented in Chapter 3 (see also Pew Center on the States 2012b). This means that the registration rolls frequently overstate the number of people who are actually registered and eligible to be so. As a result, states report extremely high registration rates. Two states – Alaska and Michigan – had rates greater than 100 percent of the VEP in 2008, 2010, and 2012. In 2012 New York reported a registration rate of 106 percent, and the District of Columbia reported a registration rate of 117 percent. These rates are clearly erroneous. Even if voter rolls are slightly bloated by a less-than-immediate purging of inactive voters, it is difficult to understand how the list maintenance provisions of HAVA would affect states so differently.

At the same time, several states had unbelievably low rates by this measure. In 2008, Mississippi reports that less than half of eligible voters were registered, a logical impossibility given the 61 percent turnout rate in the presidential election in Mississippi. Three other states also reported registration rates that are lower than turnout rates. There are also inexplicable variations over time. Mississippi's registration rate jumped by fifteen points between 2008 and 2010 despite a substantial decline in turnout.[8] Ohio's registration increased by thirty points. Another nine states showed less dramatic increases that nonetheless run against conventional understandings of the differences between

---

[8] It jumped again, to 94 percent, in 2012. Going back in time, the Mississippi story is even muddier (pun intended). Between 2006 and 2008 total registration dropped by 773,301. This was not a result of simply shifting voter statuses from active to inactive; both fell substantially. The state reports having a registration rate of 84.1 percent in 2006 despite turnout of just 29.4 percent that year. Paradoxically the Mississippi secretary of state reports, "Voter rolls in many counties continue to be bloated with lack of purging conducted by Election Commissioners to bring the voter rolls up to date. As of February 13, 2012, there are 16 counties which have ... more registered voters than the 2010 Census Bureau figures indicate are eligible to vote" (Mississippi Secretary of State 2012, p. 5). Similarly, New Mexico saw a surprising decrease in registration from 2006 to 2008 and then a dramatic increase in 2010. This was likely attributable to the movement of nonparticipating voters from the active to the inactive rolls; the two numbers rose and fell together. Despite these concerns, it is puzzling that neither Mississippi nor New Mexico appears to be an outlier in Catalist data analyzed by Ansolabehere and Hersh.

midterm and presidential elections.[9] While it is possible that the official registration measure gets the *ranking* of states about right (after the removal of several obvious outliers), the raw values of the variable cannot yet be viewed as accurate indicators of the actual registration rates.

Logically one might expect registration totals to track changes in a state's population. Between elections some registrants die or leave the state, while other people transition into registration eligibility by reaching age eighteen or moving into the state. These vital statistics are carefully tracked by the Census Bureau and could be used to establish a baseline for identifying reasonable changes in registration. This would need to be done between two comparable elections – say, two sequential presidential elections – rather than a presidential and a midterm year, when voters, campaigns, and political groups are less focused on registration.[10] Even without this analysis in hand, it provides an intuitive guide to assessing measures of registration. We know from Census data that population changes over a two- or four-year period should be fairly modest, usually no more than a few percentage points. All else constant, it follows that a valid measure of registration rates should roughly track those incremental changes.

The "survey" measure brings a different set of measurement concerns. By definition it relies on self-reports that are subject to error, usually overreporting. Like voter turnout, where overreporting may be a result of sample bias or something about respondents, such as faulty recall or intentional misreporting because of social desirability (Burden 2000), research shows that respondents also overreport being registered (Ansolabehere and Hersh 2011; Fullerton, Dixon, and Borch 2007). Fortunately the error appears to be much less than with turnout, although some systematic biases remain. Overreporting of registration is somewhat more common in Deep South states, where minority populations are larger and religious affiliation is more widespread (Bernstein, Chadha, and Montjoy 2003). Whereas the "official" measure appears to vary too much, it is possible that the "survey" measure varies too little because of individuals assuming that they remain registered even when they have not voted recently. For example, many respondents mistakenly believe that their registration is automatically updated when they move. Yet compared with the "official" measure, the "survey" measure has a

---

[9] No state had higher voter turnout in 2010 than 2008.

[10] Between 2008 and 2010 every state's "survey" registration rate dropped. All but ten "official" rates dropped, and most of the contrary states appear to be a result of errors.

great deal of face validity. For example, in 2008 Maine reported an unbelievable "official" rate of 95.3 percent that was paired with a more sensible "survey" rate of 86.5 percent.[11]

Both registration measures are reliable in that they provide stable estimates between the 2008 and 2010 elections. This is to be expected because population changes are slow and because most registrants vote and thus remain actively registered from one election to the next. As a scatterplot presented in Figure 2.3 shows, the "survey" measures appear to be superior because of its larger over-time correlation.[12] Both registration indicators show more stability when a state does not experience a significant midterm election that might induce more new registrations. The over-time correlations are highest for states with neither a gubernatorial nor senatorial election in 2010, lowest for states with both types of elections, and intermediate for those with either a gubernatorial or senatorial election.

Further validation of the official registration lists might be done with the Catalist measures analyzed by Ansolabehere and Hersh in Chapter 3. Catalist is a private firm that aims to clean state voter files by eliminating and correcting entries it identifies as invalid based on duplication, change of address requests, and death records, as well as commercial data on consumer behavior. These exercises allow Catalist to estimate the share of individuals in a state's voter file that is "probably dead." Surprisingly, the "probably dead" measure is negatively and significantly correlated with both registration measures in both 2008 and 2010 (correlations range between –.223 and –.412). This counterintuitive finding suggests that states with higher registration rates actually have less deadwood. This might explain outliers, such as Alaska, that have high mobility but not states, such as Oregon, with a high registration rate but also high "probably dead" rate. More exploration of these Catalist measures with overall registration rates would be helpful.

Because of the many concerns I have documented with the "official" measure, including the different standards used by states to define

---

[11] In other analyses I evaluated the over-time variance in the two registration rates. Because rates are expected to move slowly along with changes in population, a lower variance would indicate a state that it managing its list more effectively. Consistent with other evidence, variance of the "official" measure was much higher than that of the "survey" measure. Comparing the two highlighted many of the same problematic states turned up in the raw data. I thank Charles Stewart for suggesting this empirical strategy.

[12] Note that the correlation jumps dramatically to .920 after removing six outliers where states' 2008 registration rates were above 100 percent or below their turnout rates.

registration and the impossible rates some of them report, I view it as an unacceptable metric of registration rates in too many cases. As states continue to improve their voter registration lists and reporting practices, the "official" indicator is likely to improve. For the remainder of this chapter, I focus on the "survey" measure as the best source of registration rates.

In contrast to the measures of registration rates, the measure of turnout rates is more straightforward. The numerator is the total number of ballots counted (wherever it exists). For states without a separate turnout report, it is defined as the vote for president in 2008 or highest office in 2010. The denominator is the McDonald VEP measure.

The validity of the turnout measure is high. The McDonald indicator has become the standard measure employed by scholars studying elections. It is a clear improvement over older measures that relied on the VAP, as demonstrated by head-to-head comparisons (Holbrook and Heidbreder 2010). McDonald is transparent about how the VEP is created by adjusting the VAP for such things as noncitizens, overseas citizens, and ineligible felons.

The reliability of the turnout measure is high and varies in predictable ways. The over-time correlation is .895, closely mirroring that for the survey registration measure. The correlation remains high if limited to states that had either a gubernatorial or senatorial election (.785) or both kinds of elections (.784) in 2010, thus more closely approximating the intense electoral environment of the presidential campaign. The correlation is considerably lower among states with neither type of midterm election (.440, although the sample is only six states).

WHAT THEY TELL US

Although the media often write at great length about how participation in the most recent election compares with the previous one, the most important source of variation is not temporal. *Registration and turnout rates vary much more across states than over time.* The seesaw of up-and-down activity between presidential and midterm years is predictable and well understood. In contrast, the greater variation across states has received less acknowledgment than it deserves.

Figure 2.1 displays the raw data by state. Several facts are evident and will be reinforced by later analyses. There is considerable variation across states, more so with turnout than with registration. In addition, there is often a substantial gap between the registration rate and the turnout

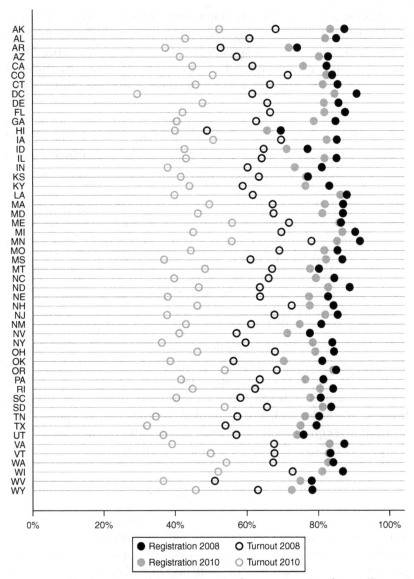

FIGURE 2.1. Registration and turnout rates in the states, 2008 and 2010. (*Sources*: Registration rates are based on the CPS's VRS. Turnout rates are provided by Michael McDonald [elections.gmu.edu].)

rate. In 2008 median state turnout was 64.0 percent, but that summary statistic disguises massive variation. On the low end were Hawaii at 40.0 percent and West Virginia at 51.2 percent; Minnesota's 78.1 percent marked the nation's highest turnout rate. In 2010, turnout ranged from a low of 29.6 percent in the District of Columbia and 32.2 percent in Texas to 55.9 percent in Minnesota and 56.0 percent in Maine.

Variability in turnout is greater in 2010 than in 2008. Although the range is a bit large in 2008, presidential turnout has a smaller standard deviation (5.8 points versus 6.2 points). This is indicative of the fact that a presidential election provides more uniformity because the same major party candidates appear on the ballot in all states. In contrast, midterm elections are subject to uneven competition, with some states having hard-fought statewide races and other states having none.

It is important to note that there is also variation within states. Shifting to a slightly different turnout measure computed at the county level (total presidential votes counted divided by the VAP) provides evidence of intrastate differences.[13] Some states show a lot of internal variation. For example, in Colorado, county turnout in 2008 ranged from 26.7 percent to 86.3 percent. States with less variation tend to be found in New England (where there are fewer counties or countylike units to generate variability) and upper Midwest states. For example, in Iowa the county range spanned from 56.1 percent to 77.5 percent. This might reflect the greater homogeneity of the Iowa population, hinting that demographics are important at the local level.

Registration rates vary less than turnout rates. In 2008 registration varied a bit more over twenty points from a low of 69.6 percent in Hawaii to 91.8 percent in Minnesota. In 2010 the overall mean turnout level was lower, but the gap between the lowest and highest registration states was about the same as in 2008. State-level factors would thus seem to have more influence on turnout than on registration.

Yet the diversity across states has generally declined over time. Figure 2.2 plots the standard deviation of state turnout rates by year.[14] As would be expected, midterms show more variability than presidential elections. Even with the unequal attention given to battleground and nonbattleground states in presidential elections, the standard deviation has nonetheless generally been a percentage point or two higher in midterms, where presumably competition is more uneven across states. The other interesting pattern is the decrease in variation over time.

[13] We must use VAP as the denominator in exploring turnout rates at the county level because VEP is not regularly calculated at that level by McDonald or by any other scholar.

[14] For this figure I used McDonald's "highest office" turnout measure rather than the "total ballots" measure, which is missing for many states. Indeed, many years have missing data for ten to fifteen states, which limits the comparability of the measure over time. Fortunately, the correlation between the two measures at the state level is .997.

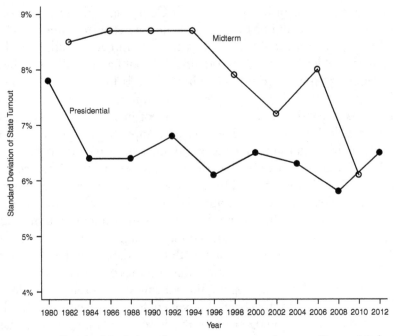

FIGURE 2.2. Standard deviation of state voter turnout, 1980–2012. (*Source*: Michael McDonald [elections.gmu.edu].)

Both presidential and midterm elections show evidence of growing uniformity among the states.[15] There has been convergence in turnout rates between the South and non-South (McDonald 2010), but that is not the whole story. In any given year the South shows more uniformity in turnout, but the decrease there is no greater than in the rest of the country.[16]

---

[15]   The last two points in both series may be anomalies or signs of more lasting changes. Midterm election variability dropped sharply in 2010, while presidential election variability reverted to earlier levels, thus causing the lines to cross for the first time in the period examined.

[16]   I defined the South as the eleven states of the Confederacy. The standard deviation of presidential year turnout in the South varies by only nine points between 1980 and 2004, with only a slight indication of downward movement. The range in the non-South during those same years is fourteen points. The 2008 election is an anomaly in the South as the standard deviation actually jumped to its highest level, a pattern not seen in other states. This appears to be because of highly competitive elections in Virginia and North Carolina.

EXPLAINING TURNOUT

The purpose of this section is to identify variables responsible for state turnout rates. State registration and turnout rates tend to persist across elections, with only modest bumps up and down caused by variation in competitiveness around those central tendencies. The main story is one of inertia, implying that contemporary variables are unlikely to have large effects on either registration on turnout.

As simple evidence for this point, consider correlations between 2008 and 2010. These are displayed as scatterplots in Figure 2.3. Despite being starkly different electoral environments – one a presidential year that favored Democrats and the other a midterm year that favored Republicans – the correlation between the two elections is high: .89 for registration and .71 for turnout. Put another way, 80 percent of the variation in registration and 50 percent of the variation in turnout can

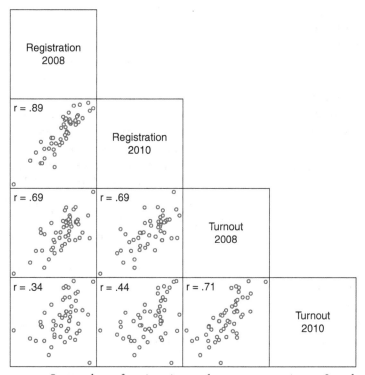

FIGURE 2.3. Scatterplots of registration and turnout rates in 2008 and 2010. (*Sources*: Registration rates are based on the CPS's VRS. Turnout rates are provided by Michael McDonald [elections.gmu.edu].)

be explained simply by knowing the state, even when comparing rather different presidential and midterm election years. When the analysis is instead based on comparing the 2008 and 2012 presidential elections, the stability in registration is relatively unaffected (correlation of .88) but the stability of turnout rises substantially to .94. This over-time consistency says that the factors that underlie state registration and turnout rates must also be sluggish.

Registration and turnout rates are also correlated with one another, but less strongly. In 2008 the correlation is .69. In 2010 it is a weaker .44 but rises to .74 in 2012. These correlations show that registering a large share of the population does not necessarily lead to high turnout. Even in presidential election years, registration "explains" only about half of the variation in turnout. Whereas registration rates are fairly uniform across the states, turnout is more variable and thus subject to state-specific factors.

What are these factors? A long line of research demonstrates that more competitive elections drive up both registration and turnout. Higher levels of competitiveness make voters aware of the importance of their votes for the outcome, provide more information via the media, and generate more elite activities, such as advertising, phone calls, voter registration drives, and other "get out the vote" (GOTV) efforts (Cox and Munger 1989; Rosenstone and Hansen 1993). Yet the impact of competitiveness should not be overstated. It is true that "battleground" states tend to have higher levels of participation than do uncompetitive states, but the variation across states far exceeds these impacts.

For a fuller accounting of turnout, I estimate multivariate statistical models of state registration rates in 2008 and 2010. These models follow common approaches in the literature (e.g., Kim, Petrocik, and Enokson 1975; Rosenstone and Hansen 1993). Independent variables represent three types of forces: election laws, demographics, and competitiveness. Election laws include the use of EDR, same day registration (SDR, or when registration is available during early voting), early voting, and vote (only) by mail.[17] These are inherently interesting because they come from state law and are under direct control of policy makers. Demographics, over which policy makers have almost no control, include median income, percent high school graduates, percent black,

---

[17] See Burden et al. (2014) for codings of these variables and additional statistical analyses that provide for clearer causal inferences. Adding a dummy variable for the South does not change the results substantially.

and percent Hispanic.[18] Finally, campaign competitiveness represents a short-term force that varies more from election to election. For 2008 it is measured as 100 − |McCain's percent − Obama's percent| according to the final Pollster.com estimate in each state. For 2010 it is measured by dummy variables indicating whether gubernatorial and senatorial elections were taking place in the state.[19] I estimate these models for both years with and without demographics. States are weighted by the total number of votes cast to alleviate heteroskedasticity and approximate individual level effects.

The results are found in Table A2.1. For ease of interpretation, I display the estimated effects of the three key election laws in Figure 2.4. The models suggest that election laws have real effects on turnout. Depending on specification, the availability of EDR increases turnout by five to ten points. SDR has a more modest effect of three to four points. In contrast, early voting tends to have no effect or even decrease turnout by several points. Vote by mail appears to have a large positive effect only in 2010, although this might be attributable to the limited leverage provided by close statewide elections in both Oregon and Washington. The main message is that at least some of the variation in voter turnout rates is under the control of state policy makers who shape election laws. Although effects on the order of three to ten points do not come close to accounting for the full extent of turnout differences between the highest and lowest states, the boost from adopting EDR or SDR is not trivial.

In contrast, demographic factors have only limited explanatory power. Few population characteristics have significant influence on turnout in either election year. Electoral competition was a somewhat more consistent turnout driver. In 2008 turnout increased by two to three points for every ten points that the gap between the major party nominees contracted. There is also some evidence that senatorial and gubernatorial elections raised turnout levels. A more subtle measure of the competitiveness of those races would likely show more convincing effects.

---

[18] I say "almost no control" because education and income levels may be affected by state policies.

[19] This is a crude measure that ignores other statewide races (including House races in states with at large districts) and does not capture the actual competitiveness of the races. Because of their imperfections, the measures should have weaker relationships with other variables than a superior measure of midterm competitiveness would.

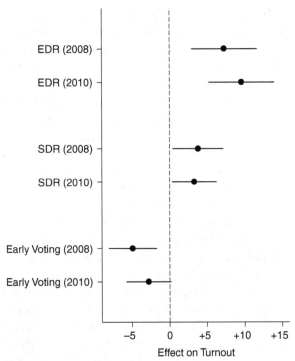

FIGURE 2.4. Effects of voting laws on turnout in 2008 and 2010.
Note: Based on models in first and third columns of Table A2.1. Dots indicate point estimates. Horizontal lines indicate 95 percent confidence intervals.

The modest role of demographic variables is striking. The limited amount of variance explained (as measured by the R^2) suggests that state "fixed effects" account for much of the difference among states. It is likely that demographic factors would be more powerful predictors at the county or municipal level, where state characteristics such as political culture are held constant.[20]

CONNECTING REGISTRATION AND TURNOUT

While some of the variation in turnout rates can be explained with election laws, competitiveness, and to a lesser degree demographics,

---

[20] Cross-sectional regressions suffer from concerns such as omitted variable bias and possible reverse causation. See Burden et al. (forthcoming) for a more sophisticated analysis that uses county data, individual level data, matching methods, and difference-in-difference models to show similar results for 2004 and 2008.

it seems that much of turnout is attributable to factors that are established before the voting period opens, especially at the prior step of voter registration. It is sensible that turnout rates are largely a result of registration rates. The correlations presented earlier suggested as much, and it is axiomatic that the number of people who vote may not exceed the number of people registered. Studies at the individual level suggest that the best predictor of voting is in fact being registered (Erikson 1981; Timpone 1998).[21] This realization naturally turns our attention toward the variables that explain registration.

Yet the connection between registration and turnout is far from perfect. States vary in the degree of "falloff" from the preelection registration rate to the turnout rate. In 2008 the mean state saw a gap of 19.7 percentage points between the two rates. This difference varied between a low of 11.8 in New Hampshire to a maximum of 29.2 in the District of Columbia.[22] The gaps are generally greater and more variable in 2010 because turnout is lower and more variable. In the midterm election, falloff in the mean state was 35.4, with a range between 25.7 points and 55.1 points. At the same time, there is substantial correlation of .64 in the 2008 falloff and the 2010 drop-off, suggesting that there is a large systematic component that is state-specific.

States with the most significant falloffs were located in the South or border states. Louisiana, Kentucky, West Virginia, Mississippi, Texas, Oklahoma, and Alabama are all in the bottom ten. States best at turning registrants into voters tend to be in the upper Midwest (Minnesota, Wisconsin, and Iowa) or Rocky Mountain region (Colorado, Idaho, Montana, and Wyoming). Eight of the top ten states have EDR, suggesting that the practice helps to prevent the "leakage" of registrants from participating on Election Day. Studies show that many Election Day registrants are in fact reregistering, usually by updating their names or addresses (McDonald 2008).

Because highly competitive campaigns mobilize more voters, it is reassuring that several of the states with lowest falloff in 2008 were in fact battlegrounds in the presidential election. But this does not appear to be the major explanatory factor because battlegrounds such as Florida and North Carolina were in the middle of the pack. Likewise,

---

[21] Brown and Wedeking (2006) find that registration is less predictive of turnout after the implementation of NVRA because it registered people less likely to vote.

[22] Alternatively, one might compute the ratio of turnout to registration. For 2008 this produces a similar ranking of states with West Virginia (.655) and the District of Columbia (.679) at the bottom and Colorado (.852) and New Hampshire (.860) at the top.

states with gubernatorial or senatorial elections in 2010 saw less falloff from the registration rate, but there were plenty of states that ran counter to this pattern.

As a final step in the analysis, I consider explanations for varying registration rates across the states. Because registration rates are much more uniform than are turnout rates, variables provide less leverage and make this a more challenging task. The specifications are identical to those in the turnout models, except that the observations are now weighted by the VEP rather than the number of people voting.

The results, which appear in Table A2.2, show several things. First, it is more difficult to explain registration than turnout. This reflects the fact that registration rates display more inertia than do turnout rates. Few variables are statistically significant, and none of the models explains much of the variation. The lack of evidence indicating that EDR and SDR affect registration rates may nonetheless be informative. It implies that one-stop registration procedures do not so much increase overall registration rates as they do increase turnout among the registered. This might be because many of these registrations involve voters updating their names or addresses. In contrast, early voting appears to have a more direct, negative effect on registration. Early voting procedures appear to reduce turnout rates primarily by reducing registration rates. More research will help clarify the precise pathways through which these election laws shape registration and turnout rates.

Demographics have little explanatory power, but that was to be expected based on earlier research (Jackson, Brown, and Wright 1998). There is evidence that registration rates are increased in states where blacks make up a larger share of the population, but not much else matters. In addition, competitive campaigns do not seem to drive up registration rates, but instead work to increase turnout among the registered.

It is possible that the way in which voter registration databases are assembled in the states affects the accuracy of the official reports of registration rates. The main distinction here is between a "top-down" system in which data are stored on centralized state hardware and a "bottom-up" system in which data are stored locally. If clerical decisions and errors are solely responsible for discrepancies in the "official" data, then the structure of state databases should not affect the "survey" registration rates. This is precisely what we find when using the EAC's codings of the state systems in its 2008 statutory overview. States with top-down systems have higher official registration rates ($r = .219$), while those with bottom-up systems have lower registration rates ($r = -.243$). In contrast, neither indicator is correlated with the self-reported measure ($r = .030$ and $.023$).[23] This would be consistent with a theory that centralized systems have more duplicate records that are not adequately purged, whereas locally based systems are subject to less uniform data entry and reporting. An alternative explanation is that top-down states are more efficient at registering people who want to be registered.

LOOKING AHEAD

Registration and turnout rates are two of the best measured, best understood, and most important indicators of democracy in the states. They are not under the complete control of election administrators, but they are affected by election laws that make registration easier or extend the voting period. Policy makers can take action to enhance turnout by adopting the proper mix of practices and backing them with adequate financial resources.

Further study is likely to identify ways in which administrators can influence voter participation. When it comes to turnout, a promising line of research examines "postregistration" actions, such as providing sample ballots or extending polling hours, that are under the control of state policy makers (Wolfinger, Highton, and Mullin 2005). Another issue to explore is inequalities in turnout. It is unclear to what degree low turnout is attributable to low participation by minority groups or those with demographic disadvantages. Such information would aid policy makers who wish to increase overall turnout and enhance the representativeness of the voting public.

Official state registration numbers are being improved, but some states have problematic voter files. Many of the official registration figures simply lack face validity. Because we know that self-reports by survey respondents are imperfect, honing the official registration rates would be valuable. At this point it is not clear whether the problems stem from the registration databases themselves or just the reporting processes. I expect these data to improve as states continue to move toward best practices. The Electronic Registration Information Center

[23] To code states I use the more definitive summaries in the text of the EAC report rather than the self-reports by states, which the EAC views as suspect, particularly when states that appear to have hybrid systems that are reported as top-down. Using the states' reports as the truth produces similar results, although stronger for top-down states and weaker for bottom-up states. Results are similar but weaker in 2010.

(ERIC), an initiative in data sharing and matching being spearheaded by seven states, is a promising avenue for enhancing the accuracy of voter rolls.

More research is required to understand the causes of registration rates. Following on the innovative analysis by Ansolabehere and Hersh in Chapter 3, one approach is to pursue metrics such as "deadwood" and duplicates in state databases to determine where problems appear. Further analysis might also consider other practices, such as purging of registration lists (cf. Rhine 1995).

Voter registration and turnout rates deserve special attention as markers of election administration performance in the states. These two measures tap most directly into the fundamental activities undertaken by members of the electorate who wish to express their preferences on Election Day. And they serve as meta-indicators that are the end result of so many other state laws, practices, and expectations. Fortunately both registration and turnout are well understood, but they also vary across the states more dramatically than is usually acknowledged, indicating that lessons may be learned from those with the highest levels of success.

3

Voter Registration: The Process and Quality of Lists

Stephen Ansolabehere and Eitan Hersh

INTRODUCTION

Voter registration is the backbone of election administration in the United States. Registration lists are used to establish eligibility to vote, to determine the offices for which one can vote, to communicate to citizens when elections occur and where and how to vote, to validate people at the polls, and to audit elections after the fact. In many ways U.S. voter registration is a remarkable system. A highly decentralized set of authorities consisting of more than 5,000 municipal and county election officials collaborate on state and local voter databases.

Election administrators and the public as a whole place a premium on accuracy of the lists. Poorly maintained lists can make it difficult for administrators to communicate with voters or to run the election at the polls. Errors in the lists used by the local election offices can prevent some legitimate voters from participating and may be abused by those seeking to perpetrate voter fraud. Election administrators devote considerable effort to continual management of the voter lists. This is a difficult task, especially in less well-staffed offices, and errors do occur. Any effort to improve the quality of lists can be greatly informed by data about the accuracy of the voter files. How common are different sorts of problems, do errors follow systematic (and possibly correctable) patterns, and what are the consequences of different sorts of errors?

To date, studies of the quality of the registration system have relied on surveys of individuals conducted by the U.S. Census and other organizations, and on intensive analyses of individual counties or states (e.g.,

The authors thank Bob Blaemire, Laura Quinn, Taylor Terry, and the staff of Catalist for their helpful guidance and cooperation.

Lichtman and Issacharoff 1993; Wolfinger and Rosenstone 1980). As far back as the 1970s, such research has documented that registration systems create barriers to participation that affect several million Americans each election (Wolfinger and Rosenstone 1980), but the surveys have not had sufficient sample sizes and statistical power to determine the origins and magnitude of specific problems, or to compare jurisdictions.

Examination of the system failures during the 2000 election identified voter registration as the single largest source of problems for voters in that election. Such revelations prompted the federal government to pass the Help America Vote Act (HAVA) in 2002, and they continue to motivate calls to improve the voter registration system today, including proposals to adopt universal registration and to force local governments to improve by ranking their performance (e.g., Gerken 2009a; Alvarez 2009; Pew Center on the States 2008). But even the post-2000 assessments (and the reform efforts that have followed in their wake) have been unable to offer a comprehensive assessment of the quality of voter registration lists in the United States.

This chapter presents a nationwide view of the accuracy of information on the voter lists. We examine the voter registration files of all the states to provide a comprehensive assessment of the validity of ten specific pieces of information on the voter files, such as addresses, birth dates, and vote histories. We compare these registration-based measures against measures originating from surveys of election officials and surveys of public opinion. The novelty of this analysis owes to the fact that the registration-based data themselves are quite new. In just the last few years, political data management firms, working with parties, campaigns, and other organizations, have accumulated all state and local voter files and have compiled the first truly national voter lists for the United States. In addition to the availability of the first national registration file, advances in computing memory and power over the past decade make it possible to access and analyze all 180 million records on the voter files and to compare them with other comprehensive data about the American public. The primary data for this assessment come through a contract with one particular firm, Catalist. Although Catalist vends data to the Democratic Party, campaign organizations, labor unions, and other groups, we have no partisan or ideological agenda in pursuing this research, nor do we have any consulting relationship with this firm.

This chapter examines data from the 2008 and 2010 election cycles. At the time of this publication, the data from the 2012 election cycle have just become available. The 2012 data reveal the same general patterns as the 2008 and 2010 data, and, in fact, the correlation from year to year of measures at the county level is quite high.

In analyzing the 180 million–plus records from the national voter registration database assembled by Catalist, this chapter makes four basic points about the administration of elections. First, we argue that the "big data" revolution in itself will lead to the improvement in election administration by allowing us, for the first time, to see the national contours of the voter registration system. Second, we argue that voter registration serves at least four separate functions, and we offer a taxonomy of those functions along with measures to assess each one. Third, by studying new measures of registration list quality, we show that individual measures are not highly correlated with one another at the state level. States that perform well on one measure are not more likely to perform well on another measure. Interpreting this empirical finding, we argue that these measures should not be added together or combined to provide overall state-by-state assessments, since aggregating uncorrelated measures cannot serve the purpose of identifying an underlying, latent measure of registration quality. Finally, we argue that scholars, advocates, and policy makers should be cautious when drawing conclusions from data that are aggregated to the state level, since aggregation can mask underlying patterns.

THE DATA

Data for this analysis come from an emerging commercial enterprise. A government-managed national voter registration system does not yet exist, but privately managed national lists have emerged to fill this void. Political campaigns, such as those conducted by the national political parties and interest groups, use public registration records as the basis for their voter contact programs. Precisely because registration records are a burden to collect and contain inaccuracies, campaigns purchase lists from professional data vendors. The vendors do the painstaking work of collecting the data, flagging address errors and typos, and identifying duplicative records, deceased voters, and movers.

There are two by-products of this effort. First, the commercial vendors have, in essence, created national voter registration lists. Second, they have conducted audits of the public lists available from local and state offices. Election data firms do this as a means of lowering costs of campaigning, for example, by getting rid of duplicate mailings or mailings to people no longer at an address. Because their customers want clean lists so that they can determine which voters to contact and which records are obsolete, these vendors have developed an extensive understanding of the quality of registration lists originating from the state and county election offices. In this analysis, we draw inferences about the quality of registration records by investigating how a state's voter registration list is transformed into a list in which obsolete records are removed and inaccuracies are identified. We examine the election data assembled by the firm and the firm's own indicators of problematic information on the lists.

Catalist, a Washington-based firm, is one of the premier political data vendors in the business. From voter registration records in every state, Catalist's team builds a nationwide voter file that is used by the Democratic Party and by interest groups on the Democratic side of the political spectrum. During the winter and spring of 2010, we conducted a detailed investigation into Catalist's data-cleansing process through an intensive study of its voter records and interviews with its senior staff.

Because of the nature of the business, Catalist, like most other political data vendors, serves only one political wing. However, after a careful study of its process, we are confident that the results described here are not affected by partisan bias. The reason for this confidence is simple: the vendor has neither cause nor much capacity to discriminate on the basis of partisanship when developing and cleaning the lists. Consider the basic method they use.

Several times a year, Catalist purchases the publicly available voter registration files made available by each state or county election office. For every voter on a list, Catalist makes a note of missing or duplicative information. Is the voter's address complete or is it missing a key piece of information such as a zip code or street address? Is the voter's birth date absent from the file? Does the voter show up multiple times in the state because the registration record from a former residence was never deleted from the file?

Catalist then cross-references the registration lists with other public records, such as the National Change of Address (NCOA) database maintained by the post office and the Social Security Death Index. Movers and deceased voters are flagged. Catalist matches the registration files to commercial records from data aggregation firms that compile lists from retailers and direct marketing companies. This allows the firm to correct the records of individuals who may have a typo in their registration record or may have registered with a nickname rather than their legal name. For example, if a voter registered with the first name "Tom," but a collection of commercial records show that his real first name is "Thomas," Catalist will note the discrepancy.

Statistical data-matching procedures are run on every voter file that Catalist processes. Catalist does not attempt to create more careful records for likely Democratic voters or likely Republican voters, nor does it attempt to conduct a more rigorous data cleansing of some states than others. Biased processing of this sort would result in less reliable data for Catalist's clients, who work to mobilize all kinds of citizens in every state, depending on the nature of independent issue campaigns. Thus, we are quite confident that analysis of Catalist's records is not biased by Catalist's political affiliations. In fact, because data vendors on both sides of the political spectrum use the same voter registration data and create lists with the same purposes in mind, we would expect an analysis of records of a Republican vendor's data to produce the same basic results. Of course, we would embrace an opportunity to study the records of a Republican vendor just as we have done with Catalist's records. We view partnerships with private data firms as a new and valuable approach to assessing public data, and we hope that it will be replicated in the future.

FOUR FUNCTIONS OF VOTER REGISTRATION LISTS

Assessing records maintained by Catalist will enable us to measure quality indicators that address four functions of the voter registration system. The first function is to map voters to precincts. To identify a voter's correct precinct, administrators need to know the address of the voter. When precincts are established, a list of all voters eligible to vote in that precinct (and to vote for the unique set of offices corresponding to that precinct) is generated. This list is used by local election offices, campaigns, and other organizations to communicate with registered voters about where, when, and how to vote. This function requires complete, mailable addresses. An address with just a street name or an address that does not correspond to a known geographic location makes it impossible to place voters in precincts.

The second function of a registration list is to authenticate voters at the polls. When a person goes to vote, poll workers verify that the person is indeed allowed to vote at that location. In every state (but North Dakota), the individual must say where he or she lives, so that the poll worker can check that the person is in the right location. Half of the states require some form of identification when voting. Names, addresses, and birth dates are used to validate a registrant's identity. A voter whose identifying data do not match registration records may encounter problems at the polls.

The third function of registration lists is to audit election results. One part of election audits involves comparison of the lists and the vote tallies: Does the total number of people recorded as having voted equal the number of ballots cast?

The fourth function is to prevent in-person voter fraud. Duplicate and obsolete records allow for the possibility that people vote multiple times in several places. To maintain clean lists, states must identify people who are registered in multiple locations in a state as well as those who have moved out of the state or have passed away. At the same time, the goal of keeping lists clean of obsolete records ought not to allow states to remove voters from lists who are legitimate voters. In recent elections, administrations that have attempted to purge voters purportedly in order to prevent fraud have been accused of purging legitimate registrants in order to satisfy political considerations. To achieve the right balance between purging obsolete records and not purging legitimate records, states can follow procedures laid out in the National Voter Registration Act (NVRA) and in state laws. Under these rules, registrants who fail to vote for a series of elections can be sequestered and eventually dropped. In order to purge voters on the basis of past voting participation, however, administrators must maintain accurate vote history data as well as an accurate record of when voters entered the registration system.

Data Quality Indicators

To assess the voter registration system in each of the four functions described earlier, we must estimate the accuracy of mailing address information, identifying information (such as birth dates), vote history records, and records indicating when people entered the registration system, as well as the incidence of obsolete and duplicative records. We have developed ten indicators to measure accuracy in each of these areas.

1. **Missing Address Information.** The number of registrants missing a city, state, or zip code field in their mailing address. Missing this information

will make it difficult for election administrators to send notifications about voting to a registrant. Additionally, a person's mailing address is usually the same as his or her registration address. Consequently, missing a city, state, or zip code could make it difficult to place a voter in a precinct.

2. **Undeliverable Addresses.** An estimate of whether a mailing address is erroneous. Catalist runs every mailing address through a U.S. post office process called CASS, the Coding Accuracy Support System. The CASS process generates an estimate of how likely it is that an address is valid. Consider an example. Suppose a voter lives at 100 Main Street; however, on account of a typo or poor penmanship, the address is listed on the voter file as 109 Maln Street. Although this address is missing no values, the CASS process might find that Maln Street does not exist in this particular city, or that Maln Street does exist but that 109 is not likely to be a viable street number on Maln. In Catalist's data, the output of the CASS process is a five-category rating: mailable, probably deliverable, possibly deliverable, probably undeliverable, or undeliverable.

3. **Birth Date Coverage.** The number of registered voters for whom Catalist does not have a record of date of birth from the voter files.

4. **Birth Date Distribution.** The percentage of people listed as being born on each day of the year. Even when a birth date is associated with a voter on the registration file, the birth date might not be correct. One good signal of the accuracy of birth date records is the distribution of voter birthdays throughout the year. Records should show that approximately the same number of registrants have a birthday on each day of the year. If a disproportionate number of voters have a listed birth date on any one day (such as January 1), this suggests inaccurately recorded data on the part of election administrators.

5. **Deceased Voters.** A blunt estimate of the number of deceased people on the rolls in each state. This measure is generated through commercial records and the Social Security Administration's Death Index. If a company, such as a telemarketing firm, attempts to contact a person and is informed that the person has died, the company will make a note in its records, and the indicator may end up in Catalist's system. The measure is not comprehensive (it does not cover all deaths), nor is it as reliable as other measures (since it comes from a combination of commercial records and official records), but state-by-state differences in the number of deceased voters identified are likely to reflect the true distribution of dead voters on the rolls across jurisdictions.

6. **Deadwood.** Catalist's estimate of whether a record is obsolete. A reg-
    istered voter's record is considered by Catalist to be "not deadwood,"
    "possibly deadwood," "probably deadwood," or "likely deadwood." The
    deadwood indicator takes into account the age of the registrant and if he
    or she is identified as deceased through commercial matches or official
    records. It also accounts for inactive registration status, though it is sen-
    sitive to the fact that some states have a very low threshold for placing
    registrants in inactive status, while other states have a high threshold or
    do not label any voters inactive. The measure further takes into account
    whether the voter has moved and has reregistered at a different address.
    Lastly, the deadwood model considers vote history. For instance, if a
    registrant has not voted even once in the last ten years, his record is
    unlikely to be current.
7. **Registration Date Coverage.** The number of registered voters for whom
    their initial date of registration is unknown.
8. **Registration Distribution.** The percentage of registrants who are listed
    with an initial registration date of January 1. January 1 is one of the least
    likely days of the year for a registration application to be processed by
    an election office. Yet, many states are in the habit of assigning January
    1 as a default registration date.
9. **Vote History Discrepancy.** The number of discrepancies between the
    ballot tally and the voter tally in the 2008 and 2006 general elections.
    In any given election, voter turnout can be calculated in two ways: by
    the number of ballots cast and by the number of voters who showed
    up (or submitted a mail ballot). These two numbers should be exactly
    the same, but they rarely are. Ballots may not be counted because of
    machine malfunctions and voters may not be counted because an elec-
    tion worker might forget to check the voter's name off on the rolls.
10. **Summary Measure.** The number of records that have been flagged as
    either deadwood or undeliverable or both.

Before delving into a state-by-state analysis of these measures, consider
some national summary statistics. Table 3.1 shows the initial number of
all registered voters in all states plus Washington, DC. It is important to
note that this number is a moving target. In many states, voter files are
changed multiple times a day as records are added and removed. This
particular snapshot of the registration system is based on data collected
from the states between March and June 2010.

The total number, 185,445,103, reflects the sum of voters in the
Catalist database at one point in time, but this number is actually

TABLE 3.1. *National summary statistics*

Number of Listed Registered Voters	185,445,103
Missing Address Information	224,046
Predicting Undeliverable	6,507,871
Missing Birth Date	24,501,377
Predicted Deceased	1,836,837
Predicted as Deadwood	6,740,264
Missing Registration Date	2,984,683
Records without Missing Address, Undeliverable, Deceased, or Deadwood Flags	169,317,778

already smaller than the total number of registrants listed in state and county voter files. This figure reflects registrants listed *after* Catalist has collapsed duplicative records. It has been difficult for us to gauge the total number of records before duplicates are identified by Catalist, but it appears that in the typical state, about 1.5 percent of records are duplicates, which would mean that the true number of listed registered voters may be closer to 188 million. Some of the quality measures we calculate cannot be identified at the level of individual voters, because they rely on distributions of grouped voters. For those that can be identified at the individual level, Table 3.1 lists national counts.

STATE-BY-STATE ANALYSIS

The basic purpose of voter registration lists is to record the names of citizens eligible to vote in order to authenticate voters. In most states if a citizen is not listed on the registration file prior to Election Day, he or she is not permitted to vote. Provisional ballots offer a fail-safe, but the voter must still be on the lists. Registration lists serve other functions, as well. Because a voter's address is listed on the file, election offices use the registration list to send important mail to voters. Voters are asked to confirm by mail that they still live at their addresses. They may be notified of upcoming elections or of changes to precinct locations. Mail-in ballots are sent out to addresses listed on a voter file. Furthermore, registration lists are used to identify and check voters in at precincts on Election Day, and election workers note on the registration file whether each citizen voted or not. A registrant's recorded vote history is used, in part, as the basis for purging obsolete records from the rolls, as stipulated in the NVRA. And, of course, registration lists are used outside of administrative purposes, most notably by political campaigns seeking to mobilize and persuade voters to vote for their candidates.

In this data presentation, we divide the administration function of voter registration lists into four broad categories. Each of the ten quality metrics fall into one or more of these categories. The fifty states and Washington, DC, are evaluated on the basis of these measures. We will make comparisons across states, but in doing so, it is necessary to keep sight of the volatile nature of registration records. States are constantly altering their voter files, such as by adding and removing voters, appending new election data, and linking information across databases. When Catalist aggregates state and county voter files, it cannot keep current with each root file's real-time changes; rather, it assembles snapshots of each state file. In reviewing our results, we caution that when comparing snapshots of state records – even if these snapshots are aggregated into a national file by a company such as Catalist – the state-by-state comparisons may look different than at a different point in time on account of volatility in the state record maintenance.

List Function #1: Assign Voters to Precincts and
Communicate with Voters by Mail

When citizens submit voter registration forms, they must be correctly assigned to their voting precincts. Because precincts are assigned to voters on the basis of their residence, proper address information is required to successfully connect a registrant to his or her voting jurisdiction. Proper address information is also required in order to contact voters by mail, which is important for notifications and mail-in ballots sent to addresses listed on the voter file. Because they both require address information, we consider these two aspects of list quality simultaneously.

Problems with address information on registration records can take two forms: address information can be missing or address information can be incorrect. Sometimes election offices process registration applications with incomplete address fields. They may neglect to note a voter's zip code, for example. Other times, because of illegible handwriting on the part of voters or faulty data entry on the part of officials, street numbers, street names, cities, and zip codes may be entered incorrectly or contain typos.

Nationwide the incidence of incomplete addresses is 1 in 1,000. That figure varies considerably across states, as depicted in Figure 3.1.

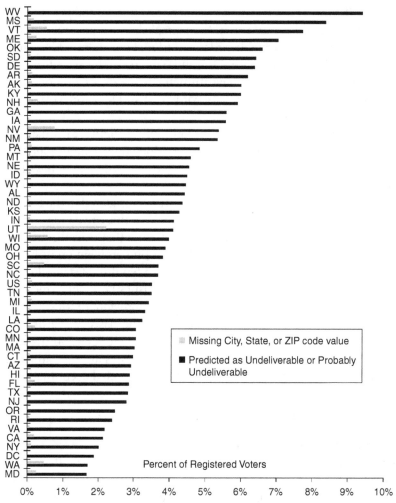

FIGURE 3.1. The accuracy of mailing addresses on voter registration files.

As is evident, in most states, mailing addresses have complete fields. Although, in general, missing address fields are not pervasive, they are clearly a problem in some states. In Utah, more than 1 in 50 of all registered voters have missing address information, and in neighboring Nevada, about 1 in 100 voters have missing data.

The second measure of address accuracy is a prediction of mailability, as defined earlier. The black bars in Figure 3.1 display the rate of undeliverable or probably undeliverable records on registration lists among the states. The incidence of unmailable addresses is one in twenty-five.

It is clear that there is a far higher incidence of undeliverable addresses than of missing address values. In the typical state, 3.5 percent of registered voters have undeliverable addresses listed. Four states – Maryland, Washington State, Washington, DC, and New York – have a rate as low as 2 percent, and fifteen states have unmailable addresses for more than 5 percent of the names on their lists, with West Virginia and Mississippi having the highest rates.

Three points are worth noting in considering Figure 3.1. First, the rate of undeliverable mail identified here does not include mail that may be undeliverable because a voter has moved residences or has died. The undeliverable mail rate depicted in Figure 3.1 is simply estimated by address information. Obsolete addresses are considered in the following, especially in Figure 3.9. Second, notice that these two measures of address quality are uncorrelated. This is a theme that runs throughout our exploration of these data. A state that has one problem on its lists is not more likely to have other problems. Only a handful of states do routinely well or routinely badly. Most of the statistics here, then, indicate specific problems that must be addressed by individual states. Third, note that voters are assigned to precincts on the basis of registration addresses, whereas the two measures identified here focus on mailing addresses. While for most voters these two addresses are the same, for some they are not. The measures should be interpreted accordingly.

List Function #2: Identify Voters at the Polls

Since the 2000 election, a large number of states have strengthened their voter identification provisions, with half now requiring that voters show identification when they vote.[1] When checking in to vote at a precinct polling location on Election Day, a voter may be asked to provide proof of identification, such as a state-issued identity card with current address or a current utility bill. This authentication process necessarily involves checking the identification against the information on the voter list, and inaccuracies can cause obstacles to voting. The statistics already presented in Figure 3.1 indicate the likely incidence of address problems. Here, we consider the likelihood of incomplete or inaccurate birth dates and flag some specific issues with the ways that state and local election offices maintain records of birth dates of voters.

---

[1] For a recent summary of voter ID legislation in the states, consult the National Conference of State Legislatures Web site, http://www.ncsl.org/default.aspx?tabid=16602.

In Figure 3.2, we show the percentage of records for which Catalist has a record of a birth date from the voter file. Aside from North Dakota, which does not maintain a traditional voter registration file, the states with the least amount of birth date coverage are Alaska, Washington, DC, and Hawaii. Thirteen other states have birth dates for fewer than 80 percent of registered voters. Most states, however, have nearly complete coverage.

Some of the states that appear to have poorer coverage of birth dates do actually maintain birth dates for voters, but they do not share this sensitive field with political parties and data vendors, presumably to protect the privacy of voters. To be clear, the data in Figure 3.2 reflects Catalist's data, not the states' data. For states that do not share the full extent of their data with vendors, some follow the path of releasing the year or month and year of birth for registrants. Twelve states are noted with blue lines in Figure 3.2 that seem to follow this practice. Of the voter registration fields we study here, birth date is unique in its sensitivity to privacy concerns, and this limits our ability to study what is going on in state records by investigating records as they appear to Catalist. We do not suspect this issue impairs our other measures in the same way.

In states that do provide exact dates of birth, we still can study the birth date accuracy. We can estimate the incidence of date of birth errors by looking at the distribution of birthdays on a state file. In general, if birth dates are entered correctly into the voter file, one would expect to see, approximately, a uniform distribution of birthdays. That is, about the same number of people are born on January 1 as January 2 as January 3, and so on. There is some expected periodicity in births by season that will make the true distribution deviate slightly from uniform, but other than this seasonal fluctuation, we expect the distribution to be relatively uniform. In Figure 3.3, for each month-day combination, we plot the percentage of voters whose birth dates fall on that day of the year. Voters with incomplete birth date information and those born on February 29 are excluded. Excluding the states with either no birth date information or with only year or month birth date information, we are left with thirty-five states to analyze in Figure 3.3.

In both the upper and lower plots in Figure 3.3, the twenty-nine states that have uniform-looking birthdays are represented in light gray lines. Most of the lines fluctuate around 0.27 percent, which is

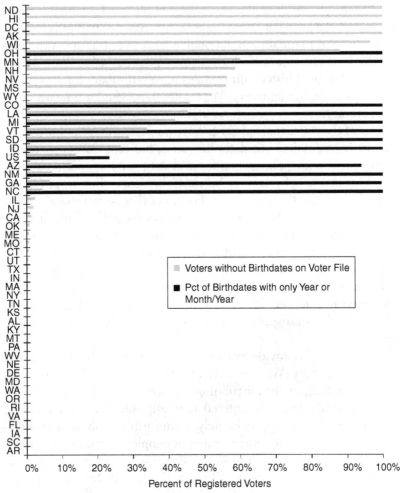

FIGURE 3.2. Birth date coverage on state voter files.

equal to 1/365. Each plot shows the distributions of three anomalous states, as they compare with the other states. However, the exceptions stand out clearly. Mississippi, Wyoming, and New Hampshire seem to have the practice of assigning the first day of each month to a disproportionate number of voters. This is apparent in the upper plot. Many more states have unusually high numbers of voters listed with birthdays of January 1, a pattern that cannot be seen clearly in the figure. Aside from Mississippi, Wyoming, and New Hampshire, the states with the highest proportion of January 1 birthdays are Missouri

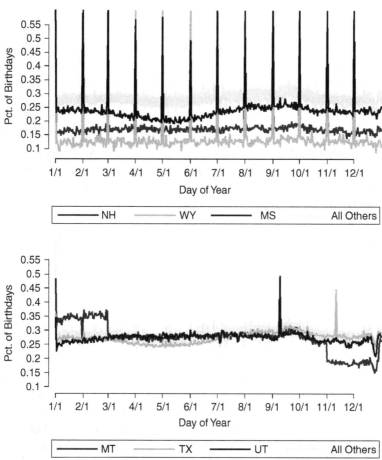

FIGURE 3.3. The distribution of voters' birthdays on registration files.

and Pennsylvania, both of which have about twice as many January 1 birth dates as would be expected under the uniform distribution. Three other oddities are noted in the lower subplot. Texas has a uniform distribution except that a large number of voters are inexplicably listed with November 11 birth dates. Utah has similar issues as Texas. And Montana has too many people born at the start of the year and too few at the end of the year. Some of these oddities may be attributable to computer programs that require election officials to enter a birth date for a voter, even if the voter did not provide a birth date. Thus, administrators type the first day of the year or the first day of the month or, perhaps in Texas, 11/11.

List Function #3: Audits of Vote Tallies

Voter files contain not only identifying information for registered voters, but also records of past and current electoral participation. These data are used to audit elections, as they provide duplicate indicators of total numbers of voters and possible evidence of problems with machines or administration.

Vote histories have a further use in purging obsolete records. One of the criterion set forth in the NVRA for when states can purge voters is if, in addition to failing to respond to communications from the election office, voters abstain from voting in two successive federal general elections. These purging provisions are implemented in different ways by the states, but their existence means that an election office needs accurate vote history data in order to clean the lists. If an election administrator does not keep track of which registrants voted and which did not in the last two federal elections, it cannot determine which records to purge.

Vote history accuracy can be observed by comparing the number of ballots cast in a particular jurisdiction and the number of voters listed as having voted. Official election results are tallied by counting ballots, but when voters walk into a polling place or submit an absentee ballot, their record is also marked that they voted. It is possible and quite common for the ballot tally and the registration record tally to be inconsistent in each other. A precinct election worker may neglect to indicate that a particular person voted, or a ballot may not be counted because of a machine malfunction. The first of these errors would result in a higher official tally than a voter file tally; the latter would generate the opposite result.[2]

To measure the discrepancy between counted ballots and counted voters, we use the following procedure. For every county in a state, we take the absolute difference between the two counts. For example, if in County X, 150 ballots were counted in the 2008 general election, but only 140 registrants residing in the county were marked as having voted, we would count the deviation as 10. Similarly, if 160 voters were counted, we would also count the deviation as 10. We then sum these

---

[2]   There is another method to gauge the accuracy of the vote tally: count the number of ballots processed by a voting machine. For example, the number of paper ballots entered into an optical scan device can give a count that might be different both from the total number of votes cast for a particular office and the total number of registrants marked as having voted.

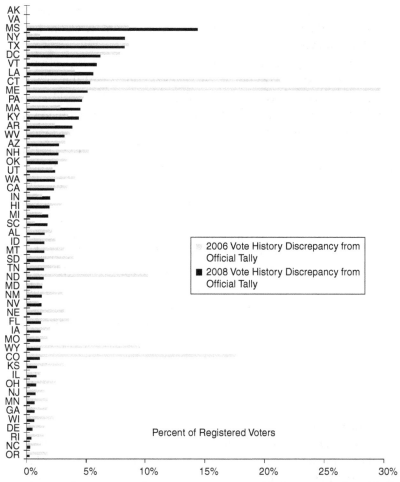

FIGURE 3.4. Discrepancies between voters counted as having voted and ballots counted.

deviations for the entire state and divide by the total number of official votes in that election. So, a discrepancy value of 5 percent is interpreted as 5 percent of votes cast in a particular state in a particular election was inconsistent with the tally of voters on the voter file. Figure 3.4 shows the discrepancy rates for the 2008 and 2006 general elections. The 2008 and 2006 vote history discrepancy rates vary considerably by state. In Oregon, North Carolina, Rhode Island, Delaware, and many other states, discrepancies are at a minimum, representing fewer than 5 percent of all votes. However, in other states such as Mississippi,

New York, and Texas, the 2008 discrepancy rate is closer to 10 percent. Note that the data necessary for this analysis are not available for the states of Virginia and Alaska.

Not every discrepancy represents a failure on the part of election officials, for two reasons. For one, a few states do not report the total tally of ballots as the official vote count.[3] Instead they merely report the number of ballots cast for the highest office on the ballot, usually president or governor. Because some voters participate in down-ballot races but abstain from the top contest, this could result in a few inconsistencies between the official turnout report and the registration list count.

The second reason why some of the inconsistencies in Figure 3.4 do not necessarily represent an administration error is that the vote tally from a registration file excludes the votes cast by citizens who were purged from the file since the election. For instance, a person who voted in 2006 but was since removed from the rolls would not be included in the count on the registration list but would have an official ballot counted. However, this presents just a minor problem since it only applies to voters who confirmed with the registrar that they moved. Because two federal elections have not yet transpired since 2006, citizens who voted in 2006 will not have been removed without their expressed consent.

List Function #4: Maintain Current Lists

The most important function of the voter registration list is to keep a current record of those eligible to vote. This means that voters who have moved and are voting in another jurisdiction should not be on the file in their original jurisdiction. It means that deceased voters should be removed from the file in a timely fashion. It also means that voters who have not moved and are not dead and wish to be registered ought not to be purged from the voter file without their consent. Keeping current lists is the most difficult task for election administrations for the basic reason that the population is fluctuating and the lists must struggle to keep up.

Deadwood and the Dead. While Catalist will remove duplicative records from their database during the cleansing process, they do not completely remove records of registered voters no matter how unlikely

---

[3] For more information, consult Michael McDonald, United States Elections Project, elections.gmu.edu.

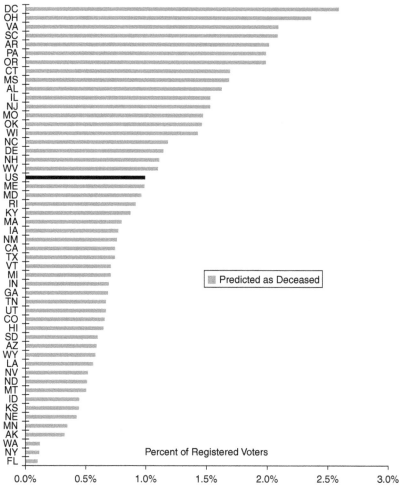

FIGURE 3.5. Identified deceased voters on registration lists.

the person is to be registered. For instance, if a voter on a registration file is 120 years old or has not voted since 1972, this record is almost surely obsolete, but instead of erasing the record from its file, Catalist flags the record with a number of indicators. Figures 3.5 and 3.6 show results from two such indicators. Figure 3.5 displays the percentage of registered voters who from commercial or official records appear to be deceased. As with some of the other measures, while the typical state has only a fraction of a percent of deceased registrants on the rolls, a few states have quite a large number of dead registrants. In particular,

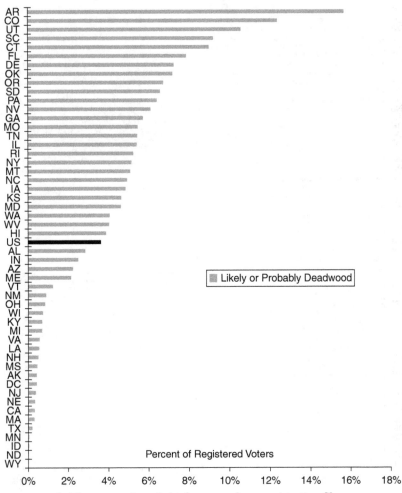

FIGURE 3.6. The proportion of obsolete records on registration files.

in Washington, DC, Ohio, Virginia, and South Carolina, more than 2 percent of registered voters are estimated to be dead.

Figure 3.6 provides another measure of obsolete records. Figure 3.6 shows the proportion of records that Catalist estimates to be definitely or probably deadwood. Values take a very wide range across states. Wyoming, which performed poorly on measures of address and birth date accuracy, performs exceedingly well in measures of deadwood. In twenty of the fifty-one jurisdictions, less than 1 percent of records look to be deadwood. An equal number of states, however, have more than 5 percent of their rolls consisting of deadwood, and in two states, Colorado and Arkansas, more than 12 percent of records appear to be obsolete.

Purging Requisites. The NVRA of 1993 sets forth guidelines to states for the purpose of removing obsolete records from the rolls. If a registrant does not confirm in writing that she or he is still a resident of a jurisdiction, she or he may only be removed from the voting file if she or he fails to respond to a mailed notice *and* fails to vote in two consecutive federal elections. In order to purge old records following these guidelines, a state not only needs to have adequate mailing address information (to contact voters) and adequate vote history data (as discussed earlier), but it also needs to keep accurate records of the length of time a voter has been on the rolls. Also if a state has Election Day registration (EDR), they are exempt from NVRA list management requirements, because the voter can correct the registration at the polls. In 2008, the states with EDR were Idaho, Iowa, Maine, Minnesota, Montana, New Hampshire, Wisconsin, and Wyoming.

Accurate records of the dates on which citizens registered are important to the purging process because if an election office does not know how long a voter has been on the rolls, it cannot know whether the voter has been eligible but abstained from two consecutive federal elections. We offer two measures that assess the accuracy of registration date records. The first is the proportion of active registered voters for whom no registration date is listed. Figure 3.7 shows the results. The New England states of New Hampshire, Vermont, Connecticut, and Maine exhibit among the highest rates of absent registration date data. In New Hampshire, nearly 40 percent of active registered voters do not have a registration date associated with their records. Oklahoma also has a high rate of missing data here. Figure 3.7 shows that Delaware has few missing values, but for nearly 25 percent of records in that state, only a month and year are listed. Dates represented only by month and year are probably sufficient for the purging process, though the practice is clearly out of synch with the rest of the nation.

A second measure of registration date accuracy is the proportion of records in which January 1 is listed as the registration date. It appears to be the practice of registrars in many states to assign voters a date of January 1 if they did not collect or report a correct date. Of course, January 1 is one of the least likely days for a voter registration application to be processed in reality. It is a federal holiday, election offices are closed, and few jurisdictions would have registration deadlines close to the date. Nevertheless,

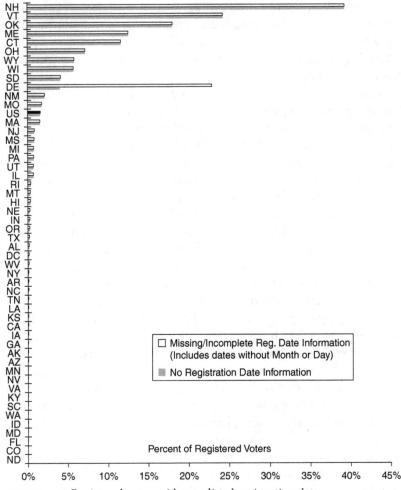

FIGURE 3.7. Registered voters without a listed registration date.

as is shown in Figure 3.8, in many states an implausibly large number of voters are listed as having registered on January 1 of a particular year. In Arkansas, New York, Wisconsin, and Massachusetts, more than 7 percent of records are listed with a January 1 registration date.

A SUMMARY INDEX OF REGISTRATION QUALITY

When this data project took form, we had assumed that some states would consistently perform well on these measures and other states

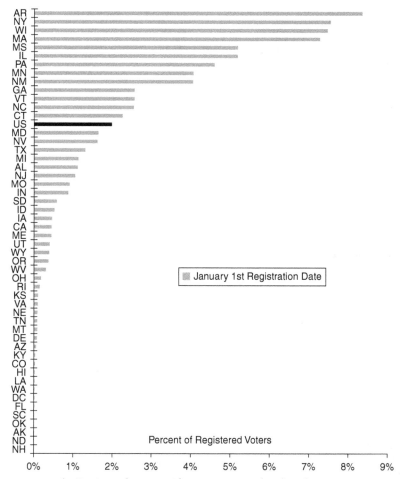

FIGURE 3.8. Registered voters with a registration date listed as January 1.

would consistently perform poorly. The reality is different. While there are some states that generally rank well across measures, for the most part states do well on some measures and poorly on others. In statistical terms, the correlation across measures is close to zero. There seems to be no underlying "quality" parameter that is captured by averaging across these measures.

Consider a few examples. Colorado has the second highest amount of deadwood on the rolls, but it also has few dead registrants on the file and it has very good registration date information. Delaware has excellent vote history data but has high levels of deadwood and undeliverable

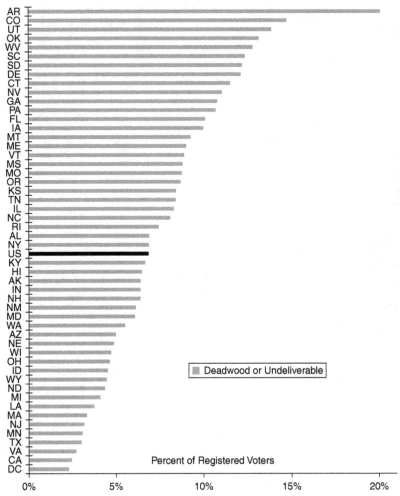

FIGURE 3.9. Registration records estimated as undeliverable or deadwood, or both.

addresses. Texas generally ranks high, except for its vote history data and its birth date distribution.

In Figure 3.9, we combine two of the more important measures described earlier. Figure 3.9 displays the percentage of registrants on a state's voter file that are either predicted as deadwood or predicted as undeliverable or both. In effect, this graph combines the data described by Figures 3.1 and 3.6. We see a wide range of values, from 2 percent of records appearing problematic in Washington, DC, to 20 percent in Arkansas.

Using a different methodological approach, in a recent study supported by the Pew Center on the States, we found results consistent with those on display in Figure 3.9. Along with our colleagues Alan Gerber and David Doherty, we audited the registration files in the state of Florida and the county of Los Angeles, California, and measured the rate of mail returned as undeliverable (Ansolabehere et al. 2010). Mail is undeliverable either because the address is incorrect (missing data or typos) or because the registrant is no longer alive or no longer at the address. Thus, the rate of undeliverable mail in that study should track with the data in Figure 3.9. In Florida we found an undeliverable rate of 9 percent (compared with 10 percent in this study) and in Los Angeles we found a rate of 5 percent, compared with 2.5 percent for California in this study.

Figure 3.9 summarizes two important scores, but because these two scores are uncorrelated with each other, the combined score obscures more than it reveals. Colorado is a case in point. In the combined measure in Figure 3.9, Colorado appears as the second worst state. This ranking obscures the fact that Colorado does better than three-fifths of the states on maintaining mailable addresses. Colorado's low score relative to the other states is attributable to its low placement on only one of these measures, not on both.

ADDITIONAL ANALYSIS OF NEW INDEX MEASURES

In addition to the quality measures we have developed, we also explore three separate measures of registration quality that have been developed by the Pew Center on the States. These measures are part of a project spearheaded by Pew to create an Election Performance Index (EPI) that will estimate the quality of U.S. election system. The quality of voter registration lists is one important piece of this puzzle.

The first measure originates from the U.S. Election Assistance Commission's (EAC's) biennial Election Administration and Voting Survey (EAVS). The measure represents the percentage of new registration applications that were rejected as invalid, according to the state election office. We have versions of this measure both from the 2008 and 2010 EAVS. The 2008 version was collected from thirty-two out of fifty-one states (plus DC) and ranges from 0 percent to 25 percent. The median state rejected 2 percent of applications. The 2010 measure was collected in forty-one states and ranges from 0 percent to 44 percent, with the median state rejecting 1 percent of applications.

The second measure comes from the Census Bureau's Current Population Survey (CPS). In November of election years, CPS respondents are asked about their experience with the voting process. The random sample of U.S. residents who tell the CPS that they did not vote in the general election are asked to identify the main reasons for their abstention. This measure of election quality represents the proportion of reported nonvoters who claim that a problem with their registration status was the reason for their failure to vote. For instance, the voter may not have received an absentee ballot or was registered in the wrong precinct. We have versions of this measure from 2008 and 2010. In 2008, the median state had 6 percent of nonvoters mentioning registration problems, ranging from 0 percent in Montana and Louisiana to 16 percent in Oregon. In 2010, the median state had only 3 percent of nonvoters mentioning registration problems, ranging from 0.003 percent in Mississippi to 13 percent in Washington State. Because this measure comes from a national survey of residents from the Census Bureau rather than of election offices, all states are represented.

The final measure from Pew represents the number of databases to which the state voter registration database is cross-checked. To assist in maintaining up-to-date records, states check their voter registration records against other governmental records. For example, they might use the U.S. post office's NCOA registry to identify voters who likely have moved homes. They might check against a driver's license database or the Social Security Death Index or other databases, as well. This measure simply represents the total number of databases used for cross-checking, as reported by states to the EAC both in 2008 and 2010. In both 2008 and 2010, the median state cross-checked against three databases, with a range of zero to six. Forty-eight states reported cross-check statistics in 2008 and fifty-one reported the statistics in 2010.

Analysis

While the cross-checking measure is fairly stable between 2008 and 2010, Pew's other measures exhibit some unstable tendencies. The measure of rejected applications shows some states reporting dramatically different numbers between 2008 and 2010. In 2008, Indiana reported that it rejected 2 percent of new registration applications (close to the median state). Two years later, Indiana reported rejecting 44 percent of new applications, by far the most of any state. Utah exhibited the opposite behavior, reporting in 2008 that it rejected 22 percent of applications and in 2010 that it rejected 2 percent of them. Similar erratic reporting is seen in Pennsylvania and Texas. If this measure accurately picks up the tendency of states to reject applications, it could surely be a useful measure of problematic registration systems. However, the outlier cases suggest that the rate of rejected applications might itself be measured with significant error.

The measure of registration problems reported on the CPS is erratic for a different reason. So few people report registration problems to the CPS that state-by-state analysis will be overwhelmed by measurement error. Nationwide, only 513 respondents reported registration problems in 2008, and only 368 reported such problems in 2012. Cutting up these data into fifty-one state units leaves subsamples that are generally too small for statistical analysis. It is not uncommon for 95 percent confidence intervals on these measures to range ten percentage points or more for within-state mean values. When the entire distribution of states is within ten to fifteen percentage points, the measures are rendered unusable for the purpose of comparing across states. Of course, the measure is still valuable as an over-time indicator of the national changes in incidence of voter registration problems.

In Table 3.2, we report pairwise correlation coefficients that summarize the relationship between the three registration measures developed by Pew. Excepting the correlation of 0.84 between the two cross-check measures, all other values are quite low. What's more, half of the values are negative and half are positive. The cross-check measures are positively correlated with rejected applications and self-reported registration problems in 2010, but are negatively correlated with those measures in 2008. Similarly, registration problems are positively correlated with rejected applications in 2008 but negatively correlated with rejected applications in 2010.

If we observe the correlation matrix for the Pew measures in addition to the measures that we developed with Catalist, there is a similar absence of any clear patterns. One way to capture underlying relationships among variables is through factor analysis or principal components analysis. Suppose we focus on 2010 data and factor analyze the following measures: (1) percent deceased, (2) percent undeliverable or probably undeliverable, (3) percent likely or probably deadwood, (4) percent with invalid addresses, (5) percent with no listed registration date, (6) percent with an incomplete registration date, (7) percent

TABLE 3.2. *Pairwise correlation coefficients for Pew EPI measures*

	Rejected '08	Rejected '10	Reg. Problems '08	Reg. Problems '10	X-Check '08	X-Check '10
Rejected '08	1.00					
Rejected '10	.30	1.00				
Reg. Problems '08	.09	−.05	1.00			
Reg. Problems '10	−.11	−.14	.32	1.00		
X-Check '08	−.33	.12	−.16	.15	1.00	
X-Check '10	−.30	.17	−.13	.06	.84	1.00

listed without a birthday, (8) percent with vote history discrepancies in 2010, (9) percent of applications rejected in 2010, (10) percent reporting registration problems in 2010, and (11) number of databases used to cross-check in 2010. If we use principal components analysis to generate factor scores on these eleven variables, five factors have an eigenvalue above 1. If these eleven measures picked up on some underlying index of registration quality, there would be only one factor with a high eigenvalue. Instead, there are five, which reflects that there is no underlying quality index that these measures collectively approximate.

Part of the problem with these indicators surely is measurement error, stemming from small samples (and misreporting) in the case of the CPS, and from probable misreporting in the EAVS (for another example of the unreliability of the EAVS, consult Ansolabehere et al. 2010). But another part of the problem is the theoretical question of what the measures are actually estimating. Is a high incidence of rejected applications a sign of a good registration system or a problematic one? Too many rejected applications might signal an overly burdensome voting requirement for voters, but too few may signal a lax system that fails to catch errors in registration applications. The same principle is at play for the other measures, as well. Is it a good sign or a bad sign if few survey respondents claim that they were unable to vote because of a registration problem? With a high mobility rate in the United States, there surely will be registered voters who show up at the wrong precinct on Election Day. If none of these individuals faces a problem casting a ballot, what exactly does this indicate?

MOVING FORWARD

The purpose of this chapter is to identify some new ways of measuring the quality of elections in the United States. By collaborating with a commercial data vendor, we have gained important insights into the voter registration data that are at the core of election administration. The measures we have described and estimated are not the only ways to assess quality, but they provide a broad and comprehensive perspective into the degree and variation of problems in voter registration files across the country.

The analysis in this chapter describes the U.S. registration system through a series of quality metrics. The chapter does not speak to the causes of why some states perform better or worse on particular measures. States and localities that have mobile populations or large numbers of elderly voters may have trouble keeping clean registration systems. Likewise, jurisdictions that lack standardization in producing government records or that use outdated database systems or that have a high incidence of clerical errors might have trouble keeping records clean, as well. Answering causal questions about why states perform the way they do on measures of registration quality is a logical next step in this research agenda. We hope that the methodological and descriptive analysis conducted here can serve as a foundation for this future work.

On each of ten items in our analysis of Catalist data, we have ranked the states in terms of the quality of their records. Every measure reveals a range of scores, and it will surely be useful for states to know where they stand relative to one another. The measures can help an election office identify areas most in need of improvement. For national policy makers and advocates, these initial results suggest that the path forward should focus on addressing each state's unique set of weak spots rather than identifying states that are overall delinquent or by proposing broad changes to election administration. This same lesson is drawn from our Catalist measures and from the survey-based measures spearheaded by Pew. It does not seem to be the case that there are good states and bad states, and that the bad states can be shamed into emulating the good states.

What is more, the states that leave control over election administration primarily in the hands of county officials do not seem to perform worse on these measures than states with centralized systems. California is known to have the most "bottom-up" registration system in the nation. There, the state election office does not input changes or updates to the files originating from the counties. And yet California performs well above average on these measures of registration quality. At the same time, in preliminary county-by-county analyses we have conducted, we find that, in general, rural counties have a greater incidence of obsolete records than urban counties.

Apart from comparing the quality of records across jurisdictions, these quality measures also offer a sense of the national average of registration data quality. Interpretations of how well or how poorly the nation is doing as a whole will differ depending on one's perspective. Our own view as informed by the data presented here is that overall the states are doing quite well. Indeed, the greatest barrier to maintaining clean election records is beyond the control of state and local governments; that voters move, die, and enter and exit the registration system means that keeping a list of eligible voters is a challenge. Given the population fluctuations, we see the rate of bad addresses, deadwood, duplicates, and dead voters to be reasonable and actually lower than expected. In the areas in which election administrators can work to make improvements, such as maintaining complete addresses, birth dates, registration dates, and vote histories, there are certainly opportunities for states to do better and for voters and advocates to demand better. We hope that these measures shed light on opportunities for reform.

4

Provisional Ballots

Michael J. Hanmer and Paul S. Herrnson

Over a decade has passed since Congress passed the Help America Vote Act (HAVA) in 2002, largely in response to the problems experienced in Florida during the 2000 presidential election. Despite the appropriation of more than $3.5 billion, there are still persistent problems with the administration of elections in the United States.[1] Some encompass technical problems involving computerized voting equipment, voter lists, and the software used to manage them, but many others are rooted in more traditional issues of candidates and political parties attempting to advantage themselves at the expense of their opponents. Indeed, contemporary elections provide many opportunities for those participating in election administration to manipulate the system intentionally for partisan advantage or to introduce inconsistencies across jurisdictions as a result of the discretion granted to state and local officials. This study focuses on a key area where partisan manipulation and local variation may be most prominent: provisional ballots.

Provisional ballots are important because they offer voters who otherwise would be denied the right to vote an opportunity to cast a ballot – at least in many cases. The Caltech/MIT Voting Technology Project (2001) provided one of the first arguments in favor of provisional voting and estimated that provisional ballots might have saved 1.5 million votes from being lost in 2000.

[1] Kevin J. Coleman and Eric A. Fischer, "The Help America Vote Act and Elections Reform: Overview and Issues" (Washington, DC: Congressional Research Service, June 27, 2011), 8–9.

We thank Charles Stewart and Barry Burden and the Pew Center on the States for including us in this project. For helpful comments, we thank Barry Burden, David Kimball, Charles Stewart, and participants at the Measures of Elections Conference June 18–19 at MIT. We thank Thad Hall for pointing us to relevant reports from Pew. For excellent research assistance, we thank Hoyoun Koh, Noah Kim, Genny Mayhew, and Jeff Taylor. All errors are our own.

We evaluate whether measures of provisional ballot usage and acceptance should be included as part of an index of election performance.
We argue that the issues surrounding measures of provisional ballot
usage and acceptance are sufficiently nuanced and, intertwined with
other aspects of election administration, that they are not suitable for an
overall index of election performance. For example, a high rate of usage
might represent a vigorous attempt to ensure that no votes are lost, while
simultaneously providing protection against fraud because the ballots
will be subject to scrutiny before being counted. On the one hand, this
example represents a well-functioning "fail-safe" mechanism used to
keep many from being disenfranchised. On the other hand, it simultaneously signals significant problems with a registration system that is
not properly recording the names of registrants, informing those with
missing information to supply the information, transmitting the names
on time to be included in the poll book, or preparing the poll books.
Similar problems exist for the rate of provisional ballot acceptance. For
example, a high rate of acceptance might signal that the system works
to count the ballots of those who the registration system failed to record
as properly registered. However, a low rate of acceptance might also signal that the system is working well, for example, by keeping those who
were not eligible to vote in a given place for a given election from doing
so. At the same time, a low acceptance rate could be a sign of a serious
flaw – insufficient time for election officials to locate the information
necessary to count the ballots from those who were actually eligible to
vote but who somehow did not show up in the poll book. Complicating
matters further is the degree to which the provisional voting measures
vary based on state laws and practice, local practice, demographics, and
political factors (see Kimball, Kropf, and Battles 2006).

This chapter is organized as follows. The first section provides an
overview of provisional ballots, including how they fit within the larger
context of election administration. It is followed by a discussion of the
measures of provisional voting and our evaluation of the role they play
in evaluating election performance. Next we examine the literature on
provisional voting. Finally, we present an empirical analysis of provisional voting in 2010 compared with previous elections.

PROVISIONAL BALLOTS IN CONTEXT

The right to vote in fair and free elections is one of the most fundamental rights of citizens in a democracy. Whether Americans identify

themselves as taxpayers, Texans, or a member of the select few who passed a naturalization test, they understand that U.S. citizenship entitles them to vote. Voting rights are both exclusive and inclusive. They belong to most but not all the population that resides on U.S. territory. Those who qualify as voters cannot be deprived of their voting rights without cause (e.g., cognitive impairments [see Link et al. 2012] or felony status in some states). From the perspective of public administration, the primary objective of the arrangements governing voting should be to allow all legal voters to cast their ballots while at the same time preventing others from voting. This is a normative goal that underlies many efforts to improve the voting process. It is usually tempered by practical obstacles, such as the costs associated with running an election. It also can be influenced by the partisan considerations of the officeholders who enact election laws, the administrators who write the regulations associated with these laws, and the election officials and volunteers who work at the polls on Election Day. Decentralized administration provides opportunities for individuals at the federal, state, and local levels to pursue partisan advantages through the electoral process.

The aforementioned considerations have a considerable impact on many aspects of voting, including those concerning provisional ballots. One purpose that provisional ballots serve is to prevent the possible disenfranchisement of voters. Section 302 of HAVA "creates the right for potential voters to cast provisional ballots in the event their names do not appear on the registration list or the voters' eligibility is challenged by an election official."[2] The U.S. Election Assistance Commission (EAC), charged with implementing HAVA, describes a provisional ballot as a "safety net" or "fail-safe" for the voter that records an individual's intent to vote and voting selections, until election officials determine whether the individual has the right to cast a ballot in the election. It allows election officials to make this judgment at a time when more perfect or complete information is made available either by the voter or the election jurisdiction. This judgment is based on voter eligibility requirements established in state and federal law. These include age, citizenship, and residency.[3] The policies and procedures for determining which provisional ballots should be counted vary by state. As we discuss in the following, the degree of variation across states, which

---

[2] See http://www.eac.gov/assets/1/Page/Best%20Practices%20for%20Provisional%20Voting.pdf. HAVA of 2002, Public Law 107–252, 42 U.S.C. 15301.

[3] HAVA establishes identification requirements for first-time voters who register by mail; many states impose stricter identification standards on all voters (see Biggers and Hanmer 2012).

stems in large part from vague language in HAVA, is considerable. Foley (2008, 76) describes the language that relates to implementation as "somewhat convoluted" and responsible for uncertainty, controversy, and litigation.

Though provisional voting is generally thought of as a fail-safe, a corresponding purpose is to provide protection against fraudulent voting. By requiring those whose eligibility is in question to cast a ballot that will not be counted until the individual casting it is verified as eligible to vote in that election, the system of provisional ballots "protects the integrity of the election itself" (Foley 2008, 75). Thus, as Foley (2008) notes, provisional voting is something of a compromise between access for individuals and protection for the system. This dual role adds complexity to attempts to use measures of provisional voting to evaluate the electoral system.

MEASURES USED AND THEIR INTERPRETATION

The typical measures of election performance related to provisional ballots are (1) the rate of provisional ballot usage (total number of provisional ballots cast divided by the total number of ballots cast) and (2) the rate of provisional ballot acceptance (total number of provisional ballots accepted divided by the total number of provisional ballots cast or the total number of ballots cast). Kimball and Foley (2009) present an additional measure that is similar to the provisional ballot acceptance rate. They explore the risk of litigation and use the "unsuccessful provisional voting rate" (the total number of rejected provisional ballots divided by the total number of ballots cast) relative to the margin of victory as an indicator of how appealing litigation over the election outcome might be.

Ideally, provisional ballots would be available but none would have to be issued as either protection against fraud or as a fail-safe. That is, in a perfectly functioning election, only those who are registered to vote would attempt to vote and all those who claim to be registered would be verified on the spot as such. Thus, it would seem that with respect to the number of provisional ballots issued, a lower percentage of provisional ballots to total ballots (i.e., a lower rate of provisional ballot usage) would indicate better performance. But matters are not so simple.

The rules, their implementation, the degree to which mistakes are made in the process of registration, and the reasons for giving out provisional ballots all play a role in determining whether a low or high rate of provisional ballot usage is a better reflection of good performance. Eligible citizens, election officials, and others who are involved with voter registration are bound to make mistakes. Provided that the particular rules in place accommodate these mistakes and poll workers provide provisional ballots according to the rules, a low rate of provisional ballot usage will signal good performance, that is, that the registration system and poll books are generally accurate, rendering the fail-safe provision largely unused. Advocates of Election Day registration (EDR) often advocate it in part because it nearly eliminates the need for provisional ballots. But if the rules are too strict or poll workers do not provide provisional ballots when they should a low rate of provisional ballot usage will signal poor performance as those who would otherwise be able to vote will be disenfranchised. There might also be cases in which citizens eligible to vote in an election, who are denied a regular ballot, who become so outraged, intimidated, or embarrassed that they do not request or accept a provisional ballot. Though this would lower the rate of provisional ballot usage, it reveals poor performance with the registration system and/or poll books.

A high rate of provisional ballot usage might also be difficult to interpret on its own. A high rate of usage reflects flexibility – a clear plus indicating that poll workers successfully implemented the fail-safe mechanism – giving those who claim to be registered an option other than going home without casting a ballot. But at the same time, if the requests are largely from those who are truly eligible to vote in a given election, a high rate of usage could indicate flaws with the system of registration and/or the poll book listings, aggressive purging by election officials, or rules for getting a regular ballot that are too strict. For example, in California, a voter who moves within the county without reregistering is guaranteed a provisional ballot and it must be counted; in many other states, that person might not be permitted to have their vote counted at all. Foley (2008) notes that after the 2004 election, Ohio increased the number of triggers for one to receive a provisional ballot to fourteen, thus creating a higher standard for getting a regular ballot. Also possible, though we do not think likely, the rate of provisional ballot usage might be inflated because of attempts by those who are not eligible for that election to vote illegally. In sum, these and other possibilities demonstrate that any measure of provisional ballot usage is an imperfect measure of policy success.

Matters are similarly complex when it comes to evaluating the rate at which provisional ballots are counted as valid. That is, one cannot simply assume that low acceptance rates are an indicator of failure and high acceptance rates for provisional ballots that were submitted are a sign of a policy success. Low acceptance rates may be partly the result of eligible voters who submitted provisional ballots but then decided not to take the additional steps required to ensure their ballots would be counted. Emotional responses, such as those suggested earlier, could account for some voters' lack of follow-up; the costs associated with carrying out the extra steps may account for the lack of follow-up by others. The interplay between a lack of knowledge among voters and the actions of partisan election officials informs another possibility raised by Stewart (2009, 1): "marginal voters [may] *think* their vote has been recorded when it is actually discarded unceremoniously." That is, though the fail-safe provides an opportunity to validate one's vote, the extra step can create a burden, confusion, or both. Moreover, when election officials fail to put sufficient time or effort into the verification process, or apply standards that are too strict, this lowers the acceptance rate and raises obvious concerns.

Though there are a number of reasons to treat low acceptance rates as an indicator of problems, a low acceptance rate could conceivably be influenced by the rejection of ballots from ineligible individuals who attempted to vote illegally – although in reality this is unlikely. High acceptance rates, on the other hand, may indicate that sloppy or partisan implementation of the law may have resulted in the counting of some provisional ballots that were cast by individuals who were ineligible to vote. In the absence of fraud, which most evidence suggests is uncommon (Minnite 2010), a high rate of provisional ballot acceptance signals both a strength and a weakness. The strength comes from the ability to rectify a mistake that a voter, the governmental agency or others involved with registration, the postal service, or poll workers made that would have otherwise left some disenfranchised. But this reveals a weakness in the system of registering and tracking registrants.

As alluded to earlier, provisional ballot submission and acceptance rates are not independent of one another and are related to other aspects of election administration, including the maintenance of voter rolls. To evaluate measures of provisional voting, both usage and acceptance should be considered together, and the following information should be collected: (1) the reasons for usage; (2) reasons for counting or not counting; and (3) number of people who declined to accept a provisional ballot when offered one. Additionally, to evaluate the overall health of the U.S. electoral system, we suggest it is necessary to go beyond this information to models of provisional ballot usage and acceptance. Finding that factors such as partisanship of the election officials and demographics influence rates of usage and acceptance would suggest problems in the system. Next we turn to the lessons learned from the literature on provisional voting.

THE STUDY OF PROVISIONAL BALLOTS

Research on provisional ballots is relatively new. As a result, little on the subject has been published thus far. But across the published research and a variety of reports there are a number of important lessons for evaluating the contributions of provisional voting to the health of the electoral system and for those continuing the study of provisional ballots.

Foley (2005) offers an informative account of the competing views leading to HAVA's provisional ballot section that provides a useful perspective for understanding the empirical work on provisional voting. He reveals that HAVA's provisional voting section was a compromise between "substantive" and "procedural" views of provisional voting. He describes the substantive view as one that leads to a system that as a practical matter allows EDR.[4] That is, whether an attempt to register was associated with a mistake in the process of pre-EDR (e.g., voter failed to fill out the form completely or the form was not transmitted from a motor vehicles office on time) or even if one never tried to register before Election Day, those who hold this view argue that anyone who meets the basic criteria for registration can cast a provisional ballot and have it counted. The procedural view takes a stricter stance on whose provisional ballot can be counted. More specifically, those who hold this view argue that only those who were officially registered to vote by the closing date for registration but because of some mistake with the voter list were not counted should have their provisional ballot counted. Foley (2005) goes on to note that though the procedural view (generally preferred by the U.S. Senate) ultimately won out over the substantive view (generally preferred by the U.S. House of Representatives), the language in HAVA leaves open the opportunity for the substantive view to prevail. Given the competing visions and HAVA's vague language

---

[4] HAVA (section 302) allows states with EDR or no registration system, per section 4(b) of the National Voter Registration Act of 1993 (NVRA) section 4(b), to comply with the provisional voting section via their state registration procedures. Maine, which had motor voter provisions in place anyway, was not granted exemption from the NVRA because not all its jurisdictions allowed EDR at the polls.

(Foley 2005, 2008) it is not surprising that the states and localities have established a variety of laws and procedures and that these factors have a strong influence on the rate of provisional ballot usage and the rate of provisional ballot acceptance.

A key factor by which provisional voting measures vary is previous history of provisional voting, that is, whether the states adopted provisional ballot procedures on their own or if they were imposed by the federal government via HAVA (Eagleton Institute of Politics, Rutgers University, and the Moritz College of Law, Ohio State University [Eagleton-Moritz] 2006; Kimball et al. 2006; Stewart 2009). That the outcomes vary along these lines is consistent with what Hanmer (2009) finds with respect to EDR and motor voter laws.

Seventeen states and the District of Columbia had some form of provisional voting prior to the enactment of HAVA. Twenty-six additional states allowed for provisional voting prior to the 2004 election. Seven states were exempt from the requirement because they either do not require voter registration (North Dakota) or allow for EDR at the polls (Idaho, Minnesota, New Hampshire, Wisconsin, and Wyoming).[5] Kimball et al. (2006) provide evidence based on the 2004 elections that provisional ballots were more likely to be submitted and counted in the states that had fail-safe voting mechanisms in place prior to the enactment of HAVA. Though Stewart (2009) uses a different measure of experience and examines provisional voting across several election cycles, he draws similar conclusions. He finds that states such as California that had liberal fail-safe voting laws prior to the enactment of HAVA typically had the highest provisional ballot rates, followed by states such as Ohio that had more limited regulations. States that made no accommodations for provisional voting prior to HAVA, such as Florida, had the lowest usage rates. His interpretation of these results was quite clear: "it defies credulity to claim that the states that had adopted provisional ballots before 2000 are now five times worse in handling voter registration than the states that adopted provisional ballots after HAVA" (2009, 4). And as Hanmer (2009) does in the context of EDR, Stewart (2009) argues that any analysis of provisional ballots take into account states' previous history with provisional voting. Results such as these underscore the earlier concerns with using provisional voting measures on their own as tools for evaluating election performance.

---

[5] Wisconsin and Wyoming do offer provisional ballots in some circumstances.

The states differ considerably in terms of the rules associated with providing and counting provisional ballots. The 2010 EAC's Election Administration and Voting Survey (EAVS) *Overview Report* (U.S. EAC 2011b) lists seven items that at least five states have to trigger use of a provisional ballot. The reasons and their frequency follow: name not on registration list (all forty-five states that are not exempt from HAVA's provisional voting requirement)[6]; voter does not have proper identification (thirty-four states); voter is challenged as ineligible (twenty-six states); voting hours were extended (twenty-two states); requested an absentee ballot but it was not yet cast (seventeen states); voter eligibility cannot be immediately established (thirteen states); and error in party listing on registration record (eleven states). Another key difference comes at the counting stage, where twenty states reported that provisional ballots cast in the wrong precinct would not be counted, four states indicated that provisional ballots cast in the wrong precinct but correct county would be counted, seven states reported that provisional ballots cast in the wrong precinct would not be counted, and a number of states highlighted circumstances in which provisional ballots cast in the wrong precinct would be counted. Several studies have shown that the rate of counting the ballots as acceptable is considerably higher in states that allow provisional ballots to be cast in the wrong precinct (Eagleton-Moritz 2006; Kimball et al. 2006).

A number of other factors related to state law and practice both directly and indirectly related to provisional voting influence provisional ballot usage and acceptance. As expected, because of the benefit of added technology, states with statewide voter registration databases were less likely to issue provisional ballots in 2004 (Eagleton-Moritz 2006; Kimball et al. 2006). The Eagleton-Moritz (2006) team also found that voter registration databases reduced the acceptance rate in states using provisional ballots for the first time. States that are subject to preclearance under the Voting Rights Act tended to accept fewer provisional ballots (Kimball et al. 2006), as were states with shorter time periods set to examine the provisional ballots (Eagleton-Moritz 2006; Foley 2008).

---

[6] Though only thirty-seven states were coded as having this trigger, further analysis revealed that state law in the states subject to HAVA's provisional voting requirements did provide for this trigger. We suspect that vague language in the survey resulted in miscoding by EAC staff in the *Statutory Overview Report* tables.

Students of U.S. elections will not be surprised that a variety of local factors also influence provisional voting. The decentralization of election administration within states gives local election officials (LEOs) latitude in administering state and federal regulations. Perhaps the most concerning factor found to influence provisional ballot usage and acceptance is the partisanship of election officials. In their extensive analysis of the 2004 election, Kimball et al. (2006) note that discretion is simply part of the process of issuing and counting provisional ballots. They first look to the rule creation stage, finding suggestive evidence that Democratic officials tend to adopt more permissive standards. At the issuing and counting stages, they find that the interplay between the partisanship of the elected official and the partisanship of the electorate is an important influence. They show that as jurisdictions lean more toward one party, the number of ballots issued and accepted increases when the election official is of the same party and decreases when the election official is a member of the other party.

There are also a host of demographic factors that affect provisional voting measures. Researchers have found that the use of provisional ballots rises as the following increase: the number of ballots cast (Kimball et al. 2006); residential mobility (Alvarez and Hall 2009; Stewart 2009); population growth (Kimball and Foley 2009); the nonwhite population (Alvarez and Hall 2009); and the percent Hispanic (Kimball and Foley 2009). And the rate of provisional ballot usage decreases as the percent sixty-five and older increases (Alvarez and Hall 2009; Kimball et al. 2006) and as median income increases (Kimball et al. 2006). With respect to acceptance, Kimball et al. (2006) find that the number of ballots counted decreases as residential mobility increases and as the percent sixty-five and older increases. Kimball and Foley (2009) also find that the unsuccessful provisional voting rate increases as the size of the population increases and as the percent black and the percent Hispanic increase.

The features described in the preceding add to the complexity of interpreting provisional voting measures. Not only do we need to look beyond the basic indicators and into related indicators, but we contend that examining the measures and their correlates across time is necessary. We now turn to an examination of provisional voting. We provide a quick look at preliminary evidence from 2012 but focus on 2010 in comparison to previous elections.

PROVISIONAL BALLOT USAGE AND ACCEPTANCE
RATES: SAME STORY, DIFFERENT ELECTION

The 2012 elections were the fifth federal elections in which HAVA's pro-visional ballot requirements were in effect. Shortly before this writing, the EAC released their 2012 EAVS. According to the survey, more than 2.6 million provisional ballots were cast in the 2012 presidential elec-tion, representing about 2 percent of all ballots cast. About 75 percent of the provisional ballots cast were fully or partially counted. As a share of total ballots cast, the District of Columbia stands out as having the highest rate of provisional ballot usage, with provisional ballots making up more than 13 percent of all ballots cast. This is a sizable increase from previous elections that is largely explained by the District's policy of issuing provisional ballots to those who register to vote or change their address on Election Day.[7] This result highlights the importance of information regarding the reasons surrounding provisional ballot usage. Figure 4.1 shows the rate of provisional ballot usage across the states in 2012. These results should be viewed with caution as the data at the time of this writing are best viewed as preliminary and subject to revision as more information becomes available. That said, it is clear that provisional ballot usage varies a great deal across the states. We now turn to a closer analysis of the 2010 midterm.

Overall, 1,061,914 provisional ballots were cast in the 2010 midterm elections.[8] This amounts to about 1 percent of ballots cast in 2010. Of those nearly 1.1 million provisional ballots cast, 703,256 (66 percent) were counted in full and another 118,052 in part, for a total acceptance rate of 77.3 percent.

To better understand the 2010 results and capture the concern with variation across the states we build on Kimball and Foley's (2009) analy-sis of the usage rate, acceptance rate, and unsuccessful provisional vot-ing rates using the state as the unit of analysis for each of the four federal elections since HAVA was implemented. Table 4.1 reproduces Kimball and Foley's (2009) results from 2004, 2006, and 2008 and adds results

---

[7] The 2012 elections marked the first presidential election in which voters in the District of Columbia could take advantage of EDR.

[8] This total excludes Idaho, Minnesota, New Hampshire, and North Dakota but includes Wisconsin and Wyoming. Though Wisconsin and Wyoming are also exempt from HAVA's provisional voting requirements, they still allow provisional voting in certain circumstances. Wisconsin had sixty-four and Wyoming had twenty-five provisional votes in 2010.

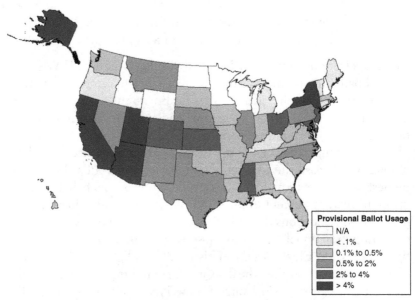

FIGURE 4.1. Provisional ballot usage by state in 2012. (*Source*: EAVS.)
Notes: Georgia is listed as N/A as the data were not reported in the EAVS.

using the 2010 EAVS. Although the results are quite similar, because the sample size and data-cleaning processes differ, we also included the 2008 results from the Measure of American Elections project's version of the 2008 EAVS (see Appendix).[9]

For almost all the measures there is little difference in the overall result across the four elections. One exception is that the median provisional ballot usage rate was lower in 2010 (0.2 percent) than it was in 2006 (0.4 percent). Though the mean is higher in the presidential elections (about 1.5 percent versus 1 percent), within election type the mean usage rate is roughly the same across years. In 2010, the mean acceptance rate (as a percentage of provisional ballots issued) across the states was 60.5 percent and the median was 63.4 percent, both of which were close to the 2006 rates.[10] And though the Kimball and Foley (2009)

[9] The Measures of Elections data, included in the appendix of this volume, were created by the editors using the reports from the EAVS. For the 2008 and 2010 elections, we also examined just the forty-one states used in Kimball and Foley's (2009) analysis of the 2004 election, but the results are similar to those using the forty-five states reported in Table 4.1. As noted earlier, because Maine was not exempt from the NVRA, we include it in our analyses.

[10] The difference in the mean acceptance rate when states are the unit of analysis and the overall national average reported in Table 4.1 stems from the aggregation method and the wide variation across the states.

TABLE 4.1. *Provisional voting measures in U.S. federal elections 2004–2010*

Replication and Extension of Kimball and Foley (2009, table 2)

	Kimball and Foley (2009)			Measures of American Elections	
	2004	2006	2008	2008	2010
Usage Rate (%)					
Mean	1.5	1.0	1.3	1.4	0.9
median	0.6	0.4	0.4	0.5	0.2
Std. dev.	1.7	1.3	1.8	1.9	1.4
Acceptance Rate (%)					
Mean	47.6	58.7	54.7	53.4	60.5
Median	49.5	61.9	48.8	48.6	63.4
Std. dev.	23.6	25.4	24.1	24.7	26.7
Unsuccessful provisional voting rate (%)					
Mean	0.5	0.2	0.4	0.4	0.2
Median	0.3	0.1	0.2	0.2	0.1

Notes: The Measure of American Elections data from EAVS exclude exempt states having EDR: Idaho, Minnesota, New Hampshire, North Dakota, Wisconsin, and Wyoming. Aggregation is done by state. That is, the results average across each state without accounting for differences in the number of ballots cast. Thus, the 2010 mean acceptance rate, 58.4 percent, represents the average of the acceptance rates across the forty-five states under consideration and not the average acceptance rate weighted by number of ballots cast. Because of what seem to be errors in the reporting of provisional ballots counted, Alabama and New Mexico are dropped from the 2008 acceptance rate calculations.

Sources: Columns 1–3 from Kimball and Foley (2009) table 2 (using EAVS 2004, 2006, 2008); Columns 4–5 from EAVS 2008, 2010, as provided by the Measures of American Elections project.

and the Measure of American Elections data used throughout this volume produce different means for 2008, regardless of which 2008 data are used, the mean and median acceptance rates for presidential elections are lower than they are for midterm elections. The story remains the same when looking to the unsuccessful provisional vote rate – in both 2010 and 2006 the mean rate was 0.2 percent and the median 0.1 percent. Again, these rates for the midterm election were lower than the rates for the president elections.

Figure 4.2 provides a visual display of the variation in provisional ballot usage across the states. The rate of usage in the states not exempt

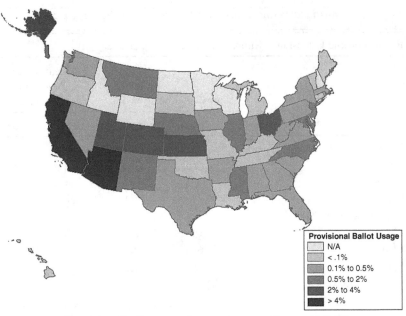

FIGURE 4.2. Provisional ballot usage by state in 2010. (*Source*: EAVS.)

from HAVA's provisional voting section ranged from a low of 0.005 percent in Vermont to a maximum of 5.2 percent in California. Two other states had usage rates at or near 5 percent of total ballots cast: Alaska (5.0 percent) and Arizona (4.7 percent). Although the reasons for these high rates might have changed, the end result has changed little as all three of these states were also in the top three in terms of usage rate in 2004 and 2008 (Kimball and Foley 2009, Figure 4.1). The remainder of the highest ten in terms of usage spread across the country: the District of Columbia (4.0 percent), Utah (3.0 percent), Ohio (2.7 percent), Colorado (2.2 percent), Kansas (2.1 percent), Maryland (2.0 percent), and Mississippi (1.6 percent). At the other end of the distribution, in addition to Vermont another seven states had usage rates below 0.05 percent: Kentucky (0.007 percent), Delaware (0.01 percent), South Dakota (0.02 percent), Louisiana (0.02 percent), Michigan (0.03 percent), Maine (0.03 percent), and Tennessee (0.04 percent). Overall, the average usage rate across the forty-five nonexempt states was 0.9 percent.

Provisional ballot acceptance rates vary even more widely across the states. Maine, which only had 159 provisional ballots accepted all of them, while Delaware accepted just 6.1 percent. Rounding out the highest ten in terms of percentage accepted are Montana (95.4 percent), Oregon (93.1 percent), the District of Columbia (92.6 percent), Maryland (91.4 percent), Colorado (90.7 percent), Alaska (90.0 percent), Ohio (88.8 percent), Louisiana (87.6 percent), and California (86.6 percent). The rest of the lowest ten in terms of percentage accepted are Kentucky (6.8 percent), Oklahoma (16.7 percent), South Dakota (18.8 percent), Texas (22.9 percent), Massachusetts (29.2 percent), Hawaii (23.7 percent), Illinois (29.8 percent), and Tennessee (35.3 percent). It is a useful reminder that here we use *highest* and *lowest* merely to describe where the states fall on the distribution, as high or low percentages on their own are not enough to assess performance.

More information is conveyed when submission and acceptance rates are evaluated together. Though it is not necessarily the case that a high level of submission will lead to a high level of acceptance, six of the states with the highest ten submission rates were also among the highest ten on acceptance rate (Alaska, California, Colorado, District of Columbia, Maryland, and Ohio). Figure 4.3 shows the relationship between the usage rate (x axis) and acceptance rate (y axis). The first thing to notice here is that most of the states have usage rates that are close to 0 percent. The red regression line indicates that, overall, there is a positive relationship between the usage and acceptance rates. Interestingly, all the states with a usage rate greater than 1 percent have acceptance rates of at least 60 percent, while states with usage rates lower than 1 percent have acceptance rates that vary across the entire range.

Figure 4.4 replicates Figure 4.3 using data from 2008.[11] By comparing the two figures, we see several similarities. In 2008, most of the states were also clustered near a usage rate of 0 percent. The relationship between usage and acceptance in 2008 is again positive with California, Alaska, Arizona, and the District of Columbia located in the top-right corner of each graph, revealing their high rates of usage and acceptance. Though the rates and relative placement differ, the same states tended to be grouped in the top-left and bottom-left quadrants, as well. For example, Delaware, Hawaii, Kentucky, Oklahoma, Texas, and South Dakota have low rates of usage and acceptance. The similarities across time suggest to us the need for additional data, highlighting the difficulty of using measures of provisional voting as part of an election performance index. Particularly useful would be data that indicate

[11] Data from Alabama and New Mexico were problematic, so we dropped these states from the figure.

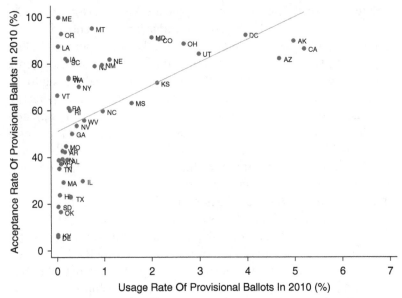

FIGURE 4.3. Provisional ballot usage and acceptance rates by state in 2010. (*Source*: EAVS.)

Notes: Acceptance rate is calculated as total number of provisional ballots accepted divided by the total number of provisional ballots cast. The correlation between the usage rate and acceptance rate is 0.52 ($p < 0.01$).

the percentage of provisional ballots issued across the various reasons for issuing provisional ballots, data that most states do not readily provide. Tracking this across time would surely provide more insight than a snapshot of a single election year. We believe data on the quality of the voter registration databases would also prove useful, especially when measures of provisional ballot usage could be examined as a function of changes in the quality of the registration databases.

We next examine rates of usage and acceptance in 2010 compared with 2008. Figure 4.5 shows the relationship of provisional voting usage in 2010 compared with 2008 by state, while Figure 4.6 shows the relationship of provisional ballot acceptance in 2010 compared with 2008. The solid lines in each figure are forty-five-degree lines that represent equal rates across the two elections. Figure 4.5 shows that there is a positive relationship between the usage rates, but that in almost every state usage was lower in 2010 than it was in 2008. Given that turnout is lower in midterm elections, this is not surprising as the 2010 election would have had fewer new registrants and fewer intermittent voters,

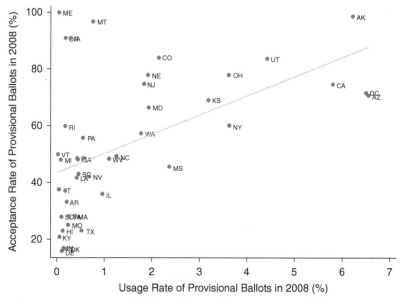

FIGURE 4.4. Provisional ballot usage and acceptance rates by state in 2008. (*Source*: EAVS.)

Notes: Acceptance rate is calculated as total number of provisional ballots accepted divided by the total number of provisional ballots cast. The correlation between the usage rate and acceptance rate is 0.52 ($p < 0.01$).

those more likely to need a provisional ballot. However, we cannot be sure that other factors are not at work.

Figure 4.6 shows that there is a positive relationship between the acceptance rates, too. However, the overall conclusion that usage rates are lower in the midterm election does not hold for acceptance rates. A large majority of the states are above or on the forty-five-degree line indicating that acceptance rates in 2010 tended to be higher in 2008. Though a variety of factors might explain this, again, our knowledge of the electorate in midterm compared with presidential elections provides some suggestions. Given that those who are more engaged are more likely to vote in a midterm election, it might be the case that individuals were more likely to follow up and provide any necessary documents to ensure their ballots would be counted. Additionally, verification might be easier in a midterm election from the perspective of the election officials; that is, the smaller turnout and smaller number of provisional ballots might have made it easier for election officials to locate the information necessary to verify registration status.

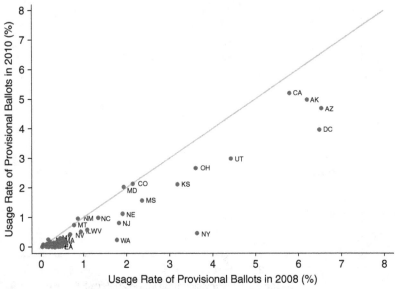

FIGURE 4.5. Provisional voting usage rates in 2008 compared with 2010 by state. (*Source:* EAVS.)

Notes: The correlation between the 2008 and 2010 usage rates is 0.95 ($p < 0.01$).

But it might also be the case that if less was at stake, election officials were more lax in counting provisional ballots as acceptable. Though these suggestions are plausible, the scatterplot reveals a fair degree of variation by state and additional analyses are beyond the scope of this chapter.

As noted earlier, state laws governing the use and counting of provisional ballots vary considerably. Table 4.2 provides the mean usage rate and acceptance rate (out of provisional ballots submitted) across six policies cited in the 2010 EAVS as triggering the use of a provisional ballot and whether the ballot will be counted if it is cast in the wrong precinct. The most noteworthy results pertain to the trigger for having requested an absentee ballot but not having cast it and for counting the ballot if it is cast in the wrong precinct. For both usage and acceptance, the results across the states that have these policies are substantively and statistically different from those that do not. In states that issue a provisional ballot when an individual requested an absentee ballot but did not vote, the usage rate is nearly three times as high as in states that do not cite this trigger (1.59 percent versus 0.54 percent) and the acceptance rate is seventeen percentage points higher (71.18 percent versus

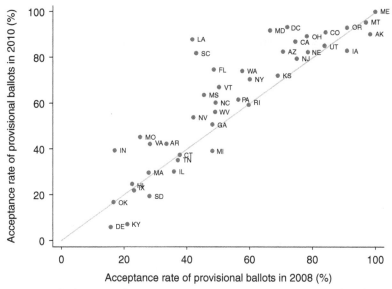

FIGURE 4.6. Provisional voting acceptance rates in 2008 compared with 2010 by state. (*Source*: EAVS.)

Notes: Acceptance rate is calculated as total number of provisional ballots accepted divided by the total number of provisional ballots cast. The correlation between the 2008 and 2010 acceptance rates is 0.88 (*p* < 0.01).

54.03 percent). The results for accepting ballots cast in the wrong precinct are even more striking. The twenty-one states that allow for this have a usage rate four times higher than states that do not (1.56 percent versus 0.39 percent) and an acceptance rate twenty-seven percentage points higher than the twenty-four states that do not count provisional ballots cast in the wrong precinct (74.92 percent versus 47.89 percent). The large differences across these two state-level policies demonstrate one of the complications of using state-level measures of provisional voting to evaluate election administration performance and call attention to the need for more detailed data on the reasons associated with provisional ballot usage and acceptance.

We conclude with an examination of one of the key factors found to influence provisional voting – when the state adopted provisional voting. We follow the Eagleton-Moritz (2006) measures of "old" and "new" but add Maine to the list of "old" states, where *old* indicates that the state had some variant of fail-safe voting by 2001 (i.e., before HAVA) and *new* indicates that the state did not have a fail-safe mechanism

TABLE 4.2. *Provisional ballot usage and acceptance rates across state policies in 2010*

State Policy		Usage Rate (submitted/ turnout, %)	Acceptance Rate (counted/submitted, %)
Registration reflects error in party listing	No (35)	0.96	60.65
	Yes (10)	0.87	60.00
	Diff	0.09	0.65
	p-value	0.87	0.95
Voter eligibility cannot be immediately established	No (33)	0.87	57.54
	Yes (12)	1.13	68.68
	Diff.	−0.27	−11.14
	p-value	0.58	0.22
Challenge of voter as ineligible	No (21)	0.73	57.40
	Yes (24)	1.12	63.22
	Diff.	−0.39	−5.82
	p-value	0.36	0.47
Voter does not have proper identification	No (13)	0.71	55.03
	Yes (32)	1.03	62.73
	Diff.	−0.32	−7.70
	p-value	0.49	0.39
When voting during extended polling hours	No (24)	0.82	62.26
	Yes (21)	1.07	58.51
	Diff.	−0.25	3.75
	p-value	0.55	0.64
Voter requested absentee ballot but has not cast it	No (28)	0.54	54.03
	Yes (17)	1.59	71.18
	Diff.	−1.05	−17.15
	p-value	0.01	0.04
Counted if cast in wrong precinct[#]	No (24)	0.39	47.89
	Yes (21)	1.56	74.92
	Diff.	−1.17	−27.03
	p-value	0.00	0.00

Notes: Includes forty-five states, which exclude Idaho, Minnesota, New Hampshire, North Dakota, Wisconsin, and Wyoming. Entries are state's mean percentage for each measure. Numbers in parentheses in the second column presents frequencies. Differences are calculated as percentage in the "No" row minus the percentage in the "Yes" row. #: Coded as "Yes" if counted either automatically or conditionally; p-values are for two-tail tests.
Source: EAVS.

prior to HAVA.[12] Our results are consistent with previous research: the rate of provisional voting usage and acceptance is substantially higher in the states that had previous experience with provisional voting. With respect to usage, the old states had an average usage rate of 1.38 percent, while the new states averaged 0.34 percent, a difference that is statistically significant (p = 0.015, two-tailed). In other words, the rate of provisional voting in old states was nearly four times larger than in the new states. The acceptance rates were also substantively and statistically different across the old and new states. While the old states had an average acceptance rate of 68.56 percent, the new states had a rate of 46.68 percent, a difference of nearly twenty-two percentage points (p = 0.005, two-tailed). Burden's chapter in this volume also finds that inertia plays a significant role with respect to issues of voter registration. In other words, election administrators tend to respond slowly to new rules. Given how closely tied the voter registration and provisional voting processes are, it is not surprising to find similar results in each of these areas of election administration. The persistence of the gaps between the "old" and "new" provisional voting states in the fourth election since HAVA was implemented underscores our earlier argument that additional information should be brought to bear when using provisional voting to evaluate election performance. It also reinforces Stewart's (2009) concern that provisional voting implementation is lacking and his call for greater attention to the differences in outcomes based on experience with provisional voting.

CONCLUSION

Provisional ballots provide eligible individuals who might otherwise be turned away with the opportunity to vote and have their vote counted. But their use varies considerably across and within states, suggesting that it is a function of many other aspects of election administration and politics more generally. That the patterns overall have not changed much suggests that some problems have yet to be fixed, or that others have failed to be anticipated and avoided.

Our empirical results further our concern with provisional voting usage and acceptance as measures of election performance in

[12] The Eagleton-Moritz measure was based on a 2001 report by electionline.org and the Constitution Project, "Election Reform Briefing: The Provisional Voting Challenge." See www.pewtrusts.org/uploadedFiles/ProvisionalVoting.pdf.

the United States. Though we believe measures of provisional voting should be included in the evaluation of elections, we simply need more information to put the measures in proper context. Among the most useful factors that would contribute to a better understanding are the reasons for issuing the provisional ballot and the reasons why it was or was not counted. The EAVS data provide a broad look at this. In 2010, provisional ballots were rejected because the voter was not registered in the state (45 percent), registered but in the wrong jurisdiction (7 percent), registered in the wrong precinct (11 percent), failed to provide identification (2 percent), submitted an incomplete or illegible ballot or envelope (4 percent), or other reasons (32 percent). Unpacking these other reasons deserves further attention.

Relatedly, the number of names purged from voter rolls and the reasons for the purge might help locate the source of difficulty with the voters or the administration of the rolls. Additionally, differences in the policies governing the maintenance of voter rolls would also help us understand usage and acceptance rates better. After all, most provisional ballots are distributed in response to polling place challenges that call into question the accuracy of an official voter list. State requirements for voter registration and voter identification also vary and might need to be taken into consideration. Another set of factors include differences in the norms associated with the conduct of elections, and politics more generally, across the states. As mentioned earlier, institutional and partisan considerations also are important. Chief among these are electoral competition, whether one or both major parties exercise some control over statewide offices or the state legislature, the methods used to select the officials who make and administer the policies that govern elections, and the size and density of election jurisdictions.

5

Mail Ballots in the United States: Policy Choice and Administrative Challenges

Christopher B. Mann

One of the most dramatic changes in voting in the United States over the last two decades has been the growth in the number of voters casting ballots by mail with every successive election cycle. In recent years, an increasing number of states have changed laws to allow voters to cast mail ballots without an excuse, to allow voters to "permanently" request mail ballots for all future elections, and even to switch to "all-mail" voting. Casting ballots by mail involves major changes in the mechanics of obtaining, completing, and submitting ballots compared with the in-person voting system used in the United States for more than a century (Ewald 2009; Keyssar 2009). Given the large and growing proportion of ballots cast by mail, it is vital to understand the effect of these policy changes on election administration and determine how well states administer this distinctive method of voting.

In the 2012 general election, thirty states allowed voters to request mail ballots without providing a reason for using a mail ballot (National Conference of State Legislatures 2012). Eight states allowed voters to request mail ballots for every election (permanent mail voter status). In-person voting was not available in Oregon or Washington: ballots were mailed to all voters that could be returned by mail or in special ballot drop boxes.[1] Twelve additional states allowed counties and cities to conduct similar mail ballot elections in specific types of primary, local, and off-year elections.

---

[1] In-person voting is available in limited cases with accessible technology for disabled voters in Oregon and Washington.

Barry Burden, Martha Kropf, John Love, Charles Stewart, and the participants in the Measure of Elections Conference at MIT provided valuable feedback on this chapter. I thank the team at MIT for their efforts to compile and clean a variety of data sources related to election administration and the Pew Center on the States for their financial support. Errors in fact or judgment are the author's sole responsibility.

Unfortunately, research about voting using mail ballots has not kept pace with state policy changes or with the growing task of administering mail ballots. Research on in-person voting is not readily transferable to mail voting because many of the central elements of in-person voting are missing, including polling place location and quality, poll workers, waiting time in line, and voting machines.[2] Simultaneously, mail voting raises new considerations about the usability of ballots, verification of identity, and reliability of mail delivery.

This chapter addresses fundamental questions about mail ballot policy choices and administrative performance. States have one of four types of mail voting systems for domestic voters: (1) traditional absentee voting; (2) *election-specific* vote-by-mail; (3) *permanent* vote-by-mail; and (4) postal voting. I define these systems in more detail in the following.

The federal Uniformed and Overseas Citizens Absentee Voting Act (UOCAVA) creates a separate system of mail ballots for military members and U.S. citizens living outside the United States. This UOCAVA system is addressed by Thad Hall in Chapter 6 in this volume because the federal law governing voting by overseas citizens is different from most domestic mail voting designed by the states, and states have little policy or administrative discretion over UOCAVA voting.

This chapter uses state-level comparisons of mail ballot use, ballot return rates, and ballot rejection rates obtained from the U.S. Election Assistance Commission's (EAC's) biennial Election Administration and Voting Survey (EAVS) to demonstrate the similarities within and differences between the four systems of domestic mail voting. Election administration problems – and their solutions – are products of policy choice and administrative performance. Election administration performance examines how well the voting process is run *within* the parameters of policy choices made by state legislatures, and thus is best assessed among states with the same mail voting system. Conversely, the effects of policy choices about mail voting are seen by comparing different mail voting systems.

---

[2] Elements of election administration, such as voter registration, communication/education about how to vote, and vote counting, that are separate from the casting of ballots remain similar.

TABLE 5.1. *Definitions of systems for administering mail ballots*

Term	Definition
Absentee Voting	Mail ballots are only available to voters who meet statutorily defined reasons for being unable to appear at their assigned polling places on Election Day.
Vote-by-Mail (*Election-Specific Vote-by-Mail*)	Any registered voter can request a mail ballot without providing a reason or excuse. Requests for ballots can be valid for an election cycle, an election year, or a specific election, depending on state law.
Permanent Vote-by-Mail	Any registered voter may request a mail ballot for all future elections, without providing a reason or excuse.[a] Permanent mail voter status is a voluntary choice, and layered on top of the election-specific vote-by-mail system.
Postal Voting	All registered voters are sent a ballot by mail. In-person voting with voting machines/polling booths is not available to the general public.

[a] Some absentee voting states have permanent absentee lists for voters who have a permanent reason why they are unable to vote in person. I do not consider these states as permanent vote-by-mail.

DEFINING FOUR SYSTEMS OF MAIL VOTING

State policies define four systems of administering mail ballots identified by why voters receive a ballot in the mail: (1) traditional absentee voting, (2) *election-specific* vote-by-mail, (3) *permanent* vote-by-mail, and (4) postal voting.[3] Policy choice about why voters receive a mail ballot leads to significant differences in which and how many voters use mail ballots (Alvarez, Levin, and Sinclair 2012; Barreto et al. 2006). These differences present different administrative challenges under each system.

The first step to better understand mail voting is clarity in the terminology. Table 5.1 summarizes definitions of the four systems. To this point there has been no consensus among policy makers, election administrators, or scholars about terminology for describing mail voting policy. The same term often refers to different procedures in different states, or different terms refer to the same procedure in different states.

[3] All states allow voters to return mail ballots by mail or by hand, although the locations to which ballots can be hand-delivered vary across states.

I use the terms *mail ballots* and *mail voting* to refer to any ballots delivered to the voters by mail, under any system governing who can receive mail ballots.

States have moved through a progression of legislative policy changes from traditional absentee voting toward postal voting. This pattern in the historical development of election policy does not imply this succession of policy changes is inevitable or normatively desirable. These policy changes do not necessarily have popular support before they are passed, but they receive popular support once in place (Alvarez et al. 2011). States may skip steps, or even reverse this progression.[4] Nevertheless, historically, every state has moved through this developmental sequence to their current mail voting system. Table 5.2 summarizes the mail voting system currently available in each state (and measures of mail voting discussed in this chapter).

The first system, traditional absentee voting, began with efforts by Abraham Lincoln's Republican Party to ensure that Union soldiers fighting in the Civil War would be able to vote in the 1864 federal elections.[5] For almost 150 years, states have had statutorily defined grounds to request an absentee ballot in lieu of appearing in person on Election Day. These reasons include limited mobility stemming from health or disability, and being away from the polls because of military service, poll worker service, education, or employment.[6]

The requirement to provide a reason for requesting a mail ballot largely depends on the honor system because election officials lack resources to investigate whether voters' reasons are legitimate. In some absentee voting jurisdictions, mail ballot requests have been increasing over time. Some observers think voters in these jurisdictions want the convenience of mail ballots and are willing to stretch the truth in providing a reason. However, it is also possible that more voters believe they have legitimate reasons to request mail ballots. Either way, the requirement to provide a reason for requesting a mail ballot may be eroding, and with it the major policy distinction between absentee voting and the vote-by-mail system.

---

[4] One recent example of a small reversal of this trend is 2013 legislation passed in North Carolina requiring mail ballots to have signatures from two witnesses or a notary.

[5] Given ongoing partisan conflicts about pre–Election Day voting, it is worth noting that partisan motivations have been part of mail voting policy debates from the very beginning.

[6] Several states, including Michigan, Tennessee, and Texas, provide an age threshold as an "excuse," which may be an assumption that senior citizens are more likely to face health or mobility challenges.

TABLE 5.2. *Mail voting systems and mail voting data by state*

Election	Mail Voting System	Share of Ballots Cast by Mail			% of Mail Ballots Not Returned			% of Returned Mail Ballots Rejected			% of Returned Mail Ballots Rejected for Missing Deadline			% of Returned Mail Ballots Rejected for Missing Signature		
		2008	2010	2012	2008	2010	2012	2008	2010	2012	2008	2010	2012	2008	2010	2012
AK	Vote-by-Mail	8.7%	7.2%	8.2%	16.5%	15.6%	15.5%	2.1%	2.9%	3.2%	0.3%	0.0%	0.0%	0.1%	0.3%	0.0%
AL	Absentee Voting						12.8%									
AR	Absentee Voting	1.8%	2.4%	2.6%	16.8%	9.7%	9.1%	3.1%	5.0%	3.0%	0.7%	0.9%	1.0%	4.4%	1.0%	1.0%
AZ	Perm. Vote-by-Mail	52.4%	61.5%	65.9%	6.4%	23.1%	19.7%	0.6%	0.8%	0.8%	0.1%	0.3%	0.3%	0.2%	0.3%	0.3%
CA	Perm. Vote-by-Mail	42.9%	48.8%	50.0%	16.2%	30.9%	29.4%	2.2%	1.4%	0.9%	0.3%	0.5%	0.4%	0.2%	0.2%	0.4%
CO	Perm. Vote-by-Mail	62.2%	68.5%	68.1%	9.0%	22.0%	12.5%	0.5%	0.6%	0.9%	0.1%	0.1%	0.1%	0.1%	0.2%	0.1%
CT	Absentee Voting	8.8%	5.7%	7.5%	-4.9%	6.5%	8.7%	2.1%	1.9%	2.0%		1.9%				
DC	Absentee (2008) Vote-by-Mail (2010, 2012)	11.1%	2.5%	3.8%	3.7%	32.7%	28.2%	8.6%	8.6%	3.5%	0.3%	0.5%	0.8%		5.4%	0.8%
DE	Absentee Voting	4.9%	3.6%	4.6%	3.6%	4.5%	7.6%	1.6%	1.2%	1.2%	1.6%	1.1%	1.2%	0.0%	0.1%	1.2%
FL	Vote-by-Mail	21.5%	22.4%	26.6%	14.1%	29.0%	18.2%	1.0%	1.4%	0.9%	0.3%	0.7%	0.4%	0.3%	0.4%	0.4%
GA	Vote-by-Mail	52.3%	29.7%	48.8%	1.6%	2.6%	1.7%	0.2%	0.1%		0.1%	0.0%		0.0%	0.0%	
HI	Perm. Vote-by-Mail	21.2%	30.1%	35.7%	15.0%	7.7%	9.8%	0.8%	0.9%	0.7%	0.1%	0.3%	0.4%	0.1%	0.1%	0.4%
IA	Vote-by-Mail	38.1%	31.9%	42.5%	5.1%	6.0%	7.0%	0.7%	1.2%	1.2%	0.1%	0.3%	0.2%	0.0%	0.3%	0.2%
ID	Vote-by-Mail	29.1%	19.5%	24.3%	3.3%	6.6%	3.3%	0.5%	1.6%	0.6%	0.3%	0.5%	0.4%	0.1%	0.1%	0.4%
IL	Absentee (2008) Vote-by-Mail (2010, 2012)	3.3%	3.7%	2.0%	6.8%	17.3%	0.7%	0.2%	2.0%		0.2%			0.1%		
IN	Absentee Voting	15.8%	10.3%	19.0%	3.7%	0.5%	0.7%	10.9%	3.9%	2.1%	0.1%	0.1%	0.2%	0.1%	1.8%	0.2%

(continued)

117

TABLE 5.2 *(continued)*

Election	Mail Voting System	Share of Ballots Cast by Mail			% of Mail Ballots Not Returned			% of Returned Mail Ballots Rejected			% of Returned Mail Ballots Rejected for Missing Deadline			% of Returned Mail Ballots Rejected for Missing Signature		
		2008	2010	2012	2008	2010	2012	2008	2010	2012	2008	2010	2012	2008	2010	2012
KS	Vote-by-Mail	23.3%	17.8%	16.3%	6.5%	16.3%	30.2%	1.4%	2.7%	3.6%	0.7%	0.7%	1.2%	0.5%	0.9%	1.2%
KY	Absentee Voting	6.1%	4.8%	1.8%	5.9%	2.8%	.	1.7%	1.7%	5.4%	0.3%	0.2%	0.7%	0.9%	1.1%	0.7%
LA	Absentee Voting	14.4%	10.1%	2.1%	2.6%	6.1%	21.7%	0.7%	0.6%	5.4%	0.4%	0.3%	2.2%	0.1%	0.1%	2.2%
MA	Absentee Voting	6.5%	5.1%	8.1%	9.1%	5.9%	8.2%	1.0%	0.1%	1.0%	.	0.7%	0.8%	.	0.1%	0.8%
MD	Absentee (2008) Vote-by-Mail (2010, 2012)	7.3%	4.5%	5.1%	9.3%	14.6%	12.5%	1.0%	1.3%	1.1%	0.3%	0.8%	0.6%	0.4%	0.3%	0.6%
ME	Vote-by-Mail	31.5%	24.3%	25.5%	2.8%	3.7%	3.2%	0.8%	0.8%	1.2%	0.1%	0.2%	0.2%	0.2%	0.4%	0.2%
MI	Absentee Voting	24.9%	23.1%	25.7%	2.5%	4.6%	2.9%	0.7%	0.7%	0.6%	0.4%	0.4%	0.4%	0.0%	0.1%	0.4%
MN	Absentee Voting	10.9%	5.9%	8.7%	-74.0%	7.1%	4.3%	2.8%	5.9%	2.9%	0.3%	0.6%	0.7%	1.2%	0.6%	0.7%
MO	Absentee Voting	9.6%	5.7%	8.9%	6.5%	3.7%	4.6%	1.8%	1.8%	2.0%	0.5%	0.6%	0.7%	0.1%	0.3%	0.7%
MS	Absentee Voting	5.1%	2.5%	6.9%	15.4%	-2.7%	3.9%	4.1%	6.1%	3.3%	0.5%	0.1%	0.1%	0.1%	0.2%	0.1%
MT	Perm. Vote-by-Mail	42.2%	45.8%	57.8%	4.1%	9.2%	9.3%	0.9%	0.5%	0.3%	0.1%	0.2%	0.1%	0.1%	0.2%	0.1%
NC	Vote-by-Mail	4.5%	2.0%	4.5%	14.5%	11.8%	10.7%	11.9%	1.4%	1.1%	.	0.3%	0.4%	0.6%	0.2%	0.4%
ND	Vote-by-Mail	23.7%	26.9%	28.7%	6.4%	6.1%	5.5%	0.5%	0.3%	0.4%	0.0%	0.1%	0.1%	0.1%	0.0%	0.1%
NE	Vote-by-Mail	21.5%	16.1%	24.9%	4.0%	8.2%	10.6%	1.1%	1.3%	1.9%	0.6%	0.3%	0.3%	0.3%	0.3%	0.3%
NH	Absentee Voting	9.6%	6.3%	9.0%	4.7%	5.3%	4.7%	1.8%	2.3%	2.6%	0.6%	1.0%	1.2%	0.4%	0.4%	1.2%
NJ	Perm. Vote-by-Mail	3.7%	5.2%	7.5%	43.4%	21.9%	15.6%	.	2.9%	2.3%	1.2%	0.5%	0.4%	.	0.8%	0.4%
NM	Vote-by-Mail	20.1%	12.9%	10.0%	16.6%	14.7%	.	0.8%	2.9%	1.4%	0.2%	2.9%	0.7%	0.4%	.	0.7%

NV	Vote-by-Mail	8.3%	7.9%	7.5%	8.8%	14.1%	15.0%	6.3%	1.7%	1.5%	0.7%	1.2%	0.8%	0.6%	0.2%	0.8%
NY	Absentee Voting		2.3%	3.7%	.	22.4%	13.0%	3.8%								
OH	Vote-by-Mail	28.5%	21.5%	22.1%	1.7%	8.3%	6.4%	1.6%	1.7%	1.0%	0.3%	0.6%	0.5%	0.1%	0.1%	0.5%
OK	Vote-by-Mail	4.9%	8.9%	4.4%	17.0%	8.1%	15.6%	2.7%	1.3%	3.1%	1.0%	0.4%	1.0%		0.1%	1.0%
OR	Postal Voting		0.3%	99.0%	100.0%	42.8%	.	1.8%		1.0%		1.0%			0.5%	
PA	Absentee Voting	4.6%	3.0%	4.3%	11.3%	10.8%	12.1%	0.7%	1.9%	0.7%	0.6%	1.7%	0.6%	0.1%	0.1%	0.6%
RI	Absentee Voting	3.9%	3.3%	5.3%	100.0%	10.8%	9.9%		1.1%	1.3%				0.6%		
SC	Absentee Voting		11.2%	6.3%	2.6%	3.3%	3.2%	0.3%	0.4%	0.2%	0.3%	0.4%	0.2%		0.2%
SD	Vote-by-Mail	18.5%	18.1%	13.6%	2.5%	0.3%	2.2%	0.3%	0.3%	0.2%	0.4%	0.2%	0.1%	0.1%	0.1%	0.1%
TN	Absentee Voting	2.4%	1.3%	2.2%	.	6.6%	7.4%	3.7%	0.8%	1.1%	1.5%	0.3%	0.7%	0.5%	0.4%	0.7%
TX	Absentee Voting	3.9%	3.8%	2.8%	8.7%	8.3%	6.3%	4.6%	1.6%	1.6%	2.5%	0.4%	1.3%	0.7%	0.6%	1.3%
UT	Vote-by-Mail	8.4%	13.6%	18.1%	25.3%	30.8%	22.6%	2.0%	1.3%	1.1%	0.6%	0.7%		0.1%	0.4%
VA	Absentee Voting	13.4%	4.9%	10.8%	7.3%	3.7%	4.0%	1.3%	0.5%	0.5%	0.9%	0.0%	0.1%	0.4%		0.1%
VT	Vote-by-Mail	27.3%	18.0%	20.7%	3.1%	5.1%	3.4%	1.3%	2.5%	0.7%	0.5%	0.4%	0.2%	0.2%	0.2%	0.2%
WA	Postal Voting[a]	87.2%	96.0%	97.0%		28.8%	18.1%	1.4%	1.0%		0.5%	0.2%	0.2%	0.2%	0.2%
WI	Vote-by-Mail	21.1%	10.5%	21.4%	99.6%	5.8%	6.7%	2336 2.6%	1.2%	0.6%		0.1%	0.1%	0.1%		0.1%
WV	Absentee Voting	1.7%	0.6%	2.0%	18.4%	13.2%	9.1%	3.1%	2.0%	0.2%	1.1%	1.2%	0.1%	0.1%	0.0%	0.1%
WY	Vote-by-Mail	25.0%	21.2%	26.1%	2.8%	4.5%	2.7%	0.4%	0.5%	0.3%	0.3%	0.3%	0.1%	0.0%	0.0%	0.1%

Source: Data from the 2008, 2010, and 2012 EAVS by the U.S. EAC.

Notes: [a]Washington allowed counties to choose whether to conduct elections using Postal Voting in 2008 and 2010. Pierce County was the only counties to use the default Permanent Vote-by-Mail system prior to the 2011 state legislation requiring all counties use Postal Voting in 2012.

State legislatures create the second system, *election-specific* vote-by-mail (or simply "vote-by-mail") by removing the traditional absentee voting requirement that voters must provide a reason for requesting a mail ballot. Thus, it is sometimes called "no excuse absentee voting." In a vote-by-mail system, any registered voter can request a mail ballot for upcoming elections. The basic rationale for this policy change is increasing convenience for voters. Election officials have mixed opinions about mail voting under a vote-by-mail system, with the costs of administering a separate method of voting (including postage costs) weighed against voter convenience and the benefits of centrally processing ballots.

Under a no excuse vote-by-mail system, the population of voters sending mail ballots grows larger and more diverse than under the traditional absentee voting system. As the proportion of voters using mail ballots increases over time, the mail voting population includes increasing numbers of less engaged, less motivated, and less knowledgeable voters.

The third system, *permanent* vote-by-mail, allows voters to record a standing request for a mail ballot for every future election. Permanent mail voter status is voluntary and layered on top of an election-specific vote-by-mail system. Some election officials promote permanent mail voting status to voters and lobby for policy change in state legislatures. The permanent vote-by-mail system reduces their workload of processing mail ballot requests because of a growing set of repeat mail ballot voters for each election cycle; they might also prefer the central control of ballot preparation, delivery, acceptance, and counting (Cuciti and Wallis 2011; Mann and Sondheimer 2009). However, some election officials have concerns about higher costs of administering mail ballots as a separate election system, including the postage costs. Political and civic organizations promote permanent mail voting status as a way to encourage their supporters to participate in all types of elections. As a result, the proportion of the electorate using mail ballots tends to rise above the levels in election-specific vote-by-mail systems. This expansion of the size of the mail voting population also further increases the diversity of the mail ballot population.

The fourth system, postal voting, delivers ballots to *all* voters by the mail. In the 2012 general election, postal voting was used statewide in Oregon and Washington and in portions of California, Idaho, Minnesota, Nebraska, and Nevada, where county election officials may designate precincts containing a small number of voters to use postal voting. Colorado adopted postal voting in 2013 for all future elections and previously allowed counties to choose postal voting except for even-year general elections.[7] Advocates of postal voting among election officials and policy makers argue the system saves money compared with in-person voting and provides improved centralized ballot processing. Postal voting systems also have "traditional absentee" provisions that allow voters to request mail ballots be delivered somewhere other than a voter's registration address. With postal voting, the population receiving mail ballots is identical to the registered voter population, and therefore more diverse than under other systems.

MEASURING IMPACTS OF MAIL BALLOT POLICY AND ADMINISTRATION

Studying the impact of mail voting requires measures of outcomes that are comparable across jurisdictions and primarily influenced by policy or administration. Studying administrative performance requires comparisons within each of the four mail voting systems to identify the influence of election administration within similar rules. Good measures of *administration* should reflect steps in the voting process that are largely under the control of election officials. For example, rejection of ballots provides a reasonable measure of administration because election officials have significant discretion over implementation of mail voting (design of ballots, instructions, etc.) to influence voter behavior. Election officials also have some discretion over the process for rejection or acceptance of each ballot. Good measures of *policy* impacts should have minimum reliance on administrative performance to avoid conflating the rules and their implementation. Policy measures may reflect how voters and campaigns interact with opportunities created by policy choice, as well as depend directly on policy parameters. For example, the mail ballot use rate depends on the policy choices about who can use mail ballots.

Like many other aspects of election administration, there is a shortage of systematically collected data about mail voting (Gerken 2010). The best available source is the EAVS conducted by the U.S. EAC following each federal election cycle. In particular, section C of the EAVS collects data from local election officials (LEOs) on the number

<hr>

[7] Colorado's postal voting law is unusual in requiring *delivery* of a mail ballot to all voters, but it also requires county election officials to provide all voters with the opportunity to vote on an electronic voting machine at voting service centers open prior to and on Election Day.

of mail ballots sent to voters, returned by voters, and rejected/accepted as valid ballots. The mail ballot rejection subsection also disaggregates the reasons for rejection. This chapter focuses on the available EAVS data before turning to suggestions about additional data measuring the impact of mail ballots that could provide insights on policy choices and administrative performance.

Table 5.3 describes the data and procedures used to calculate the five measures of mail voting discussed in the following. Unfortunately, the data collection process for the EAVS is challenged by the absence of standardized terminology for mail ballot administration and by incomplete response to survey items by election officials. If jurisdictions do not report data using the EAVS's intended definition or fail to report data, it undermines the validity of measures for capturing the intended outcome – but only for those jurisdictions. Therefore, the EAVS data in this chapter have been cleaned by Charles Stewart and Stephen Pettigrew (Pew Charitable Trusts, Pettigrew, and Stewart 2013a, 2013b, 2013c) to correct or remove any clearly suspect data, plus additional corrections or exclusions noted in the figure notes. Thus, these are the best available data on mail voting across the United States.

The far-right column of Table 5.3 reports correlations in the state-level measures among the 2008, 2010, and 2012 EAVS. In addition to the strong correlation between elections for the proportion of ballots cast by mail, the EAVS data are strongly correlated with estimates based on voter responses to the 2008 and 2012 Survey on the Performance of American Elections (SPAE) (Stewart 2008, 2013) and the 2008, 2010, and 2012 Census Voter and Registration Survey (U.S. Census Bureau 2008, 2010, 2012). The strong correlation in the proportion of ballots cast by mail is expected, and therefore encouraging, because the proportion of mail ballots is determined largely by the mail ballot system. The weaker correlation in unreturned ballots between the elections likely reflects, at least in part, the great variation in salience in states based on the competitiveness of midterm senatorial or gubernatorial races. Optimistically, the weaker correlations in unreturned ballots and rejected ballots reflect election-to-election improvements in handling mail ballots. Realistically, scanning Table 5.2 reveals many year-to-year state-level shifts that are difficult to explain. This suggests that weaker correlations may be partly attributable to errors in reporting these more detailed outcomes for mail ballots. The consistent patterns in these measures seen in the figures below suggest that errors in data reporting

TABLE 5.3. *Measures of mail voting*

Measure	Numerator in Measure	Denominator in Measure	Correlation: 2008 & 2010	Correlation: 2008 & 2012	Correlation: 2010 & 2012
Proportion of Ballots Cast by Mail *Among All Ballots Cast*	Valid mail ballots counted in the election (EAVS section C, question 4a)	Total participants in the election (EAVS section F, question 1a)	0.964	0.971	0.980
Unreturned Mail Ballot Rate *Among Mail Ballots Sent*	Mail ballots sent minus mail ballots returned in the election (EAVS section C, questions 1a & 1b)	Mail ballots sent in the election (EAVS section C, question 1a)	0.514	0.391	0.791
Rejected Mail Ballot Rate *Among Mail Ballots Returned*	Mail ballots rejected for any reason (EAVS section C, question 4b)	Mail ballots returned in the election (EAVS section C, question 1b)	0.496	0.235	0.506
Rejected Mail Ballot Rate because of Missed Deadline *Among Mail Ballots Returned*	Mail ballots rejected for missing ballot return deadline (EAVS section C, question 5a)	Mail ballots returned in the election (EAVS section C, question 1b)	0.211	0.431	0.240
Rejected Mail Ballots Rate because of No Signature *Among Mail Ballots Returned*	Mail ballots rejected for not having a valid signature (EAVS section C, question 5b)	Mail ballots returned in the election (EAVS section C, question 1b)	0.117	0.106	0.761

Notes: Numerator and denominator explain the EAVS data used to calculate each measure. Correlations between statistics for each election were calculated using each state weighted equally. Rates $< = 0$ or $> = 100$ percent are excluded from correlations (and subsequent figures) as likely data reporting errors. The EAVS state-level estimates of the proportion of ballots cast by mail are highly correlated with estimates from the 2008 and 2012 Performance of American Elections Surveys and the 2008, 2010, and 2012 U.S. Census Voter and Registration Surveys.

Source: Data from the 2008, 2010, and 2012 EAVS by the U.S. EAC.

are adding noise to averages (i.e., reducing measure reliability), but the measures are capturing the intended outcomes (measure validity).

The assessment of mail voting policy begins with the most intuitive measure: the proportion of ballots cast by mail. The use of mail voting is a key consequence of the four mail voting systems. For this measure, the total number of ballots cast is used as the denominator, rather than total eligible voters, to avoid confounding the choice of *how* to vote with the choice of *whether* to vote. Policy choices about mail voting may contribute to the voters' decisions about participating, but only modestly in federal general elections. Once a voter has decided to cast a ballot, mail voting policy has a clearer influence on how ballots are cast.

Among states within each voluntary mail ballot system (excluding postal voting), there is considerable variation in use of mail ballots. Voluntary use of mail ballots tends to grow over time because a large proportion of voters who try mail voting continue to use it in future elections (Mann and Sondheimer 2009). However, this growth does not occur at the same rate across states or even within states from election to election. The activity of campaigns, civic groups, and election officials to encourage use of mail ballots explains some of this variation. Recruitment to use mail ballots has proven effective for increasing mail ballot use (and total turnout) in multiple field experiments (Arceneaux, Kousser, and Mullin 2012; Mann 2011; Mann and Kalla 2013; Mann and Mayhew 2012, 2013; see also Oliver 1996). Voter education communication by election administrators also significantly influences the use of mail ballots, even when not influencing overall turnout (Michelson et al. 2012; Monroe and Sylvester 2011).

The second measure, the rate of unreturned mail ballots, reveals incomplete participation by voters who request mail ballots but fail to cast them. However, unreturned ballots measure different things under each system because the system determines the breadth of the population sent mail ballots. Thus, the denominator (mail ballot sent) and numerator (unreturned mail ballots) shift simultaneously across mail voting systems. Unreturned ballots in postal voting states measure everyone who decides not to participate in the election because everyone is sent a mail ballot. Given the high levels of nonparticipation in U.S. elections, the rate of unreturned ballots among mail voters will be large. Unreturned ballots in absentee voting and vote-by-mail states are registered voters who expressed a desire to vote at some point in the election cycle but did not fulfill this intent before Election Day. Given the proximate interest demonstrated by requesting a ballot, the proportion of voters in these systems who fail to return their mail ballots should be relatively small. In addition to failure to return the ballot because of disinterest, procedural errors by voters, election officials, or the U.S. Postal Service will cause some ballots to be unreturned. The proportion of unreturned mail ballots in permanent vote-by-mail states will fall in between because the recipients of mail ballots will include people who requested ballots for that election (or would have done so if not for permanent mail voter status) and people who would not have requested a ballot (e.g., presidential election "surge" voters who do not vote in midterm elections).

Careful consideration of unreturned ballots also highlights a significant problem in trying to use a measure such as unreturned ballots for assessing mail voting versus in-person voting as a policy choice. In-person voting has no measure of initiating the voting process equivalent to a request for a mail ballot and therefore no measure of incomplete voting actions. How many voters make an effort to find their polling place, but do not go to the polls? How many voters plan to go to the polls but run out of time on Election Day? Surveys attempt to measure intentions or initial steps toward voting, but there is no reason to believe marginal voters will be any more honest about intention than the well-known shortcomings in honest reporting whether they actually voted (Ansolabehere and Hersh 2012). Unreturned mail ballots may indicate procedural errors by voters, election officials, or the U.S. Postal Service that prevent completing the mail voting process, or they may be a positive indicator of unconsummated attempts to participate. Either way, in-person voting has no measure comparable to unreturned mail ballots.

The final step in casting a mail ballot is the rejection or acceptance of a returned ballot as valid by the LEO. Because there are so many reasons to reject ballots, total ballot rejection rate is not a useful measure to assess policy choice or administrative performance. Moreover, interpretation of whether the rejection of ballots is "good" and "bad" is confounded by prior assumptions about voter fraud. Some ballots may be correctly rejected as fraudulent, but other rejected ballots are from legitimate voters who simply make procedural mistakes. Fortunately, data from the EAVS provide the reasons officials reject mail ballots. These reasons have clear links to steps in the mail voting process. Two of these reasons are promising measures because they are unlikely to be indicators of fraud: (1) ballots rejected for being returned after the deadline and (2) ballots rejected without voter signatures.

The number of ballots rejected for a nonmatching signature is an example of the ambiguity between measuring fraud and voter error. A nonmatching signature is facial evidence the ballot was not completed by the correct voter (i.e., that fraud may have occurred). Thus, high rates of rejection for nonmatching signatures may be an indication of good performance in preventing fraudulent ballots from being cast. On the other hand, nonmatching signatures may be innocent errors by legitimate voters. Signatures on file with election officials can become outdated as handwriting changes over time – especially among older voters. Young voters might not have well-established, replicable signatures. Voters may make mistakes, such as using new names because of marriage or divorce, using nicknames, including or omitting initials or middle names, and so on. The incidence of these problems can be reduced by improved instructions from election officials and communication with voters to correct problems such as outdated signatures. In these cases, excluding otherwise legitimate ballots on the technicality of nonmatching signatures does not seem desirable. Therefore, inverse to the fraud-based judgments above, high rejection rates for nonmatching signatures indicate poor mail ballot administration.

Equivalent measures to these types of ballot rejections do not exist for in-person voting. The equivalent of mail ballots returned after the deadline would be something like people who meant to go to the polls but did not remember until the morning after Election Day. The equivalent of unsigned ballots and nonmatching signatures would be people who are turned away at the polls for inadequate identification. Provisional ballots provide a partial measure of this situation, but not everyone without proper identification completes a provisional ballot (by voter or poll worker choice) and provisional ballots are used for other problems at the polls. Counting all individuals turned away for inadequate identification is difficult to do reliably and is not currently done systematically. Moreover, identification requirements are not applied consistently by poll workers (Atkeson et al. 2010), whereas central processing of mail ballots increases the likelihood of consistent and rigorous signature validation. Overall, mail voting allows us to measure more steps in the voting process than in-person voting. This difference in measurability is important to remember to avoid biased inferences from apples-to-oranges comparisons when tallying up data on observed problems with mail voting and in-person voting.

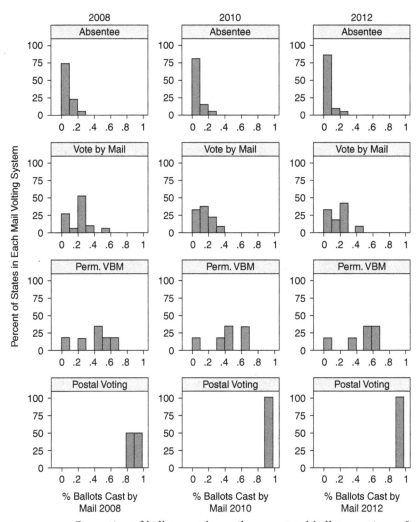

FIGURE 5.1. Proportion of ballots cast by mail among total ballots cast in 2008, 2010, and 2012, by mail voting system. (*Source:* 2008, 2010, and 2012 EAVS, U.S. EAC.)

Notes: States reporting data: 2008 = 47; 2010 = 50; 2012 = 50. New York did not report mail ballot data in 2008. Michigan has more than 20 percent mail ballots under absentee voting, but Michigan allows anyone over age sixty-five to request a mail ballot without an additional reason.

CHOICE OF MAIL VOTING SYSTEMS AND MAIL BALLOT USE

Data from the 2008, 2010, and 2012 EAVS demonstrate the significant differences in the proportion of ballots cast by mail across the four systems for administering mail ballots.[8] Figure 5.1 shows the proportion of ballots cast by mail in each state in the 2008 and 2010 general elections. The observed data cannot tell us if policy choices caused these differences in mail ballot use or if differences in mail ballot use led to policy choices. However, there are clearly distinct levels of mail ballot use in each system.

Scanning down the columns for the 2008, 2010, and 2012 elections in Figure 5.1, the pattern of mail voting rates in the four systems is consistent. States with traditional absentee voting are clustered on the left side of each graph, with an average proportion of ballots cast by mail of 7.4 percent in 2008, 5.4 percent in 2010, and 6.8 percent in 2012. In states with a vote-by-mail system, the proportion of ballots cast by mail shifts significantly to the right, with an average proportion of ballots cast by mail of 21.9 percent in 2008, 17.4 percent in 2010, and 18.4 percent in 2012. The states with permanent vote-by-mail systems shift significantly farther right, with an average proportion of ballots cast by mail of 37.4 percent in 2008, 43.3 percent in 2010, and 47.5 percent in 2012. The two postal voting states appear at the right edge of the graphs as expected.

Comparing the two elections, the proportion of ballots cast by mail is lower in the 2010 midterm election than the 2008 or 2012 presidential elections in traditional absentee voting and vote-by-mail systems. Just as citizens are less likely to vote in midterm elections, they are less likely to request mail ballots. The rightward shift in postal voting states is an artifact of the final two counties in Washington utilizing postal voting after 2008.[9] On the other hand, in the permanent vote-by-mail states where voters automatically received mail ballots, the proportion of ballots cast by mail went up across all three elections (rightward shift in the

---

[8] The differences in the distributions of the proportion of ballots cast by mail from one system to the next are statistically significant in state-level data, according to Kolmogorov-Smirnov tests: absentee voting versus vote-by-mail, 2008 $p < 0.001$, 2010 $p < 0.001$; vote-by-mail versus permanent vote-by-mail, 2008 $p = 0.063$, 2010 $p = 0.006$; permanent vote-by-mail versus postal voting 2008 $p = 0.065$, 2010 $p = 0.065$.

[9] Washington is coded as a postal voting system, although King and Pierce Counties did not require postal voting in 2008 and Pierce County did not require postal voting in 2010. The 2010 and 2012 EAVS data for Oregon are corrected to reflect all-mail voting, since the state reported only "absentee ballots" delivered by mail rather than all ballots delivered by mail.

distribution). Thus, permanent vote-by-mail states appear to retain mail voters in the participating electorate. This pattern highlights the importance of attending to differences between the mail voting systems, since the finding is specific to permanent vote-by-mail and not generalizable to absentee or vote-by-mail.[10]

DIFFERENCES IN UNRETURNED MAIL BALLOTS

Figure 5.2 shows the distribution of unreturned ballots in 2008, 2010, and 2012 for each system of administering mail ballots. The postal voting states, Oregon and Washington, are omitted from this and all remaining figures because their responses to the 2008, 2010, and 2012 EAVS were based on "absentee" mail ballots (sent somewhere other than the registration address) rather than the full set of mail ballots sent to regular voters.[11]

In the 2008 presidential election, the distribution of unreturned ballots is statistically indistinguishable across the three voluntary mail voting systems, although permanent vote-by-mail appears to have a higher rate of unreturned ballots than the other voluntary mail voting systems. The average rate of unreturned ballots among mail ballots sent is: absentee voting 7.7 percent, vote-by-mail 8.5 percent, and permanent vote-by-mail 15.7 percent.[12] In the 2010 midterm election, mail voting systems that permitted broader access to mail ballots appear somewhat likely to have higher rates of unreturned ballots, shown by the rightward shift in the distributions across the three mail voting systems: absentee voting 7.2 percent, vote-by-mail 11.2 percent, and permanent vote-by-mail 19.1 percent.[13] In the 2012 presidential election, the pattern falls between the prior two elections, with a marginally significant rightward shift toward more unreturned ballot rates in systems with broader

---

[10] Other research suggests the pattern of retaining voters occurs in postal voting systems, as well (e.g., Kousser and Mullin 2007).

[11] Washington provided data for Figures 5.2 to 5.5 on the 2010 EAVS, but this single state-year observation for postal voting is omitted from the figures. These data are reported in Table 5.2.

[12] Kolomgorov-Smirnov tests of the differences in the distributions of unreturned ballots in 2008 indicate no statistically significant change: absentee voting versus voting by mail p = 0.857 and for voting by mail versus permanent voting by mail p = 0.268.

[13] The shifts are marginally statistically significant in the state-level data, according to Kolomgorov-Smirnov tests of the differences in the distributions of unreturned ballots in 2010: for absentee voting to voting by mail p = 0.176 and for voting by mail to permanent voting by mail p = 0.076.

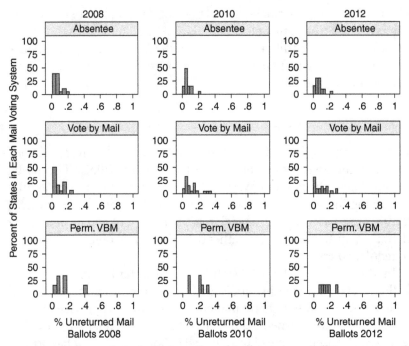

FIGURE 5.2. Proportion of unreturned mail ballots among ballots sent in 2008, 2010, and 2012, by mail voting system. (*Source*: 2008, 2010, and 2012 EAVS, U.S. EAC.)

Notes: States reporting data: 2008 = 47; 2010 = 49; 2012 = 49. Postal voting excluded because Oregon and Washington do not report unreturned ballots among regular mail ballots. They only report unreturned ballots for absentee voters receiving ballots somewhere other than the registration address. States reporting negative rates or 100 percent of mail ballots are unreturned are excluded. The outlier in 2008 permanent vote-by-mail is New Jersey, which held its first election with permanent vote-by-mail after initiating the reform in 2007, so voter confusion may explain the high rate.

populations: absentee voting 7.3 percent, vote-by-mail 10.7 percent, and permanent vote-by-mail 16.0 percent.[14]

From a policy perspective, the data on unreturned mail ballots suggest mail voting policy with broad access results in higher proportions of unreturned ballots, although the statistical relationships are relatively

[14] The shifts are marginally statistically significant in the state-level data, according to Kolomgorov-Smirnov tests of the differences in the distributions of unreturned ballots in 2010: for absentee voting to voting by mail p = 0.160 and for voting by mail to permanent voting by mail p = 0.109.

weak. Critics of mail voting may point to the increase in unreturned mail ballots as a problem with the vote-by-mail and permanent vote-by-mail systems. However, since the denominator of mail ballots cast increases much more rapidly than the numerator of unreturned ballots across the mail voting systems, it is not clear what to make of this pattern. Absentee voters have generally met more burdensome requirements than vote-by-mail voters to receive a ballot, so it is not surprising that they are less likely to fail to return a ballot. The apparently higher rates of unreturned ballots under permanent vote-by-mail likely reflect ballots that are sent but not successfully delivered to voters who move or die between elections, as well as changes of interest in participating from one election to the next. These voters who no longer exist are a list maintenance challenge orthogonal to the method of voting. Although unreturned ballots do not seem desirable from any perspective, extensive research on the effects of different mail voting systems has found no evidence of a decrease in turnout (e.g., Berinsky, Burns, and Traugott 2001; Burden et al., forthcoming; Fitzgerald 2005; Gronke et al. 2008; Gronke, Galanes-Rosenbaum, and Miller 2007; Gronke and Miller 2012; Hamner and Traugott 2004; Karp and Banducci 2000, 2001; Richey 2008), and some research suggests that turnout may increase in some elections (e.g., Berinsky 2005; Gerber, Huber, and Hill 2012; Kousser and Mullin 2007; Oliver 1996; Southwell and Burchett 2000). Given the well-established finding of null or slightly positive effects on total turnout from reforms expanding mail ballot access, it seems likely that the people who fail to return their ballots would have also failed to show up at their polling places. Therefore, mail voting seems to be making disinterest in voting and/or procedural errors in casting a ballot observable in the form of unreturned ballots but not making voters significantly less likely to participate.

The range of unreturned ballot rates *within* each system suggests unreturned ballots may be a valuable indicator of administrative performance. However, its value as a measure of election administration performance will depend on establishing a clear link between particular aspects of administering mail ballots and failure to return them. To some degree, reducing unreturned ballots may require campaign like interventions to influence individual voting behavior rather than simply altering mail ballot administration.[15]

---

[15] For example, see Mann and Sondheimer 2013 on a field experiment showing a reduction in unreturned ballots caused by phone calls from a county election official reminding voters to return their ballots.

LEARNING FROM REJECTED MAIL BALLOTS

Examining the rejection rate for mail ballots across the four mail administration systems again shows notable differences in the distribution: the
rejection rate appears to decrease as access to mail ballots increases.[16]
This is seen in the leftward shift in the distributions of Figure 5.3 when
going from absentee voting to postal voting. Note that the horizontal
axis for Figure 5.3 is only 0 percent to 25 percent rather than 0 percent
to 100 percent in Figures 5.1 and 5.2.

An array of factors influences the total ballot rejection rate in
Figure 5.3. Fortunately, the different reasons for rejecting ballots
reported in the EAVS are linked to specific steps in the mail voting
process. Although returning a ballot on time and properly signed to
verify its authenticity is certainly the voter's responsibility, election officials can reduce the odds of late and/or unsigned ballots by providing
clear instructions, establishing convenient ballot drop boxes, working
with the U.S. Postal Service to ensure prompt delivery, and reminding
mail ballot voters about deadlines and signature requirements (Mann
and Sondheimer 2013). Figure 5.4 shows the incidence of rejection of
mail ballots for arriving after the deadline is lower in mail voting systems with greater use of mail ballots. (Note that the horizontal axis
for Figures 5.4 is only 0 percent to 10 percent rather than 0 percent to
100 percent as in Figures 5.1, 5.2, and 5.5 or 0 percent to 25 percent in
Figure 5.3.) Figure 5.5 shows lower rejection rates attributable to missing signature in mail voting systems with greater use of mail ballots.

Because the measures of reasons for rejecting mail ballots have considerable range, especially in absentee voting and vote-by-mail states, they
seem likely to be useful in assessing administrative performance. First,
these measures identify jurisdictions with low rates of rejection for tardy
returns or unsigned ballots in states where "best practices" might be
established. Second, they provide accountability and actionable information to election officials who need to improve mail ballot administration because of growing demand for mail voting. Furthermore, these
measures serve as "canaries in the coal mine" for other aspects of mail
ballot administration. Local election administrators could "teach to the
test" by focusing on specific reasons for rejecting ballots, but it seems

---

[16] The shifts are only marginally statistically significant in the state-level data, according to
Kolomgorov-Smirnov tests of the differences in the distributions of rejected ballots in all
three elections.

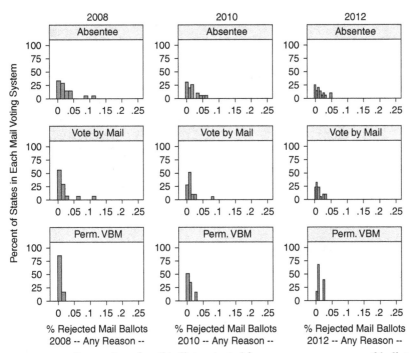

FIGURE 5.3. Proportion of mail ballots rejected for any reason among mail ballots returned in 2008, 2010, and 2012, by mail voting system. (*Source*: 2008, 2010, and 2012 EAVS, U.S. EAC.)

Notes: States reporting date: 2008 = 45; 2010 = 49; 2012 = 46. Postal voting excluded because Oregon and Washington do not report rejected ballots among regular mail ballots. States reporting negative rates or 100 percent of mail ballots as rejected are excluded. The 2008 outliers for vote-by-mail (North Carolina and Nevada) and absentee voting (Indiana) were states with heavy mobilization by the Obama for President campaign. DC was an outlier in absentee voting in 2008 and vote-by-mail in 2010.

more likely that changes to address these specific issues will improve other areas of mail ballot administration, as well.

It may initially seem odd that a policy choice to *increase* mail ballot use will *reduce* rejection of mail ballots. The most likely explanation is that election officials and voters learn over time to reduce the problems that lead to ballot rejections. When mail ballots are a small portion of overall ballots, improving the administration of mail ballots and offering voter education about mail voting are unlikely to receive attention from election officials. However, as the proportion of mail ballots increases across the mail voting systems, election officials have greater incentives and pressures to improve administration of mail ballots and to invest

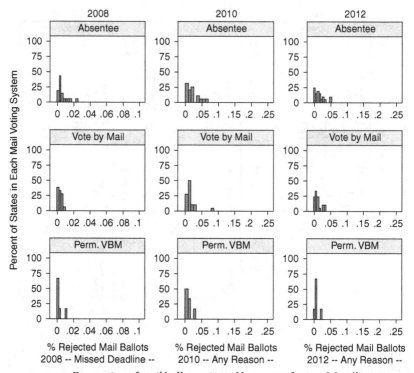

FIGURE 5.4. Proportion of mail ballots rejected because of missed deadline among mail ballots returned in 2008, 2010, and 2012, by mail voting system. (*Source:* 2008, 2010, and 2012 EAVS, U.S. EAC.)

Notes: States reporting data: 2008 = 42; 2010 = 45; 2012 = 43. Postal voting excluded because Oregon and Washington do not report rejected ballots among regular mail ballots. States reporting negative rates or 100 percent of mail ballots as rejected are excluded.

in voter education. As more voters use mail ballots repeatedly, individuals learn to avoid mistakes that lead to ballot rejection. Knowledge of proper mail voting procedures is also likely spread through social networks and the efforts of political and civic organizations. In short, a policy choice to make mail ballots more broadly available creates incentives and pressures for election officials and voters to do a better job implementing mail voting.

ADDITIONAL MEASURES OF MAIL VOTING

The available data describe only limited aspects of mail voting. Concerns about fraud are at the center of current policy debates regarding mail voting, so it would be helpful to find reliable and valid measures that

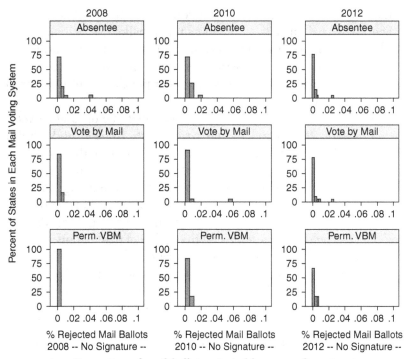

FIGURE 5.5. Proportion of mail ballots rejected because of no signature among mail ballots returned in 2008, 2010, and 2012, by mail voting system. (*Source*: 2008, 2010, and 2012 EAVS, U.S. EAC.)

Notes: States reporting data: 2008 = 38; 2010 = 43; 2012 = 43. Postal voting excluded because Oregon and Washington do not report rejected ballots among regular mail ballots. States reporting negative rates or 100 percent of mail ballots as rejected are excluded. The 2008 absentee voting outlier is Arkansas. The 2010 vote-by-mail outlier is DC.

provide more windows into the mail voting process. Although a wide variety of data could be useful, the most valuable data would also include measures of (1) requests for mail ballots, (2) residual votes on mail ballots, and (3) additional information about the acceptance of mail ballots.

The first step in casting a mail ballot under the absentee voting, vote-by-mail, and permanent vote-by-mail systems is requesting the ballot. Data on the number of requests received and accepted would provide useful information on policy choices and administrative performance. Request acceptance is determined by policy choices about valid reasons for requesting mail ballots, time limits on when requests can be made, required information, and the format of requests. These policy choices may have impacts on the rate of mail ballot use, the incidence of subsequent problems with mail ballots, and the cost of administering mail voting. Administrative performance in handling requests could be assessed among jurisdictions with similar policies about requests to identify best practices.

A major criticism of mail voting is an elevated rate of residual votes on mail ballots (e.g., Kimball and Kropf 2008; Kousser and Mullin 2007; Stewart 2011). Because mail ballot voters complete their ballots at home, they cannot ask questions of poll workers and are not subject to the warnings from in-person voting machines about making too many or too few selections. However, this does not mean residual voting on mail ballots is intractable. Systematic collection of residual vote data on mail ballots would allow research on the design of mail ballots, instructions sent to mail ballot voters, voter education efforts, and other steps to reduce this problem. Developing best practices for policy makers and administrators could reduce the mail ballot residual vote rate, just as voting machine improvements have reduced residual vote rates for in-person voting.

The available measures of ballot acceptance overlook important policy and administrative distinctions in the acceptance process. The rejection of mail ballots received without signatures or with nonmatching signatures is guided by policy directives and administrative discretion. Some jurisdictions have procedures to obtain missing or nonmatching signatures, whereas others do not. These procedures are similar to verifying provisional ballots for in-person voting. Unfortunately, there is no widespread collection of data on the initial and final status of ballots received. This chapter used data on missing signatures as reported by LEOs, presumably after any steps taken to obtain a correct signature. Collecting procedures for correcting signatures and data on ballot status before and after such effects would provide important insights about policies and implementation with potential to reduce a significant problem with mail ballots.

Given the worries about the potential for fraud with mail ballots, finding reliable measures of fraud in mail ballots is important. However, it is extremely difficult to measure fraud in any type of voting. Successful fraud is, by definition, undetected. As noted earlier, measures such as rejecting ballots for nonmatching signatures may combine malignant attempts at fraud and innocent reasons for nonmatching signatures, with no empirical tools to separate fraud and error. Further, depending on prior assumptions, measures indicating detected fraud may be interpreted as the tip of a larger unseen problem or as evidence that fraud has been prevented. In short, measuring fraud in mail voting is just as slippery and contested as it is for every other method of voting (Alvarez, Hall, and Hyde 2009; Minnite 2010).

NEXT STEPS IN STUDYING THE MAIL VOTING
POLICY AND ADMINISTRATION

Relative to its growth among voters and the expansion among states, mail voting has received little attention in research on voting reforms, voting behavior, or campaigns. Future research on mail voting must move beyond the question of whether expanding access to mail ballots increases turnout. Scholarly research has been mired in a debate about whether there is an increase in turnout from changing mail voting policy to expand access to mail voting (e.g., Barreto et al. 2006; Bergman and Yates 2011; Berinsky 2005; Berinsky, Burns, and Traugott 2001; Burden et al., forthcoming; Fitzgerald 2005; Gerber, Huber, and Hill 2012; Gronke et al. 2008; Gronke, Galanes-Rosenbaum, and Miller 2007; Gronke and Miller 2012; Hamner and Traugott 2004; Karp and Banducci 2000, 2001; Oliver 1996; Richey 2008; Southwell 2009, 2010a; Southwell and Burchett 2000). The absence of an effect on turnout does not mean mail voting has no effect on other aspects of voting behavior, conduct of campaigns (Dunaway and Stein 2013), and election administration.

This chapter has made a strong case that mail voting is not a single voting reform, but is more appropriately viewed as a feature of four distinct systems with different rules governing the access to mail ballots. These systems present distinct administrative burdens and challenges and require different institutional capacities for successful administration. First, research on mail voting must stop using the "pre–Election Day voting" or "convenience voting" typology that lumps together mail voting and early in-person voting. This typology is useful for looking at the spread of policy reforms and (possibly) for campaign effects, but not for studying election administration or voting behavior. Behaviorally and administratively, mail voting is a different animal from early in-person voting and Election Day voting.

Second, research on mail voting should be careful about which mail voting system is under investigation and especially about the limits of generalizability of findings across the distinct mail voting systems.

Because it seems likely the use of mail ballots will continue to grow within each system for the foreseeable future, research is needed on how to improve each mail voting system. Research can assist policy makers by examining the benefits and problems in each mail ballot voting system. Research can also identify best practices for administering mail ballots under different sets of policy constraints on mail voting.

Many promising areas for future research parallel other research on election administration. For example, the design of mail ballots and instructions should be subject to the same type of usability analysis as in-person voting technologies (e.g., Herrnson et al. 2008; Michelson et al. 2012; Stewart 2011). Similar to the extensive research on the time needed for UOCAVA voters to receive and return ballots, research on when to send mail ballots to domestic civilians is needed to determine if changes in mail voting timelines could reduce the number of unreturned ballots.

An important step for future research on mail voting is the use of individual-level data. For in-person voting, many types of problems are hard to track because the incidents are not linked to specific individuals. We would like to know who has difficulty finding the polling place, who runs into problems with identification, and who struggles with voting machine technology. For mail ballots, many more steps in the voting process are (or can be) recorded at the individual level. LEOs often collect individual-level data as part of administering mail ballots. Unfortunately, this individual-level information has not been utilized much for research on mail voting because it rarely leaves each local election office. The opportunities for measuring steps in the mail voting process at the individual level could provide more refined measures than possible with in-person voting. These refined measures could improve understanding of problems in attempting to vote, who these problems happen to, and how these problems could be resolved by policy choice or administrative action.

CONCLUSION

Mail voting is here to stay, and to grow, despite the failure of mail voting reforms to deliver increased turnout and the occurrence of many election administration problems. Mail voting is a growing part of the landscape of election administration in the United States because voters like the convenience once they try it, and election administrators like the central processing of mail ballots and potential cost savings.

Four distinctive systems define who can use mail ballots in U.S. elections. The policies governing who can request, or must be sent, mail ballots alter the population using mail ballots and the scope of problems arising from the use of mail ballots. The selection effects on who uses mail ballots from the four systems require evaluating administrative performance within each of the systems separately. Although the available data to measure the performance of mail ballot administration are meager, there are already some useful measures for evaluating state performance. However, more data are needed to inform policy choices and improve administration of this growing method of voting.

The data presented in this chapter suggest that policy reforms to promote more widespread use of mail ballots will result in improved mail ballot administration. However, a closer look is not so rosy. Voters in states still using an absentee voting system for mail ballots have the highest rate of problems, although the impact is limited by the constraints on who can access mail ballots. If more voters seek mail ballots despite the limits under absentee voting, and anecdotal evidence suggests more voters are doing so in many places, then increasing numbers of mail ballots will be cast in states where they are most likely to encounter problems. Innovations in administering mail ballots may trickle down to absentee voting jurisdictions, but it is more likely that the limited ballot access of absentee voting systems will prevent achieving the level of mail ballot use that appears to incentivize and demand better handling of mail ballots.

The proportion of mail ballots has not yet reached the threshold at which election officials take steps to improve mail ballot administration. If the history of mail voting policy reforms is a guide, permanent vote-by-mail is likely to come slowly, if at all, to many states. Consequently, mail ballot use will increase steadily but without the accelerant of permanent mail ballot status to draw attention to mail ballot administration. It seems more likely that absentee voting states will adopt the vote-by-mail system, and thereby add to the conundrum of growing mail ballot use without commensurate steps to reduce problems. This combination of policy and administrative inertia with dynamic growth in mail voting rates is a recipe to increase the incidence of mail ballot problems. The increase in mail-ballot-related problems will continue until mail ballot usage becomes large enough to motivate LEOs to take the necessary steps to improve administration, or until voters learn the hard way to avoid these problems.

Yet the lower incidence of rejected mail ballots under permanent vote-by-mail and postal voting in recent elections should not be seen as a panacea. There is no guarantee that other states will match this performance if they adopt these mail voting systems. However, the current relative success of permanent vote-by-mail and postal voting states offers the opportunity to identify best practices that can inform policy about and administration of mail ballots.

Casting ballots by mail is a large and growing feature of elections in the United States, and it is a process that is quite different from in-person voting. Unfortunately, research on mail voting has not kept pace with the spread of mail policy reform or the growing use of mail ballots. Understanding voting requires more data collection and careful analysis to inform the increasing use of mail ballots and the spread of policy changes that expand mail ballot use.

6

Voting from Abroad: Evaluating UOCAVA Voting

Thad E. Hall

Federal elections in America are often very close. The National Commission on Federal Election Reform found that close elections are exceedingly common, whether they be U.S. House or Senate races or the state-by-state component of the presidential elections. Specifically, they found "a 90 percent likelihood that at least one state will have a presidential election within the one-percent technical margin of error."[1] The probability is 71 percent for U.S. Senate elections and 99 percent for House elections. In these close races, a small number of votes can change the outcome of the election.

Since the Civil War, it has been recognized that one population of voters whose participation can change the outcome of an election is military personnel. Most of the convenience voting we have today – absentee and early voting – dates back to efforts to enfranchise military voters in the 1864 election.

Recent efforts to enfranchise military personnel and the overseas civilian population have resulted in the passage of several pieces of legislation, including the Uniformed and Overseas Citizens Absentee Voting Act (UOCAVA) of 1986 and the Military and Overseas Voting Empowerment (MOVE) Act of 2009.[2] Under UOCAVA, eligible voters can complete the federal postcard application (FPCA), which allows them to simultaneously register to vote and submit an absentee ballot, or, if voters have not received a ballot from a local election official (LEO), they can complete the federal write-in absentee ballot (FWAB).

Special thanks to Jacqueline Carlton for her assistance with this chapter.

[1] See the Task Force reports from the commission, http://web1.millercenter.org/commissions/comm_2001_taskforce.pdf. The quote comes from pages 2–3.
[2] The UOCAVA statue superseded two earlier efforts to enfranchise military and civilian voters: the 1955 Federal Voting Assistance Act and the Overseas Citizens Rights Act of 1975.

These bills were intended to streamline the process of voting for covered individuals and make it easier for them to vote in federal elections. However, even with the passage of such legislation, the voting process for these individuals still has many barriers.

Understanding the problems faced by UOCAVA voters is important because they are the single most difficult voting population to serve; the challenges that they face are an extreme version of problems faced by all voters, especially absentee voters. The challenges include: (1) being properly registered, (2) getting and returning a ballot in a timely manner, and (3) accurately completing the absentee ballot envelope. Learning about the problems associated with UOCAVA voting can be used to improve our understanding of various aspects of traditional voting.[3]

This chapter provides an overview of the UOCAVA voting process and the barriers that hinder the ability of UOCAVA voters to cast a vote effectively. The focus here is on two metrics: (1) ballots returned as a percentage of ballots sent to voters and (2) the percentage of ballots counted of those sent to voters. The analysis finds that the barriers to participation by the UOCAVA population are linked to the size of their jurisdictions – larger local election offices and larger states have lower count rates than do smaller states and local election offices. The analysis also finds that state-level procedural barriers also seem to hinder easy UOCAVA voting. We also find that there are data differences between 2008 and 2010; in 2008 several states failed to report the data necessary to compute the metrics identified. The data from 2012 on UOCAVA voting show that ballot return rates were relatively similar to the rates in 2008.

UOCAVA VOTING: BARRIERS TO PARTICIPATION

The barriers to UOCAVA participation are similar today to what they have been historically: it takes time to get the blank ballot from the LEO to the UOCAVA voter and for the voter to return his or her voted ballot to the LEO. The time this takes can vary based on the type of UOCAVA voter being served. Although the UOCAVA population is generally divided into the civilian population and the military population,

---

[3] The literature on overseas voting includes Alvarez and Hall (2004, 2008); Alvarez, Hall, and Roberts (2007); Alvarez, Hall, and Sinclair (2008); Cain, MacDonald, and Murakami (2008); Coleman (2006); Hall (2008); Hall and Smith (2012); and Smith (2009).

this simplistic dichotomy misses several important distinctions between types of UOCAVA voters. As we think about ballot transit time, these barriers become important to consider.

Section 1973ff-6 of the Uniformed and Overseas Absentee Voting Act of 1976 defines the various components of the UOCAVA population.[4] In section 1973ff-6, the term *absent uniformed services voter* is defined as: "a member of a uniformed service on active duty who, by reason of such active duty, is absent from the place of residence where the member is otherwise qualified to vote." Using this terminology, both "easy and hard" military personnel populations can come under this definition.

As an illustration, consider the following four soldiers, all covered by UOCAVA, three of whom are permanently stationed at Fort Benning, Georgia, and are registered to vote in Muscogee County, Georgia, where the fort is located.

- Soldier 1 is sent to undergo training at Fort Stewart, in Liberty County, Georgia.
- Soldier 2 is deployed to the Wiesbaden Army Airfield in Wiesbaden, Germany.
- Soldier 3 is deployed to Forward Operating Base Chapman, Khost Province, Afghanistan.
- The twin brother of Soldier 3 is serving aboard the USS *Maine*, a Trident submarine that carries submarine-launched nuclear ballistic missiles.

From this example, we can see that each of these voters is quite different in how and the ease with which they can be served. Soldier 1 is technically a UOCAVA voter, but it would be easy for him or her to request a regular absentee ballot and for their spouse to forward the ballot to them. This voter may not even use the UOCAVA process to vote. Soldier 2 is a UOCAVA voter and can be served through traditional mail services in both Germany and the United States. Soldier 3 is at a forward operating base in a combat zone. Mail delivery here is intermittent.[5] Soldier 4 is in a nuclear submarine that only receives mail at designated ports of call. Otherwise, the soldier is not able to receive or

---

[4] See Title 42 (The Public Health and Welfare), chapter 20 (Elective Franchise), Subchapter I-G – "Registration and Voting by Absent Uniformed Services Voters and Overseas Voters in Elections for Federal Office."

[5] Discussions of the issues with military mail delivery include: (1) Hans A. von Spakovsky, "Society for Law and Public Policy Studies, Voting by Military Personnel and Overseas Citizens: The Uniformed and Overseas Citizens Absentee Voting Act 5," *Federalist*, January 2005; (2) H.R. Rep. No. 99–765, 10–11 (1986); (3) U.S. Gen. Accounting Office, Report No. GAO-04-484, "Operation Iraqi Freedom: Long-Standing Problems Hampering Mail

send any mail. For an election official, the first two are easier to serve than the last two, if only because of a lower ballot transit time.[6]

One solution to the ballot transit problem was initiated under the MOVE Act, which requires all election jurisdictions in all states to mail ballots to voters no less than forty-five days prior to Election Day. However, a review of the Department of Justice (DOJ) actions in 2010 related to the MOVE Act shows that many states were unwilling to comply initially with the act and the DOJ was forced to engage in legal action to develop agreements that would satisfy the requirements of the MOVE Act.[7] The MOVE Act only addresses the ballot transit time problem if all other aspects of the voting process go as planned. However, if there are problems with the voting process, an error on the FPCA, for example, then the benefits of the extra time can be negated. What is necessary then is for there to be another way for the voter and the LEO to communicate.

Hall and Smith (2012) have developed a state law facility score for each state, based on sixteen characteristics of UOCAVA voting, such as allowing the electronic transmission of certain voting materials. As shown in Table 6.1, these scores grade states on various characteristics of state law that can either facilitate or restrain LEOs in their ability to serve UOCAVA voters. For example, a state that allows for an unvoted ballot to be sent from the LEO to the voter electronically would have a higher facility score than a state that does not allow for such ballot transmissions. These facility scores also recognize that LEOs are not

Delivery Need to Be Resolved 13," 2004; and (4) Karen Jowers, "Troops Want to Know: Where's My %&#@ Mail?!" *Army Times*, May 10, 2004, 1. Also, in 2008, the Military Postal Service Agency urged all military personnel deployed to Iraq or Afghanistan to mail their ballots no later than September 30, 2008, a full thirty-five days prior to the election. (As stated on the Military Postal Service Agency Web site, http://hqdainet.army.mil/mpsa/vote.htm, when accessed on September 9, 2008.)

6   The same easy–hard dichotomy can be made for civilians overseas. The Coca-Cola executive in Toronto is going to be easier to serve than the Rio Tinto engineer working in outer Mongolia or the directional driller working on an oil rig off the coast of Nigeria.

7   See http://www.justice.gov/opa/pr/2010/October/10-crt-1212.html. The DOJ filed lawsuits against four states (Wisconsin, New York, New Mexico, and Illinois) to compel compliance with the MOVE Act and reached settlement agreements with seven other states (Alaska, Colorado, Hawaii, Kansas, Mississippi, Nevada, and North Dakota) to ensure that covered voters would receive ballots in a timely manner. These states agreed to either mail ballots by the forty-fifth day, extend the time to count ballots so the overall forty-five-day ballot transmission time was maintained, or express mail ballots that were not sent by the forty-five days prior to the election. These voters were also required to be notified of the failure of the state to comply with the MOVE Act.

TABLE 6.1. *UOCAVA facility score criteria*

Registration Score Coding Criteria		Balloting Score Coding Criteria	
Extra Identification Requirements		*Ballot Transmission Time*	
1	No extra requirements for anyone	1	Ballots sent forty-five days before election
0.5	Extra requirements for part of the population	0	Ballots sent less than forty-five days before election
0	Extra requirements		
No Registration Required / Waived / Same Day		*Notarization or Witness Requirements*	
1	Registration waived/not required for everyone	1	No signature required
0.5	Registration waived for part of the population	0	Signature required
0	Registration not waived		
Registration by Fax		*Transmission of Blank Ballot by Fax*	
1	Both civilian and military allowed	1	Both civilian and military allowed
0.5	Only military or only civilian allowed	0.5	Only military or only civilian allowed
0	No fax allowed	0	No fax allowed
Ballot Request by Fax		*Transmission of Blank Ballot by E-Mail*	
1	Both civilian and military allowed	1	Both civilian and military allowed
0.5	Only military or only civilian allowed	0.5	Only military or only civilian allowed
0	No fax allowed	0	No email allowed
Registration by E-Mail		*Return of Ballot by Fax*	
1	Both civilian and military allowed	1	Both civilian and military allowed
0.5	Only military or only civilian allowed	0.5	Only military or only civilian allowed
0	No email allowed	0	No fax allowed
Ballot Request by E-Mail		*Return of Ballot by E-Mail*	
1	Both civilian and military allowed	1	Both civilian and military allowed

(*continued*)

TABLE 6.1 *(continued)*

Registration Score Coding Criteria		Balloting Score Coding Criteria	
Extra Identification Requirements		*Ballot Transmission Time*	
0.5	Only military or only civilian allowed	0.5	Only military or only civilian allowed
0	No email allowed	0	No email allowed
Hard Copy Requirements		*Privacy Waivers*	
1	Do not require hard copy after fax/email	1	Have a privacy waiver
0	Require hard copy after fax/email	0	Do not have a privacy waiver
Citizens Born Overseas		*Expanded Use of the FWAB*	
1	Allow citizen born overseas with no residence to vote	1	States have expanded use of the FWAB
0	Do not allow citizens born overseas to vote	0	States have restricted use of FWAB
Total Possible Registration Points: 8		Total Possible Balloting Points: 8	

Source: Hall and Smith (2012).

independent actors in the voting process; LEOs are constrained by the laws and regulations that the state has adopted.

After each federal election, the Federal Voting Assistance Program (FVAP) conducts a survey of LEOs that asks an array of questions regarding the LEO's experience in the UOCAVA process, including questions about ballots transmitted, ballots received, and numerous questions related to technology use. The technology questions, much like the facility scores that can be computed from state laws (e.g., Hall and Smith 2012), can be used to see how easy or hard it is in practice for voters to communicate with their LEO using technology. As we can see in Table 6.2, local jurisdictions vary widely in their ability to support technology use in voting and this facility varies based on jurisdiction size; small jurisdictions just have less capacity compared with large jurisdiction to support certain technologies in voting.

As has been shown by Kimbell and Braybeck (2012), there are fundamental differences between jurisdictions based on size. We also know that most jurisdictions are small but that most voters live in large

TABLE 6.2. *Technology use in UOCAVA voting, small and large jurisdictions*

In 2008, did your jurisdiction:	Size of Jurisdiction – Registered Voters				
	Less than 1,000	1,000– 4,999	5,000– 25,000	More than 25,000	Total
Accept faxed FPCAs from military members in the United States, military members overseas, or civilians overseas?	16.8%	34.6%	67.4%	80.8%	44.8%
Fax blank absentee/advance ballots to military in the United States, military overseas, or overseas civilians?	2.2%	4.9%	10.4%	28.5%	9.0%
Accept faxed ballots from the military in the United States, military overseas, or civilians overseas?	7.8%	14.0%	24.9%	42.7%	19.3%
E-mail FPCAs from military members in the United States, military members overseas, or civilians overseas?	11.2%	23.4%	39.2%	53.0%	28.4%
E-mail blank absentee/advance ballots to military in the United States, military overseas, or overseas civilians?	7.7%	11.5%	21.1%	34.2%	16.3%
Accept e-mailed ballots from the military in the United States, military overseas, or civilians overseas?	6.8%	10.5%	20.4%	25.4%	14.2%

Source: FVAP Post-Election Survey, 2008.

jurisdictions. If you are a voter in a smaller jurisdiction, however, your ability to use electronic transmission – which we know facilitates lowering the ballot transit time problem – is likely to be limited.[8]

One weakness of the FVAP survey is that the data reported are aggregated by Census region, not by state, and it is not clear that the survey was designed in a way to create state-specific subsamples. However, such data can be helpful because they show how LEOs within states are serving their respective populations and the gaps between *possible* modes for ballot transmission and *actual* modes available to voters.

From the discussion in this section, there are three metrics for evaluation, as indicators of how likely it is that UOCAVA voters can cast a ballot.

1. Is the state in complete compliance with the MOVE Act, absent a consent decree or other remedial action from the U.S. DOJ?

2. How highly does the state rate on UOCAVA voting facility, based on their state law?

3. How high do the LEOs rate in a state on UOCAVA voting facility, based on their actual ballot transmission abilities?

BARRIERS TO EVALUATING UOCAVA VOTING

Although the barriers to effective UOCAVA voting have been studied, there are still several barriers to evaluating the UOCAVA voting process. In this section, we review these barriers and consider whether each barrier is surmountable. Finally, we discuss how each barrier affects the potential metrics we identified in the previous section.

The Problem of Estimating the Size of the UOCAVA Population

The largest barrier to evaluating UOCAVA voting is that, for any given jurisdiction, it is not possible to know the size of the potential UOCAVA voting population with any reasonable degree of reliability. The most common estimate of the UOCAVA population nationwide is that it consists of between 6 million and 7 million individuals, of which approximately 5 million are of voting age. Specifically, there are an estimated 2 million overseas citizens of voting age, 1.4 million military service members, and 1.3 million military dependents of voting

---

[8] See Alvarez and Hall (2004, 2008) and Hall and Smith (2012) for a discussion of ballot transit.

age. The military population includes soldiers and sailors deployed overseas, as well as deployed away from their home base but still in the United States. The civilian population includes business executives, missionaries serving in various locales, members of the U.S. government workforce – from spies to diplomats – students studying abroad, and expatriates who have made a decision to live abroad.[9]

The estimate of the UOCAVA population is large because the size of the civilian population has proven very difficult to estimate. The U.S. Census has attempted on several occasions to quantify the UOCAVA population using various survey techniques and has found such efforts to be relatively futile.[10] As a part of the Secure Electronic Registration and Voting Experiment (SERVE), in 2003 researchers attempted to use data from the states, the FVAP, and other sources to estimate the size of the potential UOCAVA voting population across election jurisdiction and to project the number of likely UOCAVA voters in a given jurisdiction. The researchers found that such estimates and projections were very difficult to calculate, given the poor data that exist on UOCAVA voters and the mobility of these voters.[11]

In addition, there are limits to evaluating UOCAVA voting within a given jurisdiction because UOCAVA voters can vote using several modes, not just through the UOCAVA process. A UOCAVA voter does not have to register using the FPCA. For example, they could register using online voter registration or could already be registered and just request an absentee ballot and have that ballot sent to them by a spouse or family member. This is likely to be a relatively small number and to be random in distribution, meaning that it will be less problematic than the overall population estimation problem.

[9] For various estimates of the size of the UOCAVA population, see Derek B. Stewart, Dir., Def. Capabilities and Mgmt., Testimony before Committee on Armed Services, U.S. Senate, in U.S. Gen Accountability Office, Report No. GAO-06-1134T, "Elections: DOD Expands Voting Assistance to Military Absentee Voters, but Challenges Remain 1," 2006; GAO-06-521, "Elections: Absentee Voting Assistance to Military and Overseas Citizens Increased for the 2004 General Election, but Challenges Remain," April 7, 2006; "Americans Abroad: People & Groups," http://www.anamericanabroad.com/demographics.html; and GAO-06-521, "Elections: Absentee Voting Assistance to Military and Overseas Citizens Increased for the 2004 General Election, but Challenges Remain," April 7, 2006.

[10] See, for example, GAO-04-898, "2010 Census: Counting Americans Overseas as Part of the Decennial Census Would Not Be Cost-Effective," August 19, 2004, and GAO-04-1077T, "2010 Census: Counting Americans Overseas as Part of the Census Would Not Be Feasible," September 14, 2004.

[11] These estimates were calculated by R. Michael Alvarez (Caltech) and Thad E. Hall (University of Utah) as a part of their evaluation of the SERVE project. The memo that reports these findings is available upon request from the authors.

EVALUATING UOCAVA VOTERS – DATA SOURCES

There are two primary data sources for information about UOCAVA voters and the voting process. First, there are surveys conducted of UOCAVA voters by the FVAP. These surveys provide attitudinal data regarding voting experience for military personnel, for overseas civilians, for overseas civilians who work for the federal government, for LEOs, and for voting action officers (both military and with the Department of State). The usefulness of these surveys as instruments for evaluating American democracy is somewhat limited, given the sample size and the quality of the surveys.

Federal Voting Assistance Program Surveys

For example, the 2008 Post-Election Voting Survey of Uniformed Service Members is a survey of military personnel conducted by the Defense Manpower Data Center in the Department of Defense. It asks an array of interesting questions about the military voting experience, but the survey has certain limitations – several of which could be easily overcome – for use as measures of performance of states in the UOCAVA process. The limits to the survey include:

1. It does not report data by state, only by region of the United States.
2. It does not report clearly if a military person in the survey is or is not covered by UOCAVA at the time of the 2008 election.
3. The survey asks about satisfaction with various aspects of the voting process but does not ask an overall satisfaction question.
4. It does not include individuals in forward combat positions, such as Iraq, Afghanistan, or on board certain ships.
5. The sampling frame is not focused on states but is focused on military personnel characteristics, meaning that some states are likely undersampled.
6. The survey does not control for deployment status in the survey, thus there is not a specific question that actually gets at whether a person is covered under UOCAVA.[12]

---

[12] The closest question is question 12: On November 4, 2008, were you stationed in the United States or overseas? If you were stationed aboard a ship, indicate whether your homeport country was the United States or overseas. (Responses: United States or Overseas.) However

The survey also has data on whether voters received their absentee ballots, returned their absentee ballots, and whether they used the FWAB if they did not receive their absentee ballot. The data suggest relatively large variations – by at least five percentage points at the regional level – of voters not receiving their absentee ballots and similar differences in ballot return rates. There is also wide variation in the use of the FWAB, which may be related to voter information available from states regarding what to do if there is a balloting problem. Ideally, this survey would allow researchers to link voters and their LEOs so that it would be possible to examine whether voting experiences are related to the attributes of the voters (where they are located, their interest in politics, etc.) or to attributes of the LEOs (such as their state facility scores and their actual capacity for serving voters through alternate technologies).

The civilian survey that accompanies the military survey is much more problematic to use as a source of data about civilian UOCAVA voters. As was noted before, it is not possible to know the correct denominator for the survey, so it is impossible to know if the sampling for the survey and the subsequent weighting for the survey are accurate. These problems make the civilian survey a poor candidate for an instrument for measuring UOCAVA voting.

Election Assistance Commission Surveys

The Election Assistance Commission (EAC) collects data on UOCAVA voters from states and localities as a part of the Election Administration and Voting Survey (EAVS).[13] While there are challenges in using the EAVS, on net those challenges do not outweigh the insights one can gather from this data set. Thus, this chapter focuses on the section of the report related to UOCAVA voters, especially data regarding the number of ballots sent to UOCAVA voters, the number of ballots returned by these voters, and the number that are counted.

---

being stationed in the United States does not mean a soldier is not covered under UOCAVA, as noted previously.

[13] See http://www.eac.gov/research/election_administration_and_voting_survey.aspx for a complete description of the EAC surveys. For our purposes, the EAC survey has several issues, including a question as to how they aggregate data for some states with small election jurisdictions (e.g., Michigan or Wisconsin), and the quality of the data provided by the LEOs who respond to the survey.

Metric 1: Ballots Returned

It is possible to calculate the efficacy of the UOCAVA process by determining the percentage of ballots that were sent out to voters and subsequently returned. To calculate this, you need a numerator (the number of ballots returned to the LEO) and a denominator (number of ballots sent out to voters from a LEO). As shown in Table 6.3, the numerator and denominator can be calculated very simply, focusing just on raw ballots sent to voters and ballots received back by the LEO. This metric could be made more accurate by taking into account ballots that were returned as either undeliverable or spoiled. We could also include FWAB, which the voter can self-generate, into the numerator.

Metrics 2 and 3: Ballots Rejected

The ballots rejected metric can also be computed several ways. Metric 2 is to use the number of ballots rejected as the numerator and the number of ballots returned and submitted for counting as the denominator. Metric 3 is to use the same numerator but use the total number of ballots sent as the denominator. Metric 3 provides a broader measure of the rate of problems that might exist in the UOCAVA voting process in a jurisdiction, as it shows the difference between the number of ballots sent out and the number counted, including problems related to mail delivery, bad addresses, and ballot rejections.

EVALUATING UOCAVA VOTING WITH EAC DATA

In the bottom half of Table 6.3, we see that, in 2008, only 6 percent of local jurisdictions did not report the number of UOCAVA ballots sent to voters, 11 percent did not report the number of ballots returned and submitted for counting, and 18 percent did not report the number of ballots rejected. However, by 2010, we see that the number of jurisdictions not reporting needed data has declined dramatically. The states that had less than 85 percent of local jurisdictions reporting the necessary data in either 2008 or 2010 were Alabama, Arkansas, Connecticut, Hawaii, Illinois, Indiana, Kentucky, Mississippi, New Mexico, Oregon, Rhode Island, South Dakota, Virginia, Vermont, Washington, West Virginia, and Wyoming. By 2012, only Alabama, Illinois, Mississippi,

TABLE 6.3. *Data availability for EAC-based metrics of UOCAVA voting*

Numerator	Denominator	
Ballots Returned	All Ballots Sent by LEO	
Ballots Rejected	All Ballots Sent by LEO	
Ballots Rejected	Returned by Voters and Submitted for Counting	
	2008 EAVS	2010 EAVS
Variable	Missing Cases	Missing Cases
Total UOCAVA Ballots Rejected	826 (17.85%)	265 (5.73%)
Total UOCAVA Ballots Returned and Submitted for Counting	488 (10.54%)	112 (2.42%)
Total Ballots Sent Out	269 (5.81%)	123 (2.66%)
Overall	826 (17.85%)	273 (5.90%)

Source: 2008 and 2010 EAC EAVS.

New Mexico, and Vermont had fewer than 85 percent of jurisdictions failing to report UOCAVA voting data.[14]

UOCAVA voters infrequently come from small jurisdictions. Figure 6.1 shows that 30 percent (50 percent) of all local jurisdictions in 2008 (2010) reported ten or fewer UOCAVA ballots transmitted; 40 percent (60 percent) of jurisdictions reported sending fewer than fifteen ballots. A small number of larger jurisdictions serves most UOCAVA voters. Focusing on these jurisdictions could be an important aspect of measuring UOCAVA voting.

Tables 6.4 through 6.6 present basic data by year, by state, regarding the number of UOCAVA ballots transmitted to voters (Table 6.4), the number of ballots submitted for counting (Table 6.5), and the percentage of ballots rejected (Table 6.6). There are three key findings from these tables. First, there is a large decline – often more than 50 percent – in the number of ballots sent to voters between 2008 and 2010 (Table 6.4). If we compare data from 2012 and 2008, we find that the number of UOCAVA ballots sent to voters declined in thirty-one states and increased in thirteen states (with six states not reporting appropriate

---

[14] For the 2012 UOCAVA survey, the data for Texas are problematic and therefore not reported.

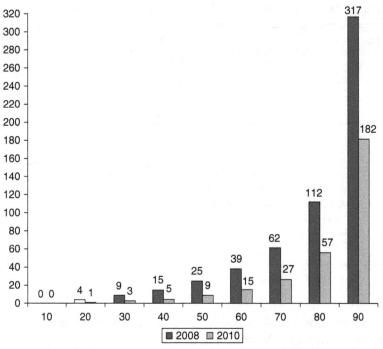

FIGURE 6.1. Number of ballots sent to UOCAVA voters by LEOs, 2008 and 2010. (*Source*: 2008 and 2010 EAC EAVS.)

data). This decline suggests that the section of the MOVE Act eliminating the requirement in Help America Vote Act (HAVA) that UOCAVA voters be sent absentee ballots for two federal election cycles after they send in a FPCA did reduce the number of UOCAVA ballots being sent to voters. When we consider forty of the states who have data on the percent of ballots returned as a percent of ballots sent, we see that twenty-six states have higher ballot return rates in 2012 compared with 2008 and fourteen states have lower return rates. This finding also suggests that more ballots were being returned after the MOVE Act was implemented.

Second, in midterm election years, the number of ballots submitted for counting can often be relatively low. In 2010, fifteen states received fewer than 1,000 UOCAVA ballots for counting (Table 6.5). Third, between 2008 and 2010, ballot rejection rates often varied widely within and across states (Table 6.6). For example, Indiana rejected 28.4 percent of ballots in 2008 but only 6.8 percent in 2010. By contrast, Wisconsin

TABLE 6.4. *UOCAVA ballots sent out, by state by year*

	2008	2010	2012		2008	2010	2012
AK	13,766	9,515	11,935	NC	19,109	12,648	19,869
AR	6,515	1,212	2,505	ND	1,339	266	1,606
AZ	14,322	8,080	13,221	NE	3,352	1,798	2,346
CA	102,983	89,582	112,355	NH	4,221	2,345	4,572
CO	16,251	10,650	24,937	NJ	18,725	11,720	15,247
CT	5,341	1,099	5,152	NV	7,483	2,140	6,449
DE	2,115	1,603	1,810	NY	–	54,495	56,694
FL	121,395	75,268	115,114	OH	32,334	9,771	19,499
GA	25,035	20,059	20,492	OK	8,368	4,847	6,683
HI	3,800	563	2,995	OR	12,179	13,757	17,895
IA	5,877	3,003	4,474	PA	40,279	23,043	28,922
ID	3,679	2,042	2,730	RI	1,125	471	1,734
IN	15,420	19,052	8,194	SC	12,134	1,757	8,695
KS	6,621	4,487	4,377	SD	3,461	758	2,014
KY	6,576	1,452	4,412	TN	18,686	4,383	15,725
LA	9,221	16,267	7,417	TX	91,106	69,526	77,333
MA	16,900	2,924	10,139	UT	4,859	2,940	5,150
MD	17,459	10,693	17,063	VA	41,762	18,369	33,257
ME	2,095	1,347	4,479	WA	61,934	52,892	72,554
MI	21,299	4,533	17,248	WI	10,102	4,077	2,122
MN	15,869	3,124	13,642	WV	4,194	798	9,450
MO	16,561	8,624	11,586	WY	1,710	913	1,920
MT	5,385	3,791	6,571				

Source: 2008, 2010, and 2012 EAC EAVS.

rejected just 3.9 percent of ballots in 2008 but 12.1 percent in 2010. For states that reported data for both 2008 and 2010, half had higher rejection rates in 2008 and half had higher rates in 2010.

When comparing the percent of UOCAVA ballot that were rejected in 2012 election with the percent of ballots in 2008 that were rejected, we see that, in twenty-four states, the percent of ballots rejected declined from 2008 to 2012 and in thirteen states the percent of ballots rejected increased. (The remaining thirteen states were missing the appropriate data from one of the two election years.)

Table 6.7 shows the correlations between the percentage of UOCAVA ballots not returned and the percentage of UOCAVA ballots rejected,

TABLE 6.5. *UOCAVA ballots submitted for counting, by state by year*

	2008	2010	2012		2008	2010	2012
AK	12,103	5,083	10,596	MT	3,640	1,535	4,532
AR	4,863	596	2,138	NC	13,137	2,913	15,718
AZ	9,171	2,643	9,445	ND	1,018	183	1,325
CA	69,823	25,208	63,193	NE	2,713	646	2,003
CO	13,289	4,548	17,363	NH	3,462	1,237	4,007
CT	–	690	4,563	NJ	12,811	2,933	10,827
DE	1,722	603	1,750	NV	4,675	1,638	6,110
FL	97,278	30,459	87,661	NY	–	22,303	39,214
GA	17,229	4,031	13,415	OH	27,469	3,869	15,709
HI	2,375	371	2,018	OK	6,672	1,432	5,790
IA	4,760	1,446	5,009	OR	–	4,813	11,749
ID	3,085	1,184	2,524	PA	31,970	8,125	20,033
IN	8,145	1,878	7,195	RI	–	302	1,158
KS	5,296	1,398	4,131	SD	2,933	617	1,607
KY	5,236	1,101	3,842	TN	15,434	3,117	12,911
LA	6,538	2,165	4,785	TX	69,837	17,863	41,804
MA	13,931	1,975	8,348	UT	3,219	823	3,612
MD	14,419	3,713	14,461	VA	29,258	3,737	27,812
ME	2,092	659	3,336	WA	45,302	21,049	47,521
MI	16,444	3,219	13,733	WI	7,570	1,573	1,681
MN	12,091	2,125	11,374	WV	3,199	510	6,765
MO	13,785	3,403	9,920	WY	1,328	472	1,533

Source: 2008, 2010, and 2012 EAC EAVS.

on the one hand, and various factors that might influence these rates, on the other. (These correlations are shown for both 2008 and 2010.) Looking first at the correlates of ballots not being returned, we see that the primary correlate is absentee ballots not being returned. There are weak indications that the registration facility score could be negatively correlated with not returning ballots, and there are mixed indications when we consider the role that different types of voter registration systems – top-down, hybrid, or bottom-up systems – may have in ensuring that ballots are sent to the correct people (and then returned). The correlates for the percent of UOCAVA ballots rejected are not clear in the 2008 data. However, in the 2010 data, we can see some clear correlates that are statistically significant and substantively significant, as

TABLE 6.6. *Percent UOCAVA ballots rejected of ballots submitted, by state by year*

	2008	2010	2012		2008	2010	2012
AK	4.3	4.25	8.25	MT	6.71	3.78	0.73
AL	–	–	–	NC	7.94	8.38	0.90
AR	5.86	4.19	9.35	ND	2.26	0.55	1.36
AZ	1.91	3.56	0.94	NE	7.85	11.61	4.89
CA	5.67	4.47	8.29	NH	4.36	4.28	16.85
CO	5.81	2.99	1.08	NJ	2.94	4.53	1.63
CT	–	3.3	8.17	NM	–	19.02	–
DE	7.38	4.31	9.77	NV	12.86	12.39	3.91
FL	2.38	4.11	2.93	NY	–	1.82	2.93
GA	2.26	4.71	0.19	OH	4.88	5.58	2.31
HI	–	6.2	0.00	OK	5.95	8.52	5.73
IA	8.13	3.73	6.13	OR	–	0	2.08
ID	12.77	20.95	13.59	PA	0.67	1.86	1.60
IL	2.98	4.58	–	RI	–	3.39	0.00
IN	28.39	6.82	24.00	SC	3.09	2.04	–
KS	10.1	3.58	3.99	SD	–	7.69	3.17
KY	–	7.45	8.04	TN	5.38	3.85	5.79
LA	6.91	10.12	4.28	TX	6.45	4.92	–
MA	7.39	7.95	0.52	UT	4.22	2.19	1.58
MD	8.57	15.54	11.32	VA	7.78	–	6.26
ME	5.59	5.01	7.94	VT	5.99	9.26	–
MI	9.05	8.85	8.70	WA	–	1.3	1.10
MN	6.36	7.34	7.63	WI	3.92	12.08	6.96
MO	4.61	7.7	3.90	WV	–	7.29	0.18
MS	–	25.17	–	WY	–	1.88	3.33

Source: 2008, 2010, and 2012 EAC EAVS.

well. The most significant variables are for ballot facility – states that have laws that make it easy to register, easy to transmit ballots, and easy to return ballots have lower rejection rates.

Testing the factors that lead to more ballots being returned or fewer ballots being rejected requires a multivariate analysis. In the analysis, the dependent variables are the percent of ballots not returned and the percent of ballots rejected. In order to make these two variables better fit the assumptions for a regression analysis, both variables are logged.

TABLE 6.7. *Correlates for ballot return rates and ballot rejection rates*

2008	Percent Not Returned			Percent Rejected		
	p	Sig.	N	p	Sig.	N
Percent UOCAVA Ballots Not Returned				0.41	0.01	37
Percent UOCAVA Ballots Rejected	0.41	0.01	37			
Percent Absentee Ballots Rejected	0.27	0.10	38	0.24	0.16	34
Percent Absentee Ballots Not Returned	0.33	0.05	37	−0.17	0.34	33
Registration Facility Score	−0.18	0.23	44	−0.11	0.53	37
Balloting Facility Score	0.09	0.56	44	0.19	0.26	37
Total Facility Score	−0.04	0.77	44	0.07	0.70	37
Top-Down Registration	−0.08	0.60	42	0.20	0.25	35
Hybrid Registration System	0.24	0.12	42	−0.17	0.34	35
Bottom-Up Registration System	−0.10	0.53	42	−0.10	0.57	35
Number of State Database Links	0.24	0.13	42	0.14	0.43	35
Total Number of Registered Voters	0.25	0.11	44	−0.14	0.41	37

2010	Percent Not Returned			Percent Rejected		
	p	Sig.	N	p	Sig.	N
Percent UOCAVA Ballots Not Returned				0.20	0.18	48
Percent UOCAVA Ballots Rejected	0.20	0.18	48			
Percent Absentee Ballots Rejected	0.37	0.01	46	−0.15	0.34	45
Percent Absentee Ballots Not Returned	0.01	0.96	44	0.04	0.82	43
Registration Facility Score	−0.22	0.13	49	−0.28	0.05	48
Balloting Facility Score	−0.03	0.83	49	−0.31	0.03	48
Total Facility Score	−0.14	0.33	49	−0.35	0.01	48
Top-Down Registration	0.08	0.56	49	−0.04	0.79	48
Hybrid Registration System	0.12	0.41	49	−0.09	0.52	48
Bottom-Up Registration System	−0.22	0.13	49	0.14	0.35	48
Number of State Database Links	0.50	0.00	49	0.03	0.82	48
Total Number of Registered Voters	0.38	0.01	49	0.10	0.48	48

Source: 2008 and 2010 EAC EAVS.

For the ballot return rate model, we include independent variables for ballot facility scores related to registration and voting, voter registration system characteristics (examining bottom-up or hybrid voter registration systems), and a state's registered voter population as a proxy for

TABLE 6.8. *2008 regressions, ballots not returned, and ballots not counted*

a. Rate of Ballots Not Returned

Dependent Variable: Percent of Ballots Not Returned, by State (Logged)

	Coefficient	Standard Error	*p*-value
Total Voters in State (millions)	0.019	0.011	0.103
Registration Facility Score	−0.072	0.034	0.041
Ballot Facility Score	0.042	0.028	0.140
Hybrid Voter Registration System	0.216	0.126	0.094
Bottom-Up Voter Registration System	−0.208	0.114	0.077
Constant	3.268	0.147	0.000
N	39		
Adjusted R²	0.175		

b. Ballot Rejection Rates

Dependent Variable: Percent of Ballots Not Counted, by State (Logged)

	Coefficient	Standard Error	Significance
Total Voters in State (millions)	−0.031	0.028	0.265
Ballot Facility Score	−0.024	0.072	0.741
Constant	1.803	0.377	0.000
N	36		
Adjusted R²	−0.02		

Source: 2008 EAC EAVS.

size. For the ballot rejection rate model, we include just two variables: the size of the state's voter registration population and its ballot facility score for voting. Data from both 2008 and 2010 are presented, but, given the relatively poor quality of the 2008 data, the analysis focuses on the findings contained in the 2010 data.

Table 6.8 presents the findings from 2008 and Table 6.9 presents the findings from 2010. In the ballot return rate model for 2008, having a higher registration facility score lowers the percentage of ballots that are not returned. There is also some evidence that a state having a bottom-up voter registration system may lower the rates of ballots that are not returned. For the ballot rejection rate model in 2008, neither of the variables is significant.

In the ballot return rate model for 2010, a larger population increases the percentage of ballots not returned. In addition, as was suggested in the 2008 model, a state with a bottom-up voter registration system has

TABLE 6.9. *2010 regressions, ballots not returned, and ballots not counted*

a. Rate of Ballots Not Returned

Dependent Variable: Percent of Ballots Not Returned, by State (Logged)

	Coefficient	Standard Error	Significance
Total Voters in State (millions)	0.044	0.015	0.01
Registration Facility Score	−0.055	0.036	0.14
Ballot Facility Score	0.032	0.033	0.35
Hybrid Voter Registration System	0.064	0.156	0.68
Bottom-Up Voter Registration System	−0.310	0.153	0.05
Constant	3.959	0.221	0.00
N	46		
Adjusted R²	0.274		

b. Ballot Rejection Rates

Dependent Variable: Percent of Ballots Not Counted, by State (Logged)

	Coefficient	Standard Error	Significance
Total Voters in State (millions)	0.01	0.03	0.74
Ballot Facility Score	−0.15	0.07	0.05
Constant	2.42	0.45	0.00
N	41		
Adjusted R²	0.10		

Source: 2010 EAC EAVS.

lower rates of ballots that are not returned. For the ballot rejection rate model, having a higher ballot facility score lowers the percentage of ballots that are rejected.

Figure 6.2 graphically presents the changes in the percentage of ballots not returned in 2008 and 2010. One clear finding in this graphic is that the percentage of ballots not returned in 2010 is much higher in 2010 compared with 2008. In 2008, only one state – Indiana – had a percentage of ballots not returned of more than 40 percent; in 2010, roughly three-fourths of all states have ballot nonreturn rates exceeding 40 percent. There is clearly a difference in the UOCAVA voting experience between 2008 and 2010, based on ballot nonreturn rates.

There are several possible reasons for this difference. Nonpresidential election years have lower turnout generally. It may be that voters were

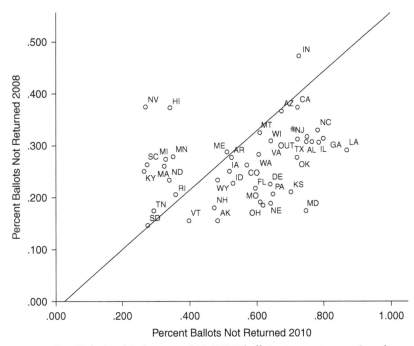

FIGURE 6.2. Relationship between UOCAVA ballot return rates, 2008 and 2010. (*Source*: 2008 and 2010 EAC EAVS.)

less mobilized to vote – both personally motivated and motivated by political parties/candidates – in the 2010 election compared with in 2008. There may also have been individuals who registered to vote as a UOCAVA voter in 2008 who were no longer at the address in question in 2010. Given the mobility of UOCAVA voters, mobility could affect ballot return rates. Better data on ballots that are returned undeliverable by jurisdiction would help determine if this is an accurate interpretation of this finding.

Figure 6.3 presents the percentage of ballots rejected in 2008 and 2010. The data in the scatterplot are highly clustered between 10 percent for both elections. Some states, such as Wisconsin, Maryland, Idaho, and Indiana, had rates that moved relatively significantly between 2008 and 2010. In the case of Indiana, the rate moved from almost 30 percent in 2008 to less than 10 percent in 2010. By contrast, the rates in Wisconsin, Maryland, and Ohio rose between 2008 and 2010.

The UOCAVA voting problem centers on the ballot transit times that occur in transmitting ballots and other materials between the voter and

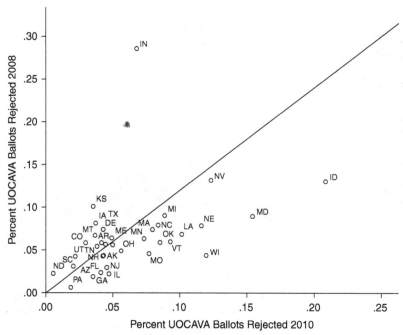

FIGURE 6.3. Relationship between UOCAVA ballot rejection rates, 2008 and 2010. (*Source*: 2008 and 2010 EAC EAVS.)

the election official (e.g., Hall 2008). It is, therefore, helpful to compare the problems within states across the two modes of absentee voting. Figure 6.4 compares ballot return rates for absentee and UOCAVA voters in 2008; Figure 6.5 does the same for 2010. In both 2008 and 2010, the percent of UOCAVA not returned is markedly higher than is the percentage of traditional by mail ballots not returned. In 2008, only New Jersey has a significantly higher percentage of traditional ballots not returned compared with UOCAVA ballots. In 2010, all states have higher percentages of UOCAVA ballots not returned. In many cases, fewer than 10 percent of traditional absentee ballots are not returned, but more than 50 percent of UOCAVA ballots in these same states are not returned.

Figure 6.6 compares ballot count rates for 2010.[15] The ballot rejection rates for UOCAVA voters and traditional absentee voters are different, with the data skewed toward UOCAVA voters having higher rejection

---

[15] Given the similarity of ballot rejection rates between 2008 and 2010, the rates are only shown for 2010, as this year has the best data.

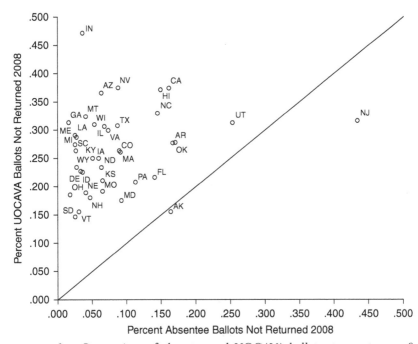

FIGURE 6.4. Comparison of absentee and UOCAVA ballot return rates, 2008. (*Source*: 2008 and 2010 EAC EAVS.)

rates compared with traditional absentee votes. Note that only Arkansas and Minnesota had rejection rates for traditional absentee ballots that equaled or exceeded 5 percent. By contrast, twenty-two states had UOCAVA ballot rejection rates exceeding 5 percent. UOCAVA voters are more likely to have their ballots rejected compared with traditional absentee voters.

CONCLUSIONS

The problems facing UOCAVA voters continue to relate to ballot transit time. The ability of a voter to get the ballot delivered to them from the LEO and then return the ballot to the LEO remains difficult. Compared with a traditional absentee voter, the UOCAVA voter is much less likely to return his or her absentee ballot and is much more likely to have a successfully returned ballot rejected and not included in the final tabulation.[16]

---

[16] This finding comports with the work of Alvarez, Hall, and Sinclair (2008), who found that, in Los Angeles County, UOCAVA voters were least likely to return their ballots and least likely to have their returned ballots included in the canvas.

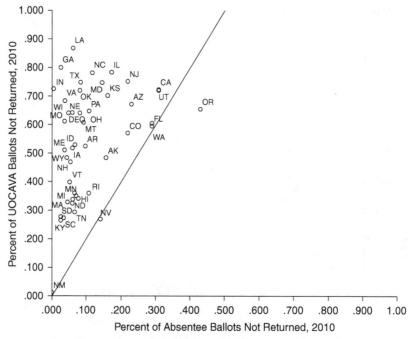

FIGURE 6.5. Comparison of absentee and UOCAVA ballot return rates, 2010. (*Source*: 2008 and 2010 EAC EAVS.)

There are state-level factors – captured in the registration and ballot facility scores – that can affect the ability of LEOs and voters alike to make the UOCAVA process work. States that have more liberal ballot transit rules are also more likely to see voters have their ballots included in the final tabulation. There is also some evidence that having more liberal registration facility rules increases the likelihood that ballots will be returned. However, this analysis considers only a single presidential election and a single off-year federal election. A more robust analysis would have at least two of each type of election, especially since the data show great variation in the levels of participation among UOCAVA voters between the two elections. Simply put, off-year elections and presidential elections have different dynamics that need to be better studied in regard to the UOCAVA voter.

It is important to note that this analysis is at the state level and there are LEO-level capacity issues that can affect whether UOCAVA voters can actually take advantage of the technologies that make ballot transmission easier. If state law allows for ballots to be faxed but the

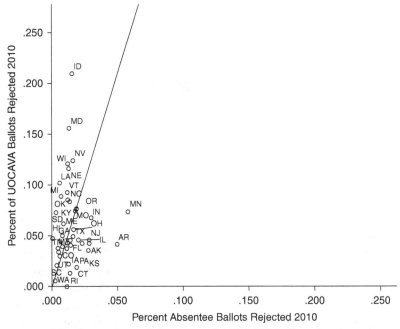

FIGURE 6.6. Comparison of absentee and UOCAVA ballot rejection rates, 2010. (*Source*: 2008 and 2010 EAC EAVS.)

LEO does not have a fax machine appropriate for the process, then the state law making fax ballot return possible is for naught. This issue is also in need of better systematic study, preferably within the context of the EAC postelection surveys. The study of UOCAVA voting will be easier with better data that allow for the calculation of better metrics. The number of ballots returned as undeliverable, for example, is critical for knowing how well the UOCAVA system works. However, this study does provide helpful information regarding policy factors at the state level that help to facilitate UOCAVA voting.

7

Polling Place Practices and the Voting Experience

Robert M. Stein and Greg Vonnahme

Americans are changing in terms of when and where they vote. We endeavor to find out whether these changes have affected the voting experience. Americans offer myriad reasons for not voting (Current Population Survey [CPS] 2004, 2006, 2008, 2010).[1] Most of these excuses are beyond immediate remedy. There may be one exception: the way we conduct and administer our elections. Voting place practices have undergone considerable change in the last decade and may offer the most immediate if not direct means of enhancing the voters' experience at their polling places and possibly voter participation. In this chapter, we ask whether contemporary polling place practices are related to the experiences voters have when voting and whether these practices directly or through voter experiences and other covariates have a non-trivial and appreciable effect on the likelihood of voting.

Our thesis is that when and where voters cast their ballot significantly impact the voter's experience and the likelihood an eligible voter will actually vote. We find that when voters have a choice of where and when to vote rather than being limited to voting on one day and at a location most proximate to their residence, they are more likely to report a positive voting experience and are more likely to vote. Specifically we find that voters who cast a ballot before Election Day report a more positive voting experience than Election Day voters. Further we find that voters report more favorable voting experiences when they vote in larger voting places – voting places that are more centrally located, where

---

[1] These include disaffection from candidates, government, and politics; conflict with work, school, shopping, and other preferred activities; illness, bad weather, forgetfulness, and the inconvenience of polling place locations; hours of operation; uncooperative poll workers; and limited parking at and transportation to voting place locations.

voters work, shop, recreate, and travel, and that have accessible parking, a large number of voting stations, and a large number of poll workers.

The plan of the chapter is as follows. In the next section, we review the research on recent trends in electoral administration and their impact on voter experiences and participation. Then we offer a general explanation for how electoral administration and specifically polling place practices and traits shape voter experiences and the likelihood of voting. We offer several hypotheses about alternative polling place practices and their effect on voter experiences, voter evaluations of their voting experience and voter turnout. We test our hypotheses in the following section with data from the 2008 Survey of the Performance of American Elections (SPAE). We conclude with a discussion of how our findings might be used for designing polling place operations.

WHEN, WHERE, AND HOW WE VOTE: A REVIEW
OF THE LITERATURE

Where, when, and how we ballot has become highly variable. We don't all vote on the same day. We vote at a host of different places and on a cornucopia of different types of voting equipment, ranging from paper ballots to sophisticated electronic voting machines.

Does this matter? Researchers have found these individual changes in how we conduct our elections have mixed and often marginal effects on voter experiences and likelihood of voting. However, there is some evidence to suggest that combinations of when, where, and how we vote have nontrivial impacts on voter satisfaction and likelihood of voting.

When We Vote

When we vote is no longer confined to just the first Tuesday after the first Monday in November. In 2008 the proportion of votes cast before Election Day had increased to 30 percent (McDonald 2008). In nine states,[2] more than half of all votes cast in the 2008 presidential election were cast before Election Day (McDonald 2008). As of 2008, more than half of the states, thirty-one, permitted no excuse in-person early voting (Cemenska et al. 2009).[3] Though all states permit absentee voting

[2] Colorado, Florida, Georgia, New Mexico, North Carolina, Oregon, Tennessee, Texas, and Washington.
[3] In-person early voting comprises the larger proportion of votes cast before Election Day. Oregon only has vote-by-mail and several states, including Colorado, have permanent mail-in

by mail, twenty-seven states allow their voters to request an absentee ballot without providing any excuse (Cemenska et al. 2009). In fifteen states, voters can permanently request that an absentee ballot be sent to their homes before every election without having to make separate ballot requests for each election. And all Oregonians have voted by mail exclusively since 1998.

The share of the electorate that voted prior to Election Day remained high in 2012. Data from the CPS reveal that more than 31 percent of voters in 2012 cast their ballots before Election Day. Data from the 2012 SPAE show that sixteen states had a majority of voters cast their ballots by mail or in-person early. The data also show significant early and mail voting in key states such as Iowa (47 percent), Ohio (48 percent), Florida (64 percent), and Colorado (80 percent). In addition, Maryland became the thirty-second state to adopt in-person early voting in 2010.

Though extremely popular with voters (Southwell 2004), pre–Election Day voting reforms to allow no excuse voting by mail (Berinsky, Burns, and Traugott 2001; Oliver 1996), all-mail voting (Kousser and Mullin 2007; Richey 2008), and in-person early voting (Gronke et al. 2007; Karp and Banducci 2001; Neeley and Richardson 2001; Stein 1998; Stein and Garcia-Monet 1997) have had mixed and limited effects on voter turnout. Neeley and Richardson report "that early voting merely conveniences those who would have voted anyway" (2001, 381). Stein (1998) reports that voter turnout among resource-poor voters does not benefit from the adoption of in-person early voting. Most research has shown that pre–Election Day voters are disproportionately likely to have voted in the past than Election Day voters (Berinsky 2005; Hanmer and Traugott 2004; Southwell and Burchett 2000), but Barreto et al. (2006) find that as the use of pre–Election Day voting has increased over time in California, this bias has largely disappeared. Southwell and Burchett (2000) and Richey (2008) offer a dissent from this finding for all-mail voting. Studying voter turnout in forty-eight Oregon elections "all-mail elections increased registered voter turnout by 10 percent over the expected turnout in a traditional polling place election" (Southwell and Burchett 2000, 76). Berinsky et al. find that "contrary to the expectations of many reformers VBM [voting by mail] advantages the resource-rich by keeping them in the electorate and VBM does little to change the behavior of the resource-poor. Simply put, electoral

voting, which accounts for a little more than half of all votes cast in the 2008 Colorado presidential election.

reforms have only been used by those who otherwise would have been most likely to vote without them" (2001, 178).

Where We Vote

The effect of when we vote on voter experiences may be mitigated by where we vote. Stein and Garcia-Monet (1997) report that the location and setting of early voting places has a significant and independent effect on voter turnout. They report that locations familiar to and frequented by voters, including grocery stores, shopping malls, social service agencies, and mobile voting centers, have a significant effect on increasing voter turnout in Texas counties. This would suggest that voters who travel to locations for one purpose, such as shopping, are more likely to vote if the same location is also a voting place. Other research (Berger, Meredith, and Wheeler 2008) has shown that voting place locations, specifically churches, can exert a significant and independent effect on vote choices.

A recent election innovation adopted in Colorado, Indiana, and Texas, and under consideration in several other states (e.g., Arizona and Iowa), replaces traditional precinct-based voting places with Election Day vote centers (EDVCs). EDVCs are non-precinct-based locations for voting on Election Day. The sites are fewer in number than precinct voting stations, centrally located to major population centers (rather than distributed among many residential locations), open to all voters in a county, and rely on countywide voter registration databases accessed by electronic poll books (i.e., ePollbooks). Voters in the county are provided ballots appropriate to their specific voting jurisdiction. Of course, this mode of balloting is what early voters are afforded before Election Day in *early* vote centers. Unlike in-person early voting and mail-in voting, vote centers replace traditional Election Day precincts.

To accommodate changes in when and where individuals are able to vote on Election Day, election administrators have sought new venues at which to locate polling operations, a practice largely aped from in-person early voting place locations. In the past, the modal location for a polling place was a neighborhood elementary school within a short distance of voters' residences. These locations were hardly spacious and not intended for adult patrons. Parking was limited to the space needs of a small teaching and administrative staff. Limited parking and floor space for machines and poll workers often conspired to produce long lines and waiting times to vote. With the adoption of in-person early voting and EDVCs election officials sought new polling locations, including retail stores, bus stations, hotels, and supermarkets (Gronke et al. 2007; Shambon and Abouchar 2006; Stein 1998; Stein and Garcia-Monet 1997; Stein and Vonnahme 2012a).[4]

We can identify among the enhanced opportunities to vote before and on Election Day two traits that may increase voter satisfaction and likelihood of voting. Moreover, these traits – openness and centralization of voting place locations – can be used as a metric for assessing the effectiveness of voting places. Openness allows individuals to vote at any location throughout the county rather than be restricted to voting at only one location near the voter's residence. This openness is expected to increase voter satisfaction and turnout by lowering transportation and information costs as voters can go to any location that is most familiar and convenient for them or locations frequented during the course of their daily activities (e.g., working, shopping, and recreating). The openness of voting place locations can be thought of as more convenient to voters.[5]

The second characteristic of vote centers is centralization. *Centralization* refers to polling locations that are fewer in number and located in larger and more visible sites. Centralization also exists to varying degrees in precinct-based polling locations. Centralization may have several positive effects on voter participation (Stein and Vonnahme 2008). Larger and more visible sites can reduce informational costs that voters incur when attempting to find a polling location, and they offer more available parking. Centralization also allows for better-equipped polling locations to efficiently process voters. With more staff at each polling location, poll workers will be able to specialize in certain tasks, such as checking in voters or assisting them with their ballots, which should lead to more efficient operations and improved service to voters.

It may seem contradictory to expect voter satisfaction and participation to increase when jurisdictions reduce the number of polling places. Previous research on the location of Election Day voting places suggests that several other considerations might be operating to both enhance and constrain the likelihood of voting. Brady and McNulty

---

4   Local school districts are reluctant to allow voting on their campuses because of the security challenges it poses for their students and staff.

5   *Convenience* is defined as anything that is intended to save resources (i.e., reduce opportunity costs). In this regard, convenience can be thought of a solution to rivalrous activities, that is, an activity whose performance prevents or limits another activity from being performed.

(2011) suggest that voting place locations and changes in voting place locations impose two types of costs on the likelihood that voters will vote: *search* and *transportation*. The first is related to informational costs of correctly identifying one's new voting location. The second is related to the time, effort, and expense required to travel to a voting place, measured by the distance of a voting place location from a voter's residence.

An increase in this distance is thought to increase the cost of voting by increasing the travel time a voter must expend getting to their designated polling place. Brady and McNulty find evidence to support the significant and nontrivial effect polling place location has on both voter turnout and performance, measured by change in the outcome of some elections. Moreover, other research in the extant literature provides supporting evidence of these findings (Gimpel and Schuknecht 2003; Haspel and Knotts 2005; McNulty, Dowling, and Ariotti 2009). What is not well studied is how attributes of convenience voting, in the context of centralization and openness, operate to affect the likelihood an individual will vote, especially infrequent voters. Properly implemented, polling place centralization coupled with the option of voting at any location – openness – should enhance the voting experience and increase the likelihood of voting.

Conventional precinct consolidation creates two challenges for voters: (1) finding a specific new voting polling place and (2) increased average distance to travel to the polling place. Together, centralization and openness address both of these problems. First, voters may go to any of numerous, visible, and conveniently located locations rather than finding a specific new location. In other words, in-person early voting and EDVCs mean there are multiple correct answers to the question of where to vote rather than a single new answer that the voter must correctly identify. Second, both in-person early voting and EDVCs make the measurement of distance from residence to precinct polling place obsolete. Since voters may choose any polling place (in the jurisdictions where they are registered), the relevant distance measure is between where they are when they decide to vote and the nearest voting location. The "nearest" location may not be defined by linear distance, but instead by travel time, deviation from rivalrous activities, or other metrics considered most salient by the voter. Furthermore, the timing of when to vote on or before Election Day and the distance to a polling place have two-way causation because the decision of when to vote is conditional on how costly it will be to get there and vice versa.

The reduction in the number of voting places, along with allowing voters to vote at any location, is often accompanied by a significant change in the location, staffing, and equipping of EDVCs that increases their convenience. A smaller number of larger voting places centrally located to where voters, work, shop, and travel outside Election Day, with a larger number of poll workers, parking places, and voting machines, lessens the likelihood that voting on a Tuesday will conflict with other daily activities. The configuration and location of EVDCs may even complement these nonvoting activities. The size and location of EVDCs makes these voting places more convenient to voters and positively effects voter turnout. Of course, we are not suggesting that the establishment of a single voting place to service all voters (e.g., a sports stadium) is the ideal means of conducting an election. The optimal balance between the location and size of voting places needs to be identified for each jurisdiction. For example, Colorado requires a minimum of one EDVC for every 5,000 registered voters.

How We Vote

The method for casting a ballot has changed significantly since the contested 2000 presidential election. With the adoption of the Help America Vote Act (HAVA), punch card technology and lever voting machines have been replaced in most jurisdictions with optically scanned paper ballots and electronic voting machines (i.e., direct recording electronic voting machines, or DREs). These technologies are associated with a significant improvement in voter satisfaction – voter confidence that their ballot will be counted accurately, reduced time to cast a ballot, and fewer residual votes, as is discussed by Stewart in Chapter 9 (Alvarez, Hall, and Llewellyn 2008). Of greater relevance to election administration are under-votes that occur despite the voters' wish to register a choice for a given office. For example, new voting technologies, unfamiliar even to the most frequent voter, can lead voters to unintentionally fail to record their preferred vote choice. Over-votes are most often attributed to ballot design, voting technologies, and the interaction of these factors with voter attributes, such as education, age, and related physical acuity. Here human factors interact with technology and ballot design to produce errors similar to those observed with the use and operation of consumer products (Everett, Byrne, and Greene 2006; Greene, Byrne, and Everett 2006; Laskowski et al. 2004; Roth 1998).

Using different methodologies (experimental and aggregate studies) and research settings (precincts, cities, and states), as well as a mix of different voting technologies, the extant research has found that paper ballots, both hand counted and optically scanned, are significantly superior to lever machines, DREs, and punched cards in reducing residual votes (Ansolabehere and Stewart 2005; Asher 1982; Kimball, Owens, and Keeney 2004; Knack and Kropf 2003; Nichols and Strizek 1995; Shocket, Heighberger, and Brown 1992; White 1960). Other researchers, however, find that voter confidence was significantly greater with optically scanned paper ballots (Alvarez, Hall, and Llewellyn 2008) while usability ratings were higher with electronic voting machines (Stein et al. 2008).

These different and contrasting findings for voting technology's effect on the residual vote and voter evaluations may reflect the influence of the interaction between different voting technologies and local election administration. Moreover, the actual influence of voting technology on residual votes may be exaggerated. Voters "may intentionally abstain in a particular race" (Ansolabehere and Stewart 2005, 369) because of a lack of interest or information or a preferred choice among the contesting candidates. These conditions cannot be attributed to any particular voting technology or readily measured with aggregate/precinct level designs.

Ansolabehere and Stewart (2005) offer an important qualification about their own and the extant literature's conclusions about the effect of voting technology on residual votes. "It appears that most of what influences whether votes get counted is due to population dependent factors that are distinct from the type of voting technology used" (2005, 383). They conclude:

> The incidence of uncounted and spoiled ballots depends strongly and systematically on "county" in addition to equipment. ... We conjecture that this county effect is substantially the result of local *institutions* of electoral administration, such as the administration of local polling places or advance instruction to voters. (2005, 386)

We concur with this perspective. Moreover, we believe the technology voters use to cast their ballots is made more accessible, error-free, and positively evaluated by voters with effective management and administration of the voting experience. The availability of experienced and knowledgeable poll workers who can assist voters with new and/or unfamiliar voting technologies enhances the voting experience and reduces voter errors, such as under- or over-counts on their ballots. These conditions are thought to be more prominent at centralized and open voting places.

RESEARCH HYPOTHESES, DESIGN, AND MEASURES

The concepts of centralization and openness in the operation and administration of polling place locations allow us to identify polling place practices that should meet with greater voter approval and in turn enhance electoral participation. More specifically, greater opportunities to vote before Election Day – in-person early voting and absentee voting by mail – should reduce the time to vote and enhance voter–poll worker interactions. For election administrators, the opportunity to distribute the vote over a longer period of time reduces the demands on polling place locations and persons staffing these locations. Elections require skilled personnel who are knowledgeable and conversant in election law to maintain computer-based voting and registration databases. A larger number of relatively small voting places works against the efficient and effective use of election personnel. Conversely, a smaller number of larger voting places enables local election officials (LEOs) to maximize the use of their scarce personnel and reduce operational costs, all to the benefit of voters.[6]

We suspect that centralized and open polling places will benefit infrequent voters and persons less attentive and interested in politics. Infrequent voters are less familiar with voting place locations, procedures, and the equipment on which to vote. The infrequency of voting becomes path dependent and increases the likelihood that these eligible voters will be more easily deterred from voting when confronted with obstacles and impediments to voting, such as long lines, scarce parking, and less accessible locations at which to vote. The prior voting history of frequent voters makes them more knowledgeable about the location of voting places and the equipment on which they vote and less likely to be deterred from voting because of long lines, scarce parking, and less accessible locations at which to vote (Brady and McNulty 2011).

---

[6] Concerns are sometimes raised about the consequences of centralization on distance to polling locations. While this is an important concern about the implementation of EDVCs, we have found little evidence that vote centers substantially increase average residential distance, and, when combined with openness, we have found that a clear majority of voters do not minimize residential distance (Stein and Vonnahme 2012).

We hypothesize:

- Voters are more likely to positively evaluate their voting experience in states with centralized and open voting systems.
- Infrequent voters are less likely to cite the inconvenience of polling place locations, hours of operation, uncooperative poll workers, limited parking, and transportation to voting place locations in states with centralized and open voting systems.

Ideally we would we would test our hypotheses with data at the individual level matched with information about the voting place locations at which each voter balloted. In another paper (Stein and Vonnahme 2012b), we report tests of these hypotheses for a sample of Colorado voters who were interviewed about their voting place experiences as they left their Election Day voting place during the 2008 presidential election. Colorado is among a few states that allow their voters to choose from a number of different modes of voting, including mail-in absentee voting, permanent mail-in voting, in-person early voting, EDVCs, and traditional precinct-based Election Day voting locations. A comparison of voter experiences at voting places with different degrees of openness and centralization confirms our hypotheses for voters in the 2008 Colorado presidential election.

The Colorado study, however, may not be generalized to other states. To examine the veracity of our hypotheses for the fifty states, we test our hypotheses using the 2008 SPAE. The Internet survey (N = 10,000), conducted with 200 registered voters in each state focuses on the voting place experiences of 2008 presidential voters and the reasons given for not voting by nonvoters. Voters were asked about problems they encountered voting, including finding their polling place, time waiting to vote, assistance provided by poll workers, and use of polling machine/equipment.

Alvarez et al.'s (2012) analysis of the 2008 SPAE demonstrates that voter choices among alternative modes of voting reflect their preference for convenience over alternative explanations, including partisan and ideological preferences. This finding suggests that voters search for and choose the most convenient mode of voting. Voters should report greater satisfaction with their polling place experience in locales that design their voting places and operations to be more convenient (i.e., more open and centralized) to voters.

Our measure of polling place openness is taken from Cemenksa et al.'s (2009) *Report on 2008 Early and Absentee Voting Dataset.* The data set details state election practices. We specifically focus on the opportunity to vote at more than one location and locations proximate to where voters might travel during the day. In-person early voting and EDVCs increase these opportunities. Of course, mail-in voting does not entail voting at a polling place location. Mail-in voting opportunities reduce the demand on voting place staff and operations, presumably enhancing the experiences of a polling place voter. In-person early voting, permanent mail-in voting, and EDVCs are each a positive indicator of open voting practices. Our measure of openness is a scale score (0–4) based on whether the states allow no excuse mail-in voting, permanent mail-in voting, no excuse in-person early voting, and mail-in elections (i.e., Oregon), reflecting the opportunities that voters have to cast ballots outside traditional Election Day precincts.

We have also collected data (U.S. Election Assistance Commission [EAC] 2008) on the number of voting precincts in each county in which our sample of voters cast ballots in the 2008 presidential election. With these data, we are able to calculate two measures of centralization: population per precinct (thousands) and land area per precinct (square miles). A smaller number of larger voting places (i.e., a greater number of persons per voting place) is expected to be positively related to voters' polling place experience. We suspect that counties with a lower density of voting places have located their voting places more centrally to where voters work, shop, attend school, recreate, and travel rather than exclusively proximate to the voters' residences. We expect the density of voting locations is negatively related to the voters' experience at their polling place.[7] Our expectation is that states with open and centralized voting systems (i.e., the interaction of openness and indexes of centralization) will have a significant and independent effect on voting experiences.

Estimating the effect of state-level polling place practices on voter experiences poses several challenges. We do not have information on the practices of the polling places at which voters balloted. Generalizing to individual polling places from aggregate information (i.e., voter per precinct and precincts per square mile) is likely to be associated with larger standard errors and risks rejecting a significant effect that might be present.

---

[7]   There a significant and negative relationship between our two measures of centralization ($R = -.16$, $p < .05$).

TABLE 7.1. *Lines for early and Election Day voters in 2008*

	Early	Election Day
No line	33.46	44.21
Less than ten minutes	27.27	26.86
Ten to thirty minutes	20.71	15.80
Thirty minutes to one hour	11.52	8.87
More than one hour	7.05	4.26

Source: SPAE.

FINDINGS

Lines

To examine voters' experiences in 2008, we first consider time spent waiting in lines. The modal voter encountered no line at all in the 2008 election, despite higher levels of voter turnout than in previous elections. Of all voters surveyed in the SPAE, 41.8 percent reported that they did not encounter any line at all at their polling places. Table 7.1 shows the length of lines for early and Election Day voters. The table shows, counterintuitively, that early voters encountered longer lines than Election Day voters. Nearly 45 percent of Election Day voters encountered no line at all compared with 33 percent of early voters. Not only were early voters more likely to encounter a line, but the lines were longer than those at Election Day polling places – early voters were twice as likely to wait more than an hour to vote. This finding is unexpected for two reasons. First, in-person early voting is intended to make voting more convenient by expanding the number of days of in-person voting, but it also appears to generate systematically longer lines for early voters. The second reason that this finding is unexpected is the many alternatives associated with early voting. Early voters do not have to vote on just one day or at only one location. An early voter that encounters a long line at one location could simply vote on another day or at another location and thus avoid the long line.[8] Election Day voters have neither option as there are no other days to vote and no other available locations. Yet these responses show that many early voters do not change their behavior to avoid lines, even waiting an hour or more to vote early.

---

[8] This is not always the case as some counties provide only one early voting location.

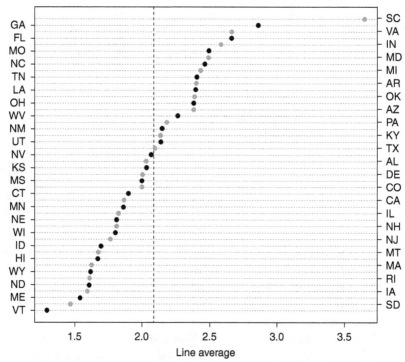

FIGURE 7.1. Polling place lines by state in 2008. (*Source*: SPAE.)
Note: The polling place lines variable was coded 1 = "not at all," 2 = "less than 10 minutes," 3 = "10–30 minutes," 4 = "31–60 minutes," 5 = "more than 1 hour."

While the categorical survey question limits responses to a maximum of one hour or more, a follow-up free-response item queried voters about wait times longer than one hour. These data show that the percentages drop off quickly. Of all interviewees, a little more than 3.8 percent reported waiting an hour and a half or more. About half that many (1.9 percent) reported waiting more than two hours and just 0.5 percent waited more than three hours. The longest reported wait time was six hours by two early voters.

Figure 7.1 shows the state averages for wait times at polling locations. One notable feature about these data is South Carolina, which had far longer lines on average than any other state. The modal voter in South Carolina waited in line more than an hour to vote (35.2 percent) and just 7.7 percent encountered no line at all.

As indicated earlier, early voting is unexpectedly related to wait times. The survey also asked voters about the source of lines at the polling locations. Of the voters who reported some wait time, 64.9 percent said that most of the wait was to check in. Only 17.7 percent said that most of the wait came after they checked in, and 16.7 percent said that the wait was about evenly divided pre- and post-check-in.

There were no notable differences in the source of lines for early and Election Day voters. The percentage citing lines to check in increases from 64.9 percent to 72.7 percent when we narrow the analysis to only those voters that waited at least thirty minutes. These results show that voter check-in is the most likely source of lines at polling locations; the availability of voting stations is significantly less likely to cause long lines. This difference is even greater at polling locations with the longest lines. Surprisingly, however, there are no differences between early and Election Day locations. Early voting check-in is procedurally more elaborate, since early voting locations are countywide and require poll workers to identify the appropriate voting district. Election Day precincts are (mostly) specific to that voting district, which should simplify voter check-in.

We also compared wait times for Election Day registration (EDR) states, which might be longer because of the additional demand on poll workers, but there was no significant difference. We also compared wait times in North Dakota with South Dakota; since North Dakota has no voter registration system, we might expect shorter wait times, but this was also not the case, as there was little difference between the two states.

To evaluate whether lines are related to other state policies, we merged the SPAE data with data on state election laws (Cemenska et al. 2009) and the number and density of precincts by county. We created two measures to reflect the centralization and openness of polling places. *Openness* refers to granting voters more opportunities to vote outside a local precinct and more days on which to vote. To construct the openness measure, we created an additive index for whether the state allowed no excuse absentee voting, permanent absentee voting, all-mail ballot elections, and in-person early voting. Higher values of the variable indicate a more open voting system. To create the measure of centralization, we obtained a count of precincts weighted by population (i.e., number of voters per precinct). Data on the number of precincts in a county were obtained from the EAC survey following the 2008 election and data on the population and land area of counties were obtained from the U.S. Census Bureau.

Regression estimates are shown in Table 7.2, column 1 for openness and column 2 for centralization.[9] These results show that openness is negatively related to wait times. States with more opportunities to vote, particularly by mail, have shorter lines. While this finding is not unexpected, it is also possible that election officials cut resources to polling place operations with more mail-in voters, such that lines could remain unchanged or even increase if the reductions are too severe, but this is not what we observe. More centralized polling locations are also associated with longer lines, as states with more voters per precinct also encounter longer wait times. Lines were also longer for non-Anglo voters, Democrats, and less frequent voters. We also included an interaction term between openness and centralization in the third column. The results from the interactive model are similar to the main effects. While centralization mitigates the effect of openness, openness continues to be associated with shorter lines even at relatively high levels of centralization.

Difficulty Finding Polling Place Location

In addition to the length of lines, we also examined whether voters had difficulty finding their polling locations. The SPAE queried voters about how difficult it was for them to find their locations. Responses were on a four-point scale and state summaries are shown in Figure 7.2.

Overall, voters had little difficulty finding their polling locations. More than 90 percent of all voters stated that it was very easy for them to find their polling locations. Election Day voters had a slightly easier time finding their polling places than early voters, but even a clear majority of early voters (more than 88 percent) had no difficulty finding their polling places.

One possible source of the difference between early and Election Day voting experiences is the type of polling location, as the ease of finding the location depended on the type of polling place.[10] Voters encountered the most difficulty finding polling locations in private homes (only 81 percent said it was very easy to find). Interestingly, the

---

[9] Results from ordered logit models were substantively the same and are available from the authors.

[10] $F_{10,\,7408} = 1.84$, $p = 0.048$.

TABLE 7.2. *Regression estimates for lines in 2008*

	(1)	(2)	(3)
Openness	−0.084***		−0.194***
	(0.014)		(0.026)
Precinct population		0.057***	−0.013
(in thousands)		(0.010)	(0.015)
Open x pop.			0.050***
			(0.009)
Habitual voter	−0.078**	−0.072*	−0.070*
	(0.036)	(0.037)	(0.037)
Residency duration	−0.108***	−0.099***	−0.105***
	(0.016)	(0.017)	(0.017)
Income	0.028***	0.025***	0.026***
	(0.005)	(0.005)	(0.005)
Non-Anglo	0.387***	0.391***	0.376***
	(0.043)	(0.045)	(0.045)
Female	−0.057*	−0.053*	−0.052*
	(0.030)	(0.031)	(0.031)
Age	0.002*	0.002*	0.002
	(0.001)	(0.001)	(0.001)
Vote margin	3.521***	3.609***	3.520***
	(0.292)	(0.298)	(0.301)
Party ID	−0.017***	−0.018***	−0.015**
	(0.006)	(0.006)	(0.006)
Partisan strength	0.023	0.022	0.019
	(0.014)	(0.015)	(0.015)
Constant	0.655***	0.375**	0.727***
	(0.155)	(0.157)	(0.165)
Observations	6,296	6,024	6,024
R-squared	0.057	0.055	0.064

Notes: *** $p < 0.01$, ** $p < 0.05$, * $p < 0.1$
Standard errors in parentheses.

second most difficult polling locations to find were located in the most public places: stores and shopping malls (86.4 percent).[11] Less than a quarter of 1 percent of Election Day voters cast ballots in a store or

[11] We expect that these facilities were easy to find, but the voting stations within the facilities may have been less visible.

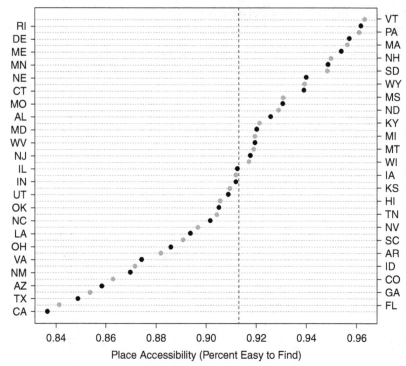

FIGURE 7.2. Ease of finding polling place locations by state in 2008. (*Source*: SPAE.)

shopping mall compared with more than 9 percent of early voters. In contrast, churches and schools were among the easiest polling locations to find and constituted more than 50 percent of Election Day voting but a little more than 5 percent of early voting. Table 7.3 shows results for first-time and repeat voters. As expected, first-time voters are significantly more likely to encounter some difficulty finding their polling locations than returning voters.

In the appendix to this chapter, we report regression estimates for the ease of finding polling locations (see Table A7.1). That analysis finds no consistent evidence that either openness or centralization is independently related to the ease of finding polling places. Centralization was negatively related to the ease of finding polling locations, but the effect is substantively small.[12] We also consider an alternative measure

[12] Moving from the least to most centralized county would only reduce the ease of finding the polling location by five-hundredths of a point on a four-point scale.

TABLE 7.3. *Ease of finding polling place by first-time and returning voter in 2008*

	First-Time Voter	Returning Voter
Very easy	81.66	91.89
Fairly easy	15.58	6.69
Somewhat difficult	2.51	1.23
Very difficult	0.25	0.20

Source: SPAE.

of centralization, which is based on the geographic area covered by the average precincts. That analysis shows the effect of geographic size of precincts is positive and statistically significant but substantively weak.

The weakness of these findings might be partially attributable to the limited variation of the dependent variable. The states with the lowest averages are Oregon and Washington, which operate a few polling places for in-person voting but conduct mostly mail ballot elections.[13] Otherwise voters across the states expressed little difficulty finding their polling locations. Partisans were no more or less likely to encounter difficulties finding their polling locations. Non-Anglo voters were somewhat more likely to have difficulties finding their polling places, as were less habitual voters and those that more recently moved to a new residence.

Polling Place Operations

The SPAE also asked voters to evaluate how well their polling places were run. The responses were on a four-point scale and state summaries are shown in Figure 7.3. Most voters stated that the polling place was run very well (over 82 percent). This proportion was slightly higher for early voters (+1.69 percent) but this difference was not significant. Figure 7.3 shows that across the states, Arizona and South Carolina had the lowest place ratings.

Regression estimates reported in the appendix (Table A7.2) indicate that states with more open voting systems received higher evaluations for their polling place operations. The results show that precinct areas also increase voter evaluations of polling place operations, and there

---

[13] In 2008, a little more than 3 percent of Oregon voters and 16 percent of Washington voters cast ballots in person.

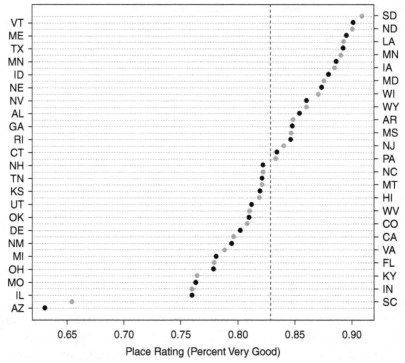

FIGURE 7.3. Polling place ratings by state in 2008. (*Source*: SPAE.)

appears to be no significant interaction with open voting systems. Partisans are no more or less likely to positively evaluate their polling places. More frequent voters, Anglos, older voters, and less residentially mobile voters evaluated polling places more positively.

There are two potential objections to these analyses. One is that the measures might be redundant, such that voters that wait in line for a long period of time will negatively evaluate polling place operations regardless of any other characteristic. Are these two survey items superfluous? The answer appears to be no, as the correlation between lines and place assessments is just 0.293.

Table A7.3 in the appendix shows regression estimates of place evaluations with the length of lines. Long wait times are associated with low place evaluations, but even the full model with all the control variables still accounts for just 10 percent of the variance in place evaluations. We also observe a difference between early and Election Day voters on this measure. Although early voters waited in longer lines, they also had a more favorable view of their polling places. Early voting might incidentally increase wait times for some voters, but those voters also appear less responsive to wait times. In contrast, Election Day voters in early voting states are less likely to encounter lines (46.6 percent encountered no line) than Election Day voters in states that do not allow in-person early voting (42 percent).

A second objection is that these findings only apply to voters. An individual might show up at a polling location and discover that there is a long line and opt out of the voting population. This person would not be able to address the wait times or the quality of the location, but his or her participation was clearly affected by polling place operations. This is a particular concern for measuring democracy, since polling locations should be accessible to everyone, including marginal and prospective voters. Is there a way to determine how nonvoters perceive polling place operations? The SPAE instrument queried nonvoters about the importance of several factors for their decision to not vote. The percentage of people citing lines as a major factor was 10.4 percent, an unfamiliar polling location was a major factor for 7.8 percent of nonvoters, and bad times or location was cited by 9.6 percent of nonvoters. Overall, 20.5 percent of nonvoters cited at least one polling place factor as a major reason for not voting.

Could openness and centralization exacerbate these problems for nonvoters? While some people, such as habitual voters, might respond very positively to openness and centralization, this might not apply to everyone, and nonvoters could be more likely to cite polling place concerns.

To examine this possibility, we conducted a bivariate analysis, using logit regression, to predict who, among the nonvoters, would cite polling place factors as a major reason for not voting. Those results, which are reported in Table A7.4 show that openness and both measures of centralization are largely unrelated to the frequency of polling place concerns of nonvoters. This allays concerns that openness and centralization could be viewed favorably by voters but create prohibitive obstacles for nonvoters.

DISCUSSION

Previous research (Stein and Vonnahme 2008, 2012b) has shown that voting place operations have a significant and positive effect on voters' evaluations of their voting experience and their likelihood of voting in subsequent elections, especially among those with a history of infrequent voting. Moreover, specific institutional arrangements, including greater opportunities for where and when to vote and the size and location of voting places, have been shown to be positively related to voting experiences and the likelihood of voting. These findings, however, are limited to just two states (Colorado and Texas). In this chapter, we asked whether previous findings about voting place operations can be generalized to other states. Lacking the granular data on voting place operations available in previous studies, we sought to correlate state- and county-level voting practices with a national survey conducted with voters in the 2008 presidential election. We find significant evidence, albeit modest and qualified, that voter experiences are more positive in states where voters have greater opportunities to vote before Election Day and at a variety of larger locations that may be more centrally located to where voters work, shop, and travel during the day. Because of our aggregated measures of voting place practices, any firm conclusion about voting place practices and their impact on voting experiences is subject to further study with more granular voting place information.

There are several findings reported in this study that underscore the importance with which voters prefer the convenience of voting before Election Day and at a variety of locations. Pre–Election Day voters reported longer waits to vote than Election Day voters. Longer waiting times to vote, however, had no appreciable effect on early voters' evaluations of their voting experiences. We conclude from these findings that early voters prefer the trade-off between longer waits to vote for the convenience of choosing when and where vote. Further evidence for voters' preference for greater convenience is the significant and positive relationship between the smaller number of larger voting places (precincts per capita) and voter evaluations.

The benefits to voters from greater convenience – openness and centralization – are not limited to states that have authorized early voting, no excuse mail-in voting, or EDVCs. States with traditional Election Day precinct operations can take advantage of greater centralization of their voting places to enhance the voting experience. Moreover, there is reason to believe that both centralization of voting place operations as well as pre–Election Day voting has a significant effect on the costs of conducting elections. The cost per vote cast and the cost per unit of benefit (e.g., time waiting in line and voter evaluation of their voting experience) are significantly lower in jurisdictions with open and centralized voting place operations (Stein and Vonnahme 2010).

Finally, there is reason to believe that how we conduct our elections, specifically allowing voters to ballot when and where they most prefer, has a significant effect on how candidates conduct their campaigns and how the media reports about electoral contests. Dunaway and Stein (2013) report that the content, quantity, and timing of campaign messages and news reporting of campaigns differ significantly between states with and without pre–Election Day voting. In states with in-person early voting and where a larger proportion of the vote is cast before Election Day, we observe a significantly greater volume of campaign news stories per day than in states without in-person early voting (one additional news story per day) and where a lower proportion of the vote is cast before Election Day (about half of an additional news story per day). Over the course of the campaign, these differences could have important implications for voter learning and engagement. Similarly, the content of campaign news coverage is significantly different in early than in nonearly voting states. Both the number and proportion of game-frame-oriented campaign news stories are significantly greater in states with both in-person early voting and where the proportion of votes cast before Election Day is higher. Understanding how voting places interact with campaigns and media coverage may help in better understanding how voters' evaluations and behaviors are shaped by how we conduct our elections.

These analyses show that two factors related to polling place operations are particularly good candidates for inclusion in a measure of democracy: lines and polling place evaluations. These two outcomes are significantly related to the openness and centralization of polling locations. There is less reason to be sanguine about the ease of finding polling locations, as the findings show a weak and inconsistent association with the way that elections are administered in the states. However, the weak relationship might have less to do with the effect of openness and centralization and more to do with the limited variation in the ease of finding polling locations. One way forward would be to continue to monitor the ease of finding polling locations to determine whether the relative constancy of voter responses persists, or if there is more variation in voter responses in less salient elections when there is less campaign activity.

8

Disability and Election Policies and Practices

Lisa Schur and Douglas Kruse

People with disabilities often face extra difficulties participating in elections. Individuals with mobility impairments, for example, may have difficulty getting to a polling place, getting inside a polling place, and using the voting equipment. People who are blind or have limited vision may have similar problems, particularly with regard to seeing the ballot and registering a choice. People with limited manual dexterity may have problems filling out a ballot or otherwise operating voting equipment, and people with cognitive impairments may have difficulty reading the ballot or understanding how to vote.

This is an important issue for American elections, in part because of the large number of people with disabilities who are eligible to vote and the likely growth in this number as the population ages. Between 35 and 46 million voting-age people with disabilities live in the United States, making them one of the largest minority groups in the country.[1] Over the past few decades, the disability rights movement has achieved many political gains, such as the passage of the Americans with Disabilities Act (ADA) in 1990. These gains have occurred despite evidence that people with disabilities are generally less likely than those without disabilities to vote or engage in other forms of political action.

---

[1] The lower number is based on six disability questions used by the Census Bureau in the 2011 American Community Survey (StatsRRTC 2012). The higher number is based on a more expansive set of disability questions in the 2005 Survey of Income and Program Participation (the 46 million figure includes only those age twenty-one or older) (Brault 2008). These estimates are similar to estimates of the number of African Americans and Hispanics living in the United States (http://www.census.gov/prod/cen2010/briefs/c2010br-02.pdf).

We appreciate the useful feedback and assistance from Barry Burden, Martha Kropf, Charles Stewart III, and Christopher Mann.

Some of the disability voting gap can be explained by lower average education levels of people with disabilities and by greater social isolation, which decreases the likelihood of political recruitment (Schur et al. 2002; Schur and Adya, 2013). The disability voting gap remains, however, after accounting for these factors. The remaining gap may be attributable in part to inaccessible polling places and other election policies or practices that create voting barriers. These not only make voting more physically difficult, but can also have discouraging psychological effects by sending the message that people with disabilities are not welcome in the political sphere (Schneider and Ingram 1993). The 2002 Help America Vote Act (HAVA) included provisions to reduce these barriers by requiring accessible voting equipment in each polling place and providing funding to increase polling place accessibility.

This chapter examines voter turnout of people with disabilities in the 2008, 2010, and 2012 elections, with special attention to the role of several election policies and practices that are under the control of policy makers and election officials: vote-by-mail systems, devices to assist people with disabilities, early voting locations, fully online registration, and Election Day registration (EDR)/same day registration (SDR). Although a number of studies have documented the generally lower voter turnout among people with disabilities, this is the first to analyze the potential effects of election policies and practices. We use the Census Bureau's Voting and Registration Supplement (VRS) data for 2008 and 2010, and the 2008 Survey of the Performance of American Elections (SPAE), matched to the U.S. Election Assistance Commission's (EAC's) data from the Election Administration and Voting Survey (EAVS) and the Statutory Overview. The effects of policies and practices may differ by type of disability, so we separately analyze six broad categories of impairments and activity limitations. We also analyze two potential indicators of election performance from the VRS, which measure the number of people who report not being registered or not voting because of illness or disability.

We find that people with disabilities were less likely to vote, but that state policies and practices can remedy much of this deficit. In the 2010 midterm elections, states that offered no excuse mail ballots or used all-vote-by-mail systems saw higher turnout among people with disabilities. Surprisingly, availability of voting devices designed for those with disabilities does not increase their levels of voter turnout. We speculate that this is attributable to lack of awareness, fear of stigmatization, and lack of knowledge among polling place officials.

THEORY AND LITERATURE REVIEW

The factors affecting political participation can be divided into three categories: resources ("Are you able to participate?"), psychology ("Do you want to participate?"), and recruitment ("Did anyone ask you to participate?") (Verba, Schlozman, and Brady 1995). Resources include time, money, and civic skills; psychological factors include political interest, civic values, feelings of efficacy, group consciousness, and commitment to specific policies; and political recruitment occurs through formal and informal networks. Research on the general population demonstrates that factors in each of these categories strongly influence the likelihood of voting (Conway 2000; Rosenstone and Hansen 1993; Verba et al. 1995).

Disability may affect voter turnout in a number of ways. Limited resources, including reduced physical stamina and mobility, can depress voter turnout. People with disabilities have lower average income and education levels than people without disabilities, and their financial resources are often further constrained by higher expenses for medical care and special equipment (WHO/World Bank 2011).

Political recruitment among people with disabilities is limited by their relative isolation. They are more likely than nondisabled people to live alone and face transportation problems and are less likely to be involved in community and social activities (Harris 2010). They have much lower employment rates, limiting their access to workplace networks that are an important source of recruitment. Physical and social isolation can be exacerbated by states' disenfranchisement of some individuals with disabilities (particularly those with cognitive impairments, such as Alzheimer's) (Carey 2009; Schriner, Ochs, and Shields 1997), frequent neglect by candidates and parties, and negative messages about disability conveyed through public policy, the media, and inaccessible polling places.

Regarding psychological factors, the stigma and discrimination associated with disability (Muzzatti 2008; Nowicki and Sandieson 2002; Schur, Kruse, and Blanck 2013; Scior 2011; Thompson et al. 2011; U.S. Commission on Civil Rights 1983; Westerholm et al. 2006a, 2006b; Yuker 1988) may combine with isolation and diminished resources to decrease feelings of personal efficacy and control and lead some people to withdraw from society and reduce their political participation (Anspach 1979). Stigma and discrimination may, however, motivate other individuals to become politically active, as shown by the growth of the disability rights movement (Anspach 1979; Scotch 1988; Shapiro 1993) and qualitative studies of disability activists (Schur 1998).

Studies over the 1992–2010 elections confirm that there is lower voter turnout among people with disabilities (reviewed in Schur and Adya, 2013). Resources, recruitment, and psychological factors all appear to contribute to this gap (Schur et al. 2002). People with disabilities have also been less likely to participate in other forms of political activity, such as contacting elected officials or contributing money to campaigns or political groups (Schur 2003; Schur et al., 2013).

Mobility problems in particular appear to contribute to low turnout of people with disabilities. Turnout appears lowest among people who report difficulty going outside their homes alone (Schur et al. 2002; Schur and Adya, 2013). As part of their mobility difficulties, about 30 percent of people with disabilities are not able to drive, and voter turnout is fifteen to twenty percentage points lower among this group. Voting by mail can be an attractive alternative for people with mobility impairments or other transportation difficulties, and voting by mail is almost twice as high among voters with disabilities (Schur et al. 2002; Schur and Adya, 2013). Even with the option of voting by mail, however, turnout is lower among people with mobility problems, suggesting greater mobility may have important social and psychological effects through increased social interaction, feelings of efficacy, and identification and engagement with mainstream society.

The turnout of people with disabilities may be discouraged by barriers getting to or using polling places. Being forced to vote by mail because of inaccessible polling places can create feelings of alienation and resentment: for example, one woman who uses a wheelchair "described the ramp at her polling place as a 'ski slope'" and now votes by absentee ballot, "which she calls a 'second-class ballot' that forces her to cast votes before she's made up her mind" (Korte, 2012).[2] The Government Accountability Office (GAO) found that while almost all polling places in 2008 had met HAVA requirements to install accessible voting systems, about half of these systems "could pose challenges for voters with disabilities to vote privately or independently" (GAO 2009b, 36); in addition, only 27 percent of polling places had no potential impediments to access by people with disabilities, a modest increase

---

[2] This feeling of alienation should be absent when everyone votes by mail, such as in Oregon and Washington.

from 2000, when 16 percent had no potential impediments.[3] In a 2000 election survey, 6 percent of people with disabilities who had voted in the past ten years reported encountering problems in voting at a polling place, while one-third of all others with disabilities said they would expect problems, compared with only 2 percent of people without disabilities (Schur, Shields, and Schriner 2005). The continuing problems in polling places were recognized in a recent U.S. District Court ruling that "cited a litany of problems: wheelchair ramps too narrow or steep, missing handicapped entrance signs, and voting booths too close to the wall for wheelchairs to get to," and ordered New York's Board of Elections to improve accessibility of polling places (Korte 2012, 4).

While there appears to be growing recognition of problems in polling place accessibility, there have been no studies on the effects of election policies and practices on the voter turnout of people with disabilities. One form of obvious exclusion comes from state laws that disqualify some people with intellectual disabilities from voting and serving on juries (Carey 2009; Sabatino and Spurgeon 2007; Schriner et al. 1997). Even where they are not expressly excluded from the political process, people with intellectual disabilities still receive "mixed messages" in laws and policies about the extent of their rights of citizenship, which can discourage turnout (Carey 2009, 9–11). Tokaji and Colker (2007) discuss the advantages of voting by mail for many people with disabilities, but also the limitations of the current vote-by-mail process. For example, people with visual or cognitive impairments may have trouble seeing or following complicated written instructions on standard mail ballots, and those with limited fine motor skills may find it hard to record their votes. When the voting process is not fully accessible, people with disabilities who want to vote may have to rely on family members or caregivers who can make informal "gatekeeping" decisions to provide or withhold assistance, or can apply pressure to vote for particular candidates, which can discourage citizens with disabilities from voting (Tokaji and Colker 2007; Wehbi and El-Lahib 2008).

There has been widespread adoption of new voting technologies, in part to meet HAVA's requirements for accessible voting systems (Stewart 2011). These technologies have been found to reduce the rate of residual

---

[3]   The GAO also noted progress in accessibility standards: "In 2008, 43 states reported that they required accessibility standards for polling places, up from 23 states in 2000. Additionally, most states reported that they used federal HAVA funds to improve the physical accessibility of polling places" (2009b, 1).

votes (Allers and Kooreman 2009; Kropf and Kimball 2011; Stewart 2006), although accuracy varies across systems (Herrnson et al. 2008). Voters tend to respond positively to computerized voting systems, although these may scare some elderly voters who are not comfortable with computers (Herrnson et al. 2008; Roseman and Stephenson 2005). The only evidence relating disability to voting technology found that people with disabilities did not differ from nondisabled voters in satisfaction with several types of vote verification systems (Herrnson et al. 2008, 131–132).

DATA SETS AND METHOD

This study analyzes three sources of data on voter turnout: the 2008 and 2010 VRSs conducted by the U.S. Census Bureau and the 2008 SPAE.[4] We also provide some descriptive results from the 2012 VRS for comparison, but at the time of writing the 2012 data set was not ready for multivariate analysis. The Census Bureau added six questions that allow one to identify disability status on the VRS starting in 2008.[5] The supplements included 92,360 people of voting age in 2008, 94,208 people of voting age in 2010, and 94,311 people of voting age in 2012. The questions allow identification of four major categories of impairment – visual, hearing, mobility, and cognitive – and two types of activity limitation – difficulty with self-care (dressing or bathing) and difficulty going outside alone. After applying VRS sampling weights, the estimated disability rates, based on those who answered affirmatively to at least one of the six questions, are 12.5 percent in 2008, 12.2 percent in 2010, and 12.8 percent in 2012.[6]

While the VRS only asks basic voting questions (e.g., whether one voted, and reason for not voting), the SPAE asks a number of questions to assess the experience of voting itself. The SPAE also includes one disability question: "Does a health problem, disability, or handicap currently keep you from participating fully in work, school, housework, or other activities?" There were 1,639 respondents who answered yes, representing 16.4 percent of the sample after applying weights.[7]

---

[4] See http://vote.caltech.edu/node/231.

[5] The questions are presented by the Bureau of Labor Statistics at http://www.bls.gov/cps/cps-disability_faq.htm#Identified.

[6] The weights are provided by the Census Bureau to account for survey sampling design and ensure the sample conforms to the known population distribution of demographic factors (age, sex, race, and ethnicity). Disability is not used in developing the weights.

[7] Statistics based on analysis of SPAE by authors. The higher rate of reported disability in the SPAE sample than in the VRS samples probably reflects the broader wording of the SPAE

We merged the voter turnout data with information on election policies and practices from the U.S. EAC, drawn from the 2008 and 2010 EAVS and the Statutory Overviews, and from Christopher Mann's data on vote-by-mail regimes that he analyzes in Chapter 5 in this volume.[8] We matched the data sets by geographical FIPS code at the lowest level possible. The match was perfect for many urban areas, but the FIPS code in the VRS often combined respondents from the balance of a state at a higher level of aggregation than in the EAVS. In these latter cases we aggregated the data in the EAVS (weighted the data by the number of voters in each reporting unit) to the higher-level FIPS codes so that they could be cleanly matched to the VRS. The result is that some of the election policy and practice figures are between 0 and 1 (for example, if 50 percent of the precincts had devices to assist voting by people with disabilities, that variable takes the value 0.5), effectively representing the probability that a voter will be covered by a particular policy or practice. The aggregation necessarily introduces some measurement error, which will tend to bias the coefficients toward zero, which makes statistically significant coefficients all the more noteworthy.[9]

RELATIONSHIP BETWEEN DISABILITY AND VOTER TURNOUT

Citizens with disabilities were less likely than those without disabilities to report voting in the 2008, 2010, and 2012 elections. The bivariate tabulations in Table 8.1 show that their overall voting rate was 7.2 percentage points lower than that of people without disabilities in 2008, 3.1 percentage points lower in 2010, and 5.7 percentage points lower in 2012 using the VRS measure of disability (column 2).[10] The narrowing of the overall voting gap in 2010 primarily represents a difference in the age composition of the electorate: younger people (who have a lower disability rate) had especially low turnout in the midterm election, so that older people (who have a higher disability rate) were a larger share

question that likely captures a wider range of disabilities, although with less information on type of disability. Some research finds that the Census measures do not capture a significant portion of people who consider themselves to have work-limiting disabilities (Burkhauser, Houtenville, and Tennant 2014).

[8] We thank Christopher Mann for sharing these data with us.

[9] While random measurement error biases coefficients toward zero, the bias could go either direction if the measurement error is systematic. The results are maintained when excluding the observations with values between zero and one.

[10] Surveys on voter turnout are subject to overreporting, but there is no reason to think that any under- or overreporting differs by disability status, as discussed in Schur et al. (2002).

TABLE 8.1. *Voter turnout by disability status*

	People without disabilities	Gap between People with and without Disabilities						
		Any disability	Visual	Hearing	Mobility	Cognitive	Difficulty with self-care	Difficulty going outside alone
	(1)	(2)	(3)	(4)	(5)	(6)	(7)	(8)
Among eligible population								
Voted in 2008 (VRS)	64.5%	−7.2%***	−7.7%***	−1.4%	−7.7%***	−18.4%***	−18.1%***	−18.8%***
Voted in 2010 (VRS)	45.9%	−3.1%***	−6.4%***	4.1%**	−2.4%**	−16.4%***	−13.5%***	−13.0%***
Voted in 2012 (VRS)	62.5%	−5.7%***	−5.2%***	0.7%	−6.2%***	−17.7%***	−15.8%***	−15.2%***
Among registered voters								
Voted in 2008 (VRS)	90.4%	−6.3%***	−6.1%***	−3.6%***	−7.6%***	−12.0%***	−13.4%***	−14.0%***
Voted in 2008 (SPAE)	93.7%	−6.7%***						
Voted in 2010 (VRS)	70.4%	−3.6%***	−7.7%***	0.9%	−4.5%***	−14.9%***	−14.0%***	−13.1%***
Voted in 2012 (VRS)	87.5%	−5.4%***	−6.5%***	−2.5%***	−6.5%***	−12.0%***	−12.3%***	−12.1%**
If voted, did so by mail								
2008 (VRS)	15.2%	10.6%***	13.5%***	9.7%***	12.8%***	10.1%***	23.2%***	19.6%***
2008 (SPAE)	18.0%	5.7%***						
2010 (VRS)	16.9%	10.6%***	11.1%	10.9%***	12.5%***	9.0%***	21.7%***	18.5%***
2012 (VRS)	17.3%	10.8%***	9.2%	11.1%***	13.7%***	12.8%***	22.3%***	18.7%***
Sample sizes								
2008 (VRS)	80,333	12,027	1,798	3,377	7,234	3,501	1,923	3,946
2008 (SPAE)	8,341	1,639						
2010 (VRS)	82,144	12,064	1,692	3,516	7,177	3,475	1,890	3,947
2012 (VRS)	81,855	12,456	1,811	3,707	7,421	3,615	2,035	4,142

Notes: * Significantly different from people without disabilities at p < .10 ** p < .05.

of the electorate. There were especially large voting gaps for people with cognitive impairments (18.4, 16.4, and 17.7 points in 2008, 2010, and 2012, respectively, in column 6) and difficulty in going outside alone (18.8, 13.0, and 15.2 points, in column 8), despite the availability of mail ballots. The latter result strongly suggests the importance of social or psychological factors associated with mobility outside the home, as well as potential difficulties in obtaining mail ballots. Looking just at registered voters, the turnout of people with disabilities was 6.3 percent lower in the 2008 VRS, 6.7 percent lower in the 2010 SPAE, 3.6 percent lower in the 2010 VRS, and 5.4 percent lower in the 2012 VRS (column 2). The gaps are again largest among those with cognitive impairments or who have difficulty going outside alone. Among those who voted, each of the data sets shows that people with disabilities were more likely to vote by mail; about one-fourth (23.7 percent to 28.1 percent across the four datasets) did so compared with about one-sixth of people without disabilities (15.2 percent to 18.0 percent). Voting by mail is especially high among those who have difficulty with self-care or going outside alone (columns 7 and 8).

The disability turnout gap continues to be strong when accounting for education and demographic variables, as shown in Tables 8.2 and 8.3. These regressions are probit models with standard demographic variables as controls, and they account for correlated errors at the state level. To aid in interpretation, the reported coefficients represent the marginal effects of the independent variable on the probability of voter turnout, assuming all other variables are at their mean values. Tests were made with multinomial logits to allow a more flexible specification predicting a choice among three options – voting in a polling place, voting by mail, and not voting – but the results were similar to those based on probits and are not reported here (but are available from the authors).

Among the voting-eligible population (VEP), the adjusted disability gap is 8.8 percentage points in 2008 (column 1) and 9.9 points in 2010 (column 3). The widening of the 2010 gap from the simple tabulations in Table 8.1 (from 3.1 to 9.9 points) reflects the effect of controlling for age: older people are more likely to vote in general, and people with disabilities are older on average, so age has a positive statistical effect on their basic turnout number, but that effect disappears once age is controlled.[11] When the separate types of disability are used as predictors

---

[11] Both the age and age squared coefficients, and the change in the disability coefficient when inserting the age terms, are statistically significant at $p < .0001$.

TABLE 8.2. *Predicting voter turnout among eligible population*

Coefficients represent marginal effects on probabilities based on probit regressions. Dep. var. = voted.

	Means		2008 VRS		2010 VRS	
Indep. vars.	No disab.	Disab.	(1)	(2)	(3)	(4)
Disability						
Any disability	0.000	1.000	-0.088 (12.73)**		-0.099 (15.46)	0.003 (0.29)
Hearing impairment	0.000	0.267		0.013 (1.09)		-0.041 (3.13)**
Visual impairment	0.000	0.151		-0.021 (1.46)		-0.095 (9.69)**
Cognitive impairment	0.000	0.294		-0.073 (6.11)**		-0.030 (2.94)**
Mobility impairment	0.000	0.607		-0.026 (3.35)**		-0.062 (3.54)**
Difficulty w/self-care	0.000	0.165		-0.057 (4.23)**		-0.106 (7.36)**
Difficulty going outside alone	0.000	0.339		-0.123 (10.37)**		
Other demographics						
Female	0.517**	0.545	0.035 (9.72)**	0.038 (10.09)**	0.000 (0.10)	0.001 (0.44)
Age	44.7**	60.6	0.009 (12.52)**	0.008 (12.04)**	0.018 (17.96)	0.017 (17.17)**
Age squared	2276.5**	3988.9	0.000 (6.43)**	0.000 (5.93)**	0.000 (9.94)	0.000 (9.24)**
Black	0.120**	0.077	0.059 (5.85)**	0.060 (5.93)**	0.027 (1.88)	0.029 (2.04)**
Other race/ethnicity	0.058**	0.046	-0.146 (15.29)**	-0.145 (15.25)**	-0.127 (8.44)	-0.126 (8.27)**
Hispanic	0.097**	0.046	-0.074 (2.23)**	-0.073 (2.20)**	-0.067 (2.84)	-0.066 (2.84)**

(continued)

TABLE 8.2 (continued)

Coefficients represent marginal effects on probabilities based on probit regressions. Dep. var. = voted.

Indep. vars.	Means		2008 VRS		2010 VRS	
	No disab.	Disab.	(1)	(2)	(3)	(4)
Education						
High school degree	0.311**	0.363	0.139 (12.69)**	0.136 (12.80)**	0.152 (14.19)	0.149 (14.37)**
Some college, no degree	0.209**	0.176	0.254 (22.40)**	0.251 (22.83)**	0.273 (24.37)	0.270 (24.30)**
Associate's degree	0.093**	0.075	0.254 (22.24)**	0.252 (22.68)**	0.290 (23.55)	0.288 (23.53)**
Bachelor's degree	0.198**	0.091	0.316 (23.64)**	0.315 (24.15)**	0.361 (24.39)	0.359 (24.38)**
Graduate degree	0.096**	0.052	0.319 (25.20)**	0.318 (25.65)**	0.396 (23.79)	0.394 (24.16)**
Pseudo R-sq.			0.090	0.092	0.115	0.117
n	80,333	12,027	92,360	92,360	94,208	94,208

Notes: * Significant at $p < .10$ ** $p < .05$ (z-statistics in parentheses).

TABLE 8.3. *Predicting voter turnout among registered voters*

Coefficients represent marginal effects on probabilities based on probit regressions. Dep. var. = voted.

Indep. vars.	2008 VRS (1)	2008 VRS (2)	2010 VRS (3)	2010 VRS (4)	2008 SPAE (5)	2008 SPAE (6)
Disability						
Any disability	-0.063 (16.32)**		-0.113 (14.06)**		-0.061 (8.62)	-0.041 (6.03)
Hearing impairment		-0.004 (0.57)		-0.023 (1.98)**		
Visual impairment		-0.006 (0.75)		-0.054 (3.07)**		
Mental/emotional impairment		-0.034 (3.84)**		-0.074 (5.30)**		
Mobility impairment		-0.038 (6.44)**		-0.061 (6.18)**		
Difficulty w/self-care		-0.021 (2.29)**		-0.045 (2.43)**		
Difficulty going outside alone		-0.063 (7.83)**		-0.099 (5.65)**		
Other demographics						
Female	0.010 (5.24)**	0.012 (5.99)**	-0.021 (5.82)**	-0.019 (5.57)**	-0.012 (2.53)**	-0.008 (1.72)*
Age	0.005 (10.97)**	0.005 (10.28)**	0.015 (14.57)**	0.014 (13.71)**	0.002 (1.86)*	0.001 (0.07)
Age squared	0.000 (7.02)**	0.000 (6.33)**	0.000 (7.89)**	0.000 (6.97)**	0.00000 (0.57)	0.00001 (1.48)
Black	0.049 (8.10)**	0.049 (8.28)**	0.044 (3.64)**	0.046 (3.80)**	0.005 (0.64)	0.010 (1.39)
Hispanic	-0.021 (0.88)	-0.021 (0.85)	-0.026 (0.75)	-0.026 (0.74)	-0.014 (1.13)	-0.012 (1.07)

(continued)

TABLE 8.3 (continued)

Coefficients represent marginal effects on probabilities based on probit regressions. Dep. var. = voted.

Indep. vars.	2008 VRS (1)	2008 VRS (2)	2010 VRS (3)	2010 VRS (4)	2008 SPAE (5)	2008 SPAE (6)
Other race/ethnicity	−0.041 (7.81)**	−0.040 (7.64)	−0.055 (3.57)**	−0.053 (3.48)**	−0.014 (1.35)	−0.014 (1.37)
Education						
High school degree	0.043 (7.41)**	0.042 (7.19)**	0.098 (9.05)**	0.095 (8.93)**	0.031 (3.46)**	0.026 (2.97)**
Some college, no degree	0.074 (13.80)**	0.073 (13.72)**	0.154 (15.48)**	0.151 (15.06)**	0.048 (6.11)**	0.040 (5.25)**
Associate's degree	0.072 (17.83)**	0.072 (17.53)**	0.154 (14.38)**	0.152 (13.93)**	0.041 (5.34)**	0.035 (4.34)**
Bachelor's degree	0.104 (16.82)**	0.103 (16.76)**	0.215 (17.43)**	0.213 (17.17)**	0.063 (8.86)**	0.054 (7.53)**
Graduate degree	0.095 (17.92)**	0.094 (18.06)**	0.226 (17.20)**	0.224 (17.29)**	0.052 (6.96)**	0.045 (5.71)**
Income (15 category dummies)	No	No	No	No	No	Yes
Pseudo R-sq.	0.082	0.085	0.089	0.091	0.124	0.142
n	66,700	66,700	62,437	62,437	9,979	9,971

Notes: * Significant at p < .10 ** p < .05 (z-statistics in parentheses).

in columns 2 and 4, turnout is estimated to be lowest among those who have difficulty going outside alone. Interestingly, there appears to be no voting gap between people with hearing impairments and those without disabilities, which may reflect fewer voting barriers for people with hearing impairments and/or the influence of Deaf culture (with a capital *D*) which rejects the idea that deafness is a disability and encourages political action based on Deaf identity (Padden and Humphries 2006).

The basic patterns are similar when limited to registered voters, as shown in Table 8.3. The estimated disability voting gap is 6.3 points in the 2008 VRS and 11.3 points in the 2010 VRS (columns 1 and 3). It is noteworthy that these gaps are similar to those estimated among the full VEP in Table 8.2, indicating that the disability voting gap primarily reflects low turnout among registered voters with disabilities, rather than low registration rates. Those with hearing impairments again have the smallest gaps relative to those without disabilities (columns 2 and 4), although, unlike in Table 8.2, there is a significant gap in 2010. The lowest turnout is among those with difficulty going outside alone. While the SPAE uses a different measure of disability, the estimated turnout gap in 2008 is similar between the VRS (6.3 points) and SPAE (6.1 points, in column 5). This figure is reduced to 4.1 points but remains highly statistically significant when controlling for income levels in the SPAE (column 6), indicating part of the lower turnout can be accounted for by the lower average income of people with disabilities (consistent with Schur et al. 2002).

The disability gap in voter turnout may reflect both direct and indirect effects of disability and omitted variables. These data sets do not measure political recruitment and feelings of political efficacy that are important predictors of turnout. The relative social isolation of people with disabilities is linked to lower levels of political recruitment, and people with disabilities have lower levels of external political efficacy. Past research finds, however, that controlling for these variables does not close the turnout gap (Schur et al. 2002).

REASONS FOR NOT VOTING

What reasons do people report for not registering or voting? Those who were not registered in the VRS were asked "Which of the following was the MAIN reason (you/name) (were/was) not registered to vote?" Table 8.4 shows that the most common reason given by both people

TABLE 8.4. *Reported reasons for not being registered or voting*

| | 2008 VRS | | 2010 VRS | | 2008 SPAE | | 2012 VRS | |
	With disability (1)	Without disability (2)	With disability (3)	Without disability (4)	With disability (5)	Without disability (6)	With disability (3)	Without disability (4)
Why not registered to vote								
Permanent illness or disability	25.9%**	1.3%	22.9%**	1.3%	na	na	24.5%***	1.2%
Not interested in the election or not involved in politics	32.7%**	42.5%	38.2%**	47.6%	na	na	32.1%**	45.2%
Did not meet registration deadlines	7.4%**	16.1%	6.8%**	13.7%	na	na	9.0%**	15.6%
Not eligible to vote	5.9%**	8.4%	4.6%**	6.7%	na	na	6.0%**	7.5%
My vote would not make a difference	3.6%**	4.2%	4.2%	3.7%	na	na	4.3%	4.8%
Did not know where or how to register	2.7%**	4.0%	3.6%**	5.4%	na	na	4.1%**	4.8%
Did not meet residency requirements/did not live here long	1.8 %**	4.0%	2.3%**	4.9%	na	na	1.2%**	3.5%

Difficulty with English	1.8%	1.4%	1.9%	1.7%	na	na	1.5%	1.6%
Other reason	18.2%	18.1%	15.6%	15.0%	na	na	17.4%	15.8%
n	2184	10735	2494	13592			2324	1118
Why didn't vote if registered								
Illness or disability (own or family's)	44.0%**	9.6%	39.6%**	7.2%	42.0%**	14.2%	43.6%**	8.2%
Not interested, felt my vote wouldn't make a difference	9.5%**	15.5%	12.4%**	17.6%	37.6%	42.8%	12.3%**	17.0%
Didn't like candidates or campaign issues	13.9%	13.9%	9.1%	8.8%	23.8%**	38.2%	9.7%**	13.8%
Too busy, conflicting work or school schedule	4.0%**	22.3%	8.4%**	30.5%	8.4%	11.4%	5.9%**	22.4%
Forgot to vote (or send in absentee ballot)	1.1%**	3.2%	6.4%**	8.5%	31.9%**	16.2%	2.8%**	4.3%
Transportation problems	7.0%**	1.9%	6.1%**	2.0%	13.9%	20.2%	6.1%**	2.8%
Out of town or away from home	3.8%**	10.8%	4.3%**	10.3%			3.1%**	10.1%
Registration problems (i.e., didn't receive absentee ballot, not registered in current location	3.5%**	7.1%	3.1%	3.4%			4.0%**	6.0%
Registration problems					21.4%	19.9%		

(continued)

TABLE 8.4 (continued)

	2008 VRS		2010 VRS		2008 SPAE		2012 VRS	
	With disability (1)	Without disability (2)	With disability (3)	Without disability (4)	With disability (5)	Without disability (6)	With disability (3)	Without disability (4)
Didn't receive absentee ballot, or too late					26.0%	20.0%		
Inconvenient hours, polling place or hours or lines too long	2.3%	3.0%	0.7%**	2.4%			2.0%	2.9%
Inconvenient hours or polling place					15.7%	21.8%		
Lines too long					15.5%*	24.4%		
Bad weather conditions	0.3%	0.2%	0.4%**	0.1%	10.1%	7.8%	0.6%	0.9%
Wrong ID					10.0%	14.1%		
Didn't know where to vote					13.2%**	23.7%		
Other	10.6%	12.5%	9.5%	9.2%			10.0%	11.8%
n	1,276	4,991	2,386	13,968	167	396	1,437	6,499

Notes: * Significant difference at p < .10 ** p < .05.

with and without disabilities was "not interested in the election or not involved in politics." Among people with disabilities, roughly one-third reported this in 2008, 2010, and 2012 (33 percent, 38 percent, and 32 percent respectively, compared with 43 percent, 48 percent, and 45 percent among people without disabilities), while about one-fourth gave the next most common reason of "permanent illness or disability" (26 percent, 23 percent, and 25 percent) (columns 1 and 3). Only 1.2 percent or 1.3 percent of non-registered people without disabilities cited "permanent illness or disability" in 2008 to 2012.

This rationale for not registering is subject to different interpretations. Some who give this reason may in fact not be allowed to vote because they have a significant mental impairment that disqualifies them from voting according to state law (Carey 2009). This is unlikely to apply to more than a tiny fraction of the respondents. Those citing "permanent illness or disability" may do so as a result of perceived barriers in registering or barriers in voting that make registration seem pointless. In addition, some people may use illness or disability as a justification or excuse for not being registered, just as some people report having a work disability as a justification for not being employed (Banks et al. 2005).

Among those who were registered but did not vote, Table 8.4 shows that in all four data sets, about two-fifths of people with disabilities (between 39.6 percent and 44.0 percent) gave "illness or disability (own or family's)" as the reason for not voting. This was also given as a reason for not voting by roughly one-tenth of people without disabilities (7.2 percent to 14.2 percent). As with reasons for not registering, people may report this because of perceived barriers or difficulties in voting (e.g., inaccessible polling places or a sudden illness on Election Day) and/or simply as a convenient justification for not voting.

POTENTIAL MEASURES OF ELECTION PERFORMANCE

The two disability-related reasons for not voting in Table 8.4 are potential indicators of the performance of American elections. Ideally, people with disabilities will have unfettered access to the political process to the same extent as people without disabilities, and they will not face barriers that prevent or discourage exercising the right to vote. Conceptually, an election performance measure should indicate any disparity in the difficulty of voting for people with and without disabilities.

The lower voter turnout of people with disabilities (as found in Tables 8.1 to 8.3) reflects both direct and indirect barriers. The direct barriers are in the election process, creating extra difficulties for people with disabilities who want to vote. Examples of these types of barriers are physical impediments in polling places for people with mobility impairments, difficulty in understanding and operating voting equipment, the inability for blind citizens to fill out a confidential ballot with standard equipment, and negative attitudes or ignorance of poll workers. These direct barriers may be alleviated or eliminated by election policies and practices that increase accessibility of the voting process.

Indirect barriers to voting may operate through social and economic factors that affect voter turnout. For example, lower turnout among people with disabilities is partly attributable to their lower average education and income levels (Schur et al. 2002), which may reflect discrimination or other difficulties in obtaining high-quality education and well-paying jobs. Lower turnout also reflects transportation barriers and greater isolation of people with disabilities that decreases social networks and the likelihood of political recruitment. A wide variety of evidence points toward social and economic barriers, such as employment discrimination, that can indirectly influence voting (for a review, see Schur, Kruse, and Blanck 2013).

It would be ideal to have two types of indicators: one measuring direct barriers to voting, and one measuring both direct and indirect barriers. Indirect barriers, however, are difficult to quantify. For example, while the evidence indicates prejudice appears to play a role in the low employment and earnings of people with disabilities (e.g., Johnson and Lambrinos 1985), it does not permit straightforward measurement of that role and its relationship to voter turnout (although factors such as education capture some of this relationship).

It is more feasible to measure direct barriers to voting, and also more useful to policy makers and election officials who want to identify barriers they can decrease or eliminate. One indicator of direct barriers comes from reports of actual or expected voting difficulties experienced by people with and without disabilities. Using a series of detailed questions about voting difficulties in the 2012 elections, a national household survey found that nearly one-third (30 percent) of voters with disabilities who voted at a polling place reported one or more difficulties in voting, compared with 8 percent of voters without disabilities (Schur, Adya, and Kruse 2013).[12] Among those who had not voted at a polling place in

---

[12] The survey was designed by the authors as part of the Research Alliance for Accessible Voting, with funding from the EAC.

the last ten years, 40 percent of people with disabilities said they would expect to encounter some type of difficulty in voting at a polling place, compared with 1 percent of people without disabilities. As noted earlier, people with disabilities are more likely to vote by mail. The 2012 survey found that 13 percent of people with disabilities who voted by mail reported some difficulty in doing so, compared with 2 percent of those without disabilities. While there are advantages to measuring voting barriers in this way, shifting conceptions and measures of disability may influence consistency over time. Nonetheless, this approach holds promise as one indicator of the performance of American elections.

Here we analyze two currently available potential measures that are reported in Table 8.4: whether a person reported not registering because of "permanent illness or disability," or reported being registered but not voting because of "illness or disability (own or family's)." We will refer to these as the "nonregistered disability measure" and "nonvoting disability measure," respectively. Two obvious advantages of these measures are that they come from a large representative sample of the population and are routinely collected following the national elections in even-numbered years.

Although these questions have reasonably good face validity, one limitation is that they only reflect barriers for those who did not vote, and do not reflect barriers faced but overcome by people with disabilities who did vote. Another limitation for the purposes of measuring election barriers is that some conditions may be so severe (e.g., being in a coma) that they prevent a person from voting no matter what policies or practices are in place. Two difficulties with the "illness or disability (own or family's)" response are that (1) that it captures temporary illnesses, such as a bad cold or the flu, and (2) captures not only the respondent's own illness or disability, but also those of a family member. These difficulties create some noise in measuring voting barriers faced by people with disabilities, although from a broader perspective it can be argued that elections should ideally be accessible to those with temporary illnesses and those who have family members with illness or disability (e.g., by making it easier to vote by mail or over the Internet), so including these two groups may contribute to a valid election performance measure.

These two measures allow the respondents to use their own definitions of disability in identifying whether it presented a problem in registering or voting. This has the potential advantage of reflecting a wider range of disabilities than can be captured in survey questions designed to measure disability, such as the Census Bureau's six questions that do not capture all types of disability. It has a potential disadvantage, however, in that the word *disability* carries stigma for many people, and many people with significant physical or mental impairments are reluctant to identify themselves as having a disability. (This may be particularly true among senior citizens who may see such impairments simply as part of getting older.) This may lead to underreporting of barriers related to disabilities/impairments as a factor in not registering or voting.

Another disadvantage is that these measures are subject to "justification bias" in which some respondents report having a disability to justify not being registered or not voting, just as some people report a disability to justify their lack of employment or their receipt of disability benefits (Banks et al. 2005).

Two important qualities of measures are reliability (consistency over time and populations) and validity (accuracy in measuring the concept). The reliability and validity of these measures are assessed in Tables A8.1 and A8.2. Ideally one would assess reliability with multiple measurements at the individual level, but those are not available, so in Table A8.1 we examine reliability by correlating state-level averages of both measures to see if there is consistency across data sets and over time. The results appear fairly promising for the nonvoting disability measure but not for the nonregistered disability measure. For the latter, one would expect a high correlation over time in reports that *"permanent* illness or disability" prevented registration, but the correlations between the 2008 and 2010 state-level averages are modest (.341 among all voting-eligible people and .324 among all nonregistered people). Despite the inclusion of temporary illnesses in the nonvoting disability measure, the correlations over time are much higher in the VRS data (.593 to .597), although the correlations between the VRS and SPAE data are lower (.107 to .479).[13]

The validity of the potential performance measures is assessed in Table A8.2 by relating them to other measures of disability. In panel A it can be seen that people with disabilities were much more likely than those without disabilities to report not being registered because of a permanent illness or disability (4.8 percent compared with 0.2 percent in both years) (columns 1–4), as well as to report being registered

---

[13] The correlations may be higher when comparing two general elections, or two midterm elections, because the composition of the voting population with disabilities appears to change between midterm and general elections, as discussed earlier.

but not voting because of an illness or disability (4.6 percent compared with 0.6 percent in 2008, and 8.1 percent compared with 1.3 percent in 2010). These strong differences by disability status also appear when the sample is confined to those who gave a reason for not being registered (row 6) and those who were registered and gave a reason for not voting (row 7).

One cause for concern over the nonvoting disability measure is that the percent of all voting-eligible people who reported this reason for not voting nearly doubled between 2008 and 2010, among people both with and without disabilities (row 2). Taken at face value, this would indicate either that the rate of illness and disability doubled or the barriers to voting doubled between these years. It is much more likely that this represents a form of justification bias, as more people in the low-turnout midterm election in 2010 used illness or disability as a convenient justification for not voting.

We take a different approach in panel B of Table A8.2 by comparing reports of disability and impairments between those who did and did not report these reasons for not being registered or voting. About three-fourths of those who reported permanent illness or disability as a reason for not being registered also reported a disability on one or more of the six questions (79 percent in 2008 and 75 percent in 2010, in row 9). A majority of this group reported difficulty in going outside alone, and mobility was the most common impairment. Among the rest of the sample, about 12 percent are classified as having a disability (row 9). Looking at the nonvoting disability measure, about half of those who reported "illness or disability (own or family member's)" as a reason for not voting also responded yes to one or more of the disability questions (52 percent in 2008 and 47 percent in 2010, in row 19). The most common type of disability among this group is again mobility impairment. The rate of disability in this group was much higher than in the rest of the sample (about 12 percent in both years, in row 19). Because the measure permits respondents to include a family member's illness or disability, row 18 breaks out the percentage of people who do not have a disability but who have a family member with a disability. Among the group giving "illness or disability (own or family member's)" as a reason for not voting, about 8 percent in both years are not classified with a disability but have a family member with one, which is only slightly higher than the 7 percent rate in the rest of the sample (row 18). A family member's disability therefore does not appear to be a large factor in responses to this question.

In summary of the reliability and validity tests, the nonregistered disability measure appears to have low reliability, while the nonvoting disability measure has reasonable reliability, based on a rough test using state-level correlations. Regarding validity, both measures are strongly related to the Census Bureau's six-question set of disability measures. One concern about the nonvoting disability measure is that the percentage reporting "illness or disability (own or family member's)" as a reason for not voting nearly doubled between the high-turnout general election of 2008 and the lower-turnout midterm election of 2010, probably indicating this measure is subject to an upward justification bias as people search for a rationale for not voting. Both of these measures will be further explored as potential performance measures in Tables 8.7 and 8.8.

ELECTION POLICIES AND PRACTICES

Do election policies and practices affect turnout for people with disabilities? We consider five types of policies and practices: (1) different systems for voting by mail; (2) availability of devices at polling places to enable voting by people with disabilities; (3) the existence of physical locations for early voting; (4) the availability of fully online registration; and (5) EDR or SDR.[14] As shown in Table 8.5 (columns of means), close to half of eligible voters in both 2008 and 2010 lived in precincts that required an excuse for an absentee ballot; about one-third were covered by no excuse vote-by-mail that has to be renewed each election; one-eighth were covered by permanent no excuse vote-by-mail; and 3 percent lived in Oregon or Washington State, where all voting is done by mail. The most common voting system at polling places is optical/digital scan.[15] Three-fourths of the eligible voters were in precincts reported to have devices to assist people with disabilities to vote, which declined to two-thirds in 2010. In both years, a little more than half of eligible voters were in precincts that had physical locations for early voting, about one-seventh had fully online registration available, and about one-eighth had EDR or SDR available.

Several of these policies and practices are associated with voter turnout, as shown in Table 8.5, which presents separate regressions by year

[14] Fully online systems allow a voter to complete the registration process via the Internet. This contrasts with partially online systems that allow a voter to use a form provided on a Web site but then require it to be printed and mailed.
[15] Because a polling place may offer more than one type of voting equipment, the proportions do not sum to 1.

TABLE 8.5. *Predicting turnout with election practices, by disability status*

Coefficients represent marginal effects on probabilities based on probit regressions. Dep. var. = voted.

	Means		All voting eligible				Just registered voters			
	2008	2010	2008		2010		2008		2010	
Sample:	All	All	No disability	Disability	No disability	Disability	No disability	Disability	No disability	Disability
			(1)	(2)	(3)	(4)	(5)	(6)	(7)	(8)
Vote-by-mail system										
Excuse required (omitted)										
No excuse, for one election	0.302	0.365	0.031 (1.93)*	0.030 (1.46)	0.002 (0.18)	0.040^^ (3.36)**	0.029 (3.68)**	0.042 (2.51)**	0.029 (2.03)**	0.067^^ (4.60)**
No excuse, permanently	0.152	0.145	0.016 (1.03)	-0.005 (0.26)	0.033 (1.86)*	0.062^^ (4.14)**	0.040 (3.39)**	0.067 (4.84)**	0.084 (3.83)**	0.155^^ (6.25)**
All-vote-by-mail	0.028	0.033	-0.007 (0.35)	-0.013 (0.45)	0.080 (2.44)**	0.138^^ (3.80)**	0.038 (3.63)**	0.075 (3.10)**	0.115 (4.08)**	0.188^^ (5.21)**
Type of voting equipment										
Optical scan (omitted)	0.847	0.744								
DRE, no voter-verified	0.351	0.335	-0.013 (0.98)	-0.023 (1.25)	-0.028 (1.77)*	-0.046 (2.01)**	0.005 (0.72)	0.007 (0.44)	-0.017 (0.80)	-0.049 (1.83)*
DRE, voter-verified	0.286	0.222	0.006 (0.52)	-0.011 (0.58)	0.009 (0.53)	-0.002 (0.07)	0.011 (1.35)	0.007 (0.41)	0.017 (0.79)	-0.001 (0.02)

(continued)

TABLE 8.5 *(continued)*

Coefficients represent marginal effects on probabilities based on probit regressions. Dep. var. = voted.

	Means		All voting eligible				Just registered voters			
	2008	2010	2008		2010		2008		2010	
Sample:	All	All	No disability	Disability	No disability	Disability	No disability	Disability	No disability	Disability
			(1)	(2)	(3)	(4)	(5)	(6)	(7)	(8)
Hybrid DRE/optical	0.304	0.242	0.001	−0.001	−0.017	−0.001	0.003	0.017	−0.014	−0.011
			(0.09)	(0.03)	(0.98)	(0.07)	(0.46)	(1.02)	(0.68)	(0.49)
Other	0.154	0.175	−0.001	0.012	0.011	−0.025	0.001	−0.001	0.013	−0.002
			(0.13)	(0.80)	(0.67)	(1.10)	(0.19)	(0.04)	(1.02)	(0.06)
Device to assist disabled	0.778	0.664	0.011	−0.003	0.027*	0.013	−0.007	−0.016	0.033*	0.011
			(1.21)	(0.24)	(2.06)	(0.76)	(1.24)	(1.12)	(2.39)	(0.56)
Early voting locations available	0.577	0.545	−0.057**	−0.043*	−0.029	−0.033**	−0.029**	−0.030**	−0.036*	−0.031
			(4.02)	(2.46)	(1.61)	(2.02)	(4.27)	(2.04)	(2.02)	(1.60)
Fully online registration available	0.154	0.146	0.003	0.017	0.034*	0.034*	−0.002	0.010	0.012	0.010
			(0.17)	(0.87)	(1.84)	(1.76)	(0.24)	(0.51)	(0.65)	(0.40)
EDR/SDR	0.124	0.122	0.021	0.00	0.034*	0.014	−0.002	−0.016	0.009	0.005
			(1.43)	(0.00)	(1.86)	(0.71)	(0.35)	(0.68)	(0.40)	(0.18)
n			76,957	11,600	82,144	12,064	56,133	8,049	54,595	7,842

Notes: All regressions include controls for gender, age and its square, education (five dummies), black, Hispanic, other race, marital status (four dummies).

** $p < 0.05$, * $p < 0.1$ Robust z-statistics in parentheses.

^^ Significantly different from no-disability coefficient (in columns 3 or 7) at $p < .05$ ^ $p < .10$.

and disability status. Looking first at all voting-eligible people, turnout among people without disabilities was higher in the states that allow no excuse mail-in ballots for one election (in 2008) or permanently (in 2010), and in the two all-vote-by-mail states in 2010 but not 2008 (columns 1 and 3). Among people with disabilities, all three of these vote-by-mail systems were linked to higher turnout in 2010 but not 2008 (columns 2 and 4). A striking finding is that the estimated effects of these vote-by-mail systems in 2010 are significantly larger among people with disabilities than among people without disabilities: for example, the all-vote-by-mail system is linked to 13.8 percent higher turnout among people with disabilities, compared with 8.0 percent higher turnout among people without disabilities.[16] The pattern is stronger when looking just at registered voters (columns 5 to 8), where all three of the vote-by-mail systems are linked to higher turnout than in excuse-required systems, in both years and for people both with and without disabilities. The 2010 coefficients are significantly larger in the disability sample than in the nondisability sample, indicating the no excuse and vote-by-mail systems appear to especially increase turnout of people with disabilities.

The other election policies and practices do not appear to be consistently related to voter turnout. Turnout was lower in precincts with physical locations for early voting, perhaps reflecting the provision of locations for early voting as part of efforts to increase turnout in low-turnout precincts.[17] Turnout did not vary substantially by type of polling place equipment available. Interestingly, having a device to assist voters with disabilities is associated with higher turnout only for voters *without* disabilities in 2010. There is no ready explanation for this. It may represent a causal effect if the devices are made available to people without disabilities to help shorten lines and waiting times, but it may also reflect a selection effect in the types of precincts that offer these devices. In separate regressions (not reported but available), we broke out the assistive devices by type of voting equipment but did not find significant disability interactions for any of the terms. The absence of a positive effect among people with disabilities may reflect a lack of outreach and information regarding the availability of these devices. Having fully online registration available is associated with higher turn-

---

[16] The differences in the three vote-by-mail coefficients between the disability and nondisability regressions are all statistically significant at $p < .01$.

[17] Studies have mixed results but on balance find that early voting does not increase turnout (e.g., Alvarez, Levin, and Sinclair 2012).

out in 2010 but not 2008, while having EDR or SDR is associated with higher turnout only for people without disabilities in 2010.

The determinants of voter turnout may differ by type of disability. Table 8.6 presents separate regressions by type of disability using 2010 data. To aid comparisons, columns 1 and 2 reproduce the results for people with and without disabilities from columns 3 and 4 of Table 8.7. The effect of being in the all-vote-by-mail states compared with excuse-required states is positive and significant for four of the disability groups (hearing, visual, and mobility impairments, and difficulty going outside), with coefficients indicating higher voter turnout ranging from 12.9 to 19.0 percentage points relative to the excuse-required system. The permanent no excuse system is also linked to higher turnout for five of the disability groups (all except those with visual impairments), while the only strongly significant coefficient for the no-excuse-for-one-election system is among people with mobility impairments. All of these coefficients are not only significantly different from zero (i.e., comparing these systems with the excuse-required system within the disability group), but are significantly different from the coefficients in the nondisability regression (i.e., comparing the effects of these systems for people with and without disabilities). While the significant coefficients are most likely to occur for people with mobility impairments, it is noteworthy that the positive effects of vote-by-mail systems do not appear to be confined to one or two disability groups, indicating that the positive effects of these alternatives to the excuse-required system appear to be broadly spread across the disability population.

Among the other policies and practices, devices to assist people with disabilities do not appear to have significant effects on voter turnout among any of the disability groups, while full online registration is linked to higher turnout among people with cognitive impairments and having EDR or SDR available is associated with higher turnout only among those without disabilities and those with hearing impairments. Having early voting centers available is actually linked to lower turnout among those with cognitive or mobility impairments.

Finally, we consider the possible effects of election policies and practices on the two potential performance measures. Table 8.7 uses the same specification as in Tables 8.5 and 8.6, but with the nonregistered disability measure as the dependent variable instead of voter turnout. Here a "good" outcome is a negative coefficient, which would support the idea that an election policy or practice decreases the percent of people not registering because of permanent illness or disability. Among

TABLE 8.6. *Predicting turnout with election practices, by type of disability*

Coefficients represent marginal effects on probabilities based on probit regressions. Dep. var. = voted. 2010 VRS data

Sample:	No disability	Disability	Hearing impairment	Visual impairment	Cognitive impairment	Mobility impairment	Difficulty with self-care	Difficulty going outside alone
	(1)	(2)	(3)	(4)	(5)	(6)	(7)	(8)
Vote-by-mail system								
Excuse required (omitted)								
No excuse, for one election	0.002	0.040^^	0.011	0.047	0.030	0.058^^	0.030	0.039
	(0.18)	(3.36)**	(0.67)	(1.67)*	(1.55)	(4.25)**	(0.92)	(1.43)
No excuse, permanently	0.033	0.062^^	0.061^^	0.032	0.085^^	0.051^^	0.104^^	0.071^^
	(1.86)*	(4.14)**	(2.59)**	(0.74)	(3.31)**	(2.38)**	(2.56)**	(2.68)**
All-vote-by-mail	0.080	0.138^^	0.151^^	0.190^^	0.032	0.208^^	0.055	0.129^^
	(2.44)**	(3.80)**	(4.11)**	(3.75)**	(1.12)	(4.10)**	(1.03)	(3.36)**
Type of voting equipment								
Optical scan (omitted)								
DRE, no voter-verified	-0.028	-0.046	-0.041	-0.058	-0.051	-0.019	-0.013	-0.065
	(1.77)*	(2.01)**	(1.37)	(1.17)	(1.71)*	(0.71)	(0.25)	(1.69)*
DRE, voter-verified	0.009	-0.002	-0.065	-0.047	0.023	0.038	0.059	0.018
	(0.53)	(0.07)	(2.02)*	(0.95)	(0.69)	(1.47)	(1.27)	(0.53)

(continued)

TABLE 8.6 *(continued)*

Coefficients represent marginal effects on probabilities based on probit regressions. Dep. var. = voted. 2010 VRS data

Sample:	No disability	Disability	Hearing impairment	Visual impairment	Cognitive impairment	Mobility impairment	Difficulty with self-care	Difficulty going outside alone
	(1)	(2)	(3)	(4)	(5)	(6)	(7)	(8)
Hybrid DRE/optical	-0.017	-0.001	0.008	0.005	0.006	0.034^^	0.067^^	-0.001
	(0.98)	(0.07)	(0.27)	(0.11)	(0.21)	(1.36)	(1.54)	(0.04)
Other	0.011	-0.025	-0.041^	-0.084^	-0.054^^	-0.014	-0.024	-0.092^^
	(0.67)	(1.10)	(1.10)	(1.70)*	(2.07)**	(0.55)	(0.70)	(3.65)**
Device to assist disabled	0.027	0.013	0.016	-0.021	-0.025^^	0.015	-0.010	0.004
	(2.06)**	(0.76)	(0.95)	(0.58)	(1.20)	(0.69)	(0.25)	(0.09)
Early voting locations available	-0.029	-0.033	0.009^	-0.021	-0.048	-0.046	-0.048	-0.043
	(1.61)	(2.02)**	(0.42)	(0.65)	(2.61)**	(2.40)**	(1.55)	(1.40)
Fully online registration available	0.034	0.034	0.024	0.010	0.061	0.025	0.045	0.008
	(1.84)*	(1.76)*	(0.80)	(0.25)	(3.27)**	(1.04)	(1.08)	(0.27)
EDR/SDR	0.034	0.014	0.056	0.024	-0.001	0.018	0.028	-0.026
	(1.86)*	(0.71)	(1.94)*	(0.47)	(0.03)	(0.66)	(1.03)	(0.96)
n	82,144	12,064	3,516	1,692	3,475	3,947	1,890	3,947

Notes: All regressions include controls for gender, age and its square, education (five dummies), black, Hispanic, other race.

** p < 0.05, * p < 0.1 Robust z-statistics in parentheses.

^^ Significantly different from no-disability coefficient in column 1 at p < .05 ^ p < .10.

TABLE 8.7. *Predicting permanent illness or disability as reason for not being registered*

Coefficients represent marginal effects on probabilities based on probit regressions, among voting-eligible population. Dep. var. = reported "permanent illness or disability" as reason for not being registered.

	2008		2010	
	No disability	Disability	No disability	Disability
	(1)	(2)	(3)	(4)
Vote-by-mail system				
Excuse required (omitted)				
No excuse, for one election	0.000	−0.019$^{\wedge\wedge}$	0.000	−0.002
	(0.15)	(2.91)**	(0.94)	(0.52)
No excuse, permanently	0.000	0.008	0.000	0.019
	(0.39)	(1.10)	(0.72)	(2.61)**
All-vote-by-mail	−0.001	0.017	0.000	0.017
	(1.76)*	(0.78)	(0.56)	(2.49)**
Type of voting equipment				
Optical scan (omitted)				
DRE, no voter-verified	0.000	0.001	0.000	0.008
	(1.60)	(0.08)	(0.42)	(1.03)
DRE, voter-verified	−0.001	−0.008	0.000	−0.004
	(2.18)**	(1.17)	(0.33)	(0.41)
Hybrid DRE/optical	−0.001	−0.001$^{\wedge\wedge}$	0.000	−0.010
	(2.40)**	(0.18)	(0.47)	(1.60)
Other	−0.001	−0.009	0.000	0.010
	(1.82)*	(1.07)	(0.95)	(1.54)
Device to assist disabled	0.000	−0.002$^{\wedge}$	0.000	−0.004
	(2.28)**	(0.30)	(0.22)	(0.91)
Early voting locations available	0.000	0.010	0.000	0.002
	(0.89)	(1.73)*	(0.74)	(0.52)
Fully online registration available	0.000	−0.011	0.000	−0.009
	(0.14)	(2.26)**	(0.28)	(2.06)**
EDR/SDR	0.000	0.015	0.001	0.011
	(0.31)	(1.73)*	(2.43)*	(1.37)
n	76,957	11,600	82,144	12,064

Notes: All regressions include controls for gender, age and its square, education (five dummies), black, Hispanic, other race.

** p < 0.05, * p < 0.1 Robust z-statistics in parentheses.

$^{\wedge\wedge}$ Significantly different from no-disability coefficient (in column 1 or 3) at p < .05 $^{\wedge}$ p < .10.

people with disabilities, the only significant negative coefficients are found for no-excuse-for-one-election systems, and for having full online registration available, in 2008 (column 2). Among people without disabilities, there is a weakly significant negative coefficient on all-vote-by-mail systems, possibly indicating that these systems provide less of an excuse for nonregistration, while there is a small positive coefficient on devices to assist people with disabilities that is difficult to interpret (perhaps representing a selection effect from precincts investing in such devices to increase registration and turnout).

When the nonvoting disability measure is analyzed, however, the results for vote-by-mail systems are striking. Table 8.8 shows that for people both with and without disabilities, and in both 2008 and 2010, all but one of the coefficients on the no excuse and all-vote-by-mail systems predict a significantly lower likelihood of not voting because of illness or disability. The magnitudes are sizable: for example, people with disabilities in the all-vote-by-mail states were 7.9 to 11.5 points less likely than those in excuse-required systems to report not voting because of illness or disability (columns 2 and 4). These regressions are restricted to registered voters, but the results hold up when the sample is expanded to include the full VEP (not reported but available). As with the predictions of voter turnout in Tables 8.5 and 8.6, the other policies and practices do not appear to have a consistent relationship to the likelihood of not voting because of illness or disability.

DISCUSSION

Overall, the results indicate that vote-by-mail systems make a difference in voter turnout, particularly among people with disabilities and particularly in midterm elections. The stronger effects found in the 2010 election may indicate easier voting by mail is especially effective in low-turnout midterm elections when people are less motivated to vote and the costs of voting are more salient. The 2010 turnout was lowest in states where people have to provide a reason for requesting mail ballots. People may be reluctant to request a mail ballot if they have to acknowledge having a disability because disability has long been recognized as a source of stigma. Not having to provide a reason for a mail ballot may remove an important barrier to voting.

Apart from the issue of disability, the finding that the all-vote-by-mail system in Oregon and Washington State was linked to higher voter turnout in 2010 but not 2008 is at odds with research by Southwell

TABLE 8.8. *Predicting registered but not voting because of illness or disability*

Coefficients represent marginal effects on probabilities based on probit regressions. Dep. var. = reported "illness or disability (own or family member's)" as reason for not voting. Restricted to registered voters.

	2008		2010	
	No disability	Disability	No disability	Disability
	(1)	(2)	(3)	(4)
Vote-by-mail system				
Excuse required (omitted)				
No excuse, for one election	−0.004	−0.018	−0.003	−0.026
	(3.82)**	(2.48)**	(1.39)	(2.41)**
No excuse, permanently	−0.004	−0.035^^	−0.007	−0.041^^
	(3.64)**	(5.91)**	(3.49)**	(4.13)**
All-vote-by-mail	−0.007	−0.079^^	−0.027	−0.115^^
	(6.17)**	(4.46)**	(6.34)**	(7.79)**
Type of voting equipment				
Optical scan (omitted)				
DRE, no voter-verified	−0.001	0.002	−0.001	0.018
	(0.66)	(0.29)	(0.19)	(1.53)
DRE, voter-verified	−0.001	0.008	−0.003	−0.018
	(0.95)	(0.93)	(1.07)	(1.57)
Hybrid DRE/optical	−0.002	−0.006	−0.003	0.003
	(1.39)	(0.81)	(1.42)	(0.23)
Other	0.001	0.004	−0.002	0.020
	(0.49)	(0.49)	(0.80)	(1.30)
Device to assist disabled	0.000	−0.004	0.000	0.005
	(0.30)	(0.83)	(0.07)	(0.39)
Early voting locations available	0.002	0.009	0.000	−0.009
	(2.60)**	(1.22)	(0.23)	(0.71)
Fully online registration available	0.000	−0.012^^	−0.001	0.007
	(0.34)	(1.95)*	(0.67)	(0.48)
EDR/SDR	0.001	0.000	−0.004	0.013^^
	(0.65)	(0.02)	(1.86)*	(0.90)
n	56,133	8,049	54,595	7,842

Notes: All regressions include controls for gender, age and its square, education (five dummies), black, Hispanic, other race.

** p < 0.05, * p < 0.1 Robust z-statistics in parentheses.

^^ Significantly different from no-disability coefficient (in column 1 or 3) at p < .05 ^ p < .10.

(2010b, 2011), who found vote-by-mail over the 2004–2008 period in Washington and the 1980–2008 period in Oregon appeared to increase turnout modestly in general elections but not in the midterm elections. Our finding of large effects in the 2010 midterm election may indicate voters became more familiar and comfortable with this method, using it to a greater extent than in prior midterm elections. This result clearly deserves further investigation.

While there has been no previous research on the effect of vote-by-mail systems on people with disabilities, the finding that easier voting by mail appears to especially increase their turnout is consistent with the finding that the turnout of other minority groups (blacks and Latinos) appears to be higher in vote-by-mail systems (Southwell 2010a).

There are no consistent findings of positive effects for the other election policies and practices. Having early voting locations available might help people with transportation or schedule problems, but the negative relationship to turnout found here probably indicates a selection effect from low-turnout precincts trying to encourage voting through opening early voting locations. Having fully online registration available is linked to higher turnout in 2010, with a similar effect for people with and without disabilities. While fully online registration can make registration easier for those with access to the Internet, people with disabilities are less likely to live in households with computers and Internet access. More than half (54 percent) of households headed by someone with a disability had no Internet access from home in 2010, compared with only 25 percent of households headed by someone without a disability (U.S. Department of Commerce 2011, 16). This digital divide limits the potential effects for people with disabilities of any policies and practices that assume Internet access.

It is somewhat surprising that the availability of devices to assist people with disabilities in voting at polling places is not associated with higher turnout. Since such devices would not be helpful in voting by mail, we also ran regressions predicting voting at a polling place, but this variable continued to be an insignificant predictor (not reported but available). One possible explanation is that the measure is noisy – election officials who checked this box on the EAVS may not have had accurate knowledge of their availability or may have been referring to different types of devices. Another possibility is that these devices may not be well advertised to potential voters, so that people with disabilities are not aware of their availability. Yet another possibility is that people with disabilities are aware of these devices but are skeptical that the devices will work or that polling place officials know how to set them up and operate them. This last possibility is indicated by many anecdotal reports of complaints following elections; for example, a disability advocate was recently quoted as saying, "Some of the machines work well. Some of the machines are a joke – a very expensive, bad joke." The article went on to note, "Accessible machines are often turned off or missing parts, and poll workers don't know how to use them" (Korte 2012, 4).

CONCLUSION

The first key finding of this study is that people with disabilities were nine to ten percentage points less likely to vote in the 2008 and 2010 elections overall, consistent with prior data on disability and voter turnout. Descriptive statistics from the 2012 election suggest that the same pattern continued in 2012. A second key finding is that voter turnout among people with disabilities in 2010 was especially high in states that allow temporary or permanent no excuse mail ballots or have all-vote-by-mail systems.

These results indicate that greater ease in obtaining mail ballots may be of extra benefit to people with disabilities, both because they do not have to go to polling places that are often inaccessible and because they do not have to provide a stigmatizing excuse for mail ballots. The findings are supported by results indicating greater ease in obtaining mail ballots is strongly associated with fewer reports of not voting because of illness of disability. While the nonvoting disability measure has limitations, it shows promise as an election performance measure.

We do not find effects on voter turnout of people with disabilities of devices in polling places to assist them in voting. This may reflect lack of awareness of availability of these devices, reluctance to stand out as "different" by using them, skepticism that polling place officials know how to operate them, or simple measurement error.

Our results indicate the lower turnout of people with disabilities is not unalterable and does not simply reflect lower interest in politics or barriers that are outside the control of policy makers and election officials. Rather, election policies and practices, particularly regarding the ease of voting by mail, appear to make a difference. This indicates that policy makers and election officials may be able to increase turnout significantly by adopting these systems, particularly in states with high percentages of people with disabilities. States may face different barriers or challenges in implementing these systems, as suggested by the GAO study that found uneven implementation of HAVA requirements (GAO 2009b). These results also strongly indicate the value of further research on the role of such policies and practices among other determinants of voter turnout among people with disabilities. This conclusion is reinforced by the finding that in 2012 nearly one-third of people with disabilities who voted at a polling place reported some type of difficulty in doing so, compared with 8 percent of voters without disabilities (Schur, Adya, and Kruse 2013).

There appears to be a trend that more states are adopting systems that make it easier to vote by mail. While this may decrease opportunities for direct face-to-face expressions of democratic participation, and these votes are at greater risk of being uncounted, these systems nonetheless appear to encourage and facilitate voting among citizens with disabilities. Given the large and growing number of people with disabilities, the social and economic disparities they have faced, and the value of including all citizens in democratic participation, it is important to ensure their voices are fully heard in the political process.

9

The Performance of Election Machines and the Decline of Residual Votes in the United States

Charles Stewart III

One of the lessons the 2000 election taught Americans is that voting machines can sometimes interfere with the conduct of elections. The Florida recount revealed that machine malfunctions (symbolized by hanging chad) and poor ballot design (symbolized by the butterfly ballot) can throw up barriers to voters who wish nothing more than to cast a ballot in an election.

The problems that beset Florida in 2000 were dramatic and compelling. Yet, once the controversy had died down, the serious question remained: Was what happened in Florida specific to the Sunshine State, or was it part of a more general malady that infected voting technology nationwide? Given the vastness of the country and the heterogeneity of how Americans vote, was there a way to put the problems brought to light in Florida in a broader context, so that this question about its general applicability to the rest of the nation could be answered?

The desire to place Florida's problems counting votes into a broader national context led to the development of a metric to assess the relative performance of voting machines, termed the *residual vote rate*. This metric can be applied to any voting machine in such a way that it is possible to compare different machines with each other, as well as different communities. The purpose of this chapter is to explore this measure in some detail, so that its use can be better understood.

To be useful, this chapter must not only define how the residual vote rate is calculated, but also illustrate what one can discern through its use. To help reach the goal of showing how the residual vote rate's value in assessing the performance of voting machines, the rest of this chapter

This revision was aided immeasurably by comments from conference participants, and especially from close readings by Barry Burden and David Kimball. All errors remain my own.

is divided into four sections. First, I define the residual vote rate metric and show how it has varied across states and across time in recent years. Second, as a prelude to using the residual vote rate to explore the performance of voting machines, I summarize the evolution of voting technology in the United States. Third, I then demonstrate how the residual vote rate can be used to examine voting machine performance at the national, state, and machine levels. Fourth, I conclude by making policy recommendations that relate to making the residual vote metric more accessible to the public and that aim at developing new ways of measuring the performance of voting machines.

MEASURING THE PERFORMANCE OF VOTING MACHINES: THE
RESIDUAL VOTE RATE

In this section I introduce the most common metric of voting machine performance now used in the United States, the *residual vote rate*, which is defined as

$$\frac{Turnout - Total\ votes\ cast}{Turnout},$$

where "total votes cast" usually refers to votes cast for candidates for president. A few studies have focused down the ballot, including referendum items (see Ansolabehere and Stewart 2005; Frisina et al. 2008; Kimball and Kropf 2008; Lott 2009; Stewart 2004; Traugott et al. 2005). However, unless I explicitly state otherwise, for the rest of this chapter, my reference to the residual vote rate will pertain particularly to the rate in the presidential election.[1]

The term is associated with work produced in the early 2000s by the Caltech/MIT Voting Technology Project (2001), and extended by scholars associated with that project (e.g., Alvarez et al. 2013; Ansolabehere and Stewart 2005; Gronke et al. 2010; Stewart 2006).[2] The idea was to measure directly how often votes were lost because of over-votes and under-votes on the ballot, which was directly at issue in the Palm Beach

---

[1] By referencing the presidential election, I am avoiding the many problems of analyzing residual vote rates during midterm elections. Because the top-of-the-ticket race varies so much across states in midterms – compared with presidential years, when the top-of-the-ticket race is always for president – cross-state comparisons of residual vote rates in midterm elections are fraught with complications.

[2] For a comprehensive review of the residual vote rate and its use in research into voting technology, see Stewart (2011).

County recount. However, it is clear that lost votes can occur for many reasons, not just because of hanging chad or the equivalent problem on other types of voting machines. For instance, poor ballot design or confusing instructions might lead voters to over-vote their ballots. The residual vote rate is agnostic about the mechanism that produces a difference between the number of people who turned out to vote and the number of valid votes cast for an office. In considering how the residual vote rate is then used to assess the performance of voting machines, it is important to recall that "performance" is a characteristic that is interpreted broadly.

Distribution of the Residual Vote Rate across Time and Space

Figure 9.1 reports the residual vote rate, calculated at the national level, from 1988 to 2012. The rate hovered around 2.5 percent in the years immediately preceding 2000. Ironically, the residual vote rate actually *fell* in 2000, compared with the three presidential elections immediately preceding it. The rate fell again in 2004, compared with 2000,

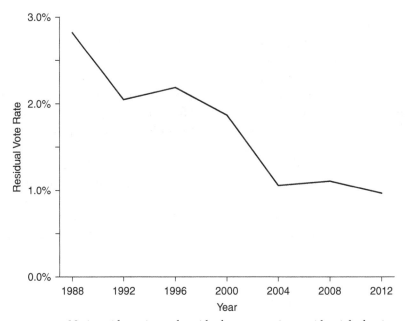

FIGURE 9.1. Nationwide estimated residual vote rate in presidential elections, 1988–2012. (*Sources*: Election Data Services [1988–1996]. State election divisions, gathered by the author [2000–2012].)

leveling off in 2008 and 2012. Viewed at its extremes during this period, from the high in 1988 (2.82 percent) to the low in 2012 (0.96 percent), the difference is 1.86 percentage points. Applied to an electorate of 130 million (i.e., 2012's turnout), that difference represents 2.4 million voters. Research reported by Ansolabehere and Stewart (2005) and Stewart (2006) suggests that about half of this reduction, or around 1 million votes, may be attributable to changes in voting technologies, particularly the abandonment of punch card machines.

The residual vote rate is not distributed uniformly across the country, as is illustrated in Figure 9.2. To show contrasts across time, Figure 9.2 shows the average rate by state in 1996, which was a year of a relatively high national residual vote rate, and 2012 to represent the new regime of relatively low rates.

A few things stand out in the comparisons in this figure. First, not all states are shaded in these maps – fourteen in 1996 and three in 2012 are unshaded. These states either did not require localities to report turnout or, in a few cases, produced turnout statistics that were clearly erroneous. Without turnout, it is, of course, impossible to calculate the residual vote rate of a state.[3]

The second thing to note is that if one had looked at the map for 1996 on the eve of the 2000 election, one could have easily picked out a set of states that were ripe for providing a voting controversy in 2000. Florida stands out, for instance, with a particularly high residual vote rate in 1996 – 2.53 percent, the eleventh highest of all the states. New Mexico, which also had its own recount controversy in 2000, had a residual vote rate of 3.34 percent in 1996, the third highest in the nation. In general, the highest rates tended to cluster in the Deep South, the industrial Midwest, and the mountain west. New England, the upper prairie states, and the far west tended to have the lowest rates.

The third thing to note is that there is a general decline in the residual vote rate across the two maps. All states but four – Kansas, Maryland, Nebraska, and Oregon – had lower residual vote rates in 2012 than in 1996. What is more, many of the states that were notoriously

---

[3] One unanswered question is whether the states that do not require localities to account for turnout independent of the number of votes cast for candidates are representative, from the perspective of the residual vote rate. A quick analysis reveals that states that did not report turnout in 1996, but that did report it in 2008, had a slightly lower residual vote rate in 2008 (1.00%), compared with those that reported the rate in both years (1.12%). For the moment, at least, it seems that the data problem has not caused a serious bias in the estimation of the nationwide residual vote rate for the past two decades, although this is a question that bears further research.

(a) 1996

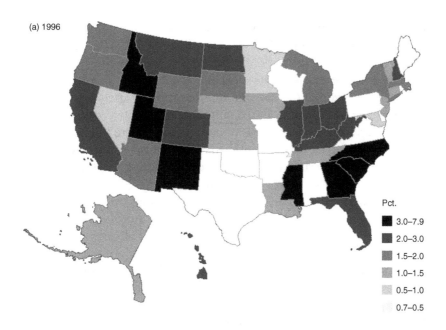

(b) 2012

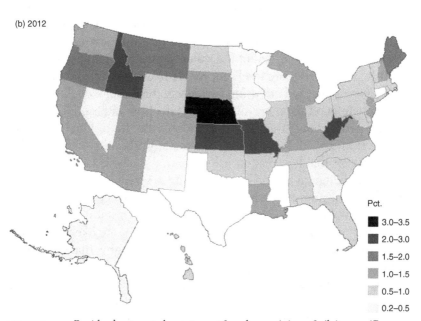

FIGURE 9.2. Residual vote rate by state, 1996 and 2012. (a.) 1996; (b.) 2012. (*Sources*: Election Data Services [1988–1996]. State election divisions, gathered by the author [2000–2012].)

Note: States shaded white did not report turnout; therefore, the residual vote rates were not calculated.

poor performers in 1996, such as New Mexico, Georgia, and Florida, had among the lowest residual vote rates in 2012.

Are There Alternatives to the Residual Vote Rate?

The residual vote rate is now the most commonly used performance measure of voting machines – so common that it holds a virtual monopoly over performance indicators. And yet it seems there should be other metrics of voting technology performance because losing votes is only one thing that can go wrong when voters use voting machines. Might not there be other measures of performance?

It is certainly true that in experimental settings, for instance, one can rely on a fuller array of measures to assess the human–machine interaction with voting technologies (Herrnson et al. 2008). However, the important question is whether such measures are possible on a national scale, lending themselves ultimately to comparisons between communities and states. No measures that are the natural by-product of running elections in all jurisdictions immediately come to mind. One could imagine that the comparison between canvassed election results and audited election results could form the basis of such a metric. However, such a metric would only be useful on a nationwide basis if all states mandated postelection audits in a uniform fashion. As it now stands, only about half of the states require such audits. As a general rule, audit results are rarely accessible to the public, and the audits themselves are carried out using a wide variety of protocols. Therefore, it is likely to be years, if ever, before postelection audits could provide another performance metric to stand alongside the residual vote rate. However, there is nothing to stop the use of the results of these audits in those states that have begun using them.

Another potential metric is time waiting to vote. Of course, this metric is hardly a pure measure of machine performance. Rather, to the degree it implicates machines, it is a measure of what it takes to *support* voting machines. Poorly performing machines are likely to induce longer lines to vote. In addition, it is possible to imagine that even *properly* performing machine types will produce lines of varying lengths, especially when the voting method requires access to a mechanical device (such as a direct-recording electronic [DRE] machine or the Los Angeles County Ink-a-Vote System), in contrast to those that could allow voters to vote anywhere there was a table.[4]

---

[4] For a thorough discussion of queue length and voting, see Allen and Bernshteyn (2006). See also Spencer and Markovits (2010) and Edelstein and Edelstein (2010).

TABLE 9.1. *Effect of voting technology on waiting time to vote,*
2008 and 2012

	Coefficient	s.e.
Voting technology		
Optical scan	Omitted category	–
Punch card	1.42	3.65
Lever	−6.69	2.44
Paper	−5.66	3.93
DRE	3.53	0.87
Year = 2012	−3.48	0.45
Constant	13.20	0.45
N	14,520	
R^2	.10	
RMSE	25.58	

Note: State fixed effects included in analysis.
Sources: Time waiting to vote taken from the 2008 and 2012 SPAE; voting
technology data gathered by the author.

Table 9.1 reports the results of two simple regressions that represent
a first attempt to assess the performance of voting machines from the
perspective of how long it takes to vote. In each case, the dependent
variable is the length of time (in minutes) respondents reported they
waited to vote in the 2008 and 2012 presidential elections. The independent variables are a series of dummy variables indicating the type
of voting machine used in the county of the respondent's residence.
I also include a dummy variable for the 2012 presidential election year.
Finally, I include state-level fixed effects, to account for unmeasured
factors that are unique to the states (such as laws that fix the allocation
of voting machines to precincts, or the prevalence of early voting).

The omitted category for the voting technology variables is optical
scanning, and thus the intercept can be interpreted as the average time
spent waiting to vote on optical scanning equipment in 2008: 13.2 minutes. The wait for lever machines was 6.7 minutes less than this, the
wait in counties with hand-counted paper was 5.7 minutes less, and the
wait for DRE machines was 3.5 minutes more.[5]

---

[5]   Only New York had mechanical lever machines, and only in 2008. Therefore, the lever
    machine coefficient can be interpreted as the average change in waiting times in New York
    that was induced by the shift to optical scanning in 2012. The negative, statistically signifi-
    cant coefficient indicates that wait times increased in New York because of this change.

The residual vote rate provides a simple and elegant way to assess the performance of voting machines, especially from the perspective of the voter hoping to have his or her vote register on Election Day. It is no doubt an imperfect measure, but no alternative has come along to supplant it or even complement it. Thus, we now turn our attention to using this measure to assess machine performance. Before doing so, it is necessary to take a quick diversion into the history of the machines we will be assessing.

CHANGES IN VOTING MACHINES OVER TIME

Voting technologies have evolved over the past century and a half. Each has arisen in response to needs defined by the political setting of the time. Because any technology interposes itself between the person and the final action, it is only to be expected that different technologies provide different opportunities to confuse and disappoint votes, just as they also respond to different felt needs of those same voters.

The earliest voting technologies were hand-counted paper-and-pencil ballots. Paper ballots for popular elections were used sporadically into the nineteenth century, with viva voce voting the norm in many places. Paper ballots printed by election officials, rather than by political parties, became ubiquitous at the end of the nineteenth century, as all states adopted some form of the Australian ballot. Although hand-counted paper ballots were for a brief period universal in the United States, by 1980 only 10 percent of American voters used this method, a fraction that dropped to less than 1 percent by 2008.

The introduction of sophisticated technology for the casting of ballots in the United States occurred in 1892, when a mechanical voting machine was first used in Lockport, New York (Saltman 2006, 112). Mechanical lever machines operate by providing an interface at the front of the machine that places the names of candidates next to levers. The levers were connected, through a series of gears and straps, to tabulator wheels that were similar to old-fashioned adding machines and car odometers. To ensure against over-voting, a series of physical devices were used to "program" the machines – for instance, to prohibit two levers from being pulled in a race for an office with a single occupant. Voters were generally able to change their votes while in the booth. With the pull of a large master lever, the mechanical counters would be incremented, the levers would be reset, the privacy curtain would be thrown open, and the machine would be ready for the next voter.

Voting devices that relied on computer punch cards were developed in the 1960s, even though the underlying technology, the Hollerith card, was developed at roughly the same time as the technology underlying mechanical lever machines. As eventually developed, punch card technologies were of two types, one relying on pre-scored cards that went by the brand name Votomatic (of Palm Beach County infamy), and another that required voters to punch through an unperforated ballot (much like the conductor's punch on a train ticket), known by the brand name DataVote. Other companies marketed their own versions of these two designs, but the Votomatic and DataVote brands so dominated that most references to punch card voting systems simply adopted these brand names as generic labels.

Also in the 1960s, vendors began developing paper-voting systems that allowed ink and pencil marks to be optically scanned by an electronic device (Jones 2010). These systems were similar to the technology used in standardized tests, which relies on "mark-sense" scanning. As with punch cards, optical scanning also comes in two major varieties. In one, the voter fills in an oval or circle next to his or her choice on the ballot, just like is done with standardized tests. In the other, the voter completes a discontinuous arrow that points to the choice she or he wishes to select; a vote is cast when the voter draws a line between an arrow's fletching and point, completing the arrow, a behavior for which there is no known analogue outside the field of voting.

The final major voting technology is the DRE. The first DREs were developed in the 1970s, emulating mechanical lever machines with push buttons replacing levers, lights replacing "X" marks, and 35 mm film replacing the mechanical wheels that counted the votes. However, as touch screen technologies and personal computers became more common and cheaper, interfaces ceased looking like full-ballot mechanical lever machines and began resembling bank ATM machines; votes ceased to be recorded physically and began to be recorded electronically.

These are the gross types of technologies. There are further refinements within each type of technology, reflecting general approaches to their implementation, and specific details that reflect the choices made by different manufactures about how to implement specific technical solutions. At the final level of detail, there are the manufacturers themselves, each of whom has had a slightly different approach to design and implementation. Before 2000, there was a dizzying array of voting machine suppliers, most of which occupied a single niche within a major voting technology type. Since 2000, there has been a steady

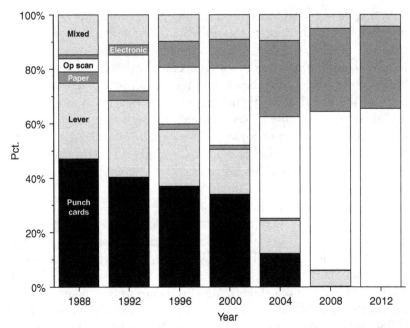

FIGURE 9.3. Voting machine usage in the United States, 1988 to 2012, as a percentage of voters. (*Sources*: Election Data Services and election returns gathered by the author from state elections divisions.)

consolidation of voting machine manufacturers, to the point that a single one currently dominates the market, Election Systems and Software (ES&S), followed by an eviscerated Premier Data Systems (the remnant of the Diebold voting machine business), and a few small niche players, such as Hart InterCivic.

Thus far I have emphasized the functional heterogeneity of voting technologies used in the United States. There is also considerable variability along the time dimension, as well. Figure 9.3 provides one view of how the use of voting machines has evolved over the past two decades. Measured by the number of voters using different technologies, at the end of the 1980s, the landscape was dominated by punch cards (dominating in the west) and lever machines (dominating in the east and south). In the 1988 election, roughly three-fourths of all voters used one of these two technologies.

If we focus on the pre–*Bush v. Gore* era, the period prior to 2000 was witnessing a gradual evolution of voting technologies, albeit within an envelope supported by stable technology-legal frameworks that had sprouted up around the country (Ansolabehere and Stewart 2008).

Mechanical lever machines were steadily giving way to DREs; the two older paper-based systems (hand-counted and punch cards) were steadily giving way to optical scanning. By 2000, optical scanning and punch cards held about two-thirds of the market, measured by voters, and three-fifths of the market, measured by jurisdictions.

Events following the 2000 presidential election conspired to accelerate the evolution of voting machine usage. Although the Help America Vote Act (HAVA) had a small role in this initial shift, more credit needs to be given to state and local officials themselves, many of whom committed to upgrading their voting equipment before the arrival of federal funds.

In the short term, there was an explosion in the use of DREs – from 2000 to 2004, their usage rates almost tripled, from 10.6 percent to 28.0 percent of voters. Almost all of this growth came at the expense of punch card systems, whose use was more than halved from one presidential election to the next, dropping from a 34.0 percent market share in 2000, to 12.2 percent in 2004.

The politics of voting machines shifted dramatically in the mid-2000s, making it more difficult for local officials to adopt DREs, as shown by the pattern of machine usage. From 2004 to the present, the adoption of new DREs has ground to a halt, owing to security controversies and to the fact that operating DREs has proven more expensive than initially thought. Indeed, 2008 represented the first presidential election in American history in which the number of jurisdictions and voters using DREs declined.[6] The growth in more modern technologies has all occurred in the optical scanning part of the market. By the 2012 election, 65 percent of voters were using optical scanning technologies to cast their ballots. DRE usage was less than half that – 30 percent of voters. Punch cards, lever machines, and hand-counted paper ballots have all virtually disappeared in federal elections.

Voting machines are not randomly distributed across states and localities. They have been chosen for a variety of reasons, ranging from the functional (a state law that mandates that all ballots be "full face" will push machine adoption in one direction, while a requirement for "office bloc" ballots will offer a wider variety of choices than a requirement for "party list" ballots) to the demographic (the smallest of communities often cannot afford any automated system, while the largest systems may find printing costs disadvantage standard optical scanning systems).

---

[6] Based on analysis of data provided by Election Data Services.

Prior to HAVA, local factors played a major role in determining which machines localities adopted. Since HAVA, differences across localities using different machines have flattened out. Prior to HAVA, DREs were used in larger counties with slightly higher incomes and more racially diverse populations. Since HAVA, optical scanners are now more likely to be used in the larger counties. The racial compositions and median incomes of counties using DREs and optical scanners are now virtually equal.

The Role of Voting Machine Heterogeneity in Assessing the Performance of Voting Machines

What is the importance of this heterogeneity, from the perspective of assessing voting machine performance using the residual vote measure? Two points seem particularly relevant. The first is that longitudinal variability in the use of voting machines has been a boon to scholars attempting to assess whether some machines perform differently than others. One of the challenges facing scholars attempting to understand the performance differences among voting machines as they are deployed in the field is the fact that they are not distributed randomly across localities. First, localities are often constrained by state laws and regulations in the machines they can choose. Second, the choice of voting equipment by localities may be correlated with factors that make it more or less likely that voters in those localities will have difficulties navigating *any* type of voting technology (Ansolabehere 2002; Garner and Spolaore 2005; Knack and Kropf 2002; Saltman 2006). Thus, if we do a cross-sectional study that correlates the types of machines localities use with performance measures, such as the residual vote rate, it is not clear whether correlations we discover are attributable to machine-related factors or simply a reflection of a spurious correlation that influence *both* the selection of voting machines *and* the ability to use voting machines without making mistakes.

Longitudinal analysis blunts this problem, although it does not eliminate it altogether. Consider two hypothetical neighboring towns that at time *t* both use hand-counted paper ballots. The choice of hand-counted paper ballots was made in the past (implicitly or explicitly) as a consequence of a long list of causal factors. In the short term, those factors are held constant *within* each community. Now, suppose that after the election in time *t*, one of the towns, Town A, switches to optical scanning. Because social-economic characteristics of towns change slowly, it is unlikely that the choice by Town A stems from a sudden shift in the types of demographic characteristics that would lead its residents to make fewer (or more) mistakes voting. Thus, if we observe in the election at time $t + 1$ that Town A's residual vote rate has plummeted, whereas the residual vote rate of Town B has remained the same, we can treat this as a quasi experiment, and consider the relative change in residual vote rates between the two towns, comparing their rates at time t to their rates at time $t + 1$, as a measure of the degree to which optical scanners induce fewer ballot mistakes, compared with paper.

A real-life example can help to illustrate this point. The example is taken from Massachusetts, which has been gathering the data that make calculating residual vote rates possible at the town level going back to the 1880s. I have assembled that data going back to 1960, along with information about the voting technology used by each town in the state.[7] In 1960, 97 percent of the state's towns, and 77 percent of its voters, voted on hand-counted paper ballots. Starting in the late 1960s, towns that used hand-counted paper began to shift to automated technologies, first punch cards (beginning in 1968) and then optical scanning (beginning in 1988). By 1996, the height of voting technology diversity in the state, 6.7 percent of voters used hand-counted paper, 17.2 percent used lever machines, 20.7 percent used punch cards, and 55.4 percent used optical scanners.

The year the greatest number of towns switched from paper ballots to punch cards – and the midpoint in the transition – was 1980, when thirty-four towns took the plunge. Of these, fifteen stayed with punch cards until they were banned by the state, following a "Palm Beach County" moment in a 1998 congressional primary.[8] In other words, we have the residual vote records of fifteen towns that all had experience with hand-counted paper from 1960 to 1976, followed by experience with punch cards from 1980 to 1996. As a comparison group, we have another 112 towns that never strayed from the use of paper throughout the entire time.

Figure 9.4 plots the residual vote rates of the two groups of towns – those that switched from paper to punch cards for the 1980 presidential

---

[7] Voting technology data were gathered using the files of the Elections Divisions of the Massachusetts secretary of state. I thank Melanie Wang for her research assistance in the data gathering process.

[8] Those towns were Bellingham, Belmont, Beverly, Cohasset, Dudley, Hull, Lowell, Maynard, Medway, Orleans, South Hadley, Swansea, Taunton, Webster, and Weston.

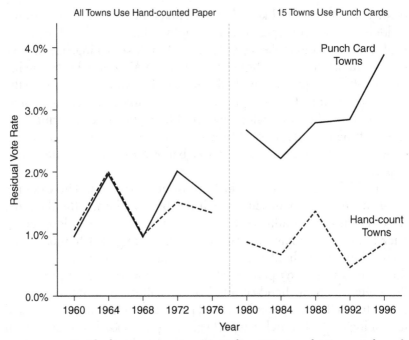

FIGURE 9.4. Residual vote rates among Massachusetts towns adopting punch cards after 1976, compared with towns that never switched from hand-counted paper ballots. (*Sources*: Massachusetts Election Statistics [P.D. 43], various years; voting machine data gathered by the author from the files of the State Elections Division.)

election and those that never switched at all.[9] Prior to the divide between the elections of 1976 and 1980, the residual vote rates of the two sets of towns were quite similar. Before 1980, the average difference in residual vote rates between the two groups was 0.11 percent higher for the punch card towns. After (and including) 1980 that difference grew to 2.04 percent, for a net shift of 1.93 percentage points. In proportional terms, the differences between the two sets of towns grew by a factor of 17.

Close examination of Figure 9.4 reveals that the residual vote rates of the two groups began to diverge somewhat in the elections of 1972 and 1976. This may, in fact, be an indication that the towns that eventually abandoned paper were beginning to experience problems that the adoption of punch cards were supposed to allay – problems that were

---

[9] The residual vote rates of the two groups are calculated by summing the turnout and "blank ballots" for each group, in each year, and dividing aggregate blank ballots by aggregate turnout. Thus, the residual vote rate in each group is weighted by the relative size of the towns contributing to the rate. (In Massachusetts, a "blank" ballot is simply the accounting difference between official turnout and the total number of legal votes cast in an election. "Blank" ballots may, in fact, include over-votes.)

not being experienced by the towns that never switched from paper. Thus, relying on the switch in voting machines is not a randomized experiment, but it may be treated as such if the choice to switch is only weakly correlated with factors that influence the residual vote rate in the cross section.[10]

In summary, longitudinal variation in the use of voting machines by states and localities provides a laboratory for researchers to assess the performance of voting machines in the field, controlling in the short term for most of the factors that might confound a cross-sectional analysis. That is the primary effect of *longitudinal* variation in voting machines on the study of their performance. What is the effect of the second major dimension of variation, among subtypes of equipment?

In theory, the presence of many different types of voting machines of each type should allow us greater precision in further specifying which *specific features* of machine design lead to more or fewer errors by voters. Indeed, there are a few clever studies that have exploited known characteristics of different machines to get at some of these differences, such as Frisina et al. (2008) and Kropf and Kimball (2011).

Studies like these are exemplary. Why are there not more of them? The primary reason is that record keeping about which machines are used by states and localities is so lousy. It is telling, for instance, that when the Election Assistance Commission (EAC) first surveyed all election jurisdictions in the United States about the voting technologies they use, the most commonly mentioned model was "N/A." In other words, it is clear that the great bulk of local officials, who were presumably responding to the survey, were not terribly aware of the distinctions between machines – or that the distinctions are not salient enough to report them to the federal government when asked.

As a consequence, most studies that use the residual vote rate to study machine performance at the national level must end up lumping quite dissimilar equipment together into single categories. "Optical scanners" include both central-count and precinct-count scanners. "DREs" lump together machines that are full-faced with those that present just one or two offices at a time; this category lumps together machines in which voters make a choice by pushing a physical button with those in which voters have to work a wheel or a joystick.

---

[10] It is possible to make an even stronger argument, which is that the abandonment of punch cards was an actual quasi-experiment, since it is clear that these towns would not have abandoned them at that time had they not been required to by the secretary of state. In a similar vein, changes away from punch cards and lever machines to new equipment *after* 2002 and the passage of HAVA more resemble quasi experiments than the changes before HAVA.

Thus, the dummy variables that indicate machine types are full of measurement error. It is well known that random measurement error attenuates the *estimated* statistical effect, compared with the *actual* statistical effect. In other words, when we estimate that (a diverse set of) punch cards, on average, produced higher residual vote rates than (a diverse set of) optical scan machines, we have to be certain that there are at least *some* comparisons involving *particular types* of punch cards and *particular types* of optical scanners in which the differences are even greater than the average differences. More troubling, when we discover that there is a tiny and statistically insignificant difference in residual vote rates between two machine types, we cannot know if this is because there really is no difference in average performance between the two machine types or if it is because the estimated differences are being underestimated because of a massive amount of measurement error.

Homogeneity cuts both ways in using the residual vote rate to assess the performance of voting machines. It helps by providing longitudinal variation, which supports analysis that treats changes to voting machines by counties and towns as quasi experiments. It hurts by pooling together voting machines that share a broad category but that differ significantly in key details of design.

VOTING TECHNOLOGY AND RESIDUAL VOTE RATES: A STATISTICAL ANALYSIS

Of most interest in this chapter is the degree to which voting machine types are associated with different residual vote rate levels. Previous research, cited earlier, suggests they are. In this section, I reproduce those findings on a focused set of observations, using election results from the two presidential elections before the passage of HAVA (1996 and 2000) and the three elections after the passage of HAVA (2004, 2008, and 2012). I start by analyzing national patterns and then move to the analysis of patterns within one state, Massachusetts. I finish by illustrating how the residual vote rate can also be used to analyze the performance of actual *machines*, in as fine a grained analysis of voting machines using the residual vote rate as possible.

Nationwide

I start at the national level. The dependent variable is the residual vote rate, defined earlier, measured at the county level. The first analysis parallels research by Ansolabehere and Stewart (2005). In addition to dummy variables for each of the major voting technology categories (optical scanning is the omitted category), there is a control for turnout (intended to capture the effects of more inexperienced voters in high-turnout years), a dummy variable for each election year (1996 is the omitted category here), and fixed effects of two types: first, an effect for each county, to capture unmeasured demographic and policy-related factors that might influence the residual vote rate, and second, a series of year × state interactions, to capture the effects of candidate competitiveness in each state in each year.

The results of the regression are reported in Table 9.2. The coefficients are largely consistent with previous research. The large coefficient associated with punch cards – 0.79 percentage points – quantifies

TABLE 9.2. *Effect of changing voting technology on the residual vote rate, 1996–2012*

	Coefficient	s.e.
Voting technology type		
Optical scanning	Omitted category	–
Punch card	0.79	0.05
Lever machine	0.03	0.09
Hand-counted paper	0.24	0.20
DRE	0.11	0.05
Pct. ballots by mail, statewide	–	–
Election year		
1996	Omitted category	–
2000	−0.47	0.58
2004	−1.14	1.73
2008	−1.37	1.63
2012	−1.39	0.56
Log (turnout)	1.31	0.18
Constant	−13.22	2.17
N	11,509	
R^2	.64	
RMSE	0.94	

Note: State × year fixed effects. Coefficient may be interpreted in terms of percentage points.
Source: Election return and voting technology data for 1996, 2000, and 2012 purchased from Election Data Systems. Data for 2004 and 2008 gathered by the author.

the large gain in terms of lost votes that was made when jurisdictions abandoned punch cards in favor of optical scanning. The coefficient associated with DREs is also positive and statistically significant, although the size of the coefficient is much smaller than that associated with punch card machines. Because the residual vote rates of all the machines except punch cards are statistically similar, this suggests that a move from punch cards to *any other technology*, notably optical scanners and DREs, also led to a substantial gain, in terms of recovering lost votes.

Voting Technology and Residual Votes in One State

In the previous section, I conducted the sort of nationwide analysis of the residual vote rate that is typically done. As noted previously, this type of analysis has to deal with a tremendous amount of heterogeneity among voting machine types and administrative practices. One hopes that through the inclusion of fixed effects for counties, some of this variability is accounted for, but it is not possible to be certain.

Another strategy for dealing with the large amount of nationwide heterogeneity is to conduct analysis explaining variation in the residual vote rate at a more granular scale, such as the state level. State-level studies of residual vote rates attributable to technology have rarely been done, probably because the number of counties within a state is small, compared with the nation as a whole. Exceptions are Stewart (2004) on Georgia and Alvarez et al. (2011) on California.

Massachusetts is one state where there is less concern about losing statistical leverage by focusing on a single state. The data are available in Massachusetts to produce a study of the same statistical power necessary to estimate residual vote rates across different voting machines with some precision. Elections are administered at the town level in the Bay State, which gives us 351 units of analysis for each election we study. Massachusetts has been gathering the necessary data to construct residual vote rate statistics going back to the nineteenth century, and I have assembled a data set of voting technologies used by the towns going back to 1960. The demographic homogeneity of Massachusetts towns is a feature of the state that has made it a laboratory for public finance economics research for decades.

At the same time, the voting technologies used in Massachusetts are less varied than the nation as a whole. For instance, the only type of lever machine used from 1960 onward was the AVM, and optical scanners

TABLE 9.3. *Effect of changing voting technology on the residual vote rate in Massachusetts, 1960–2012*

	Coefficient	s.e.
Voting technology type		
Optical scanning	Omitted category	–
Punch card	1.44	0.05
Lever machine	0.33	0.06
Hand-counted paper	0.04	0.05
Election year		
1960	Omitted category	–
1964	1.03	0.05
1968	−0.07	0.05
1972	0.80	0.05
1976	0.56	0.05
1980	−0.24	0.06
1984	−0.13	0.06
1988	0.55	0.06
1992	0.23	0.06
1996	0.49	0.07
2000	0.22	0.07
2004	−0.33	0.07
2008	−0.14	0.07
2012	−0.32	0.07
Constant	0.86	0.06
N	4,913	
R^2	.59	
RMSE	0.69	

Note: Town fixed effects. Coefficients may be interpreted in terms of percentage points.

Source: Election data taken from Massachusetts Public Document 43, various years. Voting technology data gathered by the author using the files of the Massachusetts secretary of state.

have always been used in precinct-count mode. Massachusetts is one of the rare remaining "for cause" absentee voting states, so that the confounding problems of rising vote-by-mail is not so much of an issue.[11]

Table 9.3 reports the results of a regression run on the Massachusetts data. As before, the omitted category of voting machines is optical

---

[11] In 2008, the absentee voting rate, reported by the VRS, was 5.7 percent.

scanning. Also as before, the one voting technology with a significantly worse performance level, measured by the residual vote rate, is punch cards. These results suggest that the national results are potentially robust when we take the analysis to a more finely tuned level.

One further advantage of taking the residual vote analysis to a state level is the possibility to extend the analysis to lower offices and to ballot measures. One of the factors that has limited the extension of analysis that examines voting machine performance below the presidential race is the overwhelming amount of heterogeneity in the voting booth that confounds analysis of these lesser offices. An accumulation of results from state studies can help overcome this deficiency in the research literature.

The Residual Vote Rate as a Different Sort of Individual Machine Performance

I end this section by demonstrating the value of the residual vote rate at the lowest level of disaggregation possible: the voting machine itself. The nature of election statistics makes analysis on individual machine data impractical in most settings. Furthermore, unless there are machine-specific hypotheses to be examined – such as the hypothesis that machines deployed in certain types of settings tend to produce more residual votes than machines deployed in other settings – there is little analytical advantage to analyzing the residual vote rates of individual machines.

Sometimes, however, such hypotheses *can* be tested. One such time was following the 2006 House election in the thirteenth congressional district of Florida – an election that ended up in court because of unusually high residual vote rates on DREs used for in-precinct and early voting. These high residual vote rates did not appear on absentee ballots, which were cast on optically scanned paper.[12]

A practical issue raised in the election dispute was whether the large number of under-votes, in addition to what appeared to be vote "flipping" (i.e., vote selections changing inexplicably), were attributable to calibration errors in the touch screens used on the ES&S iVotronic

---

[12] For published descriptions of this election see Frisina (2008) and Amunson (2008–2009). In the interest of full disclosure, I was an expert witness on behalf of Christine Jennings, who challenged the result of the election unsuccessfully. For my own take on the subject, see Stewart (2006).

DRE. Evidence presented at the trial court level suggested that there was something to this thought. Figure 9.5 displays the residual vote rate (in the congressional race) of all DREs used in early and in-precinct voting in Sarasota County, plotted against the day on which the voting machine was prepared to be deployed in the election. (The horizontal axis shows the number of days before Election Day.) Data tokens are proportional to the number of votes cast on the machines prepared each day.

Note the strong positive slope in this relationship. The slope coefficient, 0.28 (s.e. = 0.05) suggests that for each additional day closer to Election Day that a machine was prepared to go into the field, the expected residual vote rate increased by approximately one-quarter of one percentage point. Although this may seem like a small amount, voting machines were prepared over a one-and-a-half-month period, which results in an expected residual vote rate gap, comparing machines prepared at the end of the period with machines prepared at the beginning, of 13.2 percentage points.

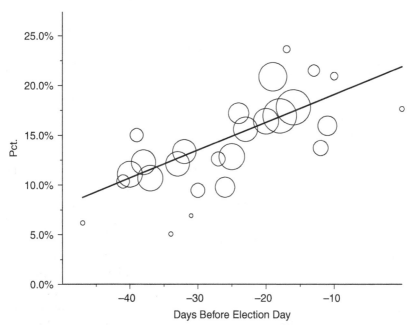

FIGURE 9.5. Residual vote rate of DREs used in Sarasota County, Florida, in the thirteenth congressional district race, 2006, as a function of the date on which the machine was "cleared and tested." (*Source*: Machine log files obtained from the Sarasota County supervisor of elections.)

The point of presenting this analysis is not to relitigate this disputed election, but, rather, to demonstrate the versatility of the residual vote metric. It is useful for more than just comparing across voting machines, or for documenting the wisdom of HAVA in mandating the retirement of punch card technologies (or the foolishness of mandating the retirement of lever machines). It is a broad-based diagnostic tool that can be used at many levels of granularity, to assess both the performance of voting equipment and the overall health of administrative practices.

Is There a Lower Bound to the Residual Vote Rate?

One question that naturally arises in the use of the residual vote rate as a diagnostic tool is what its lower bound is. A common misunderstanding of the residual vote rate is a belief in some quarters that the lower bound should be zero. However, because the residual vote rate is a composite that includes under-votes attributable to intentional abstentions, it is clear that the residual vote rate is bounded at the low end by a strictly positive number, especially in large jurisdictions. What is that number?

The first way to estimate the lower bound is through self-reported abstentions in the presidential election revealed in nationally representative public opinion surveys. Perusal of large academic studies, such as the American National Election Study (ANES) and the Cooperative Congressional Election Study (CCES), reveal that this number varies from around one-quarter of 1 percent to three-quarters of 1 percent. By this method, the lower bound should be "around" half of 1 percent, on average, year to year.

A second method is to rely on the election returns from Nevada, which allows voters to select the option of "none of these candidates" in presidential elections. This choice provides another, more reliable, estimate of the abstention rate, at least for Nevada. In 2000, 0.54 percent of Nevada voters chose this option in the presidential race, followed by 0.44 percent in 2004, 0.65 percent in 2008, and 0.57 percent in 2012. Perhaps not surprisingly, since 2000 Nevada has had among the lowest residual vote rates of any state, checking in at 0.61 percent in 2000, 0.27 percent in 2004, 0.22 percent in 2008, and 0.17 percent in 2012. Again, the returns from Nevada suggest the wisdom of the "around half of 1 percent" estimate for the residual vote rate's lower bound in presidential elections.

A third method is to examine the distribution of residual vote rates at the jurisdiction level, to ascertain whether there appears to be a

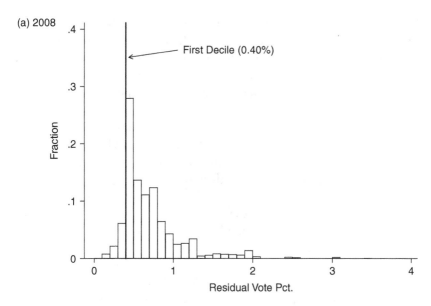

(a) 2008

First Decile (0.40%)

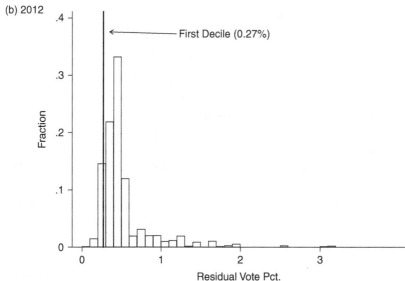

(b) 2012

First Decile (0.27%)

FIGURE 9.6. Distribution of residual vote rates in Massachusetts towns, 2008 and 2012 (towns with turnout greater than 200). (a.) 2008; (b.) 2012. (*Sources:* Massachusetts Election Statistics [P.D. 43], various years.)

practical floor to the rate in counties and towns that administer elections. Figure 9.6 shows the distribution of the residual vote rate for all Massachusetts towns with turnout levels greater than 200 voters in 2008 and 2012. Note that in these two examples (which appear to be typical), the distribution is positively skewed; in addition, on the left side of the distribution, the number of cases at the left end of the distribution drops off precipitously around the location of the first decile town. (The location of the first decile town is indicated in each distribution with a vertical line.) The first decile town had a residual vote rate of 0.40 percent in 2008 and 0.27 percent in 2012.

The shorter nationwide time series of the location of the first decile county shows a similar pattern to that of Massachusetts for the 1996–2012 period, when the two series overlap. The nationwide average for this period is 0.52 percent, almost exactly at the "half of 1 percent" floor.

We can draw two conclusions from this brief exercise. The first is that the lower bound certainly varies from year to year, and, no doubt, from jurisdiction to jurisdiction, depending on the attractiveness of the candidates at the top of the ticket. The second, though, is that in the post-HAVA period, there seems to be a lower bound at 0.5 percent. Anything well above that – to suggest another rule of thumb, a 1 percent residual vote rate – should bring further scrutiny to see what factors, beyond abstention, are leading to excessive lost votes.[13]

CONCLUSIONS AND RECOMMENDATIONS

To conclude, the residual vote rate has proven to be a valuable tool in assessing the performance of voting machines at a highly aggregated level. It helped to pinpoint the location of machine-related problems in the 2000 election and informed the drafting of the HAVA. It is an easy measure to implement and to understand. Like all measures, it must be used cautiously and with an appreciation of its limitations. With that in mind, it is a powerful and useful measure.

It is unfortunate that three states still do not report total turnout, which means that residents of those states do not have access to the most basic of machine-related performance measures. This is a problem that is easily remedied – the legislatures in those states could mandate its reporting. Given the recent concern over potential voter fraud expressed by members of state legislatures, it is surprising that such a noncontroversial tool that could also guard against fraud is not being used universally in the United States.

---

[13] In Massachusetts, the number of towns with more than 200 voters turning out in 2012 that had residual vote rates above 1 percent was 28 of 347 towns, or 8 percent of towns. Nationwide, the number of counties with more than 200 voters turning out in 2012 that had residual vote rates above 1 percent was 1,916 of 3,154 counties, or 61 percent of counties.

However, this does not let the forty-eight states and the District of Columbia that *do* report turnout off the hook. So far as I know, only one state, Florida, has begun reporting the residual vote rate on its own. Indeed, most states still keep the turnout report segregated far from the report of vote totals. The reason for this is undoubtedly administrative inertia. However, it would be an inexpensive sign of administrative far-sightedness for the secretary of state or election director to begin bringing together the data already in the state's possession to report this rate – not just for the state as a whole, but for jurisdictions within the state, as well.

Nor does the lack of widespread reporting of the residual vote rate leave the U.S. EAC off the hook. One of the provisions of HAVA was a mandate that the residual vote rate be reported on a regular basis by the EAC. That has yet to happen, and there is no indication that it will happen in the near future.

At the same time, it is important to begin building measurement strategies that go beyond the residual vote rate. As suggested in this chapter, the data generated through the growing number of postelection audits could potentially be used to develop more nuanced measures of machine performance. Other indicators covered in this volume, such as the wait time to vote or voter confidence, could also be used to assess voting machines.

The residual vote rate is a powerful measure of voting machine performance that has been used for more than a decade. Although it has its limitations, it remains the sole performance metric in many settings. If protecting the franchise is the top goal of election administration, then the residual vote rate is a particularly appropriate measure, because it is a direct measure of the degree to which the choices that voters make are actually recorded when the election is over.

Voter Confidence as a Metric of Election Performance

Paul Gronke

Public confidence in the integrity of the electoral process has independent significance, because it encourages citizen participation in the democratic process.[1]

Justice John Paul Stevens, *Crawford v. Marion County*

In the wake of the major electoral controversies of 2000 and 2004, "voter confidence" has entered the political lexicon and is altering the debate over election reform in this country. Often, voter confidence is used as a political slogan. Voter confidence may not rank with motherhood and apple pie, but surely it's something that no one opposes. Who, after all, would want a democratic electorate that did not trust the legitimacy of democratic procedures? The title of a major 2004 postelection report, *Building Confidence in U.S. Elections,* makes no bones about its underlying motive: "polls indicate that many Americans lack confidence in the electoral system.... Building confidence in U.S. elections is central to our nation's democracy" (Commission on Federal Election Reform 2005, iii). Reporters include "voter confidence" as a theme in stories about elections and election administration. A Lexis-Nexis search from 2001 to 2010 of major U.S. newspapers turned up 1,766 articles using the phrase "voter confidence," 1,542 mentions of "voter confidence" with "elections," and 291 mentions of "voter confidence" with either "election reform" or "election administration."

Policy makers, politicians, and even the Supreme Court were attentive. They believed that voter confidence would respond to reforms in election administration. Writing in 2006, Ray Martinez, then vice

Thanks to Jacob Canter and Alex Arpaia of Reed College, who provided able research support, and Michael McDonald and the editors for comments.

[1] *Crawford v. Marion County Board of Elections,* 553 U.S. 07–21, p. 13.

chairman of the Federal Election Assistance Commission, bemoaned the erosion of voter confidence:

> A *Wall Street Journal*–NBC News poll, for example, taken shortly after the 2004 presidential election, showed that more than 25% of those surveyed worried that the vote count in the 2004 presidential race was unfair. More recently, the American Bar Association released a nationally commissioned poll showing that some 20% of Americans surveyed have lingering doubts that their vote was accurately counted in the 2004 presidential election (Martinez 2006). Martinez went on to argue for a four point program of reform: election audits, conflict of interest provisions for statewide election administrators, political neutrality requirements for vendors, and disclosure requirements as a condition of voting system certification. These changes, he asserted, would restore voter confidence in the system.
>
> Jennifer Brunner, who served as Ohio's Secretary of State from 2007 to 2011, said that voter confidence would be boosted by post-election audits (Brunner 2008). Representative Rush Holt (D-NJ-12) has regularly attempted to codify "voter confidence" into law; since 2003, he has introduced and reintroduced the "Voter Confidence and Increased Accessibility Act," which implicitly assumes that moving to a system of paper ballots with voter-ver-ified paper records will improve voter confidence. Legislators in Hawaii believe that voter confidence will be boosted if voting results are publicly posted within an hour of the poll's closing, while in Tennessee, the Senate argues that discretionary use of optical scanning machines will enhance voter confidence.[2]

Finally, there is the case of photo identification at the polls. Justice Stevens, widely recognized as one of the most liberal jurists on the court until he retired in 2010, saw fit to dedicate a whole section of the *Crawford* decision to "Safeguarding Voter Confidence," and a presumed relationship between the use of photo ID and voter confidence was one of the underpinnings of the decision. That Stevens relied on voter confidence is not surprising; political debates over photo identification at the polls in Texas, Ohio, Georgia, and other states invariably have cited the restoration of "voter confidence" as a primary argument for the ID requirement.

What remains surprising about this reliance on "voter confidence" as a key indicator of the health of our democratic system and a justifi-cation for potentially restricting access to the polls is that the measure itself has been subject to little critical scrutiny. Voter perceptions may

---

[2]   These bills are SB787 from Hawaii's 2013 session and HB386 from Tennessee's 2012 session.

be only tangentially related to anything in control of election administrators. Previous scholarship has shown that voter confidence may be
prone to manipulation by partisan actors who are disgruntled about the
election outcome, by well-intentioned election reformers who are suspicious of particular voting technologies, and by media actors who spotlight a small number of cases of fraud and error without mentioning the
many elections that come off without a hitch. Even though individual
levels of voter confidence are systematically related to some aspects of
election administration, most notably the mode of casting the ballot,
they are also strongly influenced by partisan and ideological considerations. Many have noted, for instance, the common appearance of
"winner's regret": voters who cast a ballot for the losing presidential candidate are far more likely to suspect that their votes may not be counted
as cast. Sour grapes are no better for judging election performance than
they are for making wine. These results provide ready fodder for anyone
ready to attack individual attitudinal measures about election performance. These same scholars, however, have found systematic patterns
underlying the voter confidence measure that relate to election administration. Stewart shows that Oregon and Washington voters – where
vote-by-mail is mandatory – express lower levels of confidence (Stewart
2010). Finally, it is possible that the voter confidence measure is more
noise than signal, and even if there are systematic elements, they are
swamped by random variation and idiosyncratic elements.

This chapter evaluates the well-known voter confidence measure
employed by a number of scholars and election observers as a potentially key metric to gauge election performance. The chapter starts
with a methodological commentary on the development of the measure, pointing out the unusual trajectory by which the measure first
appeared in the social scientific literature. The chapter then turns to
an evaluation of the reliability and validity of the measure, paying particularly close attention to demographic and partisan factors that affect
these attitudes. Finally, it closes by asking whether state laws mandating
greater public scrutiny of vote counts and voting equipment improve
voter confidence.

Voter Confidence: From Political Slogan to Social Science Concept?

There is no shortage of political claims about voter confidence. The
selections at the start of this chapter provide just a small taste. The scholarly samplings may be less piquant, but provide more substance. Thad

Hall, a leading scholar of election administration and policy, writes that "recently, scholars have begun to study the attitudes of voters in regards to their election experience [...] these data have provided a baseline for understanding the factors that affect the confidence of voters, especially race and party affiliation." Hall argues that it is possible to link voter confidence to specific features of the voter experience such as voter–poll worker interactions or whether the voter is asked to show identification at the polls (2008, 8–9). Charles Stewart (2009) describes voter confidence as a "summary judgment of the voting experience." Lonna Atkeson (2011, 4) identifies voter confidence as a "critical property of election reform efforts," one that is used to favor "voter [*sic*] technologies that provide a verifiable vote" and a measure that provides important insights into citizens beliefs about "governmental processes" versus the more common focus on "diffuse system support . . . or external efficacy" (see also Atkeson and Saunders 2007).

Voter confidence as a social science concept remains ambiguous, however, because its meaning has changed over time. It is hard not to wonder whether "voter confidence" is a case where the cart has preceded the horse: a paucity of theorizing, conceptual development, and qualitative study but substantial quantitative measurement.[3]

We might start with the semantic approach. The term *confidence* has two dictionary definitions. The first could be termed *self-confidence*: "a feeling or consciousness of one's powers or of reliance on one's circumstances." The second meaning changes the point of reference to one's relationships with others: "a relation of trust of intimacy; reliance on another's discretion; support especially in a legislative body."[4] *Confidence*, in short, may refer either to the individual self-empowerment or a relationship of trust with other individuals, groups, or institutions. Scholarly usage of "voter confidence" prior to 2000 reflected primarily the second, social meaning of confidence. *Voter confidence* is a shorthand term used to describe trust or faith in the political system, in political parties, or in political outcomes, particularly before and after major changes in the method of allocating seats to votes (the election formula).[5]

---

[3]　Goertz writes: "concepts lie at the core of social science theory and methodology. They provide substance to theories; they form the basis of measurement; and they influence the selection of cases." His "second law" states that "the amount of attention devoted to a concept is inversely related to the attention devoted to the quantitative measure" (2005, 1–2).

[4]　Definitions from the Merriam-Webster dictionary, http://www.merriam-webster.com/dictionary/confidence.

[5]　A Google Scholar search from 1991 to 2000 returns 186 results, most of which come from articles about party politics, direct democracy, and public policy.

Voter confidence appears far more in the scholarly literature post 2000.[6] A substantial number of articles in the first few years of the decade were technical reports and documents related to electronic voting machines and contributed to the technology changes codified in the Help America Vote Act of 2002. Although Sances and Stewart (2012) note that the first appearances of items asking about a voter's confidence in the ballot count appeared in media polls in 2000, no academic surveys included the term until 2004.[7] The transition to the dominant scholarly usage among survey researchers and election analysts was led by two of the most prominent political scientists studying election administration, R. Michael Alvarez and Thad Hall, who first used the term in a 2004 publication on the California recall election (Alvarez et al. 2004). Alvarez, Hall, and Llewellyn (2008, 755) provide perhaps the most specific definition of the concept, defining "trust in the electoral process as the confidence that the voters have that their ballot is counted as intended."

Some residual disagreements on the precise meaning of the term remain, but when examined closely, these distill down to disagreements about causes, not about concepts. Atkeson, for example, argues in a series of papers that voter confidence is a "process-based" measure, one based on a citizen's direct experience with governmental functions and thus stands in contrast (and causally prior) to more system-level concepts, such as diffuse support and trust in government (Atkeson 2011; Hall, Alvarez, and Atkeson 2012). Gronke and Hicks (2009) are more skeptical, arguing that voter confidence may be part of "a bundle of attitudes about government and institutions, that generally falls under the rubric of trust in government and confidence in institutions." Atkeson has also promoted the idea that voter confidence may have different targets – one's own ballot, the ballots in a local jurisdiction, and the ballots nationwide. Sances and Stewart (2012) use a similar distinction, discriminating between "egotropic" and "sociotropic" voter confidence. Nonetheless, there has been little fundamental disagreement about the measure and little testing and comparison of alternative survey-based items.[8]

---

[6] A Google Scholar search returns 830 results from 2001 to 2010.

[7] I suspect that some conference and working papers were already appearing, but I have not to date been able to recover these via Google Scholar or other searches.

[8] This is the case in the United States even though a wider variety of evaluative measures appear in surveys conducted in other countries that often ask about election fairness, honesty, or the amount of malpractice (Gronke 2013). It is also possible, though never tested in

Voter Confidence as a Survey Measure

The most commonly used voter confidence survey item reads:

> How confident are you that your vote was [or will be] counted as intended in [the election]?
>
> 1. Very confident
> 2. Fairly [somewhat] confident
> 3. Not too confident
> 4. Not at all confident

The target of the item is "your vote" without any specific reference to one political office, and the respondent is asked if it will be "counted as intended." There have not been any attempts to test this item experimentally, including variants on the question wording, such as "counted as cast" or even "counted accurately," a usage that is common among private firms.

A recent innovative paper by Sances and Stewart (2012) took a different approach, assembling a comprehensive archive of thirty-four mainly nonacademic uses of some variant of a voter confidence item. Sances and Stewart lump the items into two broad categories: ones that ask about the respondent's own vote ("egotropic") and ones that ask about vote counting generally or nationwide ("sociotropic"). With some variations, these items usually ask, "How confident are you that your vote was [will be] accurately counted?" In 2000, two national polls (CBS and the *LA Times*) and in 2004, ABC/*Washington Post*, all included the additional prompt "your presidential vote," but none have since that year. The "sociotropic" items show more variation in question wording. Gallup/*USA Today* often used the inelegant (and potentially double-barreled) "votes will be accurately cast and counted in this year's election," while Pew, the National Annenberg Election Survey, and ABC all ask whether "votes across the country were accurately counted." Virtually all polls use the phrase "accurately counted" rather than the academic usage "as intended."[9]

---

the U.S. case, that other "sociotropic" measures of voter confidence, such as confidence that the identified winner was the actual winner as chosen by a plurality of voters, but these sorts of items have never, to this writer's knowledge, been asked.

9   Appendix 1 in Sances and Stewart (2012) contains the full list of surveys and question wordings.

Finally, Atkeson (2011) argues that voter confidence reflects the federal nature of the American electoral system. In addition to asking about one's own vote, Atkeson promotes items that ask about the confidence in the count at the local jurisdiction level and at the state level. Because Atkeson is more interested in voter confidence as an experiential, process-based attitude, these moves seem natural. On what basis can individual voters hazard an opinion about the accuracy of the vote count nationwide? By implication, Atkeson argues that we should not be surprised if these sociotropic measures are unduly influenced by diffuse attitudes, such as trust in the federal government, confidence in the performance of individual political leaders, or the outcome of the national election.

A decade after survey researchers began to ask about voter confidence, there is no consensus about question wording. Is it better to ask if your vote was counted "accurately" or "as intended"? Do citizens see discriminations between their own votes and votes counting at different levels (county versus state versus nationally)? The field would benefit from a careful assessment of these competing formulations of these survey items.

Voter Confidence over Time, Space, and Individuals

The first half of this chapter provided a critical examination of voter confidence as a conceptual category and survey measure. The rest of this chapter returns to the question that animated our opening discussion: Does voter confidence respond in systematic ways to levers that are in the control of election administrators (as Justice Stevens implicitly argued in the *Crawford* decision), or is it primarily a response to features outside the control of political actors? We would not want to evaluate the performance of American elections based on changes in consumer sentiment, for example. The focus of this analysis is to disentangle the impact of laws and policies from an individual's voting experience from more diffuse evaluations of the political system.

Specifically, in the analysis that follows, I compare four categories in terms of their impact on voter confidence:

1. **State laws.** The presence of postelection audits, required identification at the polls, and required photo identification at the polls.
2. **Mode of voting.** Voting early in person, by mail, and at the polling place.

3. **Perceptions of the voting experience.** Poll worker performance, trust in local election officials (LEOs), and reported problems with voting machines.
4. **Loser's regret and partisanship.**

These categories are ordered by the degree of control held by election administrators, state officials, and legislators. For example, the requirement for photo identification is controlled by the state legislature. If it can be shown that photo identification has no influence on voter confidence, then this ought to lessen this as a consideration in debates over ID at the polls. A local official, in most cases, does not choose the mode of balloting (except where voting by mail is mandated or where alternative modes are not available), but officials can make one or another mode more easily accessible. The third category may strike election officials as problematic; after all, do officials have any influence over how citizens evaluate poll workers or how much trust citizens express in LEOs? The answer insofar as poll workers are concerned is strongly affirmative: extensive research has demonstrated that better poll worker recruitment and training translates directly into an improved voter experience and higher confidence in election administration (Claasen et al. 2008; Hall, Monson, and Patterson 2009). While the "trust in election officials" measure is a new one, I would argue that it is also responsive to the actual performance of LEOs.[10]

The fourth category is likely the one that raises the most hackles among election administrators. They have no control over who wins or loses the election, nor do they determine the partisanship of their election constituencies. The tendency of voters to blame election administrators for their party's loss of the presidency is certainly regrettable, and, as I show in the following, there is an even more unfortunate tendency for those from the losing side to express even higher levels of concern about voter fraud.

The analysis in this chapter uses four data sources: the 2008 and 2012 Surveys of the Performance of American Elections (SPAE) and the 2008 and 2010 CCES. These surveys have been supplemented with information on state laws and procedures (audits, identification at the polls, and a photo ID requirement).

---

[10] The author added the "trust in election officials" measure to the 2008 and 2010 Cooperative Congressional Election Study (CCES) survey. The item has a long lineage in studies of citizen trust and confidence in a variety of social and political institutions, but this is the first time the target of evaluation has been LEOs.

TABLE 10.1. *Voter confidence levels*

	SPAE 2008	CCES 2008 (pre)	CCES 2008 (post)	CCES 2010	SPAE 2012
Very Confident	72.7%	47.3%	51.0%	50.4%	62.7%
Confident	94.7%	83.0%	90.7%	88.7%	90.0%
Confident (four point)	0.883	0.755	0.792	0.785	0.826
Whites	72.9%	47.3%	50.9%	56.2%	61.2%
Blacks	77.5%	52.4%	61.0%	56.1%	76.5%
Hispanics	74.6%	47.0%	48.1%	55.6%	60.8%
Other	66.0%	40.8%	34.0%	44.0%	60.2%
Male	74.6%	51.2%	52.9%	56.0%	64.7%
Female	71.7%	43.6%	49.1%	44.7%	60.9%
Republicans	71.5%	55.7%	49.1%	56.0%	53.5%
Independents	70.3%	39.2%	45.9%	40.5%	54.4%
Democrats	76.7%	48.9%	57.3%	54.5%	77.4%

Note: SPAE figures have a national weight applied. "Confident" is the percent who were "very" or "somewhat" confident. Values for race, gender, and party are the percentage "very confident." The 2008 CCES numbers are for the same respondents, that is, those who completed both the preelection and postelection version of the survey.

Voter Confidence: A First Look

A first look at the data provides some encouragement to those concerned about citizen confidence in our election system. Voter confidence is high: as shown in Table 10.1, 73 percent of respondents in the 2008 SPAE expressed a great deal of confidence, and 94.8 percent were "somewhat" or "very" confident that their ballots were counted as cast. Confidence has remained high for the past decade, as Sances and Stewart (2012) show in Table A10.1. Respondents to the 2008 and 2010 CCES expressed lower levels of confidence, a disparity that is so great that it calls for closer scrutiny.[11] Summing the top two categories ("confident") brings the three surveys more closely into agreement. Finally, confidence declined somewhat in 2012, when compared with 2008.

[11] For reasons unclear as of this writing, far fewer CCES respondents opted for the "most confident" category. The same survey firm conducted the SPAE and the CCES, so this is not a function of house effects. While the different levels of confidence are a matter of concern, the multivariate results show far less variation.

In 2008, we are able to compare voter confidence before and after the election, an alternative way to estimate "loser's regret" as well as the impact of negative voting experiences. There are only three other surveys that have this pre/post feature (see Sances and Stewart 2012, figure 6, for additional examples). The results here mirror those reported by Sances and Stewart; voter confidence increased from preelection to postelection, primarily among voters who identified with the party of the winner (Barack Obama, the Democrat) and among Independents.

Interestingly, confidence levels were significantly lower among those preelection respondents who were uncertain as to whether they would cast a ballot at all (results not reported here). Either causal ordering seems reasonable: lower confidence in the election system lowers the probability of voting, or a lower probability of voting on other grounds (e.g., disinterest, lack of knowledge, lower efficacy) is associated with lower levels of voting experiences and consequently a higher level of distrust in the machinery of democracy (Alvarez et al. 2008).

The results raise an important question: What constitutes a high level of confidence? If we add up the top two categories, voter confidence virtually never falls below 90 percent. Previous studies at local levels have found similarly high levels of confidence. Stein et al. (2008) report that 66 percent of respondents in Jefferson County, Texas, "strongly agreed" that their ballots would be counted as intended in the 2006 election, while 84 percent of respondents in two counties in New Mexico and Colorado said they were "very" or "somewhat" confident (Atkeson and Saunders 2007). Thus, even in the face of withering criticism of the elections systems by many election advocates, citizens still express robust confidence in the ability of the system to accurately count their votes.

If we concentrate only on the top category, however, confidence varies substantially across time and space, falling into the sixtieth percentage level among a number of western states, as shown in Figure 10.1 (individual estimates are reported in the methodological appendix). There are interesting and substantial changes in confidence between 2008 and 2012 in some states. The proportion of the public that was "very confident" that their ballot was counted as cast fell by 9 percent (as an average of state averages), but it declined precipitously in Florida (22 percent), Michigan (19 percent), and Rhode Island (17 percent) while remaining relatively stable in a number of other states. It is beyond the scope of this study to explore these state-by-state changes, but it is possible that important trends in voter confidence exist within states even if those trends are not readily apparent across states.

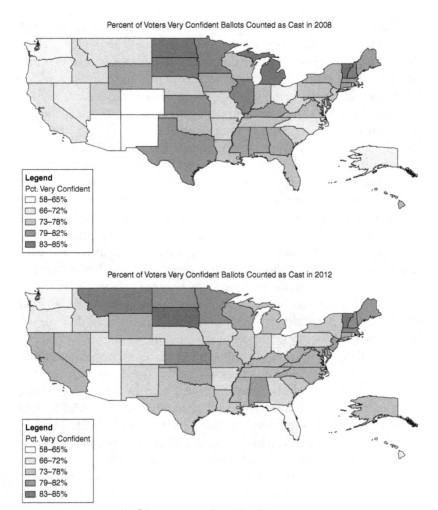

FIGURE 10.1. Voter confidence across the United States.

For the rest of this chapter, I report the percentage that responded
"very confident," and in the multivariate analyses, examine the full
four-point measure rather than collapsing the measure into two values, "confident" and "not confident."[12] It is easy to jump to conclusions
from this map, assuming that westerners are more likely to be skeptical

---

[12] I made the choice to rely on the four-point measure even though it required a more complex
statistical estimation procedure (discussed in the appendix) because when the confidence
measure was collapsed to a 0–1 scale, many covariates failed to reach statistical significance
level. Variation at the top level of confidence is meaningful. These probit analyses are available from the author.

of government, suspicious of election officials, and mistrustful of voting procedures. This is possible, but it is far more likely that the patterns shown in the map are a result of choices made among the western states to encourage voting by mail, a system that drags down voter confidence. In addition and coincidentally, many of these states voted for John McCain in 2008 and were experiencing loser's regret.

Returning to Table 10.1, previous studies (Alvarez et al. 2008) have found several demographic variables to be strongly associated with variation in voter confidence. Others, however, have found statistically insignificant effects (Atkeson and Saunders 2008). One of these is race; in particular, African-American respondents have reported notably lower rates of confidence that their ballots were correctly counted. We find diverse racial patterns in the 2008 and 2012 SPAE and the 2008 and 2010 CCES surveys. For example, racial differences in the 2008 SPAE are small, but because of the very large sample size, statistically significant. The most notable difference is between those who self-identify in an "other" racial category (any category other than white, black, and Hispanic). These respondents are far less confident that their votes will be counted accurately. The differences in 2012 are both substantively and statistically significant; while black confidence remains high after 2012, whites, Hispanics, and "other" ethnic groups all experienced substantial declines.

The oddly lower confidence levels among the "other" racial grouping are reflected in the CCES surveys. Finally, it is revealing that black and Hispanic confidence jumps dramatically after the 2008 contest (10 percent for black and 18 percent for Hispanics), while white confidence increases a more modest 6 percent. Because these measures are reported only for those who cast a ballot, we can only assume that something about the campaign and the voting experience led to these increases. The difference also highlights the importance of asking about the voter confidence at the right moment – after the election, when the voting experience is freshest in the respondents' minds.

A key finding of past studies has been that differences in voter confidence exist across voting modes. The theory is that absentee voters who lose control of their ballots earlier in the process and who have fewer interpersonal interactions with election officials (or poll workers) will express lower confidence in their vote intents being accurately recorded. Indeed, this is not an unreasonable expectation, given that absentee by mail ballots are, in fact, more likely to be challenged and less likely to be accurately counted (Alvarez, Hall, and Sinclair 2008). The pattern

TABLE 10.2. *Voter confidence and the election system*

	SPAE 2008	CCES 2008 (pre)	CCES 2008 (post)	CCES 2010	SPAE 2012
Voted for the Winner	76.6%	49.2%	58.8%	51.8%	75.9%
Voted for the Loser	69.2%	47.1%	44.1%	49.6%	49.6%
Polling Place	75.8%	46.4%	52.5%	52.8%	65.4%
Early in Person	74.8%	48.6%	52.1%	50.9%	61.9%
Vote-by-Mail	61.3%	49.5%	45.9%	48.6%	55.7%
Fraud Common	60.0%	33.8%	38.2%	–	67.6%
Fraud Not Common	77.3%	53.7%	57.1%	–	47.5%
Poll Workers Excellent	81.9%	50.5%	61.0%	57.5%	73.7%
Poll Workers Less Than Excellent	60.3%	41.5%	39.9%	41.8%	46.9%

Notes: All SPAE figures have a national weight applied. In 2010, Voted Winner = Obama vote in 2008; Poll Workers Excellent for SPAE coded "excellent" on a four-point scale; for CCES as higher than 85 on a 100-point scale. See text for changes in the "Fraud" item for the 2012 SPAE. Pre/post comparisons for the 2008 CCES are for the same respondents.

appears in the 2008 and 2012 SPAE and in the 2008 CCES postelection and 2010 CCES postelection surveys, though the magnitude of the difference is much smaller in the CCES surveys. Other patterns are also replicated in our analysis: citizens who provide a positive evaluation of poll workers express higher levels of confidence, while those who believe voting fraud is common and those whose candidate lost the presidency express lower levels of confidence.[13] It is encouraging on measurement grounds that "loser's regret" did not appear until the 2008 postelection survey, and encouraging on political grounds that regrets had mostly been forgotten by the 2010. See Atkeson (2012) for extensions of the "sore loser" argument to the sub-presidential level.

[13] In the 2008 SPAE, respondents identified the frequency of vote fraud by selecting a point on a four-point scale, running from "it almost never occurs" to "it is very common." In the 2012 SPAE, respondents were presented with six different examples of voting irregularities, such as "How often do people vote more than once?" or "How often voters are not U.S. citizens?" If a respondent thought that at least one of these occurred "often," I coded them as "worried" about fraud in 2012. Twenty-two percent of the sample fell into this category, a bit lower than the 25 percent who thought that fraud occurred "occasionally" or "often" using the four-point scale.

TABLE 10.3. *Voter confidence and election audits*

	Confidence 1 State Means	Confidence 2	
		State Means	Individual Confidence
No Postelection Audits	0.755	0.956	0.897
Postelection Audits	0.694	0.940	0.876
Difference	0.060	0.016	0.020
H (diff < 0)	0.990	0.980	1.000
H (diff! = 0)	0.004	0.025	0.000
H (diff > 0)	0.002	0.013	0.000

Source: 2008 SPAE. First two columns are based on state-level means; the final column uses individual-level data (using a national weight).

The discussion up to now may leave election officials scratching their heads. After all, it is not in their job description to make sure that voters always cast a ballot for the winner, and they are constantly being asked to provide voters more options to cast the ballot, not fewer, for the purposes of voter convenience. The next table could prompt officials to move from scratching their heads to pulling out their hair. Table 10.3 breaks down voter confidence levels by the presence or absence of statewide postelection audits. Surely no one would argue that postelection audits, procedures that have been put in place specifically to identify potential flaws or errors in the vote-counting process, ought to lower the individual voter's confidence that his or her ballot is being counted accurately.

Nonetheless, this is exactly what the data show. Table 10.3 compares voter confidence levels among states with and without audits (columns 1 and 2) and then makes the same comparison among individual respondents. While the absolute differences are small, the results are consistent: the presence of postelection audits is associated with a statistically significant drop in voter confidence. The result appears again in the multivariate models reported in the following.

Voter Confidence: A Multivariate Look

It is de rigueur for academics to call for multivariate analysis, but the results thus far are a convincing demonstration of the importance of this method. Taken at face value, Figure 10.1 indicates a crisis in voter confidence among the western states. However, once we realize that many of these states have heavy populations of McCain voters, and that more than half of the votes in the western region arrive by mail, perhaps the sense of crisis is misplaced. The multivariate analysis allows us to evaluate the relative importance of the four categories of influence, rather than examining each in isolation.

I made a number of analytical decisions to ease the interpretation of the results. First, all variables have been transformed to the 0–1 range, even demographic indicators such as age. This allows the interested reader to compare the size of the effects, with the understanding that these reflect the estimated impact of moving from the lowest to the highest value of an independent variable. Second, I have reported both ordinary least square regression results and the more complex ordered probit results in the appendix. Readers who wish to examine all the relationships should turn there. The bulk of the presentation relies on graphical representation of the most important results.[14]

Postelection Audits and Voter Identification Have Little Impact

Voter confidence is not responsive to state-mandated requirements for identification at the polls or a requirement for photo ID. While this conclusion may disappoint advocates for more widespread ID requirements, the result is consistent over two elections and across three surveys, and it remains robust to a variety of specifications. In fact, the impact of these dual requirements offset one another; the requirement for ID alone shows a weak but negative association with voter confidence, while the additional photo ID requirement displays a mildly positive relationship. None of the relationships comes close to statistical significance.

Similarly disappointing to some will be the finding of a small but statistically significant negative relationship between the existence of postelection audits and voter confidence, a finding sustained in the 2008 analyses but not in 2010. The magnitude of the effect is substantively small, 33/100ths of a single point on a 0–3 voter confidence scale. The effect is approximately one-fifth of the magnitude of the effect of voting by mail and less than one-tenth the size of loser's regret.[15] It is

[14] All the graphical presentations are based on the ordered probit estimates, and were generated using the margins command in Stata 12.

[15] Table A10.1 allows a simple comparison of effects across the full range of the independent variables. The example in the text is drawn from the first model in Table A10.1, the 2008 SPAE and all voters. The coefficient on postelection audits is –.033, which implies that changing

possible that voters are not paying attention to these requirements or do not make a connection between them and an accurate count of their individual ballot.[16] It may be that these requirements have not been in place long enough, and, in the case of audits, have not sufficiently impacted a disputed election result to affect public confidence. At least in terms of public opinion about the accuracy of the count, state laws have little discernible impact.

Managing Voter Expectations: Convenience, Competence, and Voter Confidence

Early voting methods, both early in-person and voting by mail (including no excuse absentee and Oregon and Washington's mandated vote-by-mail systems) have been growing in popularity over the past quarter century (Gronke et al. 2008), primarily for reasons of convenience to the voter but sometimes to address perceived administrative problems with Election Day voting (Gronke and Galanes-Rosenbaum 2008). The growth of convenience voting systems has not been without controversy, however, with some raising concerns about higher rates of residual votes (Gronke, Stewart, and Hicks 2010; Stewart 2010) and lower levels of voter confidence, at least among citizens who return their ballots via the post (Alvarez and Hall 2009; Alvarez et al. 2008).

The descriptive results in Table 10.2 showed that by-mail voters expressed lower levels of confidence, on average, than early in-person or polling place voters. These differences remain even after other statistical controls are put in place. Voters who cast a ballot by mail express confidence levels from 0.16 to 0.24 points lower (on a 0–3 scale) compared with polling place voters. However, all is not lost for those election officials who are, either by mandate or by choice, providing facilities for voting by mail. If officials can cultivate a strong image of trust and confidence among the electorate, this can more than offset the negative impact of convenience voting. This is illustrated in Figure 10.2, which plots the predicted probability that a voter expressed a "great deal" of confidence that his or her ballot was counted as cast, comparing between modes of balloting and for increasing levels of

the value on audits from the minimum, or 0 (no audits), to the maximum of 1, or a −0.033 drop in the voter confidence scale. The coefficients on "vote-by-mail" and "vote fraud worry" are −0.159 and −0.347, respectively.

[16] It would be interesting to investigate whether or not state-level requirements influence voter confidence in the state-level ballot count, for instance.

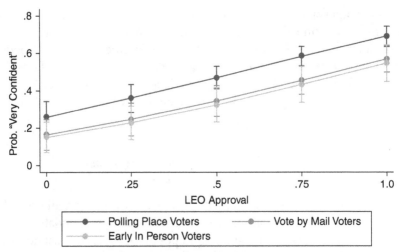

FIGURE 10.2. Voter confidence and approval of LEO.

LEO approval.[17] As the figure makes abundantly clear, the gain to be made from a positive public image – more than a 40 percent greater likelihood that a respondent would answer "very confident" – easily outweighs the difference across mode.

The other way that election officials can foster greater confidence among the voting public is by ensuring that voters have a positive experience at the polls. The poll worker bonus was as high as 20 percent in the 2008 and 2012 SPAE (see Table 10.2), and it remains a robust predictor of voter confidence in every analysis.[18] Consider, for example, voters who report that they encountered a problem with voting machines. Compared with those who reported no problems, voters with problems expressed far lower (−0.456) levels of confidence. But well-trained poll workers can make up the gap, as illustrated in Figure 10.3. As problems with voting machines are minimized, poll workers receive high scores and voter confidence nears its maximum. But if forced to make a choice between problematic machines and problematic frontline workers, the administrator looking to

---

[17] This figure and the figures in the rest of the chapter all plot the probability that a respondent would give the "very confident" answer. The figures were created using the margins and margin plot commands in Stata. The graphic represents the change in predicted probability if we change the variable or variable under question, holding all other independent variables at their average or mean value.

[18] The following discussion excludes vote-by-mail voters, since they do not have any direct poll worker experiences.

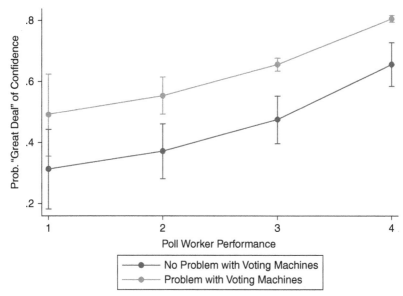

FIGURE 10.3. Voter confidence, poll workers, and voting technology.

maximize voter confidence will improve human capital before physical capital.

It is hard to minimize the relative importance of positive poll worker evaluations. Consider the two plots in Figure 10.4. The left-hand panel reports voter confidence levels across the full range of poll worker evaluations, and among respondents who expressed low, moderate, and high levels of confidence in their election officials. The right-hand panel compares the impact of poll worker evaluations with "loser's regret" and voting mode. Visual inspection of the figures and the numerical coefficient in the appendixes confirm that a positive experience with poll workers results in higher levels of confidence and is more influential than any other indicator in our model.

Other aspects of the polling place experience can also be managed by officials to improve voter confidence. In the appendix, the quantitative results show that the largest coefficients are for voters who reported having a problem with voting machines (−0.479 in 2012 and −0.267 in 2008) and voters who said they had an easy time finding the polling place (0.146 in 2012 and 0.395 in 2008). Even those indicators that might be deemed more subjective, such as confidence in the LEO and concern over ballot privacy (see the 2008 and 2010 CCES results), are more influential determinants of voter confidence than ballot mode, generalized trust in government, and partisan identity.

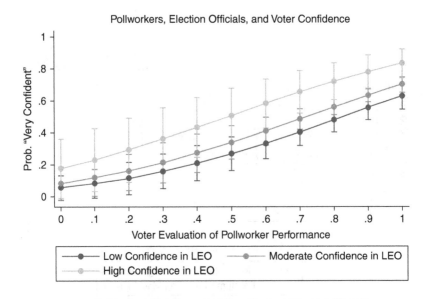

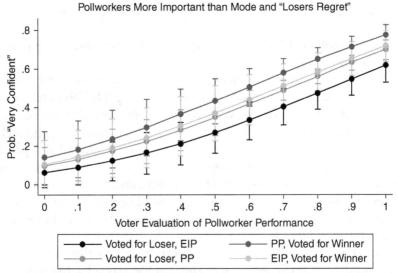

FIGURE 10.4. The impact of poll worker evaluations compared with other influences.

In short, while it is undoubtedly true that voter confidence is a subjective measure, it responds in reasonable ways to reasonable features of the election system and to characteristics and perceptions of the officials who administer that system. It is far from an incoherent jumble of emotions or short-term reactions.

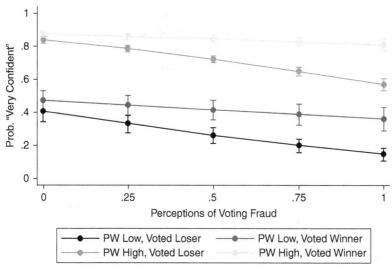

FIGURE 10.5. Poll worker quality, loser's regret, and vote fraud.

What about Voter Fraud?

We started this chapter by quoting Justice John Paul Stevens regarding photo ID in Indiana, a quote drawn from a section titled "Safeguarding Voter Confidence." Stevens's decision endorsed one of the primary arguments made by proponents of voter ID: they will deter in-person voter impersonation and, in so doing, will protect citizen confidence in the election system. Up to now, the analysis has cast some doubt on this claim, but I have left unexamined perceptions of voter fraud, regardless of the reality of voter fraud.

The analysis demonstrates that perceptions of vote fraud are a powerful force, ranking as one of the most important determinants of voter confidence. Respondents to the 2008 SPAE who think there is a lot of vote fraud are 19 percent less likely to respond "very confident" than those who believe there is not much fraud, ceteris paribus. In 2012, respondents who thought at least one of six voting irregularities occurred "often" were 17 percent less likely to be very confident.[19] Furthermore, I have uncovered a disturbing pattern to perceptions of fraud: perceptions are substantially more prevalent among those who voted for the losing candidate (in both 2008 and 2012).

Figure 10.5 compares the impact of these two attitudes, adjusting for the level of poll worker quality. This result tells two stories, one

---

[19] Results calculated from the ordered probit model in Table A10.2.

pessimistic and one optimistic. The pessimistic tale focuses on the inter-action between voting for a losing candidate and the perceptions that ballots were not counted fairly. Compare the slope of the "winner" line to the "loser" line. Among those who voted for the winning candidate, perceptions of fraud had only a minimal impact on their confidence levels. Their levels of confidence are almost completely determined by how well they evaluated their poll workers. Among those who voted for the losing candidate, however, their confidence levels declined at an accelerating rate as they also came to believe that vote fraud was more prevalent. Respondents who voted for the losing candidate and who think that vote fraud is common had only a 17 percent probability of being "very confident" that their ballots were counted as intended.

Perceptions of voter fraud and the experience of voting for the losing candidate are a potent combination that drags down citizen evaluations of the election system. Unfortunately, many political actors seem well aware of this, and, all too often, losing candidates level unsubstantiated charges of voting fraud, thus undermining citizen confidence in the system, rather than licking their wounds and returning to the electoral field of combat at the next election.

Concluding Remarks

Voter confidence is becoming a commonly used metric to evaluate the performance of American elections – a voter's perception that his ballot will or will not be counted accurately. The motivation is obvious: after the 2000 contest, and continuing in 2004, the press, bloggers, and advo-cacy groups highlighted widespread problems with voting machines and voting technology. There have been increasing calls for a "democracy index" that would help monitor election performance (Gerken 2009a; Pew Center on the States 2008). Any democracy index, however, is only as good as its components. Is voter confidence an appropriate measure of the quality of the vote count? Does it vary in reasonable ways with voter experiences, or is it prone to partisan manipulation?

Given media commentary since 2000, it is perhaps surprising to discover that voter confidence remains high, with nearly 90 percent expressing confidence that their ballots will be counted properly. On the other hand, there remain questions about what the item is mea-suring: confidence in the system by which ballots are counted, con-fidence in the probability that the voter's own ballot will be counted, or faith in the system of American elections and American democracy writ large. After all, as I have argued elsewhere (Cook and Gronke

2007; Gronke and Hicks 2009), moderately high levels of skepticism about politicians and elected officials are part and parcel of American democracy and have historically coexisted with strong levels of faith in the system as a whole. As Easton (1975) put it so effectively more than three decades ago, "system support" (support for a political system as a whole) is quite distinct from "regime support" (support for a particular political leader), party, or regime. Does the same distinction apply to voter confidence? A low level of confidence in a particular balloting system may say little about the voter's support for the overall "chain of voting."

For those who advocate the use of this item, voter confidence is strongly related to actual evaluative and experiential aspects of the election system. Voters who are concerned about fraud are, not surprisingly, also concerned about ballot integrity. Similarly, those who had a positive Election Day experience express higher levels of confidence. These patterns are reasonable and speak to the validity of this item.

Overall, the voter confidence measure is reliable and valid (see the appendix for further discussion). The voter confidence measure moves in reasonable ways, in correlation with characteristics of the election system and perceptions of the election experience. Most importantly, perhaps, the influence of poll workers, the human face of elections for most Americans, can make or break citizen confidence in the election process. That does not lead to much confidence about voter confidence as alternative voting systems, most notably voting by mail but even other remote systems such as Internet voting, become more widely adopted. Efficiency may come at the cost of confidence.

Chapter 10 Appendix

The bulk of this chapter has addressed the validity question. On the positive side of the ledger, voter confidence varies in expected ways with characteristics of the election experience, such as the mode of voting, the perceived expertise and competence of poll workers, and the presence of postelection audits.

On the negative side of the ledger, voter confidence is also strongly related to preexisting political attitudes, most notably generalized trust and confidence in government, and whether or not a voter cast a ballot for a winning candidate. To the degree that voter confidence is a function of diffuse system support and less of experiences with voting, the validity of voter confidence as a measure of the quality of the vote count may be called into question.

Multivariate Models

Two sets of multivariate models were estimated in order to understand the underlying factors that lead a voter to express a higher or lower level of confidence that his or her ballot was counted as cast.

For ease of interpretation, the interested reader will find both sets of models in the following. In all cases, the independent variables are coded to the 0–1 range so that the coefficients represent the change from the lowest to the highest value on each variable. The dependent variable, voter confidence, runs from 0 to 3.

Table A10.1 contains ordinary least squares regression estimates. The advantage of these estimates is that the reader can easily convert a coefficient into a predicted effect on voter confidence. For example, a respondent in the 2008 SPAE who was most worried about voter fraud was .347 points less confident (more than 10 percent of the total scale) than a voter who was least worried about fraud.

While regression coefficients are easily understood, the appropriate methodological specification for a limited dependent variable is a more complex statistical estimation technique called *ordered probit*. Unlike regression, probit coefficients cannot be easily translated into changes in the dependent variable. However, as in the text, all independent variables were coded to the 0–1 range. Using this alternative estimation technique changes no substantive conclusions. These results are presented for the interested reader. The graphical displays in the text are based on these models.

The models differ slightly between the 2008 and 2012 SPAE. In the 2008 SPAE, respondents were asked a five-point item regarding the frequency of fraud. In the 2012 SPAE, respondents were asked six questions about voting problems (e.g., "How often do people vote more than once?" "How often do people tamper with ballots?"). If a respondent answered "it is very common" to just one of these six items, I coded them as "worried" about fraud. Twenty-two percent of respondents said at least one violation was "very common." The most comparable proportion in 2008 is the 25 percent of respondents who said fraud was "very common" or "occasionally" common. Other coding schemes are possible, but this seemed a reasonable way to compare across the two surveys. I did not collect information on postelection audits or voter ID requirements in 2012 and did not include them in the multivariate estimates.

11

Election Data Transparency

Lonna Rae Atkeson

Providing useful information to interested parties about the election process is the responsibility of election officials. Useful information is easily accessible and transparent. This implies openness, communication, and accountability. By *accessible* and *transparent*, I mean information or data that are relatively easily available and easy to understand. Transparency invites verification. Election officials are responsible for conducting elections in a free and fair manner. To help determine that an election is free and fair, data produced during the election must be made available for independent examination. That information must be transparent.

The concepts of accessibility and transparency focus on the ease and availability of information so that those involved in the election can participate in and evaluate it. These include voters, perhaps the primary client in an election, as well as other stakeholders, including election administrators, policy makers, legislators, policy advocates, election activists, and scholars. For voters, material that assists them in the voting process, including information about the ballot, how to register, if their votes were counted, where to vote, and how to obtain an absentee ballot, are all critical pieces of information. For other stakeholders, information is needed to assess the quality of the election, for example, to determine that the election was legitimate, to verify that the candidate who received the most qualified votes won the election, and to suggest ways in which the process can be improved.

Here I examine stakeholder transparency using the Election Assistance Commission's (EAC) Election Administration and Voting

I would like to thank Alex N. Adams and Lisa A. Bryant for their assistance with this chapter. Of course, any errors are my own.

Survey (EAVS). The survey covers six broad quantitative areas, including information on registration, uniform and overseas voters, domestic absentee ballots, provisional voting, election administration, and turnout. The EAVS also has a qualitative component on state laws that I briefly examine. This latter qualitative data set is a tremendous resource for stakeholders, especially researchers, who are interested in understanding how contextual differences across states influence election administration. Finally, transparency for voters is examined with data we collected that focuses on Web-based information available to voters about the election and election process.

PROBLEMS WITH MEASUREMENT IN ELECTION ADMINISTRATION

One of the major difficulties in election administration is that there are not clear values that determine what factors are most important for determining the quality of the election (Bjornlund 2004). Moreover, we are not certain about what data generated within and across elections might be most influenced by public policy and the administration of public policy across individuals and groups. Without a well-defined set of values or a clear understanding of how the administration of elections influences metrics of value to elections, this naturally makes measuring the health of our democracy through the election process more difficult. This is true, in part, because the values that people bring to the election process are often political and therefore in conflict. For example, one broad value in elections might be that every qualified elector should participate. However, even this value is problematic since voting is not mandatory and not voting may in and of itself be a political statement. Considering a wider range of less consensual values is even more difficult.

In addition to differences in political values, there is a recurring tension in election management between the need for ballot security and ballot accessibility.[1] Both are important election administrative goals, but often they are at odds with each other. Providing easy accessibility, through such things as easier access to the ballot box, may increase opportunities for voter fraud. Fraud reduces the legitimacy of the election, so constraining opportunities for fraud through administrative and legal practices is a critical aspect of election administration. But what

[1] This form of ballot accessibility, sometimes called "convenience," is distinct from the larger issue of data accessibility that is the focus of this chapter.

does this mean for data election transparency? For example, some voters and activists see policies such as voter identification as necessary to protect the system against voter fraud, while others see it as preventing access to a fundamental political right (Liebschutz and Palazzolo 2005). Thus, the presence or absence of voter identification in a state is not a measure we can use to determine the quality of an election. States vary on how they value voter identification policies and the balance between access and integrity within their election administration, and the fact that there is no consistent interpretation makes it an unreliable indicator for inclusion in an index of election performance. However, information on voter identification policies is important to understanding the ecosystem in which election administration occurs. It likely impacts the frequency and use of provisional ballots, turnout (Alvarez and Hall 2009; Atkeson et al. 2009; Foley 2008; Kimball and Foley 2009; Kimball et al. 2006), and possibly other polling operations. Although we cannot consider the presence or absence of voter identification relevant to identifying a quality election – because as a contested idea it reflects political preferences – we can know if information on voter identification policies is transparent. This information is important to the voter and the other stakeholders. Therefore, in assessing transparency we consider only whether information on the rules relating to voter ID and other policies is transparent and accessible and do not evaluate whether or not such rules should be present.

Nevertheless, given this backdrop, there must be some concepts that are specifically related to the conduct of elections, the administration of elections, that are generic enough that they do not conflict with different people's political values. These measures would likely be narrow in scope and where the administrative process might be able to influence their outcome. Fortunately, and unlike many areas of election administration where there may be more argument and uncertainty, there is widespread consensus that more information and transparency available in the election process is better than less information and transparency. Voters and other stakeholders are important clients interested in the accessibility and transparency of elections. Voters *should* be able to determine what hurdles they need to jump through to cast a ballot and find the appropriate location or paperwork to do so. Stakeholders *should* be able to examine postelection data to determine the outcome is accurate and that procedures were followed to create a fair election environment. It is to the presence or absence of these types of data and information that I focus on for their transparency.

STAKEHOLDER TRANSPARENCY AND DATA AVAILABILITY

One historic problem with election transparency has been that election data were often created and sometimes housed at the local level because that is where the vast majority of election administration is handled. It is the local jurisdiction that organizes and implements the election. These jurisdictions present a logistical problem for the accessibility and transparency of election data because the variation in the amount of data they generate and maintain for stakeholders is very high and often is not available electronically (Gerken 2009a, 2009b; Moore 2009; Tokaji 2004–2005). For example in some jurisdictions printed reports on precinct vote totals were available, but in other jurisdictions only aggregated data at the county level were available. Moreover, these data were often not disaggregated by voting mode or other pertinent dimensions, such as provisional voters, overseas voters, or other useful delineations. Traditional practices related to institutional design and who manages elections have thus fallen short of full accessibility and transparency.

Since the 2000 election and the passage of the Help America Vote Act (HAVA) in 2002, which created the EAC, data accessibility and transparency have expanded. The EAC is an independent federal election commission whose mission is to "assist state and local election officials [LEOs] with the administration of federal elections." One aspect of their mission is to provide information on the conduct and administration of federal elections. As part of this mission since 2004, the EAC has collected data at the state and county levels on voting, elections, and election administration. The data collection is required under HAVA to meet EAC obligations "to serve as a national clearinghouse and resource for the compilation of information with respect to the administration of federal elections." It also satisfies statutory requirements related to the National Voter Registration Act of 1993 (NVRA) and the Uniformed and Overseas Citizens Absentee Voting Act (UOCAVA) (U.S. EAC 2011b). Indeed these data are used by the EAC to create three reports that are sent to Congress on the impact of the NVRA, the UOCAVA, and the HAVA (U.S. EAC 2011b). However, the content of the survey has been influenced by the needs and demands of scholars, election activists, and state and LEOs.

Two instruments have been distributed to states for completion as part of their assessment of the most recent federal elections. The first of these, the EAVS, was introduced in 2004 and has been modified after each federal election year in response to feedback from state and LEOs, political scientists, other researchers, election reform advocacy groups, the public, and boards related directly to the EAC (U.S. EAC 2011b, 3).

The quantitative data collected by the EAC include six sections:

(1) Voter registration (including total number of registered voters, total number of new registrants, total number of changes in registration, the number of inactive and active voters, total number of same day registrations [SDRs], locations where citizens registered, the number of voters sent removal notices, the number of voters removed from the voter registration and the reasons for their removal).

(2) UOCAVA data (including the number of absentee ballots sent to UOCAVA voters and whether they are uniformed services voters or civilians, the number of ballots returned by UOCAVA voters, and the number of ballots counted and rejected from UOCAVA voters, as well as the type of ballot used).

(3) Domestic civilian absentee ballots (including the number of absentee ballots sent to domestic civilian absentee voters, the number of absentee ballots returned by domestic civilians and their status, whether or not a jurisdiction has a permanent absentee voter registration list, the number of ballots counted and rejected, and the reason for ballot rejection).

(4) Election administration (including the number of precincts in each election jurisdiction, the number and type (early or Election Day) of polling places in each jurisdiction, the number of poll workers used in each jurisdiction, the ages of poll workers, and the ease of finding poll workers to work the polls).

(5) Provisional ballots (including the number of voters submitting provisional ballots, the number of ballots counted partially or fully and the number rejected, and reasons for provisional ballot rejection).

(6) Election Day activities (including turnout, turnout by voting mode [Election Day, absentee, early, UOCAVA, provisional], votes cast for the highest office on the ballot, information about first-time voters' use of electronic poll books or printed lists of voters, the type of voting equipment used, that is, direct-recording electronic machines [DREs] with or without a voter-verified paper audit trail (VVPAT), optical scan, punch card, lever, hand counts).

The second instrument is the Statutory Overview survey. This was first introduced in 2008. "The Statutory Overview gathers qualitative information on States' definitions, laws, processes, and procedures relating to the administration of elections" (U.S. EAC 2011b, ES-1). The

Statutory Overview provides important contextual data on a variety of state laws and definitions related to election administration. Because there is so much variation across states, differences between states need to be considered when understanding or trying to explain questions related to elections and election administration.

There are nine sections associated with the Statutory Overview.

(1) How states define the following terms: *over-vote, under-vote, blank ballot void* or *spoiled ballot, provisional* or *challenged ballot, absentee, early voting, active voter,* and *inactive voter.*

(2) Voter roll maintenance through the matching of voter registration databases with information from the Department of Motor Vehicles, the Social Security Administration, state public health departments, federal and state courts systems, the state police, and the U.S. Attorneys.

(3) Felon disenfranchisement and the rules associated with it and restoration of voting rights.

(4) Election counting and reporting for different voting modes and the rules associated with different voting modes. For example, whether or not an excuse is required for absentee voting.

(5) Triggers for a provisional vote and standards for counting provisional ballots.

(6) Voter identification rules for registration, in-person voting, absentee mail-in voting, and UOCAVA voting.

(7) Information on whether postelection audits are required, the scope of any such audit, the method of auditing, and any triggers that would expand or cause an audit.

(8) Polling place operations, including the frequency of poll worker training and the rules associated with polling observation.

(9) Various other data, including the processes used to capture residual votes.

ASSESSMENT OF EAC QUANTITATIVE DATA

The volume of data collected varies by state with clear improvement over time. First, I focus on a limited analysis of the 2008, 2010, and 2012 data sets to examine comparability and change over the two most recent election cycles. Second, I do a more detailed and broad analysis of the most current data that was collected for the 2010 midterm and 2012 presidential general elections. I start with the simplest approach, as discussed in the conceptual framework section, and determine whether or not the data are present or absent, and, if not present, where patterns of missing data exist either within or across states. I then examine the indicators more closely to consider which data might offer additional information that directly relates to the administration of elections. This includes identifying items that could likely vary over time in response to changes in administration rules, voter education, or poll worker training. These items provide a better indication of the quality of election administration and therefore might have value in an Election Performance Index (EPI).

COMPARING 2008, 2010, AND 2012 ACROSS FIFTEEN ITEMS

In February of 2012, Pew Center on the States published *Election Administration by the Numbers: An Analysis of Available Datasets and How to Use Them.* This report examined a variety of data, including the EAVS, for its quality and suggested future improvements. As part of its analysis, it focused on fifteen EAVS items that it describes as "basic input and output measures related to election administration workflow" (p. 50) to evaluate EAVS completeness on the most essential items. These include:

- Section A: Registration
  - Number of new registrations received
  - Number of new valid registrations
  - Number of registered voters
- Section B: UOCAVA absentee ballots
  - Number transmitted to voters
  - Number returned for counting
  - Number accepted for counting
- Section C: Civilian absentee ballots
  - Number transmitted to voters
  - Number returned for counting
  - Number accepted for counting
- Section E: Provisional ballots
  - Number submitted
  - Number accepted for counting
- Section F: Turnout
  - Number of ballots cast
  - Number cast in person on Election Day
  - Number cast in person early voting
  - Number cast absentee

For these fifteen items, Table 11.1 shows the 2008, 2010, and 2012 average completeness, the minimum percent complete, and the number of states at 100 percent.[2] It is clear from the first data column that completeness

TABLE 11.1. *EAVS Completeness across fifteen items, 2008, 2010, and 2012*

	All Fifteen Index Items	Section A – Registration	Section B – UOCAVA	Section C – Absentee	Section E – Provisional	Section F – Turnout
Average Percent Complete 2008	85	84	88	91	88	84
Average Percent Complete 2010	94	95	98	97	93	91
Average Percent Complete 2012	94	99.8	97	97	86	91
Minimum Percent Complete 2008	46	33	27	33	33	24
Minimum Percent Complete 2010	55	33	50	50	28	25
Minimum Percent Complete 2012	61	93	33	39	0	25
N (%) of States at 100% 2008	12 (24)	28 (55)	30 (59)	31 (61)	26 (51)	27 (53)
N (%) of States at 100% 2010	23 (45)	41 (80)	43 (84)	41 (81)	32 (63)	30 (59)
N (%) of States at 100% 2012	25 (49)	47 (92)	36 (71)	37 (73)	31 (61)	29 (55)

has increased over time on these fifteen items. Overall data complete-ness rates for 2008 was 85 percent, but in 2010 and 2012 it was 94 percent, an increase of nine points. We also see confirmation of improvement in the minimum percent complete, which was only 46 percent in 2008 but was 61 percent in 2012. We also see that in each biennial survey the number of states providing all the data on the fifteen items more than doubled from twelve in 2008 to twenty-five in 2012.

If we look at subsections, we find that Sections A, B, and C, informa-tion on registration, UOCAVA voters, and absentee voters respectively, saw the most significant increases in the number of states report-ing all the examined items, while provisional (Section E) and turn-out (Section F) data saw overall less improvement. Section A, which includes three questions on voter registration, was almost 100 percent complete in 2012. Sections B and C were both 97 percent complete in 2012. Section E showed a two-point decline in 2012 after a five-point increase in 2010 and Section F held study with a seven-point increase from 2008 to 2012 with an average completeness of 91 percent.

But what explains the completeness rates across these fifteen items? Could there be state characteristics that help to predict which states are more likely to respond more fully to the EAVS questionnaire? We considered the following factors that are prominent in state politics research as possible explanatory variables: state population, number of counties, the Squire index of legislative professionalism, state turnout, per capita state income, state spending per capita, percent of the state population that is white, black, and in poverty, the land area of the state in square miles, and population of the state per square mile. However, we found that none of these factors was related to EAVS reporting. Similar to mistakes on the voter registration file (Ansolabehere 2012; Chapter 3 in this volume), there appear to be no systematic features of states that help explain why some state counties report more informa-tion than other state counties.

2010 AND 2012 OVERALL COMPLETENESS BY SECTION

Although the fifteen items offer us a clear look at a specific subset of items over time, stakeholders are often interested in a variety of other data. Therefore, we now turn to a more detailed examination of the 2010

---

[2]   In 2008 the minimum percent complete excludes New York, which only provided aggregated total state data to the EAC and did not provide any county-level data. In 2010, New York complied and provided county-level data on individual items.

and 2012 EAVS with an eye on data completeness. Importantly, we note that just because states report data does not mean that the data are correct or comparable with other states, as we highlight later. For example, the survey asks states to identify the number of "new" registered voters, but that figure relies on a state's ability to know that a registration form represents a voter newly coming into the system, and not merely an update or duplicate entry. The degree to which states are able to make this assessment is unclear and is something we cannot assess in this chapter. Importantly, we note that differences in system management likely create some amount of noise in the data that researchers should be made aware of. The analysis here provides a deeper examination of the questionnaire and how states do or do not respond to it. Even with the caveat above, this is precisely the kind of information required by researchers who wish to use these data to answer questions of explanation and questions of description.

One of the first things to note about the EAVS full data set is that there is quite a bit of missing data. Unfortunately, the design of the questionnaire makes it unclear why the data are missing in many cases. The instructions state: "(2) Do not leave items blank – always provide an answer to the question asked using the 'data not available' or 'other' categories discussed below if needed. (3) Use the 'Data not available' box if the question asks for details that are not required by your state law or the question asks for information that is not currently collected." The instructions pose a few different problems for data providers and users. First, "data not available" represents two different types of problems: not required or not collected. These need to be delineated because the answers have different implications. Second, the use of "other" categories means the user has to filter through a lot of "other" data to determine what the data are characterizing and how different jurisdictions interpret the questions. In addition, given the large quantity of missing data on some responses across jurisdictions, it is not clear that the person who filled it out followed or understood the instructions. In some cases, I was left wondering if "missing" may have really meant zero, or if "data not available" really meant zero. Addressing the problems in data quality at the data collection stage would be helpful to election stakeholders.

Consider the first survey question in the EAVS asking for the total number of persons in each jurisdiction who were registered and eligible to vote in the November 2010 election. This measure is also included in the Pew subset of EAVS items discussed earlier. Importantly, every state was able to answer this question for each jurisdiction. Registration data by jurisdiction is easily available and transparent across states. Indeed, this is the most complete variable in the data set. However, the good news regarding a consistently reported figure across jurisdictions within states comes with some bad news because states use different numbers to compute the total number of registered voters. Fourteen states report active voters only (Alaska, Arizona, California, Idaho, Wyoming, Wisconsin, South Dakota, South Carolina, Kentucky, Maryland, Minnesota, New Hampshire, Ohio, Oregon); twenty-nine states report the combined total of active and inactive registered voters; two states (Pennsylvania and Texas) do not report whether they use active or inactive voters for this calculation; in four states it depends on the jurisdiction, with some jurisdictions not reporting at all and other jurisdictions reporting only active or both active and inactive (New York, 4 no reporting, 58 both; Illinois, 1 no report, 23 both, and 86 active only; Mississippi, 6 no report, 28 both, and 46 active only; Nevada, 9 both, 8 active only; Vermont, 14 no report, 202 both, 30 active only). North Dakota does not have voter registration.

The fact that different states report voter registration figures based on different definitions of registered voters reduces the reliability and efficacy of this measure, which is unfortunate. Although there is a follow-up question (A3) that asks for both inactive and active registrants, it is not entirely helpful because this variable is less complete than A1. This also is true within states as different jurisdictions appear to report using different definitions. The redundancy between questions A1 and A3 creates confusion; perhaps A3 should be the first EAVS question and questions A1 and A2 should be dropped for simplicity.

To examine completeness across the full range of items in the EAVS in both 2010 and 2012, I computed the mean completeness for each of the six sections of the survey.[3] To measure completeness, we summed the number of counties answering each question. Section A had eleven different question sections and fifty-nine total questions on registration.[4]

---

[3] I did not include questions that had the title "other" in it, since these were optional for each state.

[4] I omitted question four, which focused on SDR activities, because many states do not permit SDR.

TABLE 11.2. *EAVS completeness across all items in 2010 and 2012*

	Minimum	Maximum	Mean	Number of States at 100%	Number of States below 50%
Section A – Registration*					
2010	5%	100%	76%	10	9
2012	27%	100%	78%	4	8
Section B – UOCAVA					
2010	37%	100%	78%	5	2
2012	39%	99%	75%	0	4
Section C – Absentee					
2010	5%	100%	85%	21	5
2012	12%	100%	86%	13	6
Section D – Election Administration					
2010	8%	100%	68%	5	10
2012	6%	100%	70%	5	8
Section E – Provisional					
2010	0%	100%	80%	24	10
2012	0%	100%	76%	15	11
Section F – Turnout					
2010	25%	100%	86%	11	2
2012	17%	100%	83%	10	5

Note: North Dakota is excluded because it does not have voter registration.

Section B had eighteen different question sections with thirty-nine total questions on uniformed and overseas citizens absentee voting. Section C had five different question sections and twenty-two total questions on domestic civilian absentee ballots. Section D had five different question sections with fifteen total questions on election administration. Section E had two different section questions with thirteen total questions on provisional ballots. Section F had eight different question sections and eight total questions on Election Day activities. Table 11.2 shows the results for each section.

The range across sections is quite large and the results are very similar between 2010 and 2012. The smallest range of response is in Section B, with a range of 61 percent in 2012. Section B collects data required under the UOCAVA. State compliance with federal voting requirements may help explain why this section has the highest minimum response. Section B is followed by Section A in 2012, with a range of 73 percent, and then Section F, with a range of 75 percent. Absentee voters had a range of 88 percent in 2012 and election administration response had a range of 84 percent. Section E, provisional votes, did not change between 2010 and 2012. In both years it had a range of 100 percent.

The results between 2010 and 2012 are generally very similar and with overall high rates of completeness. The lowest section was Section D, election administration questions, which averaged 70 percent and the highest section in 2012 was Section C at 86 percent complete, which focused on questions related to absentee voting.

Despite general high-average completeness rates across sections in 2010 and 2012 there are a number of states that report on less than 50 percent of the questions. In 2012, eight states were below 50 percent on Section A, four states on Section B, six states on Section C, eight states on Section D, eleven states on Section E, and five states on Section F. Interestingly, even though Section E's range is 100, it has fifteen states in 2012 and twenty-four states in 2010 reporting nearly 100 percent of questionnaire items. Section C also has a relatively high rate of complete information with twenty-one states in 2010 and thirteen states in 2012 reporting nearly 100 percent of the requested information. Section D provides relatively poor coverage, given that only five states answered all the questions in 2010 and 2012. Section B also had a low number of states completing the items, with only five states in 2010 reporting at 100 percent and zero states reporting at 100 percent in 2012. In section A, ten states produced all the necessary information in 2010, but only four states produced all the necessary information in 2012.

Figure 11.1 shows the overall completeness rate for all sections of the EAVS in 2012. States are ordered from most to least compliant. Figure 11.2 breaks down completeness rates for each state by sections. The District of Columbia had the highest completeness rates across all items, with a score of 98 percent. New York did the worst, with reporting as low as 12 percent on Section A and as high as 49 percent in Section B. But what causes some states to report well and others to report poorly? As with the fifteen subitems discussed earlier, I examined a series of state-level characteristics to see if any correlated with reporting but found no relationships of interest. The amount of missing data does not relate to state characteristics in any obvious ways.

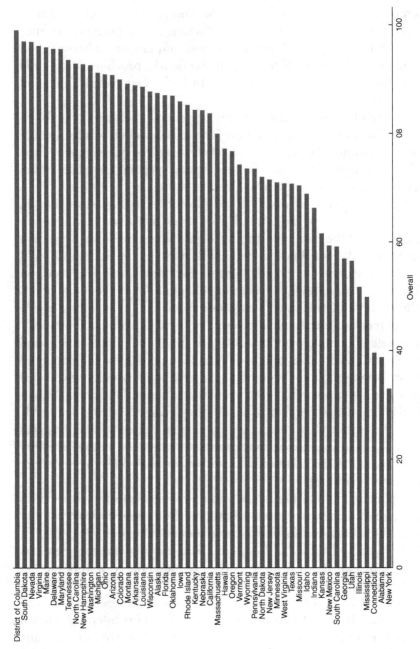

FIGURE 11.1. 2012 EAVS completeness rates by state.

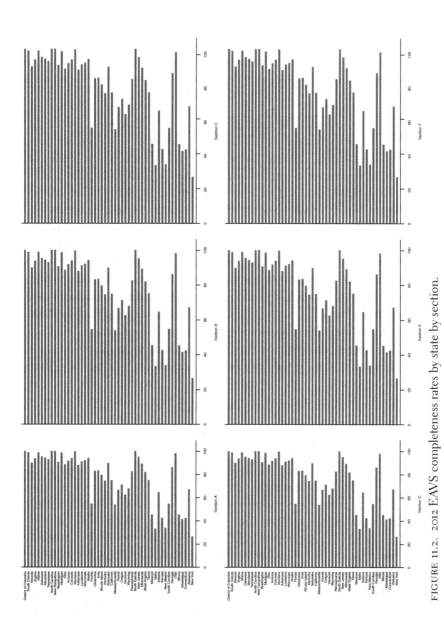

FIGURE 11.2. 2012 EAVS completeness rates by state by section.

EVALUATING TRANSPARENCY WITH THE EAC
QUANTITATIVE COMPONENT

The good news is that the EAC collects a great deal of interesting data and that with each election year more states are complying with the data reporting requests, increasing the amount of information available across jurisdictions and states. This is appealing to scholars, activists, and election officials who use these data to address questions related to elections and election administration. However, there is a great deal of unevenness across and within states in terms of reporting. This makes some items highly reliable and usable, while other items are not reliable because of their low degree of reporting compliance. In addition, the questionnaire encourages states to use the "other" categories and provide an explanation on items they cannot answer and why. These categories are difficult for researchers to code and analyze because they inevitably create unique measures as opposed to consistent ones. Jurisdictions and states should be encouraged to answer the questions posed to them with the best possible data sources and should be discouraged from using the "other" categories except when absolutely necessary.

If all the questions in the EAVS are important for transparency, then the best approach to measure data transparency within a state is to use the overall measure of transparency seen in Figure 11.2 and Table 11.2. This represents the overall level of transparency reported within the state jurisdictions. If a subset of questions such as those in Table 11.1 is deemed most important, then a presence/absence scale should be created on them. Justification for inclusion of a subset of measures needs to be well articulated and explained.

In addition, there are several measures from the EAVS that reflect broadly shared values and are likely influenced by election administration that could be important indicators of the quality of the election. One value that might be broadly accepted is that people who are qualified voters and make the effort to vote should have their votes counted. This value seems on its face nonpolitical and likely is influenced by actions taken by LEOs. With this value in mind, the following EAVS measures and their related items seem like strong candidates for inclusion in an EPI because they are transparent pieces of information that are present in or absent from the EAVS and because they provide information that tells us something about the quality of the election administrative process:

- Percent undeliverable absentee ballots
- Rejection or counting rate of absentee ballots
- Rejection or counting rate of UOCAVA ballots

- Rejection or counting of provisional rates that are directly tied to administrative or training issues, for example, missing items on the outer envelope form

Unsurprisingly, most of these items are examined as substantive indicators in other chapters of this book.

EVALUATING TRANSPARENCY WITH THE EAC QUALITATIVE COMPONENT

The contextual data from the Statutory Overview survey are important for many different stakeholders, especially academics, because they help us understand how different rules, laws, and institutions structure the election administration process and electoral outcomes. For example, states that have SDR generally have higher turnout because the costs of voting are reduced.

The contextual data are relatively complete and rich, but often not easy to work with because of the high level of detail and because the researcher must interpret many responses for placement into categories. In addition, the researcher must be sensitive to the fact that the rules and procedures as seen at the state level may vary in administrative practice at the local level.

TRANSPARENCY FOR VOTERS

In contrast with election activists, academics, and election officials, the average voter is not interested in such things as the percentage of provisional ballots or absentee ballots that are counted. In general, the voter's focus on the voting process is in advance of the election and on whether or not his or her vote was counted rather than postelection statistical analysis. Voters need easy and transparent information on how to register to vote, where to vote, and which candidates and issues will appear on the ballot. In addition, voters also need to be able to easily find information on absentee and provisional voting.

To assess transparency for voters, I collected original data during the month of September 2012 on questions related to voter information and relied on a study that was done by Pew in 2010, called *Being Online Is Still Not Enough: Reviews and Recommendations for State Election Websites 2010* (BONE II). Both data collection efforts examine each state's Web site to determine what information is available and how easy it was to access. Although these measures offer a valuable means for analysis regarding transparency for voters, it is important to note that we are relying on a single tool –the Internet – to address it. It is important to recognize that many people are still not connected to the Internet and could not avail themselves of this information and would have to use more traditional means to find information about the election, including voter registration information. Nevertheless, other tools, such as telephone calls or visits to the county clerk's office, are not easily measured. Therefore, I rely on a single tool, information on state election Web sites, which is available to likely a vast majority of potential voters to assess election transparency for voters, even though not all voters would have equal access to this information. A focus on online information is necessarily silent about other ways that potential voters might obtain election information.

The data collection was straightforward, based generally on the methodology within the first Pew study, *Being Online Is Not Enough: State Election Websites* (2008) (BONE I). I used a number of search phrases and included the state name as part of the phrase to determine how easy it was to find information needed by voters using a popular Internet search engine.

TRANSPARENCY FOR VOTERS: ONLINE SEARCHES

In the first search I focused on Web presence, using Google to search on the following phrases:

- Am I registered to vote in [state]
- Voting in [state]
- Register to vote in [state]
- Polling place in [state]
- Election candidates in [state]
- Absentee ballot in [state]
- Provisional ballot in [state]

Table 11.3 shows the results from the searches for each state. It shows that "voting in [state]," "register to vote in [state]," and "polling place in [state]" had the best search results with the appropriate state-level Web site showing up as the first results in more than seven in ten states. Considering the entire first page of results, 98 percent of appropriate state election Web sites appears. The phrases, "am I registered to vote in [state]" and "election candidates in [state]" fared more poorly. Not quite half (45 percent) of the Web pages were found in the first results for "am I registered to vote in [state]." The phrase "election candidates in [state]" did not appear as the first hit in hardly any state; only 6 percent (three states) appeared as

TABLE 11.3. *Google search phrases and results for states, 2012*

Search Term	First Result	Within First Five Results	Within First Page of Results	Not on First Page of Results	Total
Am I Registered to Vote in [State]*	45	22	0	33	100% (N = 49)
Voting in [State]	82	16	0	2	100% (N = 50)
Register to Vote in [State]*	88	8	2	2	100% (N = 49)
Polling Place in [State]**	72	6	6	16	100% (N = 49)
Election Candidates in [State]	6	48	20	26	100% (N = 50)
Absentee Ballot in [State]**	65	20	4	1	100% (N = 49)
Provisional Vote in [State]***	40	21	4	34	100% (N = 47)

Notes: *North Dakota is excluded because it does not have voter registration.
** Oregon is excluded because it uses an all-mail system.
*** Idaho, New Hampshire, and Minnesota indicate they are exempt from provisional balloting in the Statutory Overview.

the first hit when searching for information on candidates in the election. However, roughly half of the states were in the top five results with this search string and about three-quarters of states had information about candidates on the first page of results.[5] The phrase "absentee ballot in [state]" did fairly well with 65 percent of state Web sites showing up as the first results and another 20 percent within the first five and 99 percent on the first page. The phrase "provisional vote in [state]," however, fared rather poorly with one-third of state Web sites not appearing on the first page of results. About two in five states appeared as the first results with another one in five showing up within the first five results.

Aggregating across all the search terms there is a mixed picture of transparency for voters (see Table 11.4). Almost three in ten state

[5] Because the phrase "election candidates in [state]" might be awkward, I also tried "sample ballot in [state]," but it fared only slightly better. Forty percent of states did not have the correct result on the first page, though 28 percent, or fourteen states, provided the answer in the first result and another 22 percent were in the first five results, with another 10 percent on the first page.

TABLE 11.4. *Summary of Google phrases, in percentages, 2012*

Number of Items	First Result	Within First Five Results	Within First Page of Results	Not on First Page
0	2	2	0	29
1	0	0	2	41
2	16	0	0	18
3	18	6	2	8
4	29	18	8	2
5	26	22	24	2
6	8	29	37	0
7	2	23	28	0
Total	101*	100	101*	100

* Due to a rounding error.

(28 percent) Web sites are found on the first page of results, but in only one state (Virginia) did the appropriate Web site turn up as the first search result for every item.

When correlating the search phrase index with various state-level variables to determine if state characteristics are related to better Web sites, few relationships appear. Data completeness and the Google search phrase results are moderately and significantly correlated at .32. The correlation increases to .55 with the single Google search phrase "register to vote in [state]." These results suggest that it is nothing systematic about state characteristics that leads states to develop better or worse Web sites, but that states that invest more time and resources in providing information provide information to multiple targets. States in which it is easier to find information for voters on the Web are also more likely to provide information requested by the EAC on the EAVS questionnaire.

TRANSPARENCY FOR VOTERS: INFORMATION

Voters are interested in knowing if they are registered to vote, how they can register to vote if they are not, where vote centers or precincts are located if they are voting in-person either early or on Election Day, how they can vote absentee, information on provisional voting, and if their votes were counted if they voted by mail or provisionally. I examined each state's Web site and found mixed results for critical voter

TABLE 11.5. *Availability of specific voter information on state Web sites, 2012*

Does Web Site Have:	Available	Unavailable	Total
Online registration*	24	76	100% (N = 50)
Polling place locations**	94	6	100% (N = 50)
Registration verification*	82	18	100% (N = 50)
Absentee ballot information**	96	4	(100%) (N = 50)
Confirmation that absentee ballot is counted**	31	69	100% (N = 50)
Provisional voting information	72	28	100% (N = 51)
Confirmation that provisional vote is counted***	34	66	100% (N = 49)

Notes: *North Dakota is excluded because it does not have voter registration.
** Oregon is excluded because it uses an all-mail system.
*** Minnesota and Idaho are exempt from provisional voting because of their SDR policy.

information (see Table 11.5). Most states do not allow voters to register online in one easy step. Three-quarters of states do not provide an online voter registration process. Twelve states, including Arizona, California, Colorado, Indiana, Kansas, Louisiana, Maryland, Nevada, Oregon, South Carolina, Utah, and Washington, do have a fully online process to register to vote. New York also has an online process, but it is located on the Department of Motor Vehicle Web page and is not linked from the Secretary of State's page. Because of this, it is extremely difficult to find, and while technically it exists, it is not very functional and neither accessible nor transparent. Several states offer an online form that the voter has to print out and mail in, but this is not the same as a simple process that allows voters to register in one step using a Web site provided by the secretary of state or other state election official.

Nearly all states (94 percent, 45 states total) have information on polling place locations and information on casting an absentee ballot (96 percent). About four in five states include registration verification on their Web sites. However, information about whether a vote was counted is much less transparent. About two-thirds of states do not have information on whether an absentee ballot was counted (69 percent) or if a provisional vote was counted (66 percent).

TABLE 11.6. *Summary of specific voter information on state Web sites*

Frequency	Percent
0	0
1	4
2	4
3	18
4	27
5	31
6	16
Total	100

Although many states provide information on voting locations, quite a number of states do not allow for online registration or verification, and few states provide information on whether ballots cast absentee by mail or provisionally are counted or not. Given that there is some evidence in the literature that absentee voters have less confidence in their vote being counted (Alvarez et al. 2008; Atkeson and Saunders 2007), providing transparency on this issue may help to reduce the gap between in-person and absentee voters.

A summary index, shown in Table 11.6, includes all six pieces of information. It tells a mixed story about essential voter information; only 16 percent of states provide all six pieces of information, and nearly one-third of states provide five pieces of information.

TRANSPARENCY FOR VOTERS: QUALITATIVE ASSESSMENTS OF STATE WEB SITES

In contrast to objective assessments of what is available online, the usability of a Web site is a much more difficult concept to measure. This is because the concept of usability is inherently subjective. *Usability* encompasses hard-to-define concepts, including usefulness, likeability, efficiency, and intuitiveness. I measured all four of these concepts with the help of graduate research assistants who were trained to code Web sites. We used a subjective rating to assess each site, as well as several quantitative measures that were consistent with the underlying concept we were interested in measuring.

Even though our ratings were subjective, we discovered that the general usability of each elections Web site was fairly clear to us within a few minutes. First, we found that states that provided a Web site that was solely devoted to elections, instead of including information about all the secretary of state's functions and business, were easier to use. For example, focused sites, such as South Carolina's (www.scvotes.org), were more intuitive than catchall sites, such as the one from Massachusetts (www.sec.state.ma.us/ele). This also relates to a broader point: simplicity almost always provided a more usable Web site than those that were cluttered and hence made it difficult to find the necessary links of interest. A specific example of this is the inclusion of large buttons to links for common information needed by voters, where the most usable sites included these links at the top or side of all the Web pages. We found that only nineteen, or 37 percent, of states had an easy-to-find button that directed the voter to items of obvious interest to this client. Because most online information searches start with Google, the usability ratings were based partially on whether the state's election page was returned in the first couple of results for predefined search phrases. Thus, a Web site was considered especially inefficient when Google searches did not initially return the desired information. As a quantitative assessment of this feature, we counted the number of clicks it took to get to a state's voter registration information from a Google search. The mode was two clicks with twenty-eight (55 percent) states in this category. One state, South Dakota, was the first search hit. Fourteen states took three clicks, and 16 percent, or eight states, took four full clicks to find information on registering to vote. Additional frustrations were caused when commonly provided information was not online and instead the site provided a mailing address and/or phone number where the information could be requested. Similarly, links that were not intuitive or particularly well labeled that led to unintended pages were considered less usable than those sites that did not have this problem.

In terms of likability, about two-thirds of Web sites met this criteria either "a lot" or "somewhat," while about one-third were not very likable (see Table 11.7). Using the same categories, states did a bit better on intuitiveness and efficiency (see Table 11.8). About two in five states were very intuitive and efficient, and another two in five were somewhat intuitive and efficient. However, about one in six states scored poorly on this measure. More quantitatively, we found that in about fifteen states, it took a short time to find the information we needed. Another twenty states were slightly longer and were what we labeled about average. A total of sixteen states took a long time (thirteen states) or a very long time (three states). We also found that the amount of

TABLE 11.7. *How much did I like using the Web site?*

Category	Percent
A lot	10
Somewhat	56
Very little	32
Not at all	2
Total	100

TABLE 11.8. *Are tools for looking up registration, finding a polling place intuitive and efficient?*

Category	Percent
Very intuitive and efficient	40
Somewhat	44
Not very	14
Not at all	2
Total	100

TABLE 11.9. *Usability of Web site*

Category	Percent
Useful and usable, user-centered implementation	36
Might cause some frustration, but it is not fatal	38
Likely to cause initial task failures, but users can recover with a significant effort	26
Total	100

text was related to our feelings of general likability, intuitiveness, and efficiency, with more text reducing our favorability toward the Web site along these dimensions. Few states had a lot of text to read (four states, or 8 percent of states), and nineteen states had very little for us to read, which was preferred. That left most states (twenty-eight, or 55 percent of states) in the middle with some text to drudge through to find the items of interest, but not too much.

In terms of overall usability, a little more than one-third of states were seen as user centered, providing useful and usable information (see Table 11.9). Nearly two in five were somewhat frustrating, but a determined user could navigate it successfully. About one-quarter of state sites were frustrating, making it difficult to find desired information, but, with significant effort on the part of the user, the Web site was manageable. Unfortunately, this suggests that many Web sites are more difficult to navigate then they should be. In general, this suggests that states need to be more attentive to their Web sites and the quality and layout of information therein.

Evaluating Transparency for Voters

The measures we examined on Web presence and Web information are easy to obtain and simple to code. Given the criteria we used for measurement, these are highly reliable measures. They are also valid in what they measure, though we note that there are other ways for voters to obtain information and some potential voters do not have access to the Internet. Nevertheless, the ongoing expansion of the Internet and ever increasing access of this resource to potential voters makes these desirable measures of transparency.

However, we are less certain about the reliability and validity of the qualitative assessments of the Web sites. Although we found it easy to score the Web site across these measures, we note that in our discussion group that individuals had different preferences in Web site design. Intercoder reliability was not high across several measures, suggesting that Web site evaluation depends heavily on personal tastes. These differences in taste, and we imagine experience, across individuals probably matter quite a bit in these more qualitative assessments. When we correlate our usability measure with BONE I and BONE II data on usability, the Pearson coefficients are small (.16 with BONE I and .23 with BONE II) and insignificant. Of course, BONE I and BONE II data used a much different methodology and did not ask users to rate the Web site, but defined a set of terms to find on the Web site and used that information to determine usability. These factors may be important explanations for the low correlation. Second, the differences in methodology could also account for score differences. In the BONE I data, seven criteria were used for evaluating usability of state election Web sites, while ours was a user-based attitude. Nevertheless, the differences between the two, along with concerns about how user taste and experience influence perceptions of usability, lead us to evaluate the subjective measures as less reliable.

Additional testing needs to be done to determine how users vary in evaluating state election Web sites. While broad criteria that sum into an index may be an especially reliable measure, as was done in the BONE I and BONE II data, there are also strengths to an attitude-based assessment of a Web site that is global and encompasses the whole experience since that is how users interface and work with the Web.

Finally, we note that Web sites are constantly changing and so continued examination of how changes affect voters and their ability to obtain the types of information they need to be good democratic citizens needs to be monitored.

Looking Ahead

Election transparency focuses on the ease and availability of information so that qualified potential voters may easily participate in the election and election stakeholders can evaluate the election.

The indicators for election transparency are (1) data completeness rates of the EAVS, either a subset of items or the entire data set, (2) usability of state election Web sites, and (3) number of state election Web sites that have registration verification, polling place locators, online registration, information on mail-in absentee voting, and information on provisional voting.

Of the three indicators, the transparency for voter items is the most reliable. It is easily replicable across states using the same methodology and if we repeat our data collection efforts, we find consistent state-level results. The EAVS data are consistent in that the data reported are likely a good representation of state- and jurisdictional-level data. However, states are not always reporting the same measure and even within states sometimes the same measure is not being reported. Thus, there are some definitional problems within the EAVS that likely need to be addressed so that all officials are reporting the same data for each measure. Data consistency in definitions is critical for reliable and valid measures. The usability of state Web sites may be the least reliable, given that this represents a user attitude. More testing needs to be done across individuals to determine the reliability and validity of this measure as we created it.

In general, the measures within the EAVS and the statutory overview have validity. They provide information on many different aspects of the election process at the jurisdictional level. The transparency for voters' measures as tested also has validity. Voters need specific information to participate in the process, and these measures represent good indicators of the types of information they need to participate.

The most important issues surrounding the reliability of measures associated with the EAVS are completeness across jurisdictions within states and the potential different meanings behind data coded as missing in the data set. There also needs to be consistency in definitions across jurisdictions. The good news is that data completeness rates have been improving over time. However, there needs to be continued pressure from stakeholders and government for states to fully, consistently, and clearly participate.

Indicators of Election Performance

As was noted in the acknowledgments, this volume originally arose as a way to kill two birds with one stone: to help infuse additional energy into the quantitative analysis of national election policy and to help provide guidance to the Pew Charitable Trusts, which in 2012 was considering whether to launch what eventually emerged as the Elections Performance Index (EPI). At the time the papers for this volume were commissioned, Pew was considering more than twenty indicators for inclusion in the index. Although the authors were given freedom to approach the topics of their chapters how they wished, and to report on any conclusions they reached in the process of doing their analyses, each author (or set of authors) was asked to provide some assessment of the indicators that were most relevant to the topic they addressed.

Readers of this volume will recognize the independence with which the authors pursued their tasks. Some provided explicit discussions of the reliability and validity of a set of possible election index indicators, while other authors were more implicit in their assessments. It is to the credit of the authors that their analyses led to the abandonment of some of the indicators that that been proposed for the EPI. (The clearest example was a proposed indicator concerning the confidence voters had that their votes had been counted as cast. Paul Gronke's analysis in Chapter 10 provided a good argument that measures of voter confidence are important for understanding how voters think about the elections they participate in, but that survey responses to standard voter confidence questions are too influenced by partisan attitudes to be considered useful for assessing how well state and local officials run elections.) In other cases, the analysis required Pew and its advisory committee to rethink how indicators were measured, or how they were conceptualized.

Throughout this volume, the various authors made reference to the candidate indicators that were in consideration for the EPI as of the date the chapters were commissioned in the late summer of 2012. In the following pages, we report the raw state-level values of these indicators. When the chapters in this volume were originally written, only data for 2008 and 2010 were available to the authors. (Data from 2004 and 2006 were available but, as mentioned in the introduction, they were of such poor quality – especially the indicators derived from the Election Administration and Voting Survey (EAVS) – no effort was made to rest any analysis on data from those years.) After the chapters were written, the various sources that fed in data for the construction of the indicators eventually became available for the 2012 election. Most of the chapters include at least some reference to the 2012 data, though the authors were often unable to incorporate the 2012 data into their analysis.

We invite the reader to visit the EPI Web site, maintained by the Pew Charitable Trusts, for information about how the EPI was eventually constructed. Included in that Web site is a methodological appendix that addresses reliability and validity issues of most of the statewide measures addressed in this volume. A few of the indicators summarized here were not included at all in the EPI. Among these are the voter confidence and registration list deadwood measures. Some of the indicators were altered in how they were constructed. These indicators are primarily those constructed using data from the Voting and Registration Supplement (VRS) of the Current Population Survey (CPS). For these indicators, further research revealed that it was necessary to take averages across multiple years of data in order to construct a measure that had the requisite level of reliability.

INDICATOR DEFINITIONS

Percent of Voting-Eligible Population Registered to Vote

This measure was constructed using data from the VRS of the CPS. Every respondent was coded as eligible if they (1) voted (VRS item $PES1 = 1$), or (2) did not vote ($PES1 = 2$) and was not ineligible to vote ($PES3 \neq 8$). Eligible voters were coded as registered if they voted or did not vote.

Turnout as a Percentage of Voting-Eligible Population

This measure was constructed using turnout and voting-eligible population (VEP) data from the United States Elections Project Web site, http://elections.gmu.edu/voter_turnout.htm. For states that do not explicitly report turnout, turnout is measured as the total number of votes cast for president or the highest turnout office on the ballot (for off-year elections).

Percentage of New Voter Registrations That Are Rejected or Invalid

This measure was constructed using data from the EAVS. States are excluded if more than 15 percent of local jurisdictions (weighted by registration) do not report the data necessary to calculate the measure.

The numerator is the number of invalid or rejected voter registrations, other than duplicates (EAVS item A5e). The denominator is the total voter registration forms processed (A5a), less the sum of the following items: duplicate of existing valid registrations (A5d) and changes to name, party, or within-jurisdiction address change (A5f).

Percentage of Nonvoters Who State They Failed to Vote Because
of Registration Problems

This measure was constructed using data from the VRS of the CPS. Self-reported nonvoters are those who answered no to item PES1. Nonvoters because of registration problems are those who chose answer 8 ("Registration problems [i.e., didn't receive absentee ballot, not registered in current location]") to item PES4 ("What is the main reason you did not vote?"). This measure is the average of the last three presidential or midterm elections.

Deadwood on Voter Registration Lists

These measures were constructed using data provided by the firm Catalist described in Chapter 3. The two measures included here are "likely deadwood" and "probably deadwood." Data were collected in early 2010. See Chapter 3 for further information.

Number of Other Databases the State Registration Database
Is Cross-Checked Against

This measure was constructed by directly coding responses to the Election Assistance Commission's (EAC's) statutory overview, from table 5 of the EAC's biennial statutory overview report.

Percentage of Turnout That Cast a Provisional Ballot

This measure was constructed using data from the EAVS. States are excluded if more than 15 percent of local jurisdictions (weighted by registration) do not report the data necessary to calculate the measure.

The numerator is the number of people who voted using a provisional ballot (EAVS item F1e). The denominator is the total number of people who participated in the general election F1a).

Percentage of Provisional Ballots Rejected

This measure was constructed using data from the EAVS. States are excluded if more than 15 percent of local jurisdictions (weighted by registration) do not report the data necessary to calculate the measure.

The numerator is the number of rejected provisional ballots (EAVS item E2c). The denominator is the total number of voters who submitted a provisional ballot (E1).

Percentage of Civilian Absentee Ballots Returned for Counting That Are Rejected

This measure was constructed using data from the EAVS. States are excluded if more than 15 percent of local jurisdictions (weighted by registration) do not report the data necessary to calculate the measure.

The numerator is the number of rejected civilian absentee ballots provisional ballots (EAVS item C4b). The denominator is the total number of voters who participated in the general election (F1a).

Percentage of Civilian Absentee Ballots Transmitted That Are Not Returned for Counting

This measure was constructed using data from the EAVS. States are excluded if more than 15 percent of local jurisdictions (weighted by registration) do not report the data necessary to calculate the measure.

The numerator is the number of civilian absentee ballots not returned for counting, measured as the number of absentee ballots transmitted to voters (EAVS item C1a) minus the number of ballots returned for counting (C1b). The denominator is the number of absentee ballots transmitted to voters (C1a).

Percentage of UOCAVA Ballots Returned for Counting That Are Rejected

This measure was constructed using data from the EAVS. States are excluded if more than 15 percent of local jurisdictions (weighted by registration) do not report the data necessary to calculate the measure.

The numerator is the number of rejected Uniformed and Overseas Citizens Absentee Voting Act (UOCAVA) ballots (EAVS item B13). The denominator is the total number of UOCAVA ballots returned for counting (B2a).

Percentage of UOCAVA Ballots Transmitted That Are Not Returned for Counting

This measure was constructed using data from the EAVS. States are excluded if more than 15 percent of local jurisdictions (weighted by registration) do not report the data necessary to calculate the measure.

The numerator is the number of UOCAVA ballots not returned for counting, measured as the number of UOCAVA ballots transmitted to voters (EAVS item B1a) minus the number of ballots returned for counting (B2a). The denominator is the number of absentee ballots transmitted to voters (B1a).

Average Time Waiting to Vote

This measure was constructed using responses to the Survey of the Performance of American Elections (SPAE). The District of Columbia was not included in the study in 2008. Oregon and Washington are excluded because they are vote-by-mail states. The SPAE was not conducted in 2010.

Waiting times are calculated after first imputing waiting times, in minutes, based on individual responses, which were expressed in fixed categories. Respondents saying they did not wait any time to vote were assigned a value of zero, those waiting from one to five minutes were assigned the middle of the interval (i.e., three minutes), and so on. Respondents reporting they waited more than one hour were asked to report specifically how long they waited.

Percentage of Nonvoters Who Say They Didn't Vote because of Polling Place Problems

This measure was constructed using data from the VRS of the CPS. Self-reported nonvoters are those who answered no to item PES1. Nonvoters because of polling place problems are those who chose answer 10 ("Inconvenient hours, polling place or hours or lines too long") to item PES4 ("What is the main reason you did not vote?").

Percentage of Voters Who State Their Polling Places Was Easy to Find

This measure was constructed using responses to the SPAE. The District of Columbia was not included in the study in 2008. Oregon and Washington are excluded because they are vote-by-mail states. The SPAE was not conducted in 2010.

Percentages are respondents reporting it was "easy" or "very easy" to find the polling place.

Percentage of Nonvoters Who Say They Didn't Vote because of a Permanent Illness or Disability

This measure was constructed using data from the VRS of the CPS. Self-reported nonvoters are those who answered no to item PES1. Nonvoters because of permanent illness or disability are those who chose answer 1 ("Illness or disability [own or family's]") to item PES4 ("What is the main reason you did not vote?").

Residual Vote Rate

This measure was constructed using data from official election returns and turnout statistics reported by state departments of elections. The residual vote rate is not calculated in off-year elections.

The number of residual votes is defined as total turnout minus the number of votes counted for president. The residual vote rate is calculated as the number of residual votes divided by total turnout, then multiplied by 100 to make it a percentage.

Postelection Audit Required

This measure was constructed by directly coding responses to the EAC's statutory overview, from table 10 of the EAC's biennial statutory overview report.

Percentage of Voters Who State They Are Confident Their
Vote Was Counted as Cast

This measure was constructed using responses to the SPAE. The District of Columbia was not included in the study in 2008. Percentages are respondents reporting they were either "very confident" or "somewhat confident" their vote was counted as cast.

EAVS Data Completeness Rates

This measure was constructed using data from the EAVS, defined as the percentage of fifteen core measures in the EAVS that are reported by each state's counties. See Pew Charitable Trusts, *Election Administration by the Numbers.*

Usability of State Election Web Sites

This measure was constructed based on expert assessments of state election Web sites, and reported in the Pew Charitable Trust reports *Being Online Is Not Enough* (Pew Center on the States 2008) and *Being Online Is Still Not Enough* (Pew Center on the States 2011). A comparable usability assessment was not released in 2012.

Number of State Election Sites That Have Various Capabilities
on the State Election Web Site

This measure was constructed based on expert assessments of state election Web sites, and reported in the Pew Charitable Trust reports *Being Online Is Not Enough* (Pew Center on the States 2008), *Being Online Is Still Not Enough* (Pew Center on the States 2011), and *Online Lookup Tools for Voters* (2013).

Values of Election Performance Indicators Referenced in This Volume

	Percent of Voting-Eligible Population That Is Registered to Vote			Turnout as a Percentage of Voting-Eligible Population			Percentage of New Voter Registrations That Are Rejected or Invalid		
State	2008	2010	2012	2008	2010	2012	2008	2010	2012
AK	87.6%	83.5%	86.8%	68.3%	52.6%	58.9%	6.8%	8.2%	9.7%
AL	85.2%	82.1%	86.3%	61.0%	43.1%	58.9%	0.0%	0.1%	–
AR	74.2%	71.9%	75.9%	52.9%	37.5%	50.5%	–	4.5%	–
AZ	82.9%	80.3%	77.5%	57.4%	41.5%	52.9%	–	–	–
CA	82.5%	75.9%	80.1%	61.7%	45.1%	55.2%	–	–	–
CO	84.0%	82.4%	87.8%	71.6%	50.7%	70.3%	–	6.6%	1.7%
CT	85.6%	81.4%	84.5%	66.6%	46.0%	60.9%	0.4%	–	–
DC	90.9%	84.7%	92.5%	61.7%	29.6%	61.9%	–	2.9%	0.5%
DE	85.8%	81.7%	86.3%	65.8%	47.8%	62.7%	24.6%	16.0%	4.1%
FL	87.7%	81.8%	85.3%	66.6%	42.3%	63.5%	0.4%	–	6.3%
GA	84.9%	78.9%	86.3%	62.7%	40.6%	58.4%	0.1%	0.2%	–
HI	69.6%	65.8%	70.9%	49.0%	40.1%	44.2%	–	–	–
IA	85.3%	82.4%	86.5%	69.7%	50.8%	69.9%	0.8%	0.2%	46.5%
ID	77.1%	71.2%	77.1%	64.8%	42.8%	59.6%	–	–	–
IL	85.2%	81.8%	84.8%	64.3%	43.2%	58.9%	4.6%	40.4%	3.7%
IN	81.1%	73.5%	78.4%	60.3%	38.0%	55.1%	2.0%	54.5%	71.7%
KS	77.2%	76.7%	81.3%	63.5%	41.7%	56.8%	0.0%	0.0%	–
KY	83.2%	76.5%	80.8%	59.0%	44.1%	55.3%	–	20.9%	20.9%
LA	88.1%	86.2%	85.0%	61.8%	39.9%	60.4%	5.9%	5.6%	7.8%
MA	87.1%	81.9%	87.7%	67.3%	49.7%	66.3%	–	3.3%	21.8%

State	Percent of Voting-Eligible Population That Is Registered to Vote			Turnout as a Percentage of Voting-Eligible Population			Percentage of New Voter Registrations That Are Rejected or Invalid		
	2008	2010	2012	2008	2010	2012	2008	2010	2012
MD	87.0%	81.2%	87.1%	67.8%	46.5%	66.2%	–	2.1%	0.5%
ME	86.5%	86.0%	85.5%	71.8%	56.0%	68.1%	0.8%	1.0%	1.7%
MI	90.4%	86.8%	89.5%	69.7%	45.2%	64.7%	0.2%	0.3%	0.3%
MN	91.8%	85.3%	87.7%	78.1%	55.9%	75.7%	0.1%	0.2%	0.1%
MO	85.5%	81.8%	86.8%	69.1%	44.5%	62.5%	–	–	8.4%
MS	86.8%	82.2%	90.2%	61.0%	37.0%	59.7%	–	–	–
MT	80.2%	77.7%	82.7%	67.1%	48.4%	62.6%	1.0%	1.7%	1.1%
NC	84.5%	79.3%	88.8%	66.1%	39.8%	64.6%	3.3%	9.1%	4.3%
ND	88.9%	82.8%	84.2%	63.6%	46.7%	60.5%	– [a]	– [a]	– [a]
NE	82.7%	77.4%	81.5%	63.7%	38.0%	60.1%	0.5%	–	0.3%
NH	84.3%	77.6%	84.2%	72.5%	46.2%	70.1%	–	–	0.0%
NJ	85.5%	81.9%	86.5%	67.7%	37.8%	61.9%	4.5%	8.4%	8.6%
NM	80.8%	74.7%	82.5%	61.2%	43.1%	54.7%	–	–	–
NV	77.6%	71.3%	79.0%	57.2%	41.2%	57.1%	6.1%	0.4%	3.9%
NY	83.9%	78.5%	82.5%	59.6%	36.3%	53.2%	–	–	–
OH	84.4%	79.1%	85.0%	67.8%	46.2%	64.6%	–	2.3%	7.0%
OK	81.1%	70.3%	77.0%	56.3%	38.7%	49.2%	–	–	–
OR	85.0%	84.2%	85.9%	68.3%	53.9%	63.2%	–	–	–
PA	81.4%	76.3%	81.0%	64.2%	41.7%	59.4%	36.9%	55.5%	2.8%
RI	84.2%	80.5%	83.6%	62.3%	44.9%	58.0%	–	–	–
SC	80.7%	77.8%	82.5%	58.2%	40.3%	56.6%	–	–	–
SD	83.6%	81.2%	83.1%	65.6%	53.9%	59.4%	–	0.3%	–
TN	80.2%	76.3%	78.6%	57.4%	34.7%	52.2%	–	–	–
TX	79.5%	75.0%	77.1%	54.1%	32.2%	49.7%	21.3%	7.0%	57.0%
UT	75.8%	74.0%	76.8%	57.1%	36.7%	55.4%	–	2.2%	3.3%
VA	87.3%	83.2%	86.1%	67.6%	39.2%	66.4%	5.2%	2.3%	2.4%
VT	83.4%	83.1%	82.7%	67.7%	49.9%	60.4%	0.2%	–	–
WA	84.2%	82.7%	84.0%	67.3%	54.3%	64.1%	–	–	–
WI	86.9%	81.1%	87.8%	72.7%	52.1%	72.5%	–	–	0.1%
WV	78.1%	74.9%	78.9%	51.2%	36.7%	46.3%	–	0.5%	–
WY	78.3%	72.5%	74.7%	63.1%	45.8%	58.9%	–	–	–

State	Percentage of Nonvoters Who State They Failed to Vote because of Registration Problems			Deadwood on Voter Registration Lists		Number of Other Databases the State Registration Database is Cross-Checked Against[e]		
	2008	2010	2012	Likely[g]	Probably[g]	2008	2010	2012
AK	5.2%	3.5%	6.4%	0.0%	0.4%	2	1	1
AL	7.6%	7.9%	7.6%	0.2%	2.7%	4	4	4
AR	3.8%	2.5%	5.1%	1.1%	14.6%	5	5	4
AZ	9.2%	6.4%	9.0%	1.0%	1.3%	5	5	6
CA	8.6%	5.2%	9.4%	0.0%	0.3%	6	6	5
CO	6.4%	4.8%	6.4%	1.4%	11.0%	4	5	7
CT	4.7%	2.9%	4.2%	4.9%	4.1%	4	4	4
DC	10.1%	6.1%	9.3%	0.0%	0.4%	0	1	3
DE	4.8%	1.3%	5.1%	2.5%	4.7%	1	2	1
FL	9.6%	5.0%	7.8%	1.1%	6.8%	3	4	3
GA	5.8%	5.1%	6.3%	0.3%	5.4%	–	6	9
HI	6.5%	10.2%	8.2%	1.6%	2.3%	1	1	2
IA	3.8%	3.3%	1.9%	2.8%	2.0%	4	3	2
ID	2.2%	1.7%	3.2%	0.0%	0.0%	2	3	2
IL	6.4%	4.1%	6.1%	0.5%	4.9%	2	4	4
IN	6.9%	2.6%	6.5%	0.4%	2.1%	5	5	4
KS	5.1%	3.5%	6.5%	0.5%	4.1%	6	6	4
KY	5.9%	2.7%	4.5%	0.0%	0.7%	3	2	2
LA	4.5%	4.1%	3.3%	0.0%	0.6%	5	5	5
MA	8.7%	2.2%	6.8%	0.0%	0.3%	3	3	4
MD	9.2%	3.9%	6.6%	2.0%	2.6%	2	4	3
ME	1.4%	0.7%	1.2%	1.6%	0.6%	4	4	3
MI	4.7%	3.3%	3.2%	0.0%	0.7%	1	2	1
MN	1.2%	1.4%	1.2%	0.0%	0.0%	2	3	3
MO	9.9%	4.5%	7.6%	0.7%	4.8%	4	4	3
MS	8.3%	2.8%	6.5%	0.0%	0.5%	1	1	3
MT	3.7%	3.3%	5.5%	0.3%	4.8%	5	5	4
NC	7.5%	3.2%	7.7%	2.0%	3.0%	2	4	4
ND	2.3%	1.5%	2.3%	0.0%	0.0%	2	4	5
NE	7.1%	2.9%	7.9%	0.0%	0.3%	4	5	4
NH	2.2%	1.5%	2.0%	0.0%	0.5%	4	5	5
NJ	6.6%	2.9%	5.3%	0.0%	0.4%	–	5	11
NM	6.0%	3.8%	6.0%	0.1%	0.8%	–	2	0
NV	9.5%	3.4%	8.2%	0.4%	5.7%	3	3	3

State	Percentage of Nonvoters Who State They Failed to Vote because of Registration Problems			Deadwood on Voter Registration Lists		Number of Other Databases the State Registration Database is Cross-Checked Against[e]		
	2008	2010	2012	Likely[g]	Probably[g]	2008	2010	2012
NY	6.2%	2.6%	5.3%	1.7%	3.5%	3	2	2
OH	8.1%	4.7%	8.0%	0.0%	0.8%	2	3	5
OK	9.4%	5.2%	9.8%	3.0%	4.2%	4	3	3
OR	13.4%	9.4%	13.8%	0.5%	6.3%	2	2	2
PA	5.8%	3.1%	3.9%	0.6%	5.8%	3	5	4
RI	8.2%	4.5%	6.4%	3.1%	2.1%	1	1	1
SC	7.5%	6.0%	6.1%	0.8%	8.4%	1	2	1
SD	7.8%	4.7%	8.6%	2.0%	4.6%	3	3	2
TN	10.3%	5.0%	6.8%	0.6%	4.8%	0	1	1
TX	7.0%	3.0%	6.5%	0.0%	0.2%	2	1	0
UT	9.3%	3.3%	10.2%	2.2%	8.3%	2	3	2
VA	10.1%	4.4%	7.7%	0.1%	0.5%	5	6	9
VT	4.1%	3.1%	4.8%	1.2%	0.0%	2	3	2
WA	10.6%	10.2%	11.4%	0.3%	3.7%	2	3	3
WI	0.8%	1.6%	1.2%	0.0%	0.7%	4	4	4
WV	4.9%	3.3%	4.9%	0.9%	3.1%	1	2	0
WY	6.0%	2.1%	4.2%	0.0%	0.0%	3	4	4

State	Percentage of Turnout That Cast a Provisional Ballot			Percentage of Provisional Ballots Rejected			Percentage of Civilian Absentee Ballots Returned for Counting That Are Rejected		
	2008	2010	2012	2008	2010	2012	2008	2010	2012
AK	6.21%	4.98%	6.04%	0.08%	0.50%	0.08%	0.19%	0.21%	0.27%
AL	–	0.24%	0.37%	–	0.12%	0.21%	–	–	–
AR	0.20%	0.17%	0.24%	–	0.09%	0.16%	–	0.16%	0.09%
AZ	6.54%	4.67%	7.89%	1.92%	0.83%	1.42%	0.29%	0.47%	0.53%
CA	5.79%	5.19%	8.13%	0.99%	0.65%	1.36%	0.97%	0.69%	0.45%
CO	2.19%	2.15%	2.42%	0.34%	0.20%	0.38%	0.33%	0.43%	0.63%
CT	0.04%	0.08%	0.06%	0.03%	0.05%	0.05%	0.19%	0.11%	0.15%
DC	6.49%	3.96%	13.13%	1.84%	0.29%	1.10%	1.04%	0.23%	0.13%

(continued)

	Percentage of Turnout That Cast a Provisional Ballot			Percentage of Provisional Ballots Rejected			Percentage of Civilian Absentee Ballots Returned for Counting That Are Rejected		
State	2008	2010	2012	2008	2010	2012	2008	2010	2012
DE	0.09%	0.01%	0.11%	0.08%	0.01%	0.10%	0.08%	0.04%	0.06%
FL	0.42%	0.24%	0.50%	0.22%	0.06%	0.21%	0.22%	0.33%	0.24%
GA	0.44%	0.32%	–	0.23%	0.00%		0.09%	0.02%	0.02%
HI	0.11%	0.05%	0.16%	0.09%	0.04%	0.14%	0.18%	0.31%	0.25%
IA	0.28%	0.18%	0.31%	0.02%	0.03%	0.05%	0.28%	0.38%	0.51%
ID	– [b]	– [b]	– [b]	– [b]	– [b]	– [b]	0.13%	0.31%	0.14%
IL	–	–	0.82%	–	0.37%	0.57%	–	0.08%	0.08%
IN	–	0.10%	0.18%	–	0.06%	0.15%	–	0.42%	0.45%
KS	3.18%	2.11%	3.48%	0.98%	0.59%	1.21%	0.33%	0.49%	0.45%
KY	0.05%	0.01%	0.02%	0.04%	0.01%	0.01%	0.10%	0.08%	0.10%
LA	0.41%	0.02%	0.34%	0.24%	0.00%	0.21%	0.09%	0.06%	0.12%
MA	0.38%	0.12%	0.41%	0.27%	0.09%	0.30%	0.06%	–	0.08%
MD	1.92%	2.00%	2.92%	0.64%	0.17%	0.41%	0.07%	0.06%	0.06%
ME	0.04%	0.03%	0.04%	0.00%	0.00%	0.00%	0.25%	0.20%	0.30%
MI	0.08%	0.03%	0.06%	0.04%	0.02%	0.03%	0.17%	0.17%	0.17%
MN	– [b]	– [b]	– [b]	– [b]	– [b]	– [b]	0.34%	0.37%	0.26%
MO	0.23%	0.19%	0.23%	0.17%	0.10%	0.16%	0.18%	0.10%	0.18%
MS	–	–	–	–	–	–	–	–	–
MT	0.76%	0.75%	1.13%	0.02%	0.03%	0.05%	0.39%	0.22%	0.17%
NC	1.24%	0.97%	1.13%	0.63%	0.39%	0.61%	0.61%	0.03%	0.05%
ND	– [a]	– [a]	– [a]	– [a]	– [a]	– [a]	0.12%	0.08%	0.11%
NE	1.91%	1.11%	1.86%	0.42%	0.20%	0.40%	0.23%	0.21%	0.48%
NH	– [b]	– [b]	– [b]	– [b]	– [b]	– [b]	0.18%	0.15%	0.24%
NJ	1.83%	0.80%	2.65%	0.46%	0.15%	0.36%	0.17%	0.15%	0.18%
NM	0.82%	0.96%	–	–	0.19%	–	0.17%	–	–
NV	0.68%	0.41%	0.82%	0.39%	0.19%	0.48%	0.56%	0.13%	0.11%
NY	–	–	6.89%	–	–	1.81%	–	–	–
OH	3.56%	2.67%	3.69%	0.69%	0.30%	0.61%	0.46%	0.36%	0.23%
OK	0.19%	0.07%	0.40%	0.16%	0.06%	0.27%	0.14%	0.12%	0.14%
OR	0.17%	0.09%	0.10%	–	0.01%	0.00%	–	0.01%	–
PA	0.54%	0.24%	0.85%	0.24%	0.09%	0.35%	0.03%	0.06%	0.03%
RI	0.16%	0.27%	0.52%	0.06%	0.11%	0.28%	0.02%	0.04%	0.07%
SC	0.49%	–	–	0.26%	–	–	0.06%	0.05%	0.03%
SD	0.08%	0.02%	0.12%	0.04%	0.02%	0.09%	–	0.06%	0.04%
TN	0.17%	0.04%	0.29%	0.11%	0.03%	0.22%	0.10%	0.01%	0.02%

State	Percentage of Turnout That Cast a Provisional Ballot			Percentage of Provisional Ballots Rejected			Percentage of Civilian Absentee Ballots Returned for Counting That Are Rejected		
	2008	2010	2012	2008	2010	2012	2008	2010	2012
TX	0.51%	0.28%	0.64%	0.39%	0.22%	0.52%	0.20%	0.06%	0.06%
UT	4.53%	2.98%	5.23%	0.71%	0.46%	1.00%	0.18%	0.17%	0.20%
VA	0.25%	0.11%	0.33%	0.18%	0.06%	0.21%	0.18%	0.02%	0.06%
VT	0.01%	0.01%	0.01%	0.00%	0.00%	–	0.38%	0.24%	–
WA	1.76%	0.24%	0.21%	0.38%	0.06%	0.10%	0.82%	1.34%	–
WI	0.01%	0.00%	0.00%	0.00%	0.00%	0.00%	0.09%	0.13%	0.13%
WV	–	–	–	–	0.20%	–	–	0.11%	0.00%
WY	–[b]	–[b]	–[b]	–[b]	–[b]	–[b]	0.09%	0.11%	0.07%

State	Percentage of Civilian Absentee Ballots Transmitted That Are Not Returned for Counting			Percentage of UOCAVA Ballots Returned for Counting That Are Rejected			Percentage of UOCAVA Ballots Transmitted That Are Not Returned for Counting		
	2008	2010	2012	2008	2010	2012	2008	2010	2012
AK	16.5%	15.6%	15.5%	4.3%	4.2%	8.2%	15.5%	48.3%	19.3%
AL	–	–	–	–	19.2%	–	31.0%	76.4%	–
AR	–	9.7%	9.1%	–	4.2%	10.0%	29.5%	52.5%	28.2%
AZ	6.4%	23.1%	19.7%	1.9%	3.6%	1.0%	36.6%	67.3%	28.6%
CA	16.2%	30.9%	29.4%	5.7%	4.5%	8.5%	37.3%	72.2%	46.0%
CO	9.0%	22.0%	12.5%	5.8%	3.0%	3.7%	26.2%	57.0%	30.4%
CT	–	6.5%	8.7%	–	1.6%	1.0%	–	36.0%	11.5%
DC	3.7%	32.7%	28.2%	–	10.9%	1.5%	53.5%	71.2%	18.6%
DE	3.6%	4.5%	7.6%	7.4%	4.3%	9.8%	22.6%	63.9%	28.5%
FL	14.1%	29.0%	18.2%	2.4%	4.1%	3.1%	21.6%	59.6%	25.0%
GA	1.6%	2.6%	1.7%	2.3%	4.5%	2.4%	31.3%	79.9%	34.5%
HI	8.9%	7.7%	9.8%	–	6.2%	0.0%	–	34.1%	32.6%
IA	5.1%	6.0%	7.0%	8.1%	3.7%	5.9%	25.0%	55.1%	21.6%
ID	3.3%	6.6%	3.3%	12.8%	20.9%	13.6%	22.7%	52.9%	18.5%
IL	7.4%	17.3%	7.9%	3.0%	4.7%	–	30.6%	78.2%	–
IN	3.7%	–	0.7%	–	6.8%	20.6%	47.2%	73.7%	13.5%
KS	6.6%	16.3%	–	10.1%	3.6%	5.7%	24.5%	70.2%	22.8%

(continued)

State	Percentage of Civilian Absentee Ballots Transmitted That Are Not Returned for Counting			Percentage of UOCAVA Ballots Returned for Counting That Are Rejected			Percentage of UOCAVA Ballots Transmitted That Are Not Returned for Counting		
	2008	2010	2012	2008	2010	2012	2008	2010	2012
KY	6.2%	3.2%	0.0%	–	6.6%	8.1%	25.0%	26.5%	22.4%
LA	2.6%	6.1%	21.7%	6.9%	10.1%	4.3%	29.1%	86.8%	38.8%
MA	9.1%	5.9%	8.2%	7.4%	7.9%	0.5%	26.1%	32.5%	18.1%
MD	9.3%	14.6%	12.5%	8.6%	15.6%	11.2%	17.4%	74.6%	25.8%
ME	2.8%	3.7%	3.2%	5.6%	–	7.9%	–	51.1%	25.5%
MI	2.5%	4.6%	2.9%	9.1%	8.9%	8.7%	27.3%	32.8%	25.1%
MN	–	7.1%	4.3%	6.4%	7.3%	7.6%	27.8%	35.0%	21.1%
MO	4.3%	3.7%	4.6%	4.6%	7.7%	3.8%	19.1%	61.0%	21.7%
MS	–	–	–	–	–	–	–	–	–
MT	4.1%	9.2%	9.3%	6.7%	3.8%	1.0%	32.5%	60.8%	33.0%
NC	14.5%	11.8%	10.7%	7.9%	8.4%	0.9%	33.0%	78.2%	20.9%
ND	6.4%	6.1%	5.5%	2.3%	0.5%	1.4%	23.4%	33.8%	18.3%
NE	4.0%	8.2%	10.6%	7.9%	11.6%	4.6%	18.8%	63.9%	14.6%
NH	4.7%	5.3%	4.7%	4.4%	4.3%	7.3%	18.0%	47.2%	12.7%
NJ	43.4%	21.9%	15.6%	2.9%	4.5%	1.4%	31.6%	75.0%	29.0%
NM	–	0.0%	6.2%	2.0%	–	–	25.5%	–	–
NV	8.8%	14.1%	15.0%	12.9%	12.4%	4.3%	37.4%	26.9%	17.9%
NY	–	–	–	–	25.4%	17.3%	–	60.3%	30.8%
OH	5.1%	8.3%	6.4%	4.9%	5.6%	2.3%	18.5%	61.7%	20.6%
OK	17.0%	8.1%	15.6%	6.0%	8.3%	5.5%	27.7%	72.0%	31.1%
OR	–	42.8%	–	–	7.7%	2.1%	–	65.3%	34.3%
PA	11.3%	10.8%	12.1%	0.7%	1.9%	1.9%	20.6%	64.7%	30.7%
RI	2.8%	10.8%	9.9%	–	0.0%	0.2%	20.5%	35.9%	33.2%
SC	2.6%	3.3%	3.2%	3.1%	2.0%	–	26.3%	27.3%	22.3%
SD	2.5%	2.5%	2.2%	–	–	5.6%	14.7%	25.8%	21.8%
TN	–	6.6%	7.4%	5.4%	3.9%	5.9%	17.4%	29.3%	22.1%
TX	8.7%	8.3%	6.3%	6.4%	4.2%	16.4%	30.7%	74.8%	51.5%
UT	25.0%	30.8%	22.6%	4.2%	2.2%	1.6%	31.2%	72.2%	28.3%
VA	7.3%	3.7%	4.0%	7.8%	–	1.7%	29.9%	69.9%	16.9%
VT	3.1%	7.0%	4.4%	6.0%	–	1.8%	15.5%	–	21.2%
WA	13.5%	27.4%	–	1.2%	1.3%	1.1%	28.2%	60.5%	36.7%
WI	5.3%	5.8%	6.7%	3.9%	12.1%	7.1%	31.0%	64.1%	33.6%
WV	–	51.6%	8.8%	–	–	0.2%	–	33.3%	20.8%
WY	2.8%	4.5%	2.7%	–	3.4%	3.3%	23.4%	48.3%	28.5%

State	Average Time Waiting to Vote (Minutes)			Percent of Nonvoters Who Say They Didn't Vote because of Polling Place Problems			Percent of Voters Who State Their Polling Places Were Easy to Find		
	2008	2010ᶜ	2012	2008	2010	2012	2008	2010ᶜ	2012
AK	5.8		2.8	3.4%	0.6%	1.1%	99.1%		94.4%
AL	14.3		11.3	0.0%	3.0%	5.6%	96.7%		96.8%
AR	21.5		14.5	0.8%	0.5%	1.6%	97.9%		99.2%
AZ	23.7		11.9	5.3%	6.3%	4.6%	96.4%		88.2%
CA	13.6		5.8	3.6%	1.9%	1.6%	97.9%		96.3%
CO	12.6		8.6	4.3%	3.7%	2.3%	97.9%		88.2%
CT	10.1		7.4	5.5%	1.8%	1.2%	99.3%		97.3%
DC	– ᵈ		32.1	10.0%	3.7%	5.6%	–ᵉ		94.8%
DE	12.2		4.9	3.4%	1.4%	1.0%	100.0%		95.5%
FL	28.8		37.6	3.7%	2.5%	6.7%	96.2%		98.1%
GA	37.6		15.0	3.3%	2.7%	3.7%	96.6%		97.1%
HI	5.7		7.1	3.8%	6.2%	2.0%	99.4%		90.9%
IA	5.0		8.5	2.6%	3.0%	1.5%	95.4%		92.4%
ID	6.5		6.7	1.2%	2.5%	1.5%	97.6%		96.9%
IL	9.2		5.8	2.5%	1.7%	1.9%	97.8%		98.4%
IN	24.0		14.8	2.4%	5.2%	3.5%	96.1%		95.6%
KS	11.0		11.0	0.0%	1.8%	2.8%	100.0%		99.4%
KY	12.3		8.2	1.4%	3.4%	1.6%	99.0%		95.8%
LA	19.1		17.9	1.5%	1.4%	0.0%	98.8%		97.6%
MA	5.6		8.7	1.6%	2.0%	1.9%	100.0%		96.0%
MD	24.5		24.4	0.8%	3.5%	2.8%	97.5%		95.8%
ME	4.4		4.1	3.1%	1.3%	1.4%	99.3%		99.8%
MI	20.4		21.4	1.9%	1.5%	2.5%	100.0%		97.5%
MN	8.6		6.3	2.1%	0.3%	0.7%	100.0%		98.9%
MO	25.9		13.5	4.8%	3.5%	3.5%	99.2%		98.5%
MS	11.0		7.6	5.3%	1.9%	4.8%	99.1%		97.7%
MT	6.2		15.9	3.7%	0.7%	8.4%	100.0%		99.6%
NC	21.0		9.1	0.7%	2.8%	1.8%	98.4%		95.6%
ND	5.3		8.1	1.1%	4.2%	4.8%	99.6%		100.0%
NE	9.3		6.0	3.4%	1.9%	2.0%	99.3%		95.8%
NH	7.5		10.7	2.2%	1.8%	5.7%	99.4%		96.5%
NJ	7.4		4.6	0.6%	1.6%	1.6%	97.6%		98.8%
NM	12.3		6.2	2.7%	1.3%	7.8%	98.8%		96.1%
NV	12.1		7.0	0.0%	1.7%	1.0%	99.0%		98.4%

(continued)

State	Average Time Waiting to Vote (Minutes)			Percent of Nonvoters Who Say They Didn't Vote because of Polling Place Problems			Percent of Voters Who State Their Polling Places Were Easy to Find		
	2008	2010[c]	2012	2008	2010	2012	2008	2010[c]	2012
NY	8.5		9.6	5.0%	0.7%	1.2%	97.7%		97.9%
OH	15.6		12.0	1.3%	3.0%	3.1%	98.3%		97.7%
OK	22.4		15.8	1.7%	1.3%	5.9%	97.2%		96.6%
OR	n/a		n/a	1.5%	0.6%	2.8%	n/a		n/a
PA	14.5		9.1	7.2%	1.6%	2.0%	99.4%		97.5%
RI	5.2		11.5	5.9%	2.0%	4.7%	99.2%		93.7%
SC	61.5		24.5	10.3%	3.7%	4.9%	97.3%		93.6%
SD	3.9		5.2	1.8%	1.6%	2.0%	99.5%		95.9%
TN	19.4		14.7	0.8%	1.6%	1.8%	97.6%		96.4%
TX	12.0		10.7	2.3%	1.8%	2.8%	96.6%		98.1%
UT	13.7		11.0	3.4%	1.7%	5.6%	98.7%		95.7%
VA	28.7		25.8	1.3%	1.1%	4.3%	97.9%		98.1%
VT	2.5		2.3	2.7%	6.5%	3.4%	99.3%		98.3%
WA	n/a		n/a	1.1%	1.0%	0.9%	n/a		n/a
WI	7.9		9.2	3.5%	1.1%	2.9%	98.6%		98.6%
WV	15.0		10.8	1.5%	6.2%	2.8%	98.3%		98.2%
WY	5.6		4.3	2.3%	1.2%	0.0%	97.4%		96.9%

State	Percent of Nonvoters Who Say They Didn't Vote because of a Permanent Illness or Disability			Residual Vote Rate			Postelection Audit Required		
	2008	2010	2012	2008	2010[c]	2012	2008	2010	2012
AK	17.0%	11.5%	6.2%	0.3%		0.4%	1	1	1
AL	23.5%	20.4%	20.1%	–		0.6%	0	0	0
AR	20.5%	15.7%	18.1%	0.9%		0.8%	1	1	0
AZ	9.0%	5.2%	12.3%	1.2%		1.0%	1	1	1
CA	12.9%	10.2%	12.0%	1.3%		1.2%	1	1	1
CO	11.5%	7.6%	5.3%	0.9%		1.0%	1	1	1
CT	24.9%	13.6%	15.8%	–		–	1	1	1
DC	30.8%	13.7%	17.3%	0.4%		0.2%	0	1	1
DE	20.3%	14.8%	20.2%	0.3%		0.9%	1	1	1

State	Percent of Nonvoters Who Say They Didn't Vote because of a Permanent Illness or Disability			Residual Vote Rate			Postelection Audit Required		
	2008	2010	2012	2008	2010^e	2012	2008	2010	2012
FL	17.5%	11.4%	11.6%	0.7%		0.7%	1	1	1
GA	16.6%	15.6%	18.4%	0.5%		0.5%	–	0	0
HI	9.5%	13.0%	11.9%	0.5%		0.6%	–	0	0
IA	10.3%	8.8%	11.4%	0.6%		0.5%	0	0	0
ID	16.2%	7.3%	6.9%	1.9%		2.1%	0	0	0
IL	18.0%	11.8%	10.3%	1.0%		0.7%	1	1	1
IN	18.6%	12.5%	18.0%	1.9%		1.5%	0	0	0
KS	13.8%	10.6%	13.0%	–		2.2%	0	0	0
KY	20.7%	13.6%	10.7%	1.9%		1.0%	0	0	0
LA	18.2%	14.7%	16.0%	1.1%		1.0%	0	0	0
MA	25.9%	15.9%	17.5%	0.7%		0.5%	0	0	0
MD	20.2%	12.4%	15.7%	1.1%		1.0%	1	1	1
ME	16.4%	11.2%	13.4%	1.8%		1.6%	0	0	0
MI	13.6%	11.6%	16.4%	0.7%		1.0%	0	0	1
MN	18.2%	12.7%	14.9%	0.3%		0.5%	1	1	1
MO	19.4%	11.9%	15.5%	2.2%		2.9%	1	1	1
MS	22.2%	14.1%	18.6%	–		–	0	0	0
MT	9.0%	12.0%	6.7%	1.2%		1.6%	0	1	1
NC	20.1%	12.4%	18.6%	1.0%		0.8%	1	1	1
ND	12.5%	7.0%	9.2%	1.6%		0.9%	1	1	1
NE	8.7%	8.9%	8.8%	1.3%		3.5%	0	0	1
NH	19.9%	10.7%	14.2%	1.2%		1.1%	0	0	0
NJ	19.3%	8.3%	19.1%	1.8%		1.0%	–	0	0
NM	14.2%	14.5%	15.2%	0.4%		0.4%	–	1	1
NV	6.4%	7.9%	15.5%	0.2%		0.2%	1	1	1
NY	12.2%	12.6%	16.9%	1.1%		0.8%	1	1	1
OH	13.1%	10.1%	12.3%	1.3%		0.9%	0	1	1
OK	17.8%	13.1%	16.9%	–		0.6%	0	0	0
OR	7.7%	6.2%	15.2%	0.9%		1.7%	1	1	1
PA	17.4%	13.0%	12.9%	1.5%		0.7%	1	1	1
RI	23.8%	12.0%	14.0%	0.8%		0.9%	0	0	0
SC	18.5%	18.6%	22.4%	1.1%		0.9%	0	0	0
SD	9.2%	10.1%	12.5%	2.5%		1.3%	0	0	0
TN	15.1%	14.6%	15.3%	0.7%		0.9%	0	1	1

(continued)

State	Percent of Nonvoters Who Say They Didn't Vote because of a Permanent Illness or Disability			Residual Vote Rate			Postelection Audit Required		
	2008	2010	2012	2008	2010[c]	2012	2008	2010	2012
TX	14.0%	9.5%	12.4%	–		–	1	1	1
UT	19.7%	10.7%	11.5%	1.9%		1.1%	1	1	1
VA	17.9%	12.8%	19.0%	0.8%		1.1%	0	0	0
VT	4.7%	11.9%	8.0%	0.7%		0.8%	0	0	0
WA	3.3%	4.3%	2.3%	1.1%		1.5%	1	1	1
WI	17.5%	9.1%	25.4%	0.4%		0.3%	1	1	1
WV	30.2%	13.8%	18.0%	3.2%		2.1%	1	1	1
WY	11.7%	12.3%	7.6%	0.5%		0.7%	0	1	1

State	Percent of Voters Who State They Are Confident Their Vote Was Counted as Cast			EAVS Data Completeness Rates			Usability of State Election Web Sites		
	2008	2010[c]	2012	2008	2010	2012	2008	2010	2012[f]
AK	99.5%		89.7%	100.0%	100.0%	100.0%	54.3%	74.7%	
AL	97.7%		87.8%	48.6%	59.4%	58.2%	42.7%	65.7%	
AR	98.5%		86.6%	70.8%	97.7%	96.9%	41.7%	75.1%	
AZ	97.7%		86.3%	98.9%	99.1%	99.1%	52.1%	66.8%	
CA	98.0%		88.9%	96.8%	98.5%	98.3%	58.2%	59.6%	
CO	99.0%		90.8%	94.0%	100.0%	100.0%	50.9%	68.4%	
CT	99.0%		90.2%	77.7%	94.4%	77.8%	31.0%	58.0%	
DC	–[d]		94.6%	77.8%	100.0%	100.0%	56.4%	77.7%	
DE	100.0%		89.7%	100.0%	100.0%	100.0%	52.0%	68.3%	
FL	97.4%		86.2%	100.0%	88.9%	99.8%	61.3%	80.4%	
GA	96.4%		94.9%	99.9%	99.3%	83.1%	38.6%	76.8%	
HI	99.5%		90.1%	90.1%	92.6%	98.2%	45.3%	65.7%	
IA	97.5%		90.6%	94.4%	99.9%	100.0%	76.6%	81.3%	
ID	98.5%		88.1%	94.4%	94.4%	83.3%	45.6%	66.7%	
IL	97.2%		90.7%	63.9%	93.8%	82.2%	31.9%	69.8%	
IN	96.5%		91.9%	94.4%	98.3%	99.3%	58.2%	80.2%	
KS	100.0%		96.4%	88.6%	100.0%	94.4%	46.7%	76.4%	

	Percent of Voters Who State They Are Confident Their Vote Was Counted as Cast			EAVS Data Completeness Rates			Usability of State Election Web Sites		
State	2008	2010[c]	2012	2008	2010	2012	2008	2010	2012[f]
KY	99.0%	89.5%	72.2%	100.0%	100.0%	67.3%	73.5%		
LA	99.0%	90.2%	100.0%	100.0%	100.0%	46.9%	83.3%		
MA	100.0%	96.8%	66.7%	87.6%	100.0%	49.6%	62.7%		
MD	98.5%	89.3%	88.9%	100.0%	100.0%	61.6%	84.4%		
ME	99.5%	91.4%	100.0%	100.0%	100.0%	64.0%	60.3%		
MI	100.0%	92.0%	96.3%	100.0%	100.0%	59.1%	75.9%		
MN	100.0%	90.5%	96.8%	97.5%	100.0%	62.1%	90.3%		
MO	99.5%	93.0%	95.7%	97.6%	99.6%	69.8%	76.1%		
MS	97.5%	91.5%	73.6%	78.5%	64.4%	29.1%	44.2%		
MT	100.0%	93.9%	99.6%	99.9%	100.0%	48.5%	71.7%		
NC	99.0%	94.5%	100.0%	100.0%	100.0%	63.3%	80.0%		
ND	99.5%	91.6%	93.3%	86.7%	73.3%	37.8%	71.7%		
NE	99.5%	92.9%	100.0%	97.4%	98.2%	51.2%	73.1%		
NH	99.5%	96.6%	68.8%	81.3%	100.0%	30.7%	58.0%		
NJ	99.0%	92.5%	89.5%	100.0%	100.0%	64.5%	66.5%		
NM	99.0%	86.6%	81.2%	89.6%	82.2%	38.6%	53.1%		
NV	99.5%	88.6%	99.7%	98.7%	99.8%	65.9%	70.2%		
NY	97.7%	84.0%	0.0%	66.5%	83.8%	61.3%	61.4%		
OH	98.5%	88.1%	97.5%	99.1%	99.2%	57.8%	71.6%		
OK	98.5%	90.5%	94.4%	94.2%	94.4%	45.7%	52.2%		
OR	100.0%	85.6%	48.7%	90.2%	94.4%	44.3%	65.5%		
PA	99.5%	90.5%	94.4%	100.0%	100.0%	71.4%	63.0%		
RI	99.5%	94.3%	50.0%	94.4%	94.4%	50.8%	82.5%		
SC	97.9%	92.0%	88.0%	88.9%	81.8%	64.6%	71.6%		
SD	99.5%	92.8%	82.0%	96.9%	97.3%	35.9%	69.9%		
TN	98.0%	88.7%	88.4%	98.0%	99.0%	57.5%	65.2%		
TX	96.4%	92.6%	97.4%	100.0%	94.3%	71.1%	71.9%		
UT	99.0%	83.8%	97.4%	100.0%	94.4%	65.2%	75.8%		
VA	98.0%	95.4%	99.8%	89.5%	99.7%	56.2%	81.9%		
VT	99.5%	94.9%	99.1%	90.8%	92.4%	59.6%	57.5%		
WA	99.0%	83.8%	88.7%	96.5%	99.0%	64.5%	77.5%		
WI	99.0%	92.9%	86.7%	87.5%	100.0%	41.1%	79.8%		
WV	98.5%	93.5%	76.8%	81.4%	96.0%	65.4%	72.9%		
WY	99.0%	86.5%	90.5%	93.8%	93.8%	47.7%	57.4%		

	Number of the Following Capabilities on the State Election Web Site: Registration Verification, Polling Place Locators, Online Registration		
State	2008	2010	2012
AK	0	2	3
AL	0	2	4
AR	2	2	4
AZ	1	2	4
CA	0	2	0
CO	1	2	4
CT	0	2	3
DC	2	2	4
DE	1	2	4
FL	0	2	4
GA	2	2	4
HI	1	2	2
IA	2	2	3
ID	1	2	3
IL	0	2	3
IN	2	2	5
KS	1	2	4
KY	2	2	3
LA	1	2	5
MA	1	2	3
MD	2	2	5
ME	1	2	2
MI	2	2	4
MN	1	2	4
MO	2	2	3
MS	0	2	1
MT	0	2	4
NC	2	2	5
ND	— [a]	— [a]	— [a]
NE	2	2	4
NH	0	2	3

State	Number of the Following Capabilities on the State Election Web Site: Registration Verification, Polling Place Locators, Online Registration		
	2008	2010	2012
NJ	2	2	2
NM	2	2	4
NV	2	2	3
NY	2	2	2
OH	1	2	2
OK	1	2	1
OR	1	2	4
PA	1	2	3
RI	2	2	5
SC	1	2	4
SD	2	2	4
TN	2	2	2
TX	1	2	2
UT	1	2	5
VA	2	2	5
VT	0	2	0
WA	2	2	3
WI	2	2	5
WV	2	2	4
WY	1	2	1

Notes: Unless otherwise indicated, missing values are attributable to the failure of a state to provide sufficient information to the EAVS to calculate the indicator.

[a] Because North Dakota does not have voter registration, indicators involving voter registration are generally not calculated for North Dakota.

[b] Not calculated because the state has Election Day registration (EDR).

[c] Indicator based on SPAE, which was not administered in 2010.

[d] The District of Columbia was not included in the 2008 SPAE.

[e] The residual vote rate is only calculated based on the vote for president, and therefore is not calculated for 2010.

[f] The study rating the usability of state election Web sites was not conducted in 2012.

[g] See Chapter 3 for a definition of these categories.

[h] The counts for each year are taken from data reported in the EAC's Statutory Overview report for the corresponding year.

TABLE A2.1. *Explaining voter turnout across the states*

	2008		2010	
EDR	.073** (.022)	.057* (.022)	.096** (.022)	.069** (.024)
SDR	.038* (.017)	.031* (.015)	.033* (.015)	.032* (.015)
Early Voting	−.049** (.016)	−.024 (.016)	−.028* (.015)	−.011 (.015)
Vote Only by Mail	.029 (.034)	.055 (.034)	.114** (.030)	.104** (.031)
Median Income (in thousands)		.001 (.001)		.0016 (.0009)
% High School Grads		.008* (.003)		−.001 (.003)
% Black		.001 (.001)		−.001 (.001)
% Hispanic		−.0003 (.0008)		−.0016* (.0007)
Competitiveness of Presidential Election	.002** (.001)	.003** (.001)		
Gubernatorial Election			.017 (.015)	.024 (.015)
Senatorial Election			.030* (.014)	.025 (.014)
Constant	.681** (.0170)	−.026 (.273)	.391** (.017)	.426 (.242)
Adjusted R^2	.346	.493	.511	.565
Number of Cases	49	49	51	51

Notes: $^*p < .05$, $^{**}p < .01$, one-tailed test. Alaska and the District of Columbia are omitted from the 2008 models because polling was insufficient to calculate the competitiveness variable. Observations are weighted by total votes cast. North Dakota is coded as having EDR and SDR, although the state technically has no voter registration requirement but does maintain a list of registrants.

TABLE A2.2. *Explaining voter registration across the states*

	2008		2010	
EDR	.020	.035	.024	.033
	(.017)	(.017)	(.021)	(.023)
SDR	.015	.014	.001	.007
	(.012)	(.011)	(.014)	(.014)
Early Voting	−.034**	−.020	−.026*	−.010
	(.012)	(.012)	(.013)	(.012)
Vote Only by Mail	−.010	.023	.025	.061*
	(.027)	(.027)	(.0297)	(.030)
Median Income		.0013		.0011
(in thousands)		(.0007)		(.0008)
% High School Grads		.002		.002
		(.003)		(.003)
% Black		.002**		.0020*
		(.001)		(.0008)
% Hispanic		.002		−.0004
		(.003)		(.0007)
Competitiveness of	.0012	.001		
Presidential Campaign	(.0006)	(.001)		
Gubernatorial Election			−.013	−.002
			(.013)	(.013)
Senatorial Election			−.009	−.009
			(.013)	(.012)
Constant	.871**	.605**	.820**	.533*
	(.013)	(.209)	(.015)	(.213)
Adjusted R^2	.127	.279	.086	.229
Number of Cases	49	49	51	51

Notes: *$p < .05$, **$p < .01$, one-tailed test. Alaska and the District of Columbia are omitted from the 2008 models because polling was insufficient to calculate the competitiveness variable. Observations are weighted by the VEP. North Dakota is coded as having EDR and SDR, although the state technically has no voter registration requirement but does maintain a list of registrants.

TABLE A7.1. *Regression estimates for ease of finding location in 2008*

	(1)	(2)	(3)	(4)	(5)
Openness	−0.006			0.002	−0.018**
	(0.004)			(0.008)	(0.007)
Precinct population (thousands)		−0.005*		−0.002	
		(0.003)		(0.005)	
Log (precinct area)			0.012***		0.004
			(0.003)		(0.006)
Open x pop.				−0.004	
				(0.003)	
Open x area					0.005*
					(0.003)
Habitual voter	0.046***	0.047***	0.046***	0.047***	0.046***
	(0.011)	(0.012)	(0.012)	(0.012)	(0.012)
Residency duration	0.030***	0.030***	0.030***	0.029***	0.029***
	(0.005)	(0.005)	(0.005)	(0.005)	(0.005)
Income	0.002	0.003*	0.003**	0.003*	0.003**
	(0.001)	(0.001)	(0.001)	(0.001)	(0.001)
Non-Anglo	−0.056***	−0.057***	−0.052***	−0.054***	−0.052***
	(0.013)	(0.014)	(0.014)	(0.014)	(0.014)
Female	0.033***	0.035***	0.034***	0.034***	0.034***
	(0.009)	(0.010)	(0.010)	(0.010)	(0.010)
Age	0.001*	0.001*	0.001*	0.001*	0.001*
	(0.000)	(0.000)	(0.000)	(0.000)	(0.000)
Vote margin	−0.152*	−0.126	−0.102	−0.156*	−0.121
	(0.090)	(0.092)	(0.092)	(0.094)	(0.093)
Party ID	0.002	0.002	0.001	0.002	0.001
	(0.002)	(0.002)	(0.002)	(0.002)	(0.002)
Partisan strength	0.003	0.004	0.004	0.004	0.004
	(0.004)	(0.005)	(0.005)	(0.005)	(0.005)
Constant	3.799***	3.782***	3.734***	3.798***	3.771***
	(0.048)	(0.049)	(0.049)	(0.051)	(0.051)
Observations	6,287	6,016	6,016	6,016	6,016
R-squared	0.021	0.022	0.024	0.022	0.025

Notes: *** $p < 0.01$, ** $p < 0.05$, * $p < 0.1$
Standard errors in parentheses.

TABLE A7.2. *Regression estimates for evaluation of polling place operations in 2008*

	(1)	(2)	(3)	(4)	(5)
Openness	0.010*			0.013	0.006
	(0.005)			(0.010)	(0.009)
Precinct population (thousands)		−0.005		−0.002	
		(0.004)		(0.006)	
Log (precinct area)			0.024***		0.024***
			(0.004)		(0.008)
Open x pop.				−0.002	
				(0.004)	
Open x area					−0.001
					(0.004)
Habitual voter	0.026*	0.029*	0.026*	0.029*	0.026*
	(0.014)	(0.015)	(0.015)	(0.015)	(0.015)
Residency duration	0.017***	0.016**	0.017***	0.017***	0.017***
	(0.006)	(0.007)	(0.006)	(0.007)	(0.007)
Income	−0.003*	−0.003*	−0.002	−0.003*	−0.002
	(0.002)	(0.002)	(0.002)	(0.002)	(0.002)
Non-Anglo	−0.051***	−0.045***	−0.036**	−0.045**	−0.036**
	(0.017)	(0.018)	(0.018)	(0.018)	(0.018)
Female	0.014	0.013	0.012	0.013	0.013
	(0.012)	(0.012)	(0.012)	(0.012)	(0.012)
Age	0.003***	0.003***	0.003***	0.003***	0.003***
	(0.000)	(0.000)	(0.000)	(0.000)	(0.000)
Vote margin	−0.222*	−0.247**	−0.207*	−0.228*	−0.196*
	(0.115)	(0.117)	(0.117)	(0.118)	(0.117)
Party ID	0.002	0.002	0.001	0.002	0.001
	(0.002)	(0.002)	(0.003)	(0.003)	(0.003)
Partisan strength	0.005	0.007	0.007	0.007	0.007
	(0.006)	(0.006)	(0.006)	(0.006)	(0.006)
Constant	3.707***	3.738***	3.659***	3.706***	3.645***
	(0.061)	(0.062)	(0.061)	(0.065)	(0.064)
Observations	6,285	6,014	6,014	6,014	6,014
R-squared	0.015	0.015	0.021	0.015	0.021

Notes: Standard errors in parentheses.
*** $p < 0.01$, ** $p < 0.05$, * $p < 0.1$

TABLE A7.3. *Relationship between lines and evaluation of polling place in 2008*

Lines	-0.117^{***}
	(0.005)
Habitual voter	0.018
	(0.014)
Residency duration	0.004
	(0.006)
Income	-0.000
	(0.002)
Non-Anglo	-0.006
	(0.016)
Female	0.008
	(0.011)
Age	0.003^{***}
	(0.000)
Vote margin	0.189^{*}
	(0.111)
Party ID	-0.000
	(0.002)
Partisan strength	0.008
	(0.005)
Constant	3.783^{***}
	(0.057)
Observations	$6,282$
R-squared	0.102

Notes: Standard errors in parentheses.
*** $p < 0.01$, ** $p < 0.05$, * $p < 0.1$

TABLE A7.4. *Logit estimates of polling place concerns among nonvoters in 2008*

	(1)	(2)	(3)
Openness	−0.091		
	(0.106)		
Precinct population		0.064	
(thousands)		(0.080)	
Log (precinct area)			0.108
			(0.085)
Residency duration	−0.034	−0.025	−0.024
	(0.121)	(0.123)	(0.123)
Income	−0.017	−0.017	−0.009
	(0.035)	(0.035)	(0.036)
Non-Anglo	0.047	−0.059	0.037
	(0.274)	(0.283)	(0.293)
Female	−0.189	−0.171	−0.202
	(0.248)	(0.252)	(0.252)
Age	−0.044***	−0.041***	−0.041***
	(0.010)	(0.010)	(0.010)
Vote margin	0.032	0.583	0.523
	(2.404)	(2.352)	(2.356)
Party ID	0.012	0.018	0.020
	(0.053)	(0.054)	(0.054)
Partisan strength	0.224**	0.219**	0.230**
	(0.107)	(0.108)	(0.108)
Constant	0.293	−0.371	−0.496
	(1.205)	(1.161)	(1.164)
Observations	513	499	499

Notes: Standard errors in parentheses.

*** $p < 0.01$, ** $p < 0.05$, * $p < 0.1$

TABLE A8.1. *Reliability of proposed performance measures*

All calculations based on state-level means (unweighted)	Means (1)	Correlation with VRS 2010 (2)	Correlation with SPAE 2008 (3)
Among all voting eligible			
Performance measure 1: Not registered because of permanent illness or disability			
VRS 2008	0.008	0.341	
VRS 2010	0.008		
Performance measure 2: Registered but not voting because of illness or disability (own or family member's)			
VRS 2008	0.012	0.593	
VRS 2010	0.021		
Among all nonregistered			
Performance measure 1: Not registered because of permanent illness or disability			
VRS 2008	0.027	0.324	
VRS 2010	0.023		
Among all registered voters			
Performance measure 2: Registered but not voting because of illness or disability (own or family member's)			
VRS 2008	0.016	0.620	0.294
VRS 2010	0.032		0.479
SPAE 2008	0.010		
Among all registered but not voting			
Performance measure 2: Registered but not voting because of illness or disability (own or family member's)			
VRS 2008	0.151	0.597	0.107
VRS 2010	0.109		0.471
SPAE 2008	0.144		

TABLE A8.2. *Validity of proposed performance measures*

Row		2008		2010	
		No disability	Disability	No disability	Disability
		(1)	(2)	(3)	(4)
PANEL A: Breakdown of performance measures by disability status					
Among all voting eligible		100%	100%	100%	100%
1	Performance measure 1: Not registered because of permanent illness or disability	0.2%	4.8%	0.2%	4.8%
2	Performance measure 2: Registered but not voting because of illness or disability (own or family member's)	0.6%	4.6%	1.3%	8.1%
3	Voted	64.5%	57.3%	45.9%	42.8%
4	Registered but not voting because of other or unspecified reasons	6.3%	6.3%	18.1%	13.2%
5	Not registered because of other or unspecified reasons	28.4%	27.0%	34.5%	31.1%
Among all who gave reason for not being registered					
6	Performance measure 1: Not registered because of permanent illness or disability	1.3%	25.9%	1.3%	22.9%
Among all registered who gave reason for not voting					
7	Performance measure 2: Registered but not voting because of illness or disability (own or family member's)	9.6%	43.9%	7.2%	39.5%

PANEL B: Breakdown of disability status by performance measures

		Performance measure 1: Not registered because of permanent illness or disability			
		No	Yes	No	Yes
	Total	100.0%	100.0%	100.0%	100.0%
8	No disability	88.1%	20.6%	88.3%	25.0%
9	Disability	11.9%	79.4%	11.7%	75.0%

(continued)

TABLE A8.2 *(continued)*

PANEL B: Breakdown of disability status by performance measures

| | | Performance measure 1: Not registered because of permanent illness or disability | | | |
		No	Yes	No	Yes
10	Hearing impairment	3.2%	17.9%	3.3%	14.3%
11	Visual impairment	1.8%	12.1%	1.7%	12.9%
12	Mental impairment	3.3%	46.8%	3.3%	44.1%
13	Mobility impairment	7.3%	47.0%	7.0%	43.2%
14	Difficulty with self-care	1.9%	29.2%	1.7%	29.4%
15	Difficulty going outside alone	3.8%	56.1%	3.7%	55.4%

| | | Performance measure 2: Registered but not voting because of illness or disability (own or family member's) | | | |
		No	Yes	No	Yes
	Total	100.0%	100.0%	100.0%	100.0%
16	No disability	88.0%	48.4%	88.5%	53.5%
17	No family member with disability	80.7%	40.2%	81.3%	45.4%
18	Family member with disability	7.3%	8.2%	7.2%	8.1%
19	Disability	12.0%	51.6%	11.5%	46.5%
20	Hearing impairment	3.2%	12.6%	3.2%	11.1%
21	Visual impairment	1.8%	8.9%	1.6%	8.4%
22	Mental impairment	3.5%	19.1%	3.3%	16.6%
23	Mobility impairment	7.2%	39.3%	6.6%	37.0%
24	Difficulty with self-care	1.9%	18.3%	1.7%	14.2%
25	Difficulty going outside alone	3.9%	31.2%	3.6%	26.7%

TABLE A10.1. *The sources of voter confidence*

| | | 2008 SPAE | | | | 2008 CCES | | 2010 CCES | |
| | | All Voters | | Excludes VBM | | All Voters | | All Voters | |
		b	Std. Err.	b	Std. Err.	b	Std. Err.	b	Std. Err.
Demographics	Race (Black)	0.056	0.027	0.081	0.029	0.138	0.119	0.041	0.027
	Race (Hispanic)	0.032	0.038	0.042	0.042	0.155	0.084	0.042	0.042
	Income	0.084	0.028	0.108	0.032	0.292	0.139	0.036	0.035
	Education	0.073	0.028	0.063	0.031	-0.130	0.074	0.063	0.036
	Gender (Female)	-0.041	0.013	-0.063	0.015	-0.024	0.040	-0.037	0.021
	Age	0.399	0.046	0.247	0.054	0.122	0.185	0.026	0.050
Engagement	Political Interest					0.053	0.106	-0.061	0.136
Trust	Trust in Government					0.232	0.058		
	Confidence in LEO					0.281	0.096	0.244	0.036
Voting	Early In-Person Voting	-0.023	0.018	-0.035	0.018	0.005	0.077	-0.080	0.028
	Vote-by-Mail	-0.159	0.017			-0.101	0.067	-0.071	0.023
Experience	First-Time Voter	0.020	0.033	0.023	0.035				
	Problems with Machines			-0.267	0.050				
	Easy to Find Polling Place			0.395	0.075				
Results of Vote	Voted for the Winner	0.171	0.019			0.303	0.108		
Opinions on	Vote Fraud Worry	-0.347	0.021	-0.276	0.023	-0.330	0.130	0.099	0.027
Elections	Vote as a Right or Privilege							0.010	0.027

(continued)

329

TABLE A10.1 (continued)

| | | 2008 SPAE | | | | 2008 CCES | | 2010 CCES | |
| | | All Voters | | Excludes VBM | | All Voters | | All Voters | |
		b	Std. Err.	b	Std. Err.	b	Std. Err.	b	Std. Err.
	Ballot Privacy (1 = Concerned)							−0.187	0.039
	Poll Worker Performance			**0.613**	0.038				
Partisanship	Democratic	0.012	0.018	0.000	0.020	0.010	0.131	**0.042**	0.021
	Republican	**0.103**	0.018	**0.102**	0.020	**0.230**	0.118	**0.049**	0.020
	Postelection Audits	**−0.033**	0.014	**−0.033**	0.014	−0.118	0.032	0.009	0.024
	ID Required at Polls	−0.020	0.015	−0.020	0.015	−0.076	0.084	0.019	0.018
	Photo ID Required at Polls	0.034	0.024	0.034	0.024	0.066	0.098	−0.014	0.025
Constant		1.563		1.563		2.294		0.540	
N of Cases		9,120		6,815		584		656	
R-Squared		0.027		0.108		0.142		0.238	

Notes: Entries are ordinary least squares coefficients. The dependent variable is coded 0–4; all independent variables are coded to the 0–1 range.

TABLE A10.2. *The sources of voter confidence: Ordered probit results*

| | | 2008 SPAE | | | | 2008 CCES | | 2010 CCES | |
| | | All Voters | | Excludes Vote-by-Mail | | All Voters | | All Voters | |
		B	Std. Err.	b	Std. Err.	b	Std. Err.	b	Std. Err.
Demographics	Race (Black)	**0.125**	0.060	**0.186**	0.069	0.246	0.232	0.206	0.159
	Race (Hispanic)	0.091	0.083	0.138	0.097	0.250	0.172	0.222	0.237
	Income	**0.171**	0.062	**0.233**	0.075	**0.481**	0.240	0.226	0.192
	Education	**0.132**	0.062	**0.143**	0.074	-0.278	0.141	0.335	0.205
	Gender (Female)	**-0.077**	0.029	**-0.136**	0.034	-0.047	0.076	-0.232	0.117
	Age	**0.919**	0.101	**0.629**	0.126	0.226	0.358	0.174	0.278
Engagement	Political Interest					0.162	0.213	-0.238	0.627
Trust	Trust in Government					**0.422**	0.105	1.241	0.169
	Confidence in LEO					**0.571**	0.184		
Voting Experience	Early In-Person Voting	-0.064	0.040	**-0.092**	0.042	-0.034	0.138	**-0.413**	0.149
	Vote-by-Mail	**-0.345**	0.036			-0.175	0.114	**-0.352**	0.118
	First-Time Voter			0.022	0.077				
	Problems with Machines			**-0.468**	0.104				
	Easy to Find Polling Place			**0.786**	0.158				
Results of Vote	Voted for the Winner	**0.296**	0.041	**0.353**	0.049	0.238	0.104	-0.068	0.112
Opinions on Elections	Vote Fraud Worry	**-0.750**	0.045	**-0.631**	0.054	-0.601	0.252	**0.585**	0.156

(continued)

TABLE A10.2 (continued)

| | 2008 SPAE | | | | 2008 CCES | | 2010 CCES | |
| | All Voters | | Excludes Vote-by-Mail | | All Voters | | All Voters | |
	B	Std. Err.	b	Std. Err.	b	Std. Err.	b	Std. Err.
Vote as a Right or Privilege							0.050	0.151
Ballot Privacy (1 = Concerned)							-0.945	0.189
Poll Worker Performance			1.263	0.083				
Partisanship								
Democratic	0.041	0.040	0.021	0.047	-0.023	0.216	0.228	0.117
Republican	0.192	0.038	0.197	0.045	0.302	0.174	0.285	0.113
Postelection Audits	-0.077	0.029	-0.087	0.034	-0.201	0.063	0.051	0.130
ID Required at Polls	-0.053	0.030	-0.070	0.036	-0.149	0.149	0.103	0.096
Photo ID Required at Polls	0.080	0.049	0.085	0.056	0.129	0.187	-0.094	0.146
Ancillary								
Parameters								
Cut 1	-1.760		0.010		-2.090		-1.044	
Cut 2	-1.301		0.455		-1.286		-0.134	
Cut 3	-0.194		1.581		0.050		1.342	
N of Cases	9,120		6,815		584		656	

Notes: Entries are ordered probit coefficients. The dependent variable is the four-point indicator of voter confidence.

References

Adcock, Robert, and David Collier. 2001. "Measurement Validity: A Shared Standard for Qualitative and Quantitative Research." *American Political Science Review* 95: 529–546.

Allers, Maarten, and Peter Kooreman. 2009. "More Evidence of the Effects of Voting Technology on Election Outcomes,." *Public Choice* 139: 159–170.

Alvarez, R. Michael. 2009. "Measuring Election Performance," Caltech/MIT Voting Technology Project working paper, December 11.

Alvarez, R. Michael, Stephen Ansolabehere, Adam Berinsky, Gariel Lenz, and Charles Stewart, Thad Hall. 2008 Survey of the Performance of American Electorate. 2008. http://vote.caltech.edu/sites/default/files/2008%20Survey%20of%20the%20Performance%20of%20American%20Elections%20Executive%20Summary.pdf

Alvarez, R. Michael, Lonna Rae Atkeson, and Thad E. Hall. 2012. *Evaluating Elections: A Handbook of Methods and Standards.* New York: Cambridge University Press.

Alvarez, R. Michael, M. Goodrich, T. E. Hall, R. Kiewiet, and S. M. Sled. 2004. "The Complexity of the California Recall Election." *PS: Political Science and Politics* 37(1): 23–26.

Alvarez, R. Michael, and Thad E. Hall. 2004. *Point, Click, and Vote: The Future of Internet Voting.* Washington, DC: Brookings Institution Press.

2008. *Electronic Elections: The Perils and Promises of Digital Democracy.* Princeton, NJ: Princeton University Press.

Alvarez, R. Michael, and Thad E. Hall. 2009. "Provisional Ballots in the 2008 Ohio General Election," Pew Charitable Trusts, Tthe Center for the States, *Provisional Ballots: An Imperfect Solution,* at: http://www.pewcenteronthestates.org/initiatives_detail.aspx?initiativeID=54789

Alvarez, R. Michael, Thad E. Hall, and Susan D. Hyde (eds.). 2009. *Election Fraud: Detecting and Deterring Electoral Manipulation.* Washington, DC: Brookings Institution Press.

Alvarez, R. Michael, Thad E. Hall, Ines Levin, and Charles Stewart III, 2011. "Voter Opinions about Election Reform: Do They Support Making Voting More Convenient?" *Election Law Journal: Rules, Politics, and Policy* 10(2): 73–87.

Alvarez, R. Michael, Thad E. Hall, and Morgan Llewellyn. 2008. "Are Americans Confident Their Ballots Are Counted?" 2008. *Journal of Politics.* 70 (3): 754–766.

Alvarez, R. Michael, Thad E. Hall, and Brian Roberts. 2007. "Military Voting and the Law: Procedural and Technological Solutions to the Ballot Transit Problem." *Fordham Urban Law Review* 34(3): 935–996.

Alvarez, R. Michael, Thad E. Hall, and Betsy Sinclair. 2008. "Whose Absentee Votes Are Counted?" *Electoral Studies* 27(4): 673–683.

Alvarez, R. Michael, Ines Levin, and J. Andrew Sinclair. 2012. "Making Voting Easier: Convenience Voting in the 2008 Presidential Election,." *Political Research Quarterly* 65 (2): 248–262.

Ansolabehere, Stephen, and Eitan Hersh. 2011. "Pants on Fire: Misreporting, Sample Selection, and Participation." Unpublished manuscript.

    2012. "Validation: What Big Data Reveal about Survey Misreporting and the Real Electorate." *Political Analysis* 20(4): 437–459.

Ansolabehere, Stephen, Jonathan Rodden, and James M. Snyder, Jr. 2006. "Purple America." *Journal of Economic Perspectives* 20: 97–118.

Ansolabehere, Stephen, and Charles Stewart. 2005. "Residual Votes Attributable to Technology." *Journal of Politics* 67: 365–389.

Ansolabehere, Stephen, et al. 2010. "Voter Registration List Quality Pilot Studies: Report on Detailed Results." CalTech MIT Voting Technology Project Working Paper, June 8.

Anspach, Renee. 1979. "From Stigma to Identity Politics: Political Activism among the Physically Disabled and Former Mental Patients." *Social Science and Medicine* 13A: 765–773.

Arceneaux, Kevin, Thad Kousser, and Megan Mullin. 2012. "Get Out the Vote-by-Mail? A Randomized Field Experiment Testing the Effect of Mobilization in Traditional and Vote-by-Mail Precincts." *Political Research Quarterly* 65(4): 882–894.

Atkeson, Lonna. 2011. "Voter Confidence in 2010: Voter Identification, Perceptions of Fraud, Winning and Losing and the Voting Experience." Paper presented at "Aftermath of Bush v. Gore: Ten Years Later," Center for the Study of Democracy, University of California, Irvine.

Atkeson, Lonna Rae, Lisa Ann Bryant, Thad E. Hall, Kyle Saunders, and Michael Alvarez. 2010. "A New Barrier to Participation: Heterogeneous Application of Voter Identification Policies." *Electoral Studies* 29(1): 66–73.

Atkeson, Lonna Rae, R. Michael Alvarez, and Thad E. Hall. 2009. "Provisional Voting in New Mexico." Pew Charitable Trusts, the Center for the States, *Provisional Ballots: An Imperfect Solution.* http://www.pewcenteronthestates.org/initiatives_detail.aspx?initiativeID=54789

Atkeson, Lonna Rae, and Kyle L. Saunders. 2007. "The Effect of Election Administration on Voter Confidence: A Local Matter?" *PS: Political Science & Politics* 40 : 655–660.

Banks, James, Arie Kapteyn, James P. Smith, and Arthur van Soest. 2005. "Work Disability Is a Pain in the *******, Especially in England, the Netherlands, and the United States." Working Paper No. 11558. Cambridge, MA: National Bureau of Economic Research Working Papers.

Barreto, Matt A., Matthew J. Streb, Mara Marks and Fernando Guerra, 2006. "Do Absentee Voters Differ From Polling Place Voters? New Evidence from California." *Public Opinion Quarterly* 70(2): 224–234.

Berger, Jonah, Marc Meredith, and S. Christian Wheeler. 2008. "Contextual Priming: Where People Vote Affects How They Vote." *Proceedings of the National Academy of Sciences* 105: 8846–8849.

Bergman, Elizabeth, and Philip A. Yates. 2011. "Changing Election Methods: How Does Mandated Vote-By-Mail Affect Individual Registrants?" *Election Law Journal* 10(2): 115–127.

Berinksy, Adam, Nancy Burns, and Michael Traugott. 2001. "Who Votes by Mail? A Dynamic Model of the Individual-Level Consequences of Voting by Mail Systems." *Public Opinion Quarterly* 65(2): 178–197.

Berinsky, Adam J. 2005. "The Perverse Consequences of Electoral Reform in the United States." *American Politics Research* 33: 471–491.

Bernstein, Robert A., Anita Chadha, and Robert Montjoy. 2003. "Cross-State Bias in Voting and Registration Overreporting in the Current Population Surveys." *State Politics & Policy Quarterly* 21: 367–386.

Biggers, Daniel R., and Michael J. Hanmer. 2012. "Understanding the Adoption of Voter Identification Laws in the American States." Working Paper, Yale University and University of Maryland.

Bjornlund, Eric C. 2004. *Beyond Free and Fair: Monitoring Elections and Building Democracy.* Baltimore, MD: Johns Hopkins University Press.

Brady, Henry, and John McNulty. 2011. "Turning Out to Vote: The Costs of Finding and Getting to the Polling Place." *American Political Science Review* 105(1): 115–134.

Brault, Matthew W. 2008. "Americans with Disabilities 2005." Current Population Reports, P70–117, U.S. Census Bureau, Washington, DC, http://www.census.gov/prod/2008pubs/p70-117.pdf

Brennan, Jason. 2011. *The Ethics of Voting.* Princeton, NJ: Princeton University Press.

Brown, Robert D., and Justin Wedeking. 2006. "People Who Have Their Tickets but Do Not Use Them: 'Motor Voter,' Registration, and Turnout Revisited." *American Politics Research* 34: 479–504.

Burden, Barry C. 2000. "Voter Turnout and the National Election Studies." *Political Analysis* 8: 389–398.

Burden, Barry C., David T. Canon, Kenneth R. Mayer, and Donald P. Moynihan. 2014. "Election Laws, Mobilization, and Turnout: The Unanticipated Consequences of Election Reform." *American Journal of Political Science* 58: 95–109.

Burkhauser, Richard. V., Andrew J. Houtenville, and Jennifer R. Tennant. 2014. "Capturing the Elusive Working-Age Population With Disabilities: Reconciling Conflicting Social Success Estimates From the Current Population Survey and American Community Survey." *Journal of Disability Policy Studies* 24: 195–205.

Cain, Bruce E., Karin MacDonald, and Michael H. Murakami. 2008. "Administering the Overseas Vote." *Public Administration Review* 68(5): 802–813.

Caltech/MIT Voting Technology Project. 2001. *Voting: What Is, What Could Be.* http://vote.caltech.edu/sites/default/files/voting_what_is_what_could_be.pdf

Carey, Allison C. 2009. *On the Margins of Citizenship: Intellectual Disability and Civil Rights in Twentieth-Century America.* Philadelphia: Temple University Press.

Carmines, Edward G., and Richard A. Zeller. 1979. *Reliability and Validity Assessment.* Sage University Paper Series on Quantitative Applications in the Social Sciences, 07–004. Newbury Park, CA: Sage.

Cemenska, Nathan, Jan E. Leighley, Jonathan Nagler, and Daniel P. Tokaji. 2009. "Report on the 1972–2008 Early an Absentee Voting Dataset, submitted to the Pew Charitable Trusts."

Claasen, Ryan, David Magleby, Quin Monson, and Kelly Patterson. 2008. "Voter Confidence and the Election-Day Voting Experience." Paper presented at the 2008 Joint Statistical Meetings.

Coleman, Kevin J. 2006. "The Uniformed and Overseas Citizens Absentee Voting Act: Background and Issues." Congressional Research Service Report No. RS20764.

Coleman, Kevin J., and Eric A. Fischer. 2011. *The Help America Vote Act and Elections Reform: Overview and Issues*. Washington, DC: Congressional Research Service.

Commission on Federal Election Reform. 2005. "Building Confidence in U.S. Elections." Report of the Commission on Federal Election Reform, Center for Democracy and Election Management, American University. http://www1.american.edu/ia/cfer/, accessed March 1, 2014.

Conway, M. Margaret. 2000. *Political Participation in the United States*. Washington, DC: Congressional Quarterly.

Cox, Gary W., and Michael C. Munger. 1989. "Closeness, Expenditures, and Turnout in the 1982 U.S. House Elections." *American Political Science Review* 83: 217–230.

Cuciti, Peggy, and Allan Wallis. 2011. "Changing the Way Colorado Votes: A Study of Selected Reforms." Report for the Best Practices and Vision Commission, Office of the Colorado Secretary of State. http://www.sos.state.co.us/pubs/elections/

Dahl, Robert. 1971. *Polyarchy*. New Haven, CT: Yale University Press.

Dunaway, Johanna, and Robert M. Stein. 2013. "Early Voting and Campaign News Coverage." *Political Communication* 30: 278–296.

Eagleton Institute of Politics, Rutgers University, and the Moritz College of Law, Ohio State University. 2006. *Report to U.S. Election Assistance Commission on Best Practices to Improve Provisional Voting*. http://www.eac.gov/assets/1/Page/Report%20to%20the%20EAC%20on%20Best%20Practices%20to%20Improve%20Provisional%20Voting.pdf

Easton, David. 1975. "A Re-assessment of the Concept of Political Support." *British Journal of Political Science* 5: 435–457.

Erikson, Robert S. 1981. "Why Do People Vote? Because They Are Registered." *American Politics Quarterly* 9: 259–276.

Everett, S. P., Byrne, M. D., and Greene, K. K. 2006. "Measuring the Usability of Paper Ballots: Efficiency, Effectiveness, and Satisfaction." Proceedings of the Human Factors and Ergonomics Society 50th Annual Meeting. Santa Monica, CA: Human Factors and Ergonomics Society.

Ewald, Alec C. 2009. *The Way We Vote*. Nashville, TN: Vanderbilt University Press.

Fitzgerald, Mary. 2005. "Greater Convenience But Not Greater Turnout: The Impact of Alternative Voting Methods on Electoral Participation in the United States." *American Politics Research* 33: 842–867.

Foley, Edward B. 2005. "The Promise and Problems of Provisional Voting." *George Washington Law Review* 73: 1193–1205.

——— 2008. "Uncertain Insurance: The Ambiguities and Complexities of Provisional Voting." In *Voting in America: American Voting Systems in Flux: Debacles, Dangers, and Brave New Designs*, ed. Morgan E. Felchner. Westport, CT: Praeger, pp. 75–89.

Franklin, Daniel P., and Eric E. Grier. 1997. "Effects of Motor Voter Legislation: Voter Turnout, Registration, and Partisan Advantage in the 1992 Presidential Election." *American Politics Research* 25: 104–117.

Fullerton, Andrew S., Jeffrey C. Dixon, and Casey Borch. 2007. "Bringing Registration into Models of Vote Overreporting." *Public Opinion Quarterly* 71: 649–660.

General Accounting Office. 2009a. *Additional Monitoring of Polling Places Could Further Improve Accessibility*. GAO-09-941. Washington, DC: General Accounting Office.

——— 2009b. *More Polling Places Had No Potential Impediments than in 2000, but Challenges Remain*. GAO-09-685. Washington, DC: General Accounting Office.

Gerber, Alan S., Gregory A. Huber, and Seth J. Hill. 2013. "Identifying the Effect of All-Mail Elections on Turnout: Staggered Reform in the Evergreen State." *Political Science Research and Methods* 1(1): 91–116.

Gerken, Heather K. 2009a. *The Democracy Index: Why Our Election System Is Failing and How to Fix It*. New Haven, CT: Yale University Press.

Gerken, Heather. 2009b. "Provisional Ballots: The Miner's Canary for Election Administration.," Pew Charitable Trusts, The Center for the States, *Provisional Ballots: An Imperfect Solution*, http://www.pewcenteronthestates.org/initiatives_detail.aspx?initiativeID=54789

Gerring, John. 2012. *Social Science Methodology: A Unified Framework*, 2nd ed. New York: Cambridge University Press.

Gimpel, James, and Jason Schuknecht. 2003. "Political Participation and the Accessibility of the Ballot Box." *Political Geography* 22(4): 471–488.

Gimpel, James G., Joshua J. Dyck, and Daron R. Shaw. 2007. "Election-Year Stimuli and the Timing of Voter Registration." *Party Politics* 13: 351–374.

Greene, Kristen K., Michael D. Byrne, and Sarah P. Everett. 2006. "A Comparison of Usability between Voting Methods." Proceedings of the 2006 USENIX/ACCURATE Electronic Voting Technology Workshop.

Gronke, Paul, and Timothy E. Cook. 2007. "Disdaining the Media: The American Public's Changing Attitudes toward the News." *Political Communication* 24(3): 259–281.

Gronke, Paul, and Eva Galanes-Rosenbaum. 2008. "The Growth of Early and Non-Precinct Place Balloting: When, Why, and Prospects for the Future." In *The Election Law Handbook*. Chicago: American Bar Association.

Gronke, Paul, and James Hicks. 2009. "Trust in Government and Social Institutions." In *Understanding Public Opinion*, ed. Barbara Norrander and Clyde Wilcox. Washington, DC: CQ Press.

Gronke, Paul, and Peter Miller. 2012. "Voting by Mail and Turnout in Oregon Revisiting Southwell and Burchett." *American Politics Research* 40(6): 976–997.

Gronke, Paul, Eva Galanes-Rosenbaum, Peter Miller, and Daniel Krantz Toffey. 2008. "Convenience Voting." *Annual Review of Political Science* 11:437–455.

Gronke, Paul, Eva Galanes-Rosenbaum, and Peter Miller. 2007. "Early Voting and Turnout." *PS: Political Science and Politics* 40: 639–645.

2008. "Early Voting and Voter Turnout." In *Democracy in the States: Experiments in Election Reform*, eds. C. J. Tolbert, T. Donovan, and B. E. Cain. Washington DC: Brookings Institution Press, pp. 68–83.

Hall, Thad E. 2008. "UOCAVA: A State of the Research." VTP Working Paper #69. http://vote.caltech.edu/content/uocava-state-research

Hall, Thad E., and Claire Smith. 2012. "Barriers to Overseas Voting and Satisfaction with the Voting Process." Paper Presented at the 2012 Midwest Political Science Association Annual Meeting.

Hall, Thad E., J. Quin Monson, and Kelly D. Patterson. 2009. "The Human Dimension of Elections How Poll Workers Shape Public Confidence in Elections." *Political Research Quarterly* 62(3): 507–522.

Hamner, Michael, and Michael Traugott. 2004. "The Impact of Voting by Mail on Voter Behavior." *American Politics Research* 32(4): 375–405.

Hamner, Michael J. 2009. *Discount Voting: Voter Registration Reforms and Their Effects*. New York: Cambridge University Press.

Harris Interactive. 2010. *The ADA: 20 Years Later, Kessler Foundation/NOD Survey of Americans with Disabilities*. New York: Harris Interactive.

Haspel, Moshe, and H. Gibbs Knotts. 2005. "Location, Location, Location: Precinct Placement and the Costs of Voting." *Journal of Politics* 67(2): 560–573.

Henry, Ray. 2012. "Fulton County Sorts through Provisional Ballots, Certifies Election Results." *Augusta Chronicle*, November 10. http://chronicle.augusta.com/news/metro/2012-11-10/fulton-county-sorts-through-provisional-ballots-certifies-election-results

Herrnson, Paul S., Richard G. Niemi, Michael J. Hanmer, Benjamin B. Bederson, Frederick G. Conrad, and Michael W. Traugott. 2008. *Voting Technology: The Not-So-Simple Act of Casting a Ballot*. Washington, DC: Brookings Institution Press.

Highton, Benjamin. 1997. "Easy Registration and Voter Turnout." *Journal of Politics* 59: 565–575.

2004. "Voter Registration and Turnout in the United States." *Perspectives on Politics* 2: 507–515.

Highton, Benjamin, and Raymond E. Wolfinger. 1998. "Estimating the Effects of the National Voter Registration Act of 1993." *Political Behavior* 20: 79–104.

Holbrook, Thomas, and Brianne Heidbreder. 2010. "Does Measurement Matter? The Case of VAP and VEP in Models of Voter Turnout in the United States." *State Politics & Policy Quarterly* 10: 157–179.

Issacharoff, Samuel, and Allan J. Lichtman. 1993. "The Census Undercount and Minority Representation: The Constitutional Obligation of the States to Guarantee Equal Representation." *The Review of Litigation* 13(1): 1–29.

Issenberg, Sasha. 2012. *The Victory Lab: The Secret Science of Winning Campaigns*. New York: Crown.

Jackson, Robert A., Robert D. Brown, and Gerald C. Wright. 1998. "Registration, Turnout, and the Electoral Representativeness of U.S. State Electorates." *American Politics Research* 26: 259–287.

Jencks, S. F., T. Cuerdon, D. R. Burwen, et al. 2000. "Quality of Medical Care Delivered to Medicare Beneficiaries: A Profile at State and National Levels." *Journal of the American Medical Association* 284: 1670–1676.

Johnson, William G., and James Lambrinos. 1985. "Wage Discrimination against Handicapped Men and Women." *The Journal of Human Resources* 20: 264–277.

Jowers, Karen. 2004. "Troops Want to Know: Where's My %&#@ Mail?!," *Army Times*, May 10: 1.

Karlawish, Jason H., and Richard J. Bonnie. 2007. "Voting by Elderly Persons with Cognitive Impairment: Lessons from Other Democratic Nations." *McGeorge Law Review* 38: 880–916.

Karp, Jeffrey A., and Susan A. Banducci. 2000. "Going Postal: How All-Mail Elections Influence Turnout." *Political Behavior* 22 (3): 223–239.

———. 2001. "Absentee Voting, Mobilization, and Participation." *American Politics Research* 29(2): 183–195.

Keyssar, Alexander. 2001. *The Right to Vote: The Contested History of Democracy in the United States*. New York: Basic Books.

Kim, Jae-On, John R. Petrocik, and Stephen N. Enokson. 1975. "Voter Turnout among the American States: Systematic and Individual Components." *American Political Science Review* 69: 107–123.

Kimball, D. C., and B. Baybeck. 2013. "Are All Jurisdictions Equal? Size Disparity in Election Administration." *Election Law Journal* 12(2): 130–145.

Kimball, David C., and Edward B. Foley. 2009. "Unsuccessful Provisional Voting in the 2008 General Election." Pew Charitable Trusts, The Center for the States, *Provisional Ballots: An Imperfect Solution*. http://www.pewcenteronthestates.org/initiatives_detail.aspx?initiativeID=54789

Kimball, David C., and Martha Kropf. 2008. "Voting Technology, Ballot Measures, and Residual Votes." *American Politics Research* 36: 479.

Kimball, David C., Martha Kropf, and Lindsay Battles. 2006. "Helping America Vote? Election Administration, Partisanship, and Provisional Voting in the 2004 Election." *Election Law Journal* 5 (4): 447–461.

King, Gary, Robert O. Keohane, and Sidney Verba. 1994. *Designing Social Inquiry: Scientific Inference in Qualitative Research*. Princeton, NJ: Princeton University Press.

Korte, Gregory. 2012. "Study Shows Voters with Disabilities Face Access Barriers,." *USA Today*, August 9, 4.

Kousser, Thad, and Megan Mullin. 2007. "Does Voting by Mail Increase Participation? Using Matching to Analyze a Natural Experiment." *Political Analysis* 15(4): 428–445.

Kropf, Martha, and David Kimball. 2011. *Helping America Vote: The Limits of Election Reform*. New York: Routledge.

Laskowski, Sharon, Marguerite Autry, John Cugini, William Killam, and James Yen. 2004. *Improving the Usability and Accessibility of Voting Systems and Products*. Washington, DC: National Institute of Standards and Technology.

Liebschutz, Sarah, and Daniel J. Palazzolo. 2005. "HAVA and the States." *Publius* (Fall): 497–514.

Lijphart, Arend. 1997. "Unequal Participation: Democracy's Unresolved Dilemma." *American Political Science Review* 91: 1–14.

Link, Jessica N., Martha Kropf, Mark Alexander Hirsch, Flora M. Hammond, Jason Karlawish, Lisa Schur, Douglas Kruse, and Christine S. Davis. 2012. "Assessing Voting Competence and Political Knowledge: Comparing Individuals with Traumatic Brain Injuries and 'Average' College Students." *Election Law Journal*, 11: 52–69.

Mann, Christopher B. 2011. "Get the Vote in the Mail: Experiments in Getting Out the Vote using no Excuse Absentee Voting." Annual Meeting of the Southern Political Science Association, New Orleans, LA.

Mann, Christopher B., and Joshua Kalla. 2013. "Prompting Participation by Reducing Cost or Increasing Motivation: A Field Experiment on Encouraging Different Modes of Voting.". Paper presented at the Midwest Political Science Association Annual Meeting, Chicago, IL.

Mann, Christopher B., and Genevieve Mayhew. 2012. "Multiple Voting Methods, Multiple Mobilization Opportunities? Voting Behavior, Institutional Reform, and Mobilization Strategy." Paper presented at the Southern Political Science Association Annual Meeting, New Orleans, LA.

forthcoming. "Voter Mobilization Meets eGovernment: Turnout and Voting by Mail from Online or Paper Ballot Request." *Journal of Political Marketing*.

Mann, Christopher B., and Rachel M. Sondheimer. 2009. "The Role of Local Election Officials in Promoting Growth of Mail Voting." Report to Pew Center on the States, Washington, DC.

2013. "Reducing Ballot Errors & Increasing Turnout in All Mail Elections: A Field Experiment on Voter Education by the County Clerk." Paper presented at the American Political Science Association Annual Meeting, Chicago, IL.

Mathews, T. J., and M. F. MacDorman. 2012. "Infant Mortality Statistics from the 2008 Period Linked Birth/Infant Death Data Set." *National Vital Statistics Reports* 60 (5): 1–28.

McDonald, Michael P. 2002. "The Turnout Rate among Eligible Voters in the States, 1980–2000." *State Politics & Policy Quarterly* 2: 199–212.

2008. "Portable Voter Registration." *Political Behavior* 30: 491–501.

2010. "American Voter Turnout in Historical Perspective." In *The Oxford Handbook of American Elections and Political Behavior*, ed. Jan E. Leighley. New York: Oxford University Press.

McDonald, Michael P., and Samuel Popkin. 2001. "The Myth of the Vanishing Voter." *American Political Science Review* 95: 963–974.

McNulty, John, Conor Dowling, and Margaret Ariotti. 2009. "Driving Saints to Sin: How Increasing the Difficulty of Voting Disuades Even the Most Motivated Voters." *Political Analysis* 17(4): 435–455.

Michelson, Melissa R., Neil Malhotra, Andrew Healy, Donald P. Green, Allison Carnegie, and Ali Adam Valenzuela. 2012. *Election Law Journal* 11(3): 279–290.

Minnite, Lorraine C. 2010. *The Myth of Voter Fraud*. Ithaca, NY: Cornell University Press.

Monroe, Nathan W., and Dari E. Sylvester. 2011. "Who Converts to Vote-By-Mail? Evidence From a Field Experiment." *Election Law Journal* 10(1): 15–35.

Moore, Toby. 2009. "What a Better Election Data System Might Look Like." Pew Charitable Trusts, The Center for the States, *Provisional Ballots: An*

Imperfect Solution. http://www.pewcenteronthestates.org/initiatives_detail. aspx?initiativeID=54789

Munck, Gerardo L., and Jay Verkuilen. 2002. "Conceptualizing and Measuring Democracy: Evaluating Alternative Indices." *Comparative Political Studies* 35: 5–34.

Muzzatti, B. 2008. "Attitudes towards Disability: Beliefs, Emotive Reactions, and Behaviors by Non-Disabled Persons [Gli atteggiamenti verso la disabilita: Credenze, reazioni emotive e comportamenti delle persone non disabili]." *Giornale Italiano di Psicologia* 35(2): 313–333.

Myagkov, Mikhail, Peter C. Ordeshook, and Dimitri Shakin. 2009. *The Forensics of Election Fraud.* New York: Cambridge University Press.

National Conference of State Legislatures. 2012. "Absentee and Early Voting." http:// www.ncsl.org/?tabid=16604, June 1.

Neeley, Grant, and Lilliard Richardson. 2001. "Who Is Early Voting? An Individual Level Examination." *Social Science Journal* 38(3): 381–392.

Nowicki, Elizabeth A., and Robert Sandieson. 2002. "A Meta-Analysis of School-Age Children's Attitudes towards Persons with Physical or Intellectual Disabilities." *International Journal of Disability* 49(3): 243–265.

Oliver, J. Eric. 1996. "Who Votes at Home? The Influence of State Law and Party Activity on Absentee Voting and Overall Turnout." *American Journal of Political Science* 40(2): 498–513.

Padden, Carol A., and Tom L. Humphries. 2006. *Inside Deaf Culture.* Cambridge, MA: Harvard University Press.

Pettigrew, Stephen, and Charles Stewart. 2013a. "Cleaned 2008 Election Administration and Voting Survey Data." http://hdl.handle.net/1902.1/20573 UNF:5:jyQUlo+qF diGnoAFwByQ7Q== V4

2013b. "Cleaned 2010 Election Administration and Voting Survey Data." http://hdl. handle.net/1902.1/20575 UNF:5:z7VRIg5Hw25zH/oIpnEPEw== V4

2013c. "Cleaned 2012 Election Administration and Voting Survey Data." http:// hdl.handle.net/1902.1/21794 UNF:5:YSHJUa/+bD5d75pvo6ictw== Harvard Dataverse

Pew Center on the States. 2008. *Being Online Is Not Enough: State Election Websites.* http://www.pewtrusts.org/our_work_report_detail.aspx?id=45170, accessed June 14, 2012.

2011. *Being Online Is Still Not Enough: State Election Websites.* http://www. pewstates.org/research/reports/being-online-is-still-not-enough-85899376525, accessed June 14, 2012.

2012a. *Election Administration by the Numbers: An Analysis of Available Datasets and How to Use Them.* Washington, DC: Pew Center on the States.

2012b. *Inaccurate, Costly, and Inefficient: Evidence that America's Voter Registration System Needs and Upgrade.* Washington, DC: Pew Center on the States.

Pew Charitable Trusts. 2012. *Election Administration by the Numbers: An Analysis of Available Datasets and How to Use Them.* Washington: Pew Charitable Trusts.

2014. *Online Voter Lookup Tools.* http://www.pewstates.org/research/analysis/online-voter-lookup-tools-85899476858

Ponoroff, Christopher. 2010. *Voter Registration in a Digital Age.* New York: Brennan Center for Justice.

Rhine, Staci L. 1995. "Registration Reform and Turnout Change in the American States." *American Politics Research* 23: 409–426.

Richey, Sean. 2008. "Voting by Mail: Turnout and Institutional Reform in Oregon." *Social Science Quarterly* 89 (4): 902–915.

Roseman, Gary, and E. Frank Stephenson. 2005. "The Effect of Voting Technology on Voter Turnout: Do Computers Scare the Elderly?" *Public Choice* 123: 39–47.

Rosenstone, Steven J., and John Mark Hansen. 1993. *Mobilization, Participation, and Democracy in America*. New York: Longman.

Roth, Susan King. 1998. "Disenfranchised by Design: Voting Systems and the Election Process." *The Information Design Journal*, 9: 29–38.

Sabatino, Charles P., and Edward D. Spurgeon. 2007. "Facilitating Voting as People Age: Implications of Cognitive Impairment: Introduction." *McGeorge Law Review* 38: 843–859.

Sances, Michael, and Charles Stewart III. 2012. "Partisanship and Voter Confidence, 2000–2010." Paper presented at the Annual Conference of the Midwest Political Science Association, Chicago, IL.

Schneider, Anne, and Helen Ingram. 1993. "Social Construction of Target Populations: Implications for Politics and Policy." *American Political Science Review* 87(2): 334–347.

Schriner, Kay, Lisa Ochs, and Todd Shields. 1997. "The Last Suffrage Movement: Voting Rights for People with Cognitive and Emotional Disabilities." *Publius* 27(3): 75–96.

Schur, Lisa. 1998. "Disability and the Psychology of Political Participation," *Journal of Disability Policy Studies* 9(2): 3–31.

——— 2003. "Contending with the 'Double Handicap': Political Activism among Women with Disabilities." *Women and Politics* 15(2): 31–62.

Schur, Lisa, and Meera Adya. 2013. "Sidelined or Mainstreamed? Political Participation and Attitudes of People with Disabilities in the United States." *Social Science Quarterly* 94(3): 811–839.

Schur, Lisa, Meera Adya, and Douglas Kruse. 2013. "Disability, Voter Turnout, and Voting Difficulties in the 2012 Elections." Rutgers University, School of Management and Labor Relations. http://smlr.rutgers.edu/research-centers/disability-and-voter-turnout

Schur, Lisa, Douglas Kruse, and Peter Blanck. 2013. *People with Disabilities: Sidelined or Mainstreamed?* Cambridge: Cambridge University Press.

Schur, Lisa, Todd Shields, Douglas Kruse, and Kay Schriner. 2002. "Enabling Democracy: Disability and Voter Turnout." *Political Research Quarterly* 55(1): 167–190.

Schur, Lisa, Todd Shields, and Kay Schriner. 2003. "Can I Make a Difference? Efficacy, Employment, and Disability." *Political Psychology* 24(1): 119–149.

——— 2005. "Voting." In *Encyclopedia of Disability*, ed. G. Albrecht. Thousand Oaks, CA: Sage Publications.

Scior, Katrina. 2011. "Public Awareness, Attitudes and Beliefs Regarding Intellectual Disability: A Systematic Review." *Research in Developmental Disabilities* 32(6): 2164–2182.

Scotch, Richard. 1988. "Disability as the Basis for a Social Movement: Advocacy and the Politics of Definition." *Journal of Social Issues* 44: 159–172.

Shambon, Leonard, and Keith Abouchar. 2006. "Trapped by Precincts? The Help America Vote Act's Provisional Ballots and the Problem of Precincts." *NYU Journal of Legislation and Public Policy* 10: 133–194.

Shapiro, Joseph. 1993. *No Pity: People with Disabilities Forging a New Civil Rights Movement*. New York: Random House.

Smith, Claire. 2009. "Defining the Universe: The Problem of Counting Overseas Voters." *Overseas Vote Foundation Research Newsletter*, May 2–6.

Southwell, Priscilla. 2004. "Five Years Later: A Re-Assessment of Oregon's Vote by Mail Electoral Process." *PS: Political Science and Politics* 37(1): 89–93.

———. 2010a. "Voting Behavior in Vote-by-Mail Elections." *Analyses of Social Issues and Public Policy* 10(1): 106–115.

———. 2010b. "A Panacea for Latino and Black Voters? Elevated Turnout in Vote by Mail Elections," *The Social Science Journal* 47(4): 819–828.

———. 2011. "Letting the Counties Decide: Voter Turnout and the All-Mail Option in the State of Washington." *Politics & Policy* 39(6): 979–996.

Southwell, Priscilla, and Justin Burchett. 2000. "The Effect of All-Mail Elections on Voter Turnout." *American Politics Quarterly* 29(1): 72–80.

Southwell, Priscilla L. 2009. "Analysis of the Turnout Effects of Vote by Mail Elections, 1980–2007." *The Social Science Journal* 46: 211–217.

StatsRRTC. 2012. *2012 Annual Disability Statistics Compendium*. Durham: Institute on Disability, University of New Hampshire.

Stein, Robert. 1998. "Early Voting." *Public Opinion Quarterly* 62(1): 57–70.

Stein, Robert, and Patricia Garcia-Monet. 1997. "Voting Early, But Not Often." *Social Science Quarterly* 78: 657–677.

Stein, Robert, and Greg Vonnahme. 2008. "Engaging the Unengaged Voter: Vote Centers and Voter Turnout." *Journal of Politics* 7: 487–497.

———. 2010. "The Cost of Elections." Paper presented at the 2010 Meetings of the Midwest Political Science Association, Chicago, IL, April 1–4.

———. 2012a. "The Effect of Election Day Vote Centers on Voter Participation," *Election Law Journal* 11(4): 291–301.

———. 2012b. "Where, When and How We Vote: Does It Matter?" *Social Science Quarterly* 93(3): 693–712.

Stein, Robert, Greg Vonnahme, Michael Byrne, and Daniel Wallach. 2008. "Voting Technology, Election Administration, and Voter Performance." *Election Law Journal* 7(2): 123–135.

Stewart, Charles III. 2006. "Residual Vote in the 2004 Election." *Election Law Journal* 5: 158–169.

———. 2008. "2008 Survey of the Performance of American Elections." http://hdl.handle. net/1902.1/20580 UNF:5:K3Z+PFc/D3CggfRUHIytuw== V1

———. 2009. "Early-and-Late-Adopters of Provisional Ballots." Pew Center on the States. http://www.pewstates.org/uploadedFiles/PCS_Assets/2009/ProvBallots_ Stewart_essay(1).pdf

———. 2010. "More Voting By Mail? First, Consider the Hidden Costs." Web Blog Post. http://moritzlaw.osu.edu/electionlaw/comments/index.php?ID=7717, accessed March 1, 2014.

———. 2011a. "Voting Technologies." *Annual Review of Political Science* 14: 353–378.

2011b. "Adding Up the Costs and Benefits of Voting by Mail." *Election Law Journal* 10(3): 297–301.

2011c. "Voting Technologies." *Annual Review of Political Science* 14: 353–378.

2013. "2012 Survey of the Performance of American Elections." http://hdl.handle.net/1902.1/21624 UNF:5:nMKNqnHfGzpAilhPJPvE8g== V2

Thad E. Hall, R. Michael Alvarez, and Lonna Atkeson, eds. 2012. *Confirming Elections: Creating Confidence and Integrity Through Election Auditing.* New York: Palgrave Macmillan.

Thompson, Denise, Karen Fisher, Christiane Purcal, Chris Deeming, and Pooja Sawrikar. 2012. "Community Attitudes to People with Disability: Scoping Project." Available at SSRN 2014423 (2012). *U.S. Election Assistance Commission.* 2008: 2008 *Election and Administration and Voting Survey.* http://www.eac.gov/assets/1/Documents/2008%20Election%20Administration%20and%20Voting%20Survey%20EAVS%20Report.pdf

Timpone, Richard J. 1998. "Structure, Behavior, and Voter Turnout in the United States." *American Political Science Review* 92: 145–158.

Tokaji, Daniel. 2004–2005. "Early Returns on Election Reform: Discretion, Disenfranchisement, and the Help America Vote Act." *George Washington Law Review* 73: 1206–1253.

Tokaji, Daniel P., and Ruth Colker. 2007. "Absentee Voting by People with Disabilities: Promoting Access and Integrity." *McGeorge Law Review* 38: 1015–1064.

U.S. Census Bureau. 2008. "Voting and Registration Supplement to the Current Population Survey, 2008."

2010. "Voting and Registration Supplement to the Current Population Survey, 2010."

2012. "2012 Voting and Registration Supplement to CPS." https://www.census.gov/hhes/www/socdemo/voting/

U.S. Commission on Civil Rights. 1983. *Accommodating the Spectrum of Individual Abilities, Clearinghouse Publication 81.* Washington, DC: U.S. Commission on Civil Rights.

U.S. Department of Commerce. 2011. *Exploring the Digital Nation: Computer and Internet Use at Home.* Washington, DC: U.S. Department of Commerce.

U.S. Election Assistance Commission. 2008 *Election Administration and Voting Survey: Survey of Key Findings,* p. 41.

2012 *Statutory Overview Report,* pp. 10–11.

2010. "A Guide to the Election Administration and Voting Survey." http://www.eac.gov/research/election_administration_and_voting_survey.aspx, accessed June 14, 2012.

2011a. *The Impact of the National Voter Registration Act of 1993 on the Administration of Elections for Federal Office 2009–2010. A Report to the 112th Congress.* Washington, DC: U.S. EAC.

2011b. 2010 *Statutory Overview Report.* http://www.eac.gov/research/election_administration_and_voting_survey.aspx, accessed June 14, 2012.

U.S. General Accounting Office. 2004. "Operation Iraqi Freedom: Long-Standing Problems Hampering Mail Delivery Need to Be Resolved 13." GAO Publication No. GAO-04-484.

U.S. House of Representatives. 2006. H.R. REP. 99–765, 1986 U.S.C.C.A.N. 2009, House Report 99–965 of August 7, 1986 on the Uniformed and Overseas Citizens Absentee Voting Act. H.R. Rep. No. 99–765.

Verba, Sidney, Kay Schlozman, and Henry Brady. 1995. *Voice and Equality: Civic Voluntarism in American Life.* Cambridge, MA: Harvard University Press.

von Spakovsky, Hans A. 2005. "Voting by Military Personnel and Overseas Citizens: The Uniformed and Overseas Citizens Absentee Voting Act." *The Federalist Society for Law and Public Policy Studies.*

Wehbi, Samantha, and Yahya El-Lahib. 2008. "Sit (or Stand) and Be Counted! Campaigning for the Voting Rights of People with Disabilities in Lebanon." *Disability Studies Quarterly* 28(2).

Westerholm, Robert I., Laura Radak, Christopher B. Keys, and David B. Henry. 2006a. "Stigma." In *Encyclopedia of Disability*, ed. Gary L. Albrecht. Thousand Oaks, CA: Sage Publications.

2006b. "Stigma, International." In *Encyclopedia of Disability*, eds. G. Albrecht, J. Bickenbach, D. Mitchell, W. Schalick, and S. Snyder. Thousand Oaks, CA : Sage Publications, pp. 1507–1510.

Wolfinger, Raymond E., and Steven J. Rosenstone. 1980. *Who Votes?* New Haven, Conn.: Yale University Press.

Wolfinger, Raymond E., Benjamin Highton, and Megan Mullin. 2005. "How Postregistration Laws Affect the Turnout of Citizens Registered to Vote." *State Politics & Policy Quarterly* 5: 1–23.

World Health Organization/World Bank. 2011. *World Report on Disability.* Geneva: WHO and World Bank.

Yuker, Harold, ed. 1988. *Attitudes toward Persons with Disabilities.* New York: Springer.

Zaeller, Richard A., and Edward G. Carmines. 1980. *Measurement in the Social Sciences.* New York: Cambridge University Press.

Index

Citizen Voting Age Population (CVAP), 45n5
civilian overseas voting data, 144n6
  civilian absentee ballot rejection
    percentages, 302
  comparison of 2008, 2010, and 2012
    absentee ballots, 277–279
Coding Accuracy Support System
  (CASS), 67
commercial election data vendors, voter
  registration list quality and, 63–65
commercial survey research, election data
  using, 18–19
competitiveness of campaigns
  "fall-off" in turnout rates and, 56–59
  voter registration and turnout correlation
    with, 53–56
completeness of election data
  comparison of 2010 and 2012 overall
    completeness by section, 279–283, 282t
  EVAS rates for, 305
  state-based assessment, 284–285f,
    285f
  voters online searches and, 288–290
confirmatory factor analysis, state-based
  election evaluation, 28
contestation *vs.* participation principle
  (Dahl), 21
convenience in voting
  accessibility issues *vs.*, 272n1
  turnout rates and, 169–172
  voter confidence and, 263–266
  voter satisfaction and, 170n5,
    185–187
Cooperative Congressional Election Study
  (CCES)
  voter abstention data and, 244–246
  voter confidence data in, 256n11, 256–261
correlation coefficients, voter data cross-
  checking analysis, 85–88
cost analysis of elections, centralization of
  polling operations and, 185–187
counted ballot/counted voter discrepancies.
  See also recount problems, voting
    machine performance and
  provisional ballots and problems with,
    97–100
  state-by-state comparisons, 76–79, 77f
  voter confidence and, 251
county election administration
  residual vote rate analysis and, 244–246
  voter registration and turnout rate
    variations, 49–52

Crawford v. Marion County, 248–250
cross-sectional regression
  heterogeneity in voting machines and
    performance analysis using, 234–238
  voter registration and turnout
    measurement, 56n20
current list maintenance, state-by-state
  comparisons, 78–82
Current Population Survey (CPS), 10
  early voting data, 167–169
  quality measurement of, 85–88
  voter registration measurements,
    40–41, 45–49

Dahl, Robert, 21
database cross-checking systems, 85–88, 301
data sources for American elections, 9–19
  academic and commercial survey
    research, 18–19
  comparison of 2008, 2010, and 2012
    elections, 277–282, 278t
  comparison of 2010 and 2012 overall
    completeness of EAVS data by section,
    279–283, 282t
  disabled voter data, 193–194
  EAC quantitative data, assessment of,
    276–277
  Election Administration and Voting
    Survey, 12–15
  list processing and quality control
    and, 63–65
  mail ballot data shortage, 121–126
  new index measures, analysis of, 85–88
  Pew database cross-checking
    system, 85–88
  quality indicators, 66–69
  stakeholder transparency and data
    availability, 274–276
  state and local election boards, 15–18
  transparency of, 271–297
  UOCAVA data sources, 150–152
  voter's perceptions of transparency in,
    287–288
  Voting and Registration Supplement,
    9–19
deadwood
  current list maintenance and, 78–82, 84f
  factor analysis of, 85–88
  obsolete voter data, 68
  summary index of registration quality
    and, 82–85
  voter registration lists, 301

CPSIA information can be obtained
at www.ICGtesting.com
Printed in the USA
LVHW022031260722
724430LV00004B/248